DATE DUE

APR 1 2 1994	
MAR - 4 1995	
APR 1 2000	
MAY 1 4 2000	
OCT 2 1 2002	

BRODART   Cat. No. 23-221

Exits from the
Labyrinth

Exits from the Labyrinth

**Culture and Ideology in the
Mexican National Space**

Claudio Lomnitz-Adler

UNIVERSITY OF CALIFORNIA PRESS
Berkeley / Los Angeles / Oxford

University of California Press
Berkeley and Los Angeles, California

University of California Press
Oxford, England

Copyright © 1992 by
The Regents of the University of California

Library of Congress Cataloging-in-Publication Data

Lomnitz Adler, Claudio.
    Exits from the labyrinth : culture and ideology in the Mexican
national space / Claudio Lomnitz-Adler.
        p. cm.
    Includes bibliographical references.
    ISBN 0-520-07788-1
    1. Mexico—Civilizaiton—20th century. 2. Nationalism—Mexico—
History—20th century. 3. Pluraliism (Social sciences)—Mexico—
History—20th century. 4. Ethnicity—Mexico—History—20th
century. 5. Morelos (Mexico)—Civilization. 6. Huasteca Region
(Mexico)—Civilization. I. Title.
F1234.L855 1992
972.08—dc20   92-20242
                                                                       CIP

Printed in the United States of America

1 2 3 4 5 6 7 8 9

To Elena, Enrique, and Elisa

Contents

Acknowledgments

This book has been ten years in the making. During this time I have had much to be thankful for: life, health, happiness, a wife, children, friends, a family, and a job. I thank God and all of my loved ones for all of that.

On the logistic and intellectual side of things I have several debts. The Anthropology Department at Stanford University financed most of my graduate studies, including much of my field research. My uncles and aunts, Manuel, Valery, Mauricio, and Anita Adler, also helped support my research during a time of financial hardship. Parts of this work were written in the tranquil environment of El Colegio de México, an institution that provided much support. Finally, my last few years of work have been carried out in the Department of Anthropology at New York University, where I have benefitted from enormous encouragement and intellectual stimulation. Different versions and portions of this manuscript have gained from comments and criticisms from George Collier, G. William Skinner, Renato Rosaldo, Rick Maddox, Roger Rouse, Larissa Lomnitz, Fred Myers, Faye Ginsburg, Eric Wolf, Elena Climent, Jeremy Beckett, Norma Elizondo, Guillermo de la Peña and Annette Weiner. T. O. Beidelman's painstaking comments were of special value to me. Throughout most of this project I gained from the constant help and friendship of María del Carmen Hernández Beltrán. I would like to thank Stan Holwitz of the University of California Press for his encouragement, and Gregory McNamee and Rebecca Frazier for their editorial assistance. Chapter 1, "Concepts for the Study of Regional Culture," is reproduced (in a modified form) here by permission of the American Anthropological Association from the *American Ethnologist* 18:2, May 1991. Finally I would like to thank Annette Weiner and Fred Myers for their special support.

Introduction

The Project and the Labyrinth

Cada uno debe buscar a América dentro de su corazón con una sinceridad severa, en vez de tumbarse paradisíacamente a esperar que el fruto caiga solo del árbol.

Alfonso Reyes[1]

The Mexican historian Edmundo O'Gorman has argued that politics in Mexico's nineteenth century were riddled by an unresolvable paradox: conservatives wanted to adopt the economic system of Europe and the United States without substantively changing the colonial social order, while liberals wanted to adopt the United States' economic and political system while retaining Mexico's own cultural traditions. In both cases the issue was how to modernize without giving up valued aspects of Mexican culture and, conversely, how to change negative aspects of Mexican culture in order to modernize.

The political dilemmas surrounding modernization have made national culture one of the main political and intellectual obsessions in Latin America; "national culture" (be it what it may) is both a yardstick with which to evaluate modernization and an obstacle to it. People are continually preoccupied with changing some aspects of national culture and with preserving or strengthening others. In Mexico, these issues have emerged at every crucial crossroad in national history: at the time of independence, during the national dissolution that followed the Mexican-American War, under the modernizing regime of Porfirio Diaz, and in the aftermath of the Mexican Revolution. They will continue to emerge whenever there are profound processes of social change, as there are in Mexico today.

1

However, owing to the weighty political implications of each officially adopted view of Mexican national culture, the writers who have meditated on this subject have done so without resolving the theoretical obstacles that block our comprehension of the very nature of national culture. For example, in many instances, the preoccupation with national culture has been couched in an idiom of "race." Manuel Gamio, the "father" of modern Mexican anthropology, stated that the mestizo class is "the eternal rebel, the traditional enemy of the class of pure blood or foreign blood, the author and director of uprisings and rebellions and the class which has best understood the just lament of the Indian class."[2] This ideology, which became the official doctrine of the Mexican Revolutionary Party, is part of an argument about the individuality of the Mexican process: the soul of Mexican culture is Indian, and its political body is destined to be ruled by mestizos against the Europeanizing project of the lackeys of foreign imperialism. The doctrine was synthesized in Molina Enriquez's maxim, "Over time, the anvil of Indian blood will always prevail over the hammer of Spanish blood."[3] The immovable object met the irresistible force, and together they had the Mexican. Like the Spanish "hammer," the mestizo is a male spirit: assertive and political; however, the mestizo's deep allegiance is with the maternal line, with the Indians and with the soil. Thus, the racial ideology of Mexicanness can be understood as a qualified (but not absolute) critique of Westernization and imperialism.

On the other hand, Octavio Paz's famous essay on Mexican solitude was an attempt to *open* Mexican culture to the outside, not necessarily in order to adopt the culture of Europe or the United States, but rather to emerge out of that exacerbated sense of uniqueness and isolation that permeated the intellectual and political life of the postrevolutionary era (and which was, to some degree, a product of the racial definition of the Mexican). In this respect, Octavio Paz's critique was a sophisticated development of the problematics that Samuel Ramos set forth in his critique of a "Mexican inferiority complex." According to Ramos, Mexicans asserted themselves in an aggressive, macho style because they felt inferior to Europeans. Instead of focusing on inferiority, however, Paz inspected the feeling of distinctiveness that he called "solitude." In so doing he tried to reinsert the Mexican cultural process into the problematics of modernity.

A common method in all of these essays was to turn history into psychodrama, and psychodrama into interpretations of cultural practices. The "traumas" of historical "infancy" get dialectically played out from the beginnings of independence. So, Samuel Ramos—who was the founder of a kind of psychological approach to Mexican national culture—thought that Mexican family life was tainted by the traumas of conquest; Octavio Paz, on the other hand, has argued that Mexican authoritarian political culture is an unconscious reproduction of the womb of baroque order. These quasi-Hegelian dialectics of history have been painstakingly disarticulated by a more recent generation of intellectuals, who have shown that the nation is not an actor, and that ideas about national culture must be understood in the context of the national projects of dominant classes (cf. Monsivais 1982, Bartra 1987).

Yet the demystification of culture as popular psychodrama has not in the least abolished the *specific characterizations* of Mexican culture that emanated from subjectivist, voluntaristic, or idealistic culture history or pseudo-history. The paradox might be phrased as follows: the deconstruction of representations of Mexican national culture have not corroded the cultural bases that suggest the existence of national culture. In other words, the analysis of representations of national culture has not yet become a critique of national culture itself. And because of this, the criticism of works on Mexican national culture in the so-called *pensador* (intellectual-at-large) tradition has not yet replaced those works.

In short, most of the writers who have meditated on and criticized Mexican national culture have done so without resolving the theoretical obstacles that block our comprehension of the very nature of "national culture." The political importance of national culture and the difficulty in describing national culture in any terms other than the terms of nationalism has generated a circular dialectic, a vicious cycle that is built on the tensions that occur between the maze of social relations that exist within the national space and the ideologies regarding a common identity, a shared sense of the past, and a unified gaze towards the future. I call this complex of issues the labyrinth.

This book is an attempt to reframe the study of national culture. The problem I am dealing with is both political and conceptual. Its political dimension is linked to the formulation and discussion of alternate national ideologies (or of an antinational ideology). Intellectually, the issue is how to analyze culture in the national space, and how to understand the dynamic relationship between any attempt to describe national culture and the formulation of nationalist ideologies. So far, authors have addressed the political dimension of the problem without resolving the intellectual one. This book takes the opposite course.

In order to accomplish this, I have chosen to begin by rethinking cultural production in internally differentiated regional and national spaces. The book is organized in two parts. The first part is a study of cultural production and ideology in two Mexican regions: Morelos and the Huasteca Potosina. That part begins by proposing a vocabulary and a mode of analyzing culture in internally differentiated regional spaces. This theoretical discussion is followed by an ethnography and interpretation of culture and ideology in Morelos and the Huasteca. I present the meaningful historical and organizational contrasts between these two regions: the differential bases and strength of the power of the regional elites, their different relations to the state, their ethnic composition, and their relationship to national centers. The central aim is to understand the dialectics between cultural production and ideology in these complex spaces.

On the other hand, because Morelos and the Huasteca have strikingly different ways of tying in to Mexican official history and "national identity," the comparison between the two regions has many implications for the study of Mexican national culture. I take up some of these implications in part 2, where I develop an interpretation of a few aspects of Mexican national culture and of Mexican ideology. I focus on two classical issues from the essayist tradition: the history of legitimacy and charisma in Mexican politics, and the relationship between the national community and racial ideology.

The key to understanding these issues is the analysis of culture in internally differentiated regional spaces; in order to transform the findings in the essays on national culture into social scientific findings we need to be able to restore the truth that is imbedded in national myths to their rightful place. On the other hand, in order to contextualize community studies in the "larger cultural whole," or to justify historical studies in terms of their relevance for the "formation of national culture," we must have an alternate way of studying culture in internally differentiated spaces that are as complex as the national space. The study of culture and ideology in a spatial perspective has allowed me to reinterpret the existing descriptions of Mexican culture: the analysis of culture in regions is the stake that will finally put the *lo mexicano* literature to peace.

First Entrance: Anthropology

The reason why the study of national culture is currently underdeveloped is that it is part of a more general problem that social science has to confront, which is how to describe the cultural heterogeneity that arises in spaces of hegemony: anthropologists can't describe national culture, just as they can't describe the diffuse culture of a large city or of a complex region. Whereas cultural descriptions are usually constructed directly out of the actors' points of view (and from the factors that impinge on those particular points of view, as seen from fieldwork), the description of national culture, regional culture, or urban culture must focus first on the nature of those political-economic spaces as loci of cultural production and then return to specific actors' constructs.

Much of modern anthropology's task has been to remove itself from the simplistic ideas on national culture that were common in the first half of the twentieth century. During that early period, both functionalism and Boasian cultural relativism stressed the internal cultural coherence of societies, either in the form of "functional integration" or in "cultural configurations." This emphasis on a close fit between culture and society is reflected in the ambiguities of the anthropological concept of "culture," which is often used to signify simultaneously a system of signs and meanings and a people who share this system. The fact that these two notions are compounded into one word reflects a belief in an intrinsic relationship between shared mores and the construction of social and political boundaries (nationalism).[4]

It was the study of politics that undermined this view. By showing the political manipulation of cultural symbols, anthropologists questioned the conceptual models that saw harmony among a nation, its institutions, its forms of socialization, and its culture. The study of values was substituted by the study of symbolical transactions. National culture was substituted by ethnicity.

The anthropologists who did remain interested in the broad significance of culture stressed internal logic: culture is a *system* of symbols and meanings. Culture cannot be reduced to a set of flags and badges that social groups wear to distinguish themselves from others. Linguistics had proven that it was in the nature of symbols that they be complexly interrelated; particular signs may change for particular purposes, but one could not ignore the fact that the collectivities of signs were complexly interrelated. Thus, structuralism proved that culture could not be understood merely as a set of tools for interethnic politics. However, the relation between these systems of symbols and society was still a prickly topic that was most often kept undeveloped.

A telling instance of this difficulty is Lévi-Strauss's provocative aphorism, "myths think men." At one level, "myths think men" is an affirmation of the preponderance of culture (a collective creation) over individuals: individual interpretations of myths may not touch upon the full range of meaning that is implicit in the structure of a myth, but the myth will push the individual towards discovering those meaningful relationships. However, at another level, the polemical phrase is a symptom of the poverty of structuralism as a sociology of culture; "myths think men" is a defense of a method that allows structures of myths to be analyzed without too much reference to the many uses to which myths are put. Thus, the structuralist faith in the importance of collective manifestations is also a retreat from an analysis of the nature of the collectivity.

Moreover, the enormous political and economic complexities of the national space inevitably tempt anthropologists into finding method-

ological shortcuts—analyses of state rituals and myths, for example—
that seem to lead directly to national culture without explicitly confronting the national space. Although these shortcuts have produced very
significant insights on the way the state operates, they have not un-
covered the complex dialectics between statist ideologies and cultural
production in the national space. National rituals and myths do indeed
reveal general principles that operate in political society, but they cannot
easily show the ways in which those principles articulate the different
social classes and groups within the nation. They do not reveal the
structure of mediations between classes and groups in the national
space.

Some of the difficulties in analyzing national culture can be more
clearly understood if we think of the problem in Durkheimian terms:
national culture is a specific instance of "organic solidarity" (solidarity
emerges out of a sense of interdependence); however, the "subcultures"
that compose a national culture are units welded by "mechanical solidarity" (wherein solidarity emerges out of a sense of sameness). Thus, at
one level one has a collective conscience based on likeness and identification, and at another level differentiation, individuation, and a collective
conscience based on interdependence.

The main problem is that these two levels of culture are interacting:
the "mechanical" parts could certainly be broken, or at least "loos-
ened," by the interaction with other "subcultures," and therefore the
collective manifestations of the subculture would be muddy, unclear,
reflections of their allegedly homogeneous base. On the other hand, the
"organic solidarity" side of national culture is equally problematic because it is made through a division of labor that is *spatially segregated*.
The production of a loose collective conscience with a moral impulse to
individuation and interdependence could be hindered by the fact that
many of the actual communities in the nation-state are internally homogeneous. This problem calls for a sociology of the national space; structuralism and poststructuralism have only provided an analysis of the
representations of that space.[5]

Recognizing the theoretical and political difficulties of this dialectic,
the positions on national culture that have been developed by anthropologists and historians since the late seventies tend to counter the
cultural monism of nationalism with an image of culture as a set of
practices which vary greatly; the description of "culture" in a spatial
frame that is as complex as that of the "nation-state" is deemed to be
impracticable, because the "culture" in question is continuously being
transformed by such a great diversity of actors. Moreover, studies of the
history of anthropology suggest that the will to classify and analyze
national culture is closely related to processes of nation-building (cf.

Herzfeld 1982). If we seek to describe a nationally shared culture, we will only be reproducing the fundamental precept of nationalism, the notion that there is a "national soul" that is the true source of the status quo.

Not surprisingly, then, most contemporary studies of national culture center on the ideology of nationalism: how nationalists have "invented tradition," how nationalism is based on metaphors that systematically treat the nation as if it were an individual or an organism, or how nationalism juggles with the issue of cultural plurality by positing ever-"deeper" levels of national communion.

In short, this dialectic of orientations—functionalism, culture and personality, transactionalism, structuralism, and ideological criticism—has not brought us much closer to understanding regional and national cultures. Structuralism has not been able to reinstate national-culture studies because of the immense complexities in relating whatever cultural systematicity it might discover in culture to "national society." Interpretative anthropology (with its attention on "meaning" and "practice") is "deconstructive"—its forte is the contextualization and analysis of specific cultural constructs—and, as such, it depends on previous constructions that, in this case, do not exist outside of the state-linked ideology of nationalism. Anthropologists analyze the contexts and ways in which the nation is represented and the tropes that are used to connect it with everyday experiences of particular actors. This is why contemporary anthropology's rediscovery of the state has produced an image of an amorphous plurality of actors that are faced with a totalizing discourse (nationalism). National culture itself has ceased to be a legitimate topic. It has been substituted by studies of local cultures and of national ideologies.

Despite all this, national culture is still a relevant analytical category. One cannot deny the fact that there are cultural differences between different societies, that the nation-state builds on the cultural specificities of the people who inhabit the national space, that it plays with dominant cultural conceptions of family relations, hierarchy, gender, and so forth. State-building involves working with and within the cultures of the polity; the nation-state is an important political and economic matrix for the production of cultural difference and cultural homogenization.

Because of all this, a contradiction has emerged from the current underdevelopment of national culture in the social sciences, for while social scientists insist on avoiding a reified stereotype of national culture, they still depend on short encoded references to that national culture which they claim does not exist outside ideology: references to "Mexican machismo," "American individualism," "English formality," or "Japanese politeness" still seem to creep into ethnographies of those regions, even if ethnographers do not posit the existence of national culture. Social scientists assert the impossibility of dealing with the whole of national culture while benefitting from some of the insights that are to be gained from the exercise. We want to have our cake—present a purist critique of national culture—and eat it too, benefitting from a vague recognition of the properties of that national culture.

Second Entrance: "The Pensadores"

Most of the important works that deal explicitly with Mexican national culture have been written in the form of essays. Foreign commentators on Mexican intellectual life often refer to the writers of these essays, especially to the most venerated ones, as *pensadores*, a category that literally means "thinkers," and hence has some rather unflattering implications for the rest of us. Since the so-called pensadores are, frequently, literati, some of their legitimacy in the social sciences stems from the fact that they present "artistic" perceptions of social reality.

However, this is just a way of encapsulating and taming these essays. Instead of trying to separate out a set of people who, touched by a muse, produce interesting—yet always "unproved"—insights, one must recognize that the relationship between the essays on Mexican culture and social-scientific texts on Mexico is quite problematic because, on one hand, the essays invariably draw on social-science theories and empirical studies while, on the other hand, social scientists in Mexico are drawn to the essay (and to the novel) in order both to speak to a general public and to say what they truly believe, to expound a "world view."

The proliferation of the essay in the national-culture literature is an alternative to the kind of holism that is typical of traditional anthropology, a holism that does not encompass the anthropologist and his or her desire to know and to act. This is why so many of the best Latin American social scientists have suffered from literature-envy: through the essay or the novel, they have dreamed of fulfilling, not of escaping from, their sociological inclinations.[6] The transition from the production of empirical studies to the production of general interpretative essays is seen as a sign of intellectual maturity, not as a symptom of escapism.

The pull toward the essay is therefore especially strong for anthropologists who, like myself, work in their own societies. Our goal is to *remap* a vast—but familiar—terrain (national and regional culture), and so we must reconsider the "international" canons for establishing one's "right to speak" about a group of people. Do we need to chain ourselves to the methods of participant observation that have been developed since Malinowski for making the strange familiar and the familiar strange? If we do not consider this problem, we shall continually make demands on our work that are alien to the will to knowledge that lies behind it, and anthropology in the "Third World" will be simply a provider of data for our novelists. It is this particular form of schizophrenia—the uncritical acceptance of ("First World") field methods wedded to a will to knowledge that is different ("reframing the familiar")—that accounts for the mediocre attempts of the Mexican social sciences to study national culture and the persistence of the *pensador* mode at the fore of our social thought: the pensadores have not sacrificed their will to knowledge to considerations of method that have been tailored to other wills. Yet, precisely because of their proximity to public opinion, the works of pensadores rarely provoke empirical research. They are syntheses meant to be consumed in particular political conjunctures. In fact, it is fair to say that Mexican national-culture studies form a kind of "anti-tradition," for the endeavor has allowed for little *accumulation* of knowledge. Knowledge created is knowledge politically used, exploited, and (eventually) discarded into a pool of reusable symbols ("stereotypes"). The "tradition" consists more of posing an identity problem than of an increasingly precise theory of the ways in which a cultural and historical dialectic has played out into Mexico's present.

Ideas of Mexican national culture have been produced in politically constrained fields. During most periods of history, Mexican thinkers on Mexico have been caught between two forums with radically different characteristics: the national forum (with its dialectic among intellectuals, politicians, and social classes), and the international audience (with its academicians, policymakers, and journalists). During the nineteenth century, Mexican elites—like their counterparts in many other Latin American countries—were in a double bind; they could not construct an image of Mexicanness that was fashioned on their own culture because that culture was European, and so the whole argument for sovereignty from European powers was undermined. On the other hand, if they reached very directly toward popular culture, they ran the risk of being excluded from the nation that they were so intricately engaged in forging.

These dynamics were radically transformed with the Mexican Revolution. The revolutionaries' identity as mestizos allowed a reformulation of Mexican national culture as a mestizo culture. This formula resolved many of the old nationalism's problems, identified the political elite with "the people," and provided an ideological platform for a protectionist economy and a strong state. This complex conjunction of a mestizo nationalism and a "mixed economy" proved to be extremely potent; the party of the Mexican Revolution has been in power for sixty-two years.

In the past decade, however, revolutionary nationalism has been undermined because of the bankruptcy of the protectionist state and the concomitant shift toward an open economy and against state-owned enterprises. The government has not yet formulated a new nationalism; it is, in some ways, back in the double bind of nineteenth-century nationalism, while much of the opposition has rallied around a revamped version of revolutionary nationalism.

We can illustrate the sorts of political fields in which the descriptions of Mexican culture operate by analyzing the case of Jorge Portilla, a particularly interesting thinker on Mexican culture. Portilla focused his attention on *relajo,* a cultural category that means something like "chaos" except that it can be an activity (*echar relajo*) or it can describe people who are prone to that activity (*relajientos*). Relajo is what happens when people who are engaged in purposeful activity—a serious conversation, a piece of work, and the like—subvert that activity by allowing one person (a *relajiento*) to overcharge the situation with other possible meanings, thereby creating a kind of vicarious chaotic pleasure: relajo. Portilla's phenomenology of relajo is, in political terms, a call for responsibility and empowerment of (Mexican) agents; he believed that Mexico could only modernize if Mexicans succeeded in organizing the purposeful collective actions that were being undermined by the nihilism of relajo.

Portilla's phenomenology is not a sociological or a historical explanation of relajo. In fact, the phenomenon of relajo could be linked to various kinds of social causes. Relajo could be seen as a form of resistance (lack of identification with a dominant purpose) or it could be seen as a kind of defensiveness that no longer has a real social cause, an atavism (like Samuel Ramos's notion of a Mexican inferiority complex); relajo could be seen as laziness (insofar as it is a way of avoiding work), or it could be seen as a manifestation of an extreme form of selfishness and suspicion of all team efforts (*personalismo*). In other words, a single cultural phenomenon could be grist for a leftist national mill (resistance), for a rightist nationalist explanation of why Mexico does not progress (laziness or personalismo), for a colonialist legitimation of foreign intervention (laziness), and for a liberal appeal to transgress an already meaningless past (relajo as an atavism).

This example shows how national-cultural descriptions can easily free themselves from a particular political position and wander into other positions. The variety of interpretations around particular cultural traits is an integral part of what makes them "national." The dialectics of political pressure on the conformation of Mexican identity are the reason why social thought on Mexican national culture has occupied a rather broad range of discursive spaces. In fact, the dispersion of these ideas is such that there is no real analytical progress on the issue, and the cumulus of ideas on Mexican national culture is often just a pile of cliches that can be used whenever they are handy. The insistent play with particular traits by different political groups makes these traits into stereotypes. In sum, the history of social thought on Mexican culture has turned on the political tensions between different (localized) social classes, and between Mexican and foreign elites. Because social thought on national culture has served to shape, bridge, or highlight these tensions, ideas of national culture have usually affected Mexicans' ideas and representations of themselves. Moreover, once the political debates on the nature of national culture were ignited, all studies of specific aspects of culture in Mexico were transformed into a kind of reserve of raw material for these debates. That is why the dialectics of the national-culture literature have dominated Mexico's social sciences even when social scientists have attempted to steer clear of these debates; to the extent that social scientists study "Mexico," their works can be taken up in the never-ending debate.

So, for example, although the popular-culture literature that burgeoned in Mexico in the late seventies and dominated the decade of the eighties sought to counter a unitary image of Mexicanness by emphasizing the cultural pluralities that exist within the country, in fact, much of that intellectual movement has fit into a new view of Mexican national culture as being diverse yet somehow "all the more Mexican for it." The popular-culture literature has grown to feed the state's voracious appetite for new and variegated images of nationality, and the government has tended to substitute a nationalism that had a single people—the mestizo—as its hero for a vision of cultural pluralism that is still encompassed by the national state.[7]

There are several other examples of this kind of contradiction:

1. Characterizations of community cultures hinge on their insertion in an undefinable "national society"; case studies are legitimated as illustrations of a national whole which cannot itself be described without mythification. So, for example, a recent book that is a reinterpretation of the colonial period is titled *The Forging of the Cosmic Race*. The title of this prize-winning book seems to be telling a potential audience, "this book on colonial history will help you understand Mexican national culture, you will understand how Mexican national culture, as it was described by the nationalist ideologue José Vasconcelos in *The Cosmic Race*, was forged." However, each and every attempt to spell out "Mexican national culture," including Vasconcelos's notion of the "cosmic race," has been attacked through the medium of colonial and nineteenth-century history. Historians continually revive characterizations of national culture that had previously been debunked because of their alleged historical distortions; they do this because they need "national culture" to make their investigations relevant and attractive for the present.

2. (National) cultural independence is defended by intellectuals who consider attempts to define national culture to be politically harmful: traits and habits of specific groups are used to defend "national culture," while characterizations of "national culture" are inevitably considered to be stereotypical and thus harmful to the culture that is being described. The people who believe in defending national culture insist on the prejudices that inevitably result from its characterization.[8]

3. Finally, perhaps the most interesting evidence of the problem lies in the uneasy relationship that Ibero-American social scientists maintain with the so-called pensadores. The main difference between social scientists and these essayists is that the latter lend priority to their will to knowledge, to their will to speak to relevant issues, whereas social scientists lend priority to their will to method and science. The results of this relationship are complex. Because pensadores speak directly about the problem of national culture which social scientists back off from for lack of method, social scientists project onto them a kind of envy which in the end produces either a turn of Hispanic American social scientists toward the essay and the novel, often with harmful effects on the standards of empirical description, or an extreme irritation with, and rejection of, the essayists' treatment of national culture, thereby ignoring the many ideas that have been produced in this flexible genre.

For example, Aguilar Mora claims that "*The Labyrinth of Solitude* has, in fact, become a sequence of pedagogical images for after-dinner conversations; these images do not put forth very complicated conflicts, they do not postulate dialectical historical situations" (1978:25). Furthermore,

Paz confuses history with the perception of history: he takes the last two centuries of historical developments as a perceived, *represented*, object. . . . The tradition that Octavio Paz analyzes as the true tradition that runs across Mexican history is what I have called a false tradition: a projected image, a mirage, an illusion. . . . [I]t is the false image [of history] that Paz receives wholesale from the dominant ideology, the history of the dominant classes. It is unidimensional, linear, and it has a direction, an end, an objective. . . . The Indian defeat is suicidal (a self-destructive impulse of the Aztecs); Conquest is an "expression of the unitary will" of both its parties; New Spain is opposed to New England; the presence of an Indian substratum divides our religious conceptions; Sor Juana's generation denies itself: "this denial is that of the colonial world closing in on itself" . . . With the Revolution "the Mexican seeks reconciliation with his History and his origin." In this sense Zapata incarnates the return to the origin while at the same time manifesting a profound historical consciousness. Finally the Revolution is a "return to tradition, the reestablishment of links with the past that were broken in the *Reforma* and the Dictatorship, the Revolution is a search for ourselves and a return to our mother." (37–38, my trans.)

And yet this false tradition (for false it is) leads Paz to descriptions of Mexican culture that cannot be easily discarded or interpreted away as "nationalism":

> The preeminence of closure over openness . . . manifests itself . . . as a love for Forms. Forms contain and close in intimacy. . . . Indian and Spanish influence conflate in our predilection for ceremony, formulas, and order. The Mexican, despite suppositions that stem from a superficial interpretation of our history, aspires to create a world ordered by clear principles. . . . Perhaps our traditionalism—which is one of the constants in our being and what gives coherence and age to our people—begins from the love we profess to Form. . . . [T]he ritual complexities of courtesy, the persistence of classic humanism, the love of closed poetic forms (the sonnet and the *decima*, for instance), our love for geometry in the decorative arts . . . the poverty of our romanticism and the excellence of our baroque art, the formalism of our institutions and, finally, our dangerous inclination toward formulas [are a result of our love of Form and closure]. Formalism, and the specific "masks" it takes on, is liberated in the fiestas, which are a revolt, a sudden immersion in shapelessness, in life itself. (1950:46, my trans.)

It is astonishing that we can so well understand and deconstruct the fallacies in Paz's theory of the way in which Mexican culture is generated (the psychohistory of Mexico, the mechanism of "solitude," and so on) and yet find ourselves hard put to understand the meaning of the description above, and worse, why so much of it "rings true." The sociologist can point to the fallacy of pseudo-history, but she or he cannot easily account for or shrug off Paz's description of "the Mexican" (or even the contrast that Paz establishes between U.S. and Mexican culture).[9]

Thus the demise of national culture as a scientific topic has not abolished the problem of national culture itself: analytical incompetence in the question of national culture—and, as we shall see, in regional culture generally—has provoked contradictions in the theoretical and methodological frames of social scientists. These contradictions have exiled the subject from social studies, and it has found safe harbor in the interpretative essay. Although many of these essays contain important ideas and observations, they have not allowed an accumulation of knowledge because they have been too closely linked to the political needs which give rise to them. They are made to be consumed in a particular conjuncture. After they are consumed, they merely sink into the past and sit on the sediment of reusable stereotypes.

Third Entrance: Politics

In his study of nationalism in Quebec, Handler (1988:196) discusses the dialectics between a "negative vision"—which is the fear of losing one's cultural authenticity—and a state apparatus that is predicated on specifying, separating, and working on "discrete" aspects of that culture. The results of the nostalgia for national communion can be quite dangerous. Fascism and other forms of totalitarianism have usually had a component of frustrated desire for autonomy, purity, and coherence.

But is not the "negative vision"—the specter that energizes nationalism—also quite simply about losing the possibility of creating, shaping, and running one's own state institutions? The fear of having no organization to counter another community's plans for you? The fear of being ruled by foreign elites and getting ethnicity and class compounded in more disadvantageous ways? In this sense, we need to confront the different uses that cultural nationalism has in a global environment that is dominated by nation-states. Mexican nationalism, for example, is currently undergoing a profound crisis, and yet, in my opinion, the fully antinationalist stance that has emerged as the backdrop of current official policy is unrealistic. Mexico probably will not become part of—or just like—the United States. In that context, to abandon all forms of nationalism is merely to place the country at the unqualified disposal of the market and of United States policy.

The current criticism of nationalism, with its potent antitotalitarian implications, is still relatively barren in this respect. In too many cases, critiques of nationalist discourse do not fully address the available political alternatives. The essayists I have spoken of have always taken this problem seriously. Their criticisms are important because they are trying to pinpoint national problems that can reproduce only thanks to their links to widespread cultural practices, and because they attempt to subsume some of the forces of the market into the interests of the national community. As long as they are stuck (or blessed) with having their own country, Mexicans must try to take the administration of their society into their own hands, and this implies a kind of reflexive self-criticism.

In this study I hope to open doors to a critique of cultural practices in Mexico. This can only be done by placing oneself in the world of ideas, and not strictly in the national forum of discussion. The ideas in this book were developed thanks to the élan of the essayists and to the painstaking methods of anthropology. I hope to show that by bridging these two traditions, one can come closer to understanding what Mexican ideology represents.

Part One

Regional Culture

1

Concepts for the Study of Regional Culture

In this chapter I propose a terminology and conceptual framework for studying culture in internally differentiated regional spaces. I develop a notion of regional culture as culture in power-regions, and I propose, explicate, and illustrate five concepts: "intimate culture," "culture of social relations," "localist ideology," "coherence," and "*mestizaje.*" Since the discussion in this chapter is theoretical and rather abstract, I make use of a set of ethnographic examples that I will develop in subsequent chapters. The approach that I outline here is designed to specify key areas for the ethnographic description of regional culture and hegemony.

The spatial dimension of cultural production and identity is a theme that has usually been sidestepped by both regional analysts and cultural theorists. Regional analysis has always emphasized the explicit construction of schemes of regional organization, and, in so doing, it has made a substantial contribution to all anthropologies that ignore the systemic dimensions of social space.[1] However, the main thrust of regional-systems theory has been ill suited to the analysis of culture or ideology for at least three reasons: because regional analysts often presume that culture is simply a rational adaptation to economic and political forces in the regional system;[2] because the kinds of perspectives that are used in order to represent spatial structures often prejudice writers in favor of charting "observable behavior" (the eye takes precedence over the ear, counting takes precedence over interpreting, and so on);[3] and because the analysis of commercial relations has so conditioned most of regional analysis that culture is often reduced to a kind of symbolic interaction that appears to be especially "transparent" and comparable to commercial exchange: the exchange of information.[4] In its most developed versions, regional analysis has not yet reached beyond the demonstration of its relevance for explaining—in piecemeal fashion—certain cultural characteristics of groups in regions.[5]

Cultural theory has had a more varied set of problems vis-à-vis regional culture. A large proportion of cultural studies focus on discourse and rhetoric while downplaying the question of cultural production in social space. Structuralists, as we have seen, tend to view cultures as codes or as texts, thereby minimizing the "sociological" issues pertaining to the dynamics of spatial-cultural variation. Neither have poststructuralist criticism and postmodernism advanced much in this regard; given the postmodernists' emphasis on the culture of "late capitalism," they have tended to concentrate on the fragmentation of personal and group identities and on the mythification of cultures at the hands of the powerful (today's local cultures are transformed into neutered caricatures for capitalist consumption). And they have been particularly fascinated by the ways in which space and distance have been transformed by satellite communications. However, space and the relationship between culture and political and economic regions have not yet been understood, and the postmodernist assault on particular understandings of cultural boundaries has left the general issue of cultural regions (including "postmodern" cultural regions) underdeveloped.[6]

On the other hand, social analysts who have studied agency, power, culture, and ideology have examined some important dimensions of the relationship between culture and space. Bourdieu's (1979) notion of "habitus," for example, is designed to address the relations between cultural structure, the ways in which spaces are laid out, and the self (see also Bourdieu 1971). So, although the production and reproduction of social spaces are the result of the practices of people, these people are social personae whose very identities and practical orientations are influenced by the spaces in which they have been socialized (the house, the street, the temple, and so forth).[7] There is, in other words, a dialectic between person and place; because places are frames of social relations, they become imbued with the values of those relations and therefore help to create the relational values that make up the self.[8]

Throughout his many works, Foucault explores an aspect of the history of this dialectic by centering his attention on the relationships among the desire to know, the construction, expansion, and deployment of discourses, and the ways in which spaces are organized. In his historical interpretations, Foucault (see, for example, 1988) shows some of the ways in which knowledge and power have shaped and reshaped space in conformity to the (figured) ideas produced in discourse. However, it is important to bear in mind that Foucault, like Bourdieu, does not systematically explore the spatial implications of his perspective.[9] His interest lies in the connections between power, discourse, institutional transformations, and the ultimate reduction of people to conformity via the minute encoding of people's drives and desires. He pays little attention to the ways in which practices and institutions map out in actual social space, and in this the strategies of regional analysis—with its insistence on systematic observation of the interaction between *different* spatial logics within "nodal regions"—could be useful indeed.[10]

In this chapter I will develop the fundamentals of a perspective that analyzes cultural differentiation and homogenization in political-economic regions by paying strict attention to the relationship between the spatial arrangement of power relations and cultural and ideological production.[11] The end result is a framework that specifies and contextualizes the notion of hegemony. This specificity is needed for an adequate understanding of what cultural descriptions actually describe.

Culture and Communication in Regional Spaces

Contemporary societies are made up of many kinds of groups with all sorts of different relations between them; the systematicity and internal coherence of culture are problematic indeed. A recognition of the problem of systematicity and mutual use and understanding of symbols has led some anthropologists to compare culture to a *repertoire* of often dissimilar meanings and symbols. In this context, what can we possibly mean by "regional culture"? Are we looking for a "collective consciousness" or are we trying to analyze the full—heterogeneous—cultural repertoire of a region?

When we speak of regional culture, we are interested not exclusively in a common regional culture, although finding whether such a common culture exists, or if images of such a common culture exist, is part of the task involved. Rather, we seek to show how different kinds of cultural interaction map out in regional space, and from there to explore the spatial dimensions of cultural understanding.

The task is therefore twofold. On the one hand we need to explore the "political economy" of regional culture (that is, the spatial organization of the production and distribution of signs), and on the other we must explore the relationship between space and ideology. In other words, we must analyze the regional frame of cultural interaction (communication), defining the kinds of interactional contexts or frames that characterize different sorts of places; but we must do this bearing in mind the hierarchical integration of a regional culture through power. Thus, in order to define cultural "power regions" (or, to abbreviate,

"regional cultures") we need to look at the spatial dimension of communication in terms of the relations of power within those regions. This
substantive focus on power implies, of course, that the issue is not only
to note the patterns of communication but also to analyze the actual
culture that is produced.

In this section I will present an example of the way in which a dominant ideology's construction of social space is modified by the spatial
organization of the economy.[12] I hope to show that there are internal
contradictions involved in the organization of social space. In this example, there are contradictions between the legal organization of regional
space (and the ideological foundation of this legality) and the regional
structure of communication, and they illustrate the main point of this
section: that the study of cultural spaces requires equal attention to
"culture" and to "communication."

During the sixteenth century, Mexico was incorporated into the Spanish empire with the double purpose of enhancing the empire's power and
wealth and christianizing the natives. Once the Crown found its bearings
in the new situation it encountered, it attempted to introduce a kind of
"caste" society. The economy, whose dominant sectors were silver mining, hacienda production, and commerce, was to be legally organized
along "ethnic" lines. In this arrangement, Indians were to have a legal
status akin to that of legal minors, and Spaniards were to be their tutors
by means of the Church, by means of the state, and by means of their
control over property in all three dominant sectors of the economy.
Indians were to live in their native communities, where they would work
their ancestral communal holdings. There they would elect their own
communal officials from among the old Indian nobility, and these officials would be in charge of dispensing justice, enforcing laws, and collecting tribute for the Crown, the Church, and—with bureaucratic
approval—for the Spanish mine-owners and landowners.

In the area that today is called Morelos, this arrangement made for a
spatial differentiation between haciendas and the Indian Republic and
between the seats of Spanish power and the seats of Indian power.[13]
However, the symbols of Spanish-Christian domination extended over
the whole of the region via the omnipresence of the Church, for although priests kept watch over all of their flock (Spaniards as well as
Indians), they were themselves Spaniards, and were expected to *teach*
the Indians (Spanish) "civilization."

At the spatial level, this meant that the society was divided into two
poles, Spanish and Indian, each with its "exemplary centers" (see
Geertz 1983): the exemplary centers of power, where all of the recognized sorts of power (spiritual, financial, political, and racial) coincided
in the proper way; and the exemplary centers of what one might call

"well-guided Indianness" (those of the Indian Republic). The Indian pole was, of course, more problematically represented. The dramatized presentation of an Indian pole could not be achieved merely by putting all that was subordinate together; it was a matter of putting all that was subordinate in its properly subordinate place.

In the Alcaldía Mayor of Cuernavaca, the idea of the Indian Republic was synthesized in the icon of the community chest (*caja de la comunidad*). These *cajas de las comunidades*, which were meant to store the savings of the community, had three locks with three keys. One key, the "commoner's key," hung on the chest and could be used by anyone; another key was kept by the Indian governor and so represented the legitimate Indian leadership and nobility; and the third was kept by the priest. Alongside the community chest, the priest was supposed to oversee and maintain a ledger book in which all expenditures and income were reported, and the governor was supposed to inform the commoners of the state of the community's finances every year. So, in contradistinction to the exemplary centers of Spanishness, where spiritual, material, racial, and political power were meant to coincide, the exemplary centers of Indianness stressed the coexistence of Indian commoners, their legitimate representatives (the Indian officials), and the guide of the (Spanish) Church. Thus, the fundamental "skeleton" of society was meant to be ordered along the lines of two social types, each with its own place: the Spaniards in the towns, cities, and haciendas, the Indians in their communities. The Spanish towns were meant to oversee the development of the Indian communities. The Indians were meant to serve the Spaniards.

Nevertheless, despite the ideological attractions of this spatial arrangement, the Crown was often forced to recognize that this system was not adequate for the management of economic production on mines and haciendas, and so it allowed for the importation of slaves (which occupied spaces of their own) and for the hiring of (free) Indian and mestizo labor.[14] The state and the Church both moved to keep the racial and economic classes that issued from this dimension of the economic system separate from the fundamental bipolarity of the system; for example, in the village of Tepoztlán (in the current state of Morelos), mestizos often worked as muleteers or hacienda employees; in other words, they often occupied positions outside the bipolar order, or positions that served to connect between these two orders. On the other hand, when there were conflicts between a person's economic situation and his or her ethnic status, these conflicts had to be resolved via the manipulation of the legal order: mestizos purchased access to Indian barrio lands, rich Indians were sometimes considered mestizos or Spaniards, mestizos were sometimes allowed to accede to positions within the Indian structure of government, and so forth.[15]

Moreover, if we look at the way in which this political culture mapped out on the ground, we will immediately find the points of political and cultural tension in the hegemonic model. The village of Tepoztlán, for example, was the seat of the jurisdiction of the same name, and so had an Indian governor and a whole set of political offices that were occupied by the Indian nobility. Because of its position in the cultural geography of the Alcaldía Mayor, Tepoztlán should have been (and in the legal documents was usually imputed to be) a kind of "exemplary center" of the Indian pole of society. But in fact Tepoztlán was large and economically important enough to attract some of the less wealthy Spaniards of the region to it, so that, during the whole of the colonial period, Tepoztlán had both a local Indian nobility, which through political office could, at times, achieve substantial economic benefits, and a local Spanish elite, which was, to a certain extent, divorced from its "exemplary centers" (Cuernavaca, Huautla, Taxco, Mexico City, and the haciendas).[16]

This tension between the ideological-cum-legal and the economic organization of social space produced quite elaborate cultural politics among the Tepoztecan elites—including extensive manipulations of language, class, and ethnicity by the local Spanish and Indian elites alike. These manipulations were a distinct part of the local culture of Tepoztlán during the eighteenth century, and they help us to understand fundamental aspects of the local culture all the way into the present day.

The point of this example is that a description of spaces that relies solely on an analysis of the relationship between ideology, discourse, and space—with no reference to how that spatial logic maps on to other spatial logics—is deceptive. If, on the contrary, we juxtapose the spatial correlates of the hegemonic ideology with the spatial correlates of (in this case) the economic system, we quickly realize the points of tension for the reproduction of the hegemonic ideology and, *en passant,* explain some of the major elements of cultural production in the region.

Cultural, Economic, and Administrative Regions: Relations and Specificity

A regional culture is the internally differentiated and segmented culture produced by human interaction within a regional political economy. The various "cultural spaces" within a regional culture can be analyzed in relation to the hierarchical organization of power in space: within a given region one can discover similarly constituted identity groups, whose senses of themselves (their valued objects and relationships, their boundaries) are related to their position in the power region. Likewise, a regional culture implies the construction of frames of communication within and between the various identity groups, and these frames also have their spaces.

The spatial implications of ideological principles, systems of political control, and systems of economic production and circulation do not overlap with one another in a neat way, and therefore regional *culture*—with its identity groups and their communicative frames—cannot be neatly predicted from the spatial logic of ideology, state administration, or economics. In other words, it cannot be predicted using Foucault's strategy alone. Instead, these notions (the spatial logic of ideology, state administration, and economics) have to be combined—by looking at real power relations—in order to account for culture in space. And this is true not only at the level of cultural identity but also at the level of sign transmission itself.

Signs usually flow within the general bounds of regional economic and political systems. Books and leaflets must be bought or distributed in the same way as any other goods; radio and television are quick and effective ways of transmitting signs from cities to their hinterlands; state and national stations assure coverage throughout the political region; superpowers use satellites to broadcast their programs throughout the world; conversation and rumor flow through networks of relationships that also exist for economic and political interaction. Administrative control over a region will usually be asserted via sign transmission to that region or via the attempted impediment of sign transportation from competing administrative units. In summary, the spatial structure of sign distribution is related to the general economic regional structures in which sign transmission occurs; but the ways in which the various forms of sign transmission combine in any one place will be a reflection of relations of power in that place.

So, to return to our Morelos example, the hegemonic organization of the region in colonial times made for the construction of several identity groups; notably Spaniards, Indians, slaves, and mestizos. However, when these are analyzed in their places in the regional system, it becomes obvious that in certain local contexts the boundaries between these groups could break down. For example, Tepoztlán had both an Indian and a Spanish economic elite. Because these elites lived as neighbors, there were plenty of contexts in which they interacted and learned from each other; sometimes they even intermarried. Because of Tepoztlán's position in the regional economy, many members of Tepoztlán's Spanish and Indian elites were bilingual in Spanish and Náhuatl and biculturally quite adept, so that manipulation of their ethnic identities was common. This contrasts with the dynamics of boundary construction and maintenance in other areas of the regional economic system. For example, the hamlets within the jurisdiction of Tepoztlán were too small and too poor to attract Spanish settlers, and there were very few frames of communication with Spaniards. In those hamlets Indians could hardly avoid maintaining their Indianness, and the political system's primary concern was that they be properly overseen by the clergy. In other words, the communicative dimension of the economic organization of the region undermined the ideological and legal frame of sanctions on relations between castes: the dynamics of regional culture have to be understood in the light of this dialectic.[17]

Meanings

Cultural regions are inextricably linked to economic and administrative regions; however, the spatial differentiation of culture, its organizational patterns and rhythms of change, follows the beat of another drummer: the logic of symbolic interaction and of *meaning*. The cultural groups of a nodal region can be delimited according to the kinds of symbolic interaction between them and the ways in which they "share" meanings. Because "sharing" implies having common elements of what Bourdieu calls a "habitus," the life span of the person—and not only of the social group—is significant.

Regional economic and political systems are like matrices in which regional culture is produced, yet the internal workings of culture in regional space must be analyzed first in terms of the relations between symbolic interaction and the production of meaning. A cultural region entails the existence of a domain of "shared" symbols; however, the nature of this domain—what it does and does not encompass, and the characteristics of other, unshared, symbolic domains—is undetermined in the concept of regional culture. The idea of regional culture as an internally differentiated cultural space does imply, however, the existence of both a common regional culture and sets of understandings that are specific to the groups that compose the region. In fact, a regional culture will always have a degree of systematic variation in the meanings attached to the signs of even the regionally "shared" cultural domains: the production of meaning occurs within preexisting symbolic contexts, and because these symbolic contexts differ by cultural group, and even between persons occupying different positions within a group, the interpretation of regionally shared signs will tend to vary accordingly. One would expect an especially rich set of multivocal symbols in the cultural domain that is "shared" within a region.

Take, for example, the meanings and associations of the term *secretario* (secretary). In Mexico, there exists the political office of the private secretary; the president has a private secretary, ministers of state (themselves known as *secretarios*) have private secretaries, governors have secretaries, and municipal councils have secretaries. Until a few years ago, politics was strictly a male domain, and all of these secretaries were male. The positions of secretary are all positions of power, given to individuals who can help the member of the executive (president, minister, governor, municipal president) order his affairs. The secretary therefore must be literate, usually a professional, and capable of dealing with other politicians. Until about twenty-five years ago, Tepoztlán and most other relatively peripheral peasant *municipios* of Morelos often elected illiterate or barely literate peasant leaders to the municipal council. Because of this, the office of secretary was particularly important, and the secretarios often stayed in power over a number of presidential periods. The careers of secretarios at higher levels of the political hierarchy, on the other hand, were and are inextricably tied to the fates of their patrons.

In this context, the municipal secretario became, from a popular perspective, a relatively powerful figure. People needed his help for practically all bureaucratic paperwork, and used him as a go-between with other municipal officers over time. Furthermore, because secretaries often outlasted municipal presidents, they tended to develop a certain professional trustworthiness so as to inspire the confidence of incoming municipal officers. This explains, I think, the reason why I found that people in Tepoztlán and other villages of the region insisted on linking the nature of the office of secretario with what they considered the etymology of the word: he who keeps secrets. This association between secretary and secrets is not commonly made at higher levels of the political system, where literacy is taken for granted and secretaries don't know much more than what their patrons want them to know.

In sum, the regional dimension of literacy and politics accounts (in this period) for some of the multivalence of the notion of secretario: in peasant peripheries the office was both stabler and, in relative terms, more powerful than in the urban cores, and it implied a different kind of power over the populace. In the one case, the power of the secretary was and is based exclusively on his proximity to and good standing with the powerful officer; in the other it was based on his professional capacity (literacy) as well as on his permanent discretion (like that of a priest).

Thus, although the spatial organization of the economy and the polity are meaningful contexts for the production of a system of internally segmented and hierarchically interrelated cultures ("regional culture"), regional cultures operate according to their own logic, which depends partly on the constitution of communicational groups and partly on processes of transformation of meaning within and among the various groups. This is why we need to construct concepts especially attuned to the dialectics of culture, identity, and ideology in cultural regions. Definitions of bounded groups have tended to be either objectivist (class, for example) or subjectivist (ethnicity, for example); however, in a regional cultural perspective, we need to incorporate both kinds of perspectives, for the conformation of new meanings depends on both "objective" relationships (communication, frames of communication) and on how the symbolic exchanges produced in these relationships are perceived and understood (culture, ideology, identity).

Power Regions and Hegemony

Hegemony is a fundamental concept for the study of regional culture, for when we say "regional culture," we are referring not to the culture of a homogeneous group, but to culture as it exists and operates in a space that is organized by—and articulated through—class domination. In other words, class domination implies specific forms of organization of spatial systems. These forms of organization in turn imply bringing various cultural groups together in relations of power. These relations of power guarantee a certain unity of meaning within the cultural diversity implicit in the spatial segregation of classes and ethnic groups.

Yet hegemony—which, in its most abstract formulation, is a shared sense of reality that is diffusely constructed out of class domination (G. Williams 1961)—does not fit in a neat way into each specific power relation. In order to understand this, we must take into account the vertical dimension of spatial systems. Today's world is integrated into a single spatial system at the level of production; however, at the level of political power and the normative instruments of legislation, justice, and administration, the nation-state is usually the highest effective level of spatial integration.

In this context, hegemony—when it is achieved—implies power at the level of the state, and it is modified and worked on in each local context. Thus, distinct power regions below the level of the nation-state have distinct positions in the general framework of hegemony. The *municipio* of Tepoztlán in the 1860s, for example, was a small power region within a larger, Cuernavaca-centered power region, which was itself within a larger, Mexico City-centered region. At the commercial level, the *municipio* of Tepoztlán was what could be called a lower-level nodal region because the area was a small marketing region, with its central market town and its outlying hamlets. At the level of production it could be called a small region, insofar as Tepoztlán's small elite depended on the local population for the production of surplus. This very modest local dominant class, known to itself as *los notables,* was made up of small landowners, merchants and professionals, and most of them depended on their political control over the *municipio* for their own sense of importance, as well as—ultimately—for a significant portion of their income.

Given the importance of politics for this elite, its role as representative of the community was crucial, and so, during this period, the notables often represented the township against the interests of the encroaching haciendas, which were not powerful enough to control peripheral municipios such as Tepoztlán directly. In order to protect their position in the community, that is, the notables had to protect the community's interest at the regional level. They did this in part by appealing to the then recently formed national mythology issuing from Mexico City. For the first time, Tepoztlán was proudly portrayed as an Indian community with long-standing traditions, including both land rights and the right to have their own representatives. In this sense, the notables took up the role and the discourse of the old Indian principales and revamped them in the new national context.

This example illustrates the fact that a national hegemonic order provides plenty of room for—equally "legitimizable"—power struggles between different local elites. The power strategies of the three elites (Tepoztecan notables, Morelos *hacendados,* and national statesmen) implied latching on to different programs, a *sine qua non* condition for the negotiation of the position of each one of these elites in the national "whole." Hegemony, then, implies constructing a culture that gives the dominant mode of production room for expansion, but it also implies constructing institutional ideologies that mediate between the interests of the various elites and national power groups.

The dialectic between hegemony and power relations can be observed in two distinct processes: the manipulation of a dominant mythology and the development of idioms of interaction between cultural groups. The first of these involves the appropriation of local cultures and their resignification; the second involves the creation of specific, context-bound forms and frames of interaction. In what follows, I attempt to spell out the different communities that are integrated through hegemony (which can be seen as a kind of "diffused power" insofar as it links different power regions through the market and the state) and localized power. I also define the two key processes of hegemony—the manipulation of national mythology and the construction of frames and idioms of interaction between cultural groups—within regional culture.

Class Cultures, Intimate Cultures, and the Culture of Social Relations

Given the analytical primacy of hegemony and the cultural region, it is obvious that the category of class has a central position in the framework I am proposing. However, it is crucial not to conceive of a cultural region simply as the sum of a region's class cultures, for "class culture" is an a-spatial concept, which usually does not correspond to any specific set of cultural practices as observed on the ground. Because this is a common problem in the popular-culture literature, I shall spell it out further: a cultural region is a cultural space that is articulated through a process of class domination. In this process, cultural groups are subjugated, classes or castes are created, and those classes or castes are ordered in a hierarchical political-economic space. However, the main classes in a power-region will tend to exist in different kinds of localities, which can be defined through, among other things, their internal class composition. In other words, the various members of a class will live in a variety of places, alongside members of different classes. And, because symbols and meanings are created and negotiated in social interaction, the variations in the kinds of places in which members of a class live will make for corresponding variations in the culture of the class.

This argument implies that if we take a spatial view of culture, the notion of class culture can only be constructed out of the structural transformations of the symbolic production of a class in its different kinds of local interactional settings. As a corollary, it is rarely possible to speak directly of a class culture. One must begin by understanding the culture of a class in specific places in the regional political-economic organization.

Because of the confusion that can set in when we speak directly of class culture (because, again, reducing regional culture directly to class culture tends to foster an a-regional, a-spatial perspective) I have invented the term "intimate culture" to represent the real, regionally differentiated manifestations of class culture. Intimate culture is the culture of a class in a specific kind of regional setting. The various intimate cultures that correspond to a single class in a cultural region are the "transformations" of an ideally conceived "class culture." Class culture is therefore an abstract concept that must be constructed out of the observation of a region's intimate cultures.

I use the word "intimate" for this concept because localized class culture refers both to specific class-based communities (neighborhoods, settlements, people who share spaces of work or recreation), and to the culture of one's home, regardless of whether that home is socially integrated into a local class community. Localized experiences of class are not always isomorphic with particular communities, even though, in time, these communities emerge. Much of the politics of regional culture is anchored in this tension between an actor's home experience and the organization or dissolution of class-based communities. The dynamics that exist between these two aspects of intimate culture—the home and the homogeneous class community—are the basis for understanding regional cultural change. I call local class cultures "intimate" because they simultaneously evoke the home and the community.

The other concept that I propose is that of the "culture of social relations." This concept is also designed to help detect the institutional and cultural specifics of what might otherwise remain a spatially undeveloped or undifferentiated notion: hegemony.[18] The forms of interaction between intimate cultures constitute the culture of social relations. The concept is therefore bound to contexts of interaction between intimate cultures. The culture of social relations is the symbolic field in which relations of power between intimate cultures are "objectively" established.

Once ethnographically recorded and described, the culture of social relations should be analyzed in terms of two kinds of processes. The first is what Roland Barthes (1957) has called "mythification": a social class's appropriation, recontextualization, refunctionalization, and resignification of a sign or of statements. For example, in Morelos one of the contexts of interaction between various "peasant" intimate cultures and the intimate culture of urban "middle classes" (especially the middle-level bureaucracy) is political rallies where both bureaucrats and politically prominent peasants give speeches. In these speeches, peasants often petition authorities to take action on specific issues, such as land conflicts, investments for water or public works, and pensions for old Zapatista veterans. Peasants will quite overtly criticize both the bourgeois order that encroaches on peasant lands and livelihoods and bureaucratic ineptitude or corruption. At the same time, after emphasizing the peasants' rights to land and polity, they may appeal to the governors of "their land" to intercede in their favor, implying that the landowning and bureaucratic groups are not the legitimate represented peoples of the state, but only they, the heirs of Zapata, are.

This dimension of the culture of social relations, which is really a peasant rhetorical claim to priority as the true "people" of Morelos, is used as a form of interaction with government officials because the petty bureaucracy of Cuernavaca has appropriated—"stolen," Barthes would have said—the banner of Zapata and recontextualized it, placing it on the walls of its museums, on the flag of the state, and so forth. It is a key factor in the legitimation of the contemporary state. Here, then, Zapatismo underlies the "culture of social relations" because it is formally "shared"—thanks to mythification—by several intimate cultures of peasants and bureaucrats, and since it serves to conceptualize the relations between them.

In the culture of social relations that has been constructed between peasants and politicos, the latter have mythified Zapatismo in order to gain legitimacy as an elite. At the same time, the myth allows room (and terms) for negotiation between peasants and politicos, insofar as peasants can make their claims to the bureaucracy using the idiom of Zapatismo. Finally, I should emphasize that domination is reflected here not only in the construction of this (mythified) culture of social relations, but also in the production of the frames of interaction where that culture is employed. In this case, a proper analysis of the culture of social relations would have to include both the mythified culture of Zapatismo and the frames (the museums, the flag, the political rallies) in which the myths are used for transcultural communication.

Actual frames of interaction are therefore the space in which a culture of interrelations is negotiated. The forms of interaction that emerge out of contacts and negotiations between peoples are simultaneously products of each group's power resources and each group's interpretation of its position in a social order. The interpretations regarding relative positions involve, as I have shown, appropriation and recontextualization of the other's culture (mythification). They also involve imputing power and motivations to the other that in fact stem from one's own power and motivations; that is, they involve alienation and fetishism.

Let me illustrate this second ideological pillar of the culture of social relations. In the Huasteca Potosina, a tropical region on the Gulf of Mexico, the culture of social relations involves interactions between a number of cultural groups: the (dominant) ranchero and commercial class; the Huastec and Nahua Indian peasant groups; the mestizo peasant/day-laboring class; and several emergent urban groups, including industrial workers, schoolteachers, doctors, and government employees. Historically, the presence of the urban groups has been weak, and the cultural region has been shaped chiefly by the ranchero class.

Even today, the rancheros "talk down" to the Indians with an insolence that would be very rare between non-Indians. This style of interaction involves using the familiar *tú* (second-person pronoun) instead of the respectful *usted,* regardless of relative ages, and ostentatiously using one or two Indian words in a mode that is simultaneously jocular and derogatory. In commercial frames of interaction mestizos aggressively slash the suggested prices of Indian merchandise, making Indians feel that they overvalue their goods and the worth of their own work, and they pry into Indians' personal motives for entering market situations, suggesting, for example, that an Indian wants money to make a fiesta or to get drunk. In contexts of patronage, rancheros often play the role of sanctioning witness—ranchero municipal presidents preside over the Indian ritual of changing Indian officers, they are sometimes called upon to settle major disputes between Indians, and they take on counseling roles as priests and catechists or as labor patrons. Occasionally, rancheros will take formal patronage roles vis-à-vis "their" Indians (be they peons on their ranches or domestic workers), serving as godparents or as lenders of money.

In other words, long-term political relations and relations of production between Indians and rancheros are marked by patronage (except, evidently, at times of rebellion), whereas exchange relations are marked by an assortment of aggressive and predatory practices. How is this culture constructed? What are its ideological components? On the one hand, we have mythification by the mestizo in some of the following spheres. First, they transpose the image of the Indian as a self-sufficient companion of nature to the context of the market, thus facilitating the conclusion that the relationship between Indians and money relates to Dionysian impulses (money, especially for Indian men, is immoral). This mythification allows both a devaluation of Indian labor and of Indian respectability as sellers of produce. Second, they mythify the importance and role of drinking and fiestas, and this allows a view of Indian men as divorced from familial and civic responsibilities and thus as the deserving prey of organized civil society. Finally, they import the myth of the unchanging traditionalist Indian into the marketplace, including the labor market, where it is utilized to keep prices "traditional" as well as to keep Indians "in their place."[19]

Alienation and fetishism also play their roles in the construction of this culture of social relations. On the Indian side of the equation, "worldviews" sometimes place mestizo ranchers and merchants (and their Spanish language) in a mediating position between Indians and God. Among Catholics, this is formalized in Indian relations with mestizo priests and, symbolically, with Christ, but it is sometimes also ritualized or objectified in roles such as that of *el socio* (the partner), a mythical personage that intercedes for Indians before God. This internalization of the position of white men in the cosmological order is alienation: the reproduction of the world, with its rains, its crops, its diseases, and its cures, is mediated by the white man's goodwill.

On the other hand, mestizo ranchers often project their own lives of relative idleness onto that of the Indians, thereby justifying exploitation: "Indians don't have to work, they can just pull the fruit down from the trees." This is summed up in the maxim *"ellos hacen como que trabajan y nosotros hacemos como que les pagamos"* ("they pretend to work and we pretend to pay them") or in the attribution of mercantile mechanisms of profit production to the Indians' orientation to the market.[20] Alienated Indian intimate cultures fetishize the political domination of mestizos by converting this historical order into a transcendental religious order. Alienated mestizo intimate cultures subsume the Indian to the order of nature, so that Indian products are seen not as the result of valuable human labor, but as a product of nature. This view of the Indian is also reflected in the mestizos' respect for Indian knowledge of nature and healing (for a parallel case, see Taussig 1987).

In sum, the culture of social relations is an idiom of interaction between intimate cultures, produced in a set of interactional frames. The idiom of interaction is constructed through mythification; the interactional frames are constructed through institutionalization and resistance to institutionalization; and the substance of the culture of social relations is constructed within a field of power, economic and political interests, alienation, and fetishism.

The concepts of "intimate culture" and "culture of social relations" are ways of spatially specifying the idea of hegemony—an idea that implies structures of class domination in which cultural, political, and social forces interlock. Hegemony can be understood in regional cultural terms only by distinguishing those symbolic elements that are central to the articulation of regional power—whose barest manifestation is the "culture of social relations"—from the symbols that are primarily oriented toward the cultural reproduction of each localized class or ideologically bounded cultural group.

Evidently, the culture of social relations is reelaborated within each intimate culture. For example, the language of interaction between mestizos and Indians in the Huasteca has—in some historical and spatial contexts—adopted the colonially imposed culture of social relations in which mestizos speak paternalistically to Indians and Indians make signs of filial reverence to mestizos. In these contexts, mestizos are still *de razón,* a colonial term that literally means "provided with reason," and Indians are *sin razón:* irrational. This paternalistic culture of social relations is reelaborated within both Indian and mestizo intimate cultures. The patriarchal Huastec Indian family becomes a metaphor that legitimates mestizo ranchero paternalism in the Huastec cultural region. Mestizos internalize their dominant position through their identification with the major public institutions (state, media, and church), and this identification lends legitimacy to their surveillance of Indians.

At the same time, the internal (intimate) interpretations of the culture of social relations are subjected to the logic of cultural reproduction of intimate cultures. This process can create tensions for regional hegemony. For example, Huastec Indian family organization has also served as a source of ethnic identification to the *exclusion* of the regional elites, and so has become an ideological basis for class struggle or for "caste wars" in the region, as was apparently the case in Juan Santiago's revolt during the 1880s (see Márquez 1977); the predatory culture of social relations practiced by mestizos in the marketplace is opposed to the relations of kinship, equality, and reciprocity in the Indian communities.

On the other hand, mestizo paternalism has, on rare occasions, itself undermined the exploitation of the Indian. Juan Santiago's rebellion was partly inspired by a socialist-utopian mestizo priest, Zavala, who reinterpreted his assigned paternalistic role as a mandate to protect Indians against the dominant mestizo order (see Márquez 1977; Reina 1980).

The most basic element in the construction of a regional culture is the development of an idiom and a mythology for interaction between the groups that are being pulled together. I have called this conjunction of idiom and mythology the "culture of social relations." The culture of social relations is a useful point of entry for understanding hegemony because it is constructed within frames for symbolic production that are negotiated between the regional classes and groups; the culture of social relations must withstand the tensions between the interpretative demands of the dominant and subordinate "intimate cultures" of the region.

Intimate cultures are the signs and meanings that are developed by a localized class.[21] These cultures are based on localized experiences of class within a power region and are therefore closely related to status and ethnicity. Nevertheless, an intimate culture—which is an *analytical* construct—does not necessarily coincide with any particular status or ethnic group. The shapes and boundaries of ethnic groups are locally defined in political contexts; ethnic "boundaries" change continuously, and although these changes are closely related to the localized experience of class (and to its concomitant symbols, values, and institutions), the logic of boundary construction is not identical to the rhythm and direction of intimate-cultural change. Therefore the notion of intimate culture should not be reified into a notion of specific, bounded identity groups. To share a class experience implies sharing a position in space and time as well as a set of cultural understandings about that position. It does not necessarily imply the construction of social boundaries along the lines of that shared experience. In sum, intimate culture is not the same as either "class culture" or "ethnicity." In contradistinction to "class culture," intimate culture implies a specific place in a cultural region; in contradistinction to ethnicity, intimate culture is necessarily determined by class and does not always imply the existence of a bounded group.

Thus, an analysis of the conformation of a cultural region such as the Huasteca could begin by showing the expansion of Spanish and mestizo groups into the Indian region and by describing the culture of social relations and the residual, dominant, and emergent intimate cultures that ensued. However, one would yet have to show the ways in which groups define themselves and construe, legitimate, or yield to their particular places in the cultural region. This level of analysis can be encompassed by the study of what I will call "localist ideologies."

Localist Ideologies

From a pragmatic point of view, ideology is being generated whenever an individual or a group selects one aspect of a culture in order to exert power. Ideologies appeal to one set of cultural principles over other cultural principles that are applicable within the same situation (see Friedrich 1989). The cultural principles to which ideology appeals are never isolated. Rather, they form complexes, systems within a culture. Treating culture as a coherent system of symbols and meanings may be a common mistake in modern anthropology; but if the coherent system is not always there, it is at least certain that there are sets of elements within a culture that are synthesized, systematized, or ordered in various ways, and related to the interests of a group or class. Ideology is the ordering of one or several systems within a culture by arguing (often by omission) the centrality of one cultural principle over another. Ideology is accepted only if the appeal to the principles in question lends meaning to the receiver's experiences. Ideology is always drawing on past experience and reconstituting it into meaningful and coherent systems.

The articulation of intimate cultures, the creation of a culture of social relations, depends on the social relations between the groups that produce those cultures. Cultures that may have developed independently can be thrust into a single cultural region through the economic or political expansion of one group, and a culture of social relations must emerge out of the terms of interrelation between the two groups (see, for example, Sahlins 1985, Todorov 1984, Wolf 1984). On the other hand, through economic and political processes, members of a single identity group can become differentiated to the point that each develops its own intimate culture, while certain common elements remain and are constituted into a culture of social relations.

Ideology plays a key role in both the fabrication of a culture of social relations and the construction of identity groups out of intimate cultures. The culture of social relations is not an idiom or a mythology that is separate or separable from intimate cultures, just as ethnic boundaries are often constructed on the basis of intimate culture. At the same time, and this is crucial, the culture of social relations tends to favor the point of view of the dominant regional class: that class generally controls the frames of interaction for the production of the culture of social relations. Ideologies are required to ease the interpretative tensions emerging from the adoption of a culture of social relations that responds to class interests that are, in different degrees, at variance with those of intimate culture. I have called these ideologies about the nature and place of an intimate culture in the wider society "localist ideologies."

Localist ideologies are, then, a kind of reframing—from the context of intimate cultures—of the culture of social relations. The clashes and points of coincidence between localist ideologies and the culture of social relations point to the contested spaces between groups in a regional culture. Another example can clarify this. In Morelos, much of cultural hegemony is based on a "middle sector" control over the state apparatus. The culture of social relations that has emerged from the power exerted through the state has been legitimated in both "practical" and "cultural" terms. Foremost among the latter, as we have already discussed, is the state government's appropriation of Zapatismo as a regionalist movement. The government's commemoration of Zapata's birth and death dates is a ritual legitimation of the culture of social relations that characterizes the Morelos region.

If we look to the place of Zapata in each particular intimate culture, however, we can perceive the scope, limits, and tensions of cultural hegemony in the region. Peasants from Morelos' pueblos generally perceive Zapata as a regionalist and a Morelense, thus supporting hegemonic integration, and as a leader who was morally and economically superior to his followers, which in some circumstances also legitimates the culture of social relations. Another aspect of Zapatismo, however, can be and has been used as a weapon against regional hegemony: Zapata's martyrdom is construed as proof that no truly honest and selfless politician can survive. Peasant localist ideologies thus support the Morelos middle sector's hegemony to some degree, yet they maintain the right (or the potential) to delegitimize the position of the bureaucratic elite with the very myth that sustains it.

These processes of identity-building therefore tend both to name an intimate culture and—usually surreptitiously—to bind it to other classes. We have already noted that an intimate culture is not the same thing as an ethnic group; it is not even always an identity group. Ethnic groups are constituted out of intimate cultures, and the process of binding an intimate culture and transforming it into an "ethnic group" contributes to the institutionalization of shared social practices within an intimate culture. However, class differences can emerge within an ethnic group, and plenty of ethnic groups are made up of a constellation of classes. In such contexts, the intraethnic group's culture of social relations and the shared elements of the various intimate cultures *within* the ethnic group are stressed, and as a result the transclass ethnic group can, at times, make up a node of regional culture within a greater overarching regional culture.

Cuernavaca's peripheral neighborhoods provide examples of these dynamics. Since the 1960s, the city of Cuernavaca has developed neighborhoods of migrants who work as proletarians or in the so-called informal sector. Most of these migrants are peasants from the states of

Morelos, Guerrero, and Oaxaca, and many of them have used their networks of family and friends for help with the migration process. In their new settlements in Cuernavaca, however, these groups of often interrelated migrants come into contact with one another in their (localized) experience as an urban underclass. They wait for public transportation together, shop in the same stores, drink in the same bars, have the same religious institutions to choose from, live near one another, and sometimes share a workplace. All of these experiences promote the creation of an intimate proletarian-cum-service worker culture in the neighborhoods.

The specific situation of the neighborhoods has fostered differences between this emergent intimate culture and other proletarian intimate cultures in the city. For example, the first working-class neighborhoods of Cuernavaca, which were created at a time of labor shortage in local industry (1960), had more support from the unions, the industries, and the city government, so that they are, today, more prosperous and internally bounded than the emergent proletarian neighborhoods. The relative solidity of their localist ideology makes the old proletarian neighborhoods less of a marketplace for religious and political proselytizers than the emergent proletarian neighborhoods. The emergent intimate culture of the peripheral neighborhoods does not adhere to a single localist ideology. Some migrants see their situation in Cuernavaca as temporary and their cultural experience in the city as a kind of liminal period within a reproductive cycle that belongs to their peasant intimate culture of origin, whereas others have fully reoriented their experience to their new environment. The process of constructing neighborhoods is, of course, itself a force that contributes to creating a bounded identity group in each neighborhood, but creating a bounded identity group that coincides with the emergent intimate culture takes time, work, and political struggle, and it is a process that must be continually renegotiated in order to meet the ever-changing requirements of the group.

In these neighborhoods we sometimes find entrepreneurs whose fortune depends on their privileged ties to labor on the basis of "ethnic" identification. The labor relations within this ethnic situation are influenced by the cultural identification between employers and employees; relations of trust and patronage are bolstered and class strife is underplayed. This manipulation of localist ideology allows for the creation of power regions within a wider, "transethnic" power region; and we must specify the nature of these new identity-group power regions in order to carry out a proper analysis of regional culture as a whole.

The conceptual model that I am proposing here is not one in which intimate culture equals identity group, or cultural region equals the sum of identity groups that are articulated by a dominant identity group.

Defining things this way would imply losing sight of the whole dynamics of regional culture: power hierarchies are created both between and within identity groups, and a proper analysis of social boundaries therefore requires a historical understanding of the interplay between shared cultural experience (intimate culture) and the ideological construction of identity groups (localist ideology). The rhythms of transformation of intimate culture are not the same as the politics of identity. New intimate cultures can emerge and old ones can decline within an identity group that nevertheless retains its boundaries.

Regional Systems, Cultural Coherence, and Flows of *Mestizaje*

I have thus far discussed three of the major components of regional culture: localist ideology, intimate culture, and the culture of social relations. I have also shown that there are dynamic relations between these components. Localist ideologies are built out of elements of intimate cultures, but they can be used to create transclass identity groups. The culture of social relations is continuously transformed and renegotiated in order to accommodate the communicational and interpretative demands of both dominant and subordinate peoples. Because regional cultures are created out of culturally diverse pools of people who are drawn into interaction by the power of a dominant class, regional cultures are always changing, and at any point in time, we can observe the coexistence of residual, dominant, and emergent intimate cultures and localist ideologies. The culture of social relations changes along with all of these transformations.

The concept of "coherence" is fundamental to the description of these dynamics. It is a way of gauging—admittedly without a precise measurement—the mutual compatibility of the various major beliefs and institutions in an intimate culture. Because we are dealing with complex societies, "coherence" is always partial. It is a function of the position of an intimate culture vis-à-vis the regionally dominant class: to what extent is an intimate culture permeated by regional hegemonic culture? And to what extent is this permeation compatible with the basic tenets of cultural reproduction? These are the relevant questions.

Linguists have developed the notion of coherence in the context of discourse analysis (for example, Bernardez 1982, Van Dijk 1978). It is a qualitative notion that evaluates the degree to which the semantic components of a text are mutually referential. The linguistic mechanisms of mutual reference are known as mechanisms of "cohesion," and these mechanisms are words with specific linguistic functions. I use the term "coherence" in a related, but distinct fashion: coherence refers to the degree to which cultural institutions—and the beliefs produced in the context of those institutions—are mutually referential and mutually compatible.

When Robert Redfield visited Tepoztlán in 1926, economic differences had been attenuated by the Revolution, and the town's economic dependence on regional centers had diminished thanks to the combined effects of agrarian reform, the economic decline of the haciendas, and a diminished population size. At that time, the village's main social events, its fiestas, effectively linked the yearly cycle of agricultural work to the "life cycle" of all women and men. Barrio and town fiestas buttressed family and neighborhood ties through the organization of celebrations linking personal development to the lives of Jesus, Mary, and the saints. In addition, these fiestas buttressed both the internal definition of life-cycle phases (through baptism, communion, marriage, and death) and the yearly agricultural calendar. Much of the Tepoztecan local culture of the time was produced in a field made up of a specific family and neighborhood organization and the organization of agricultural and domestic work.

There were only two elements of local ritual that made no reference to the reproductive rhythms of this basic cultural cycle: the election of municipal officials and the celebration of national holidays,[22] which introduced the whole issue of the political articulation between the local culture and the regional polity. This element of incoherence was, however, subsumed in fact to the elements of the primary reproductive model. Municipal presidents were themselves peasants and not full-time officers, so their rhythms of work were linked to the agricultural calendar; and the terms for understanding local politics were embedded in the general logic of reproduction of the peasant intimate culture (see Lomnitz-Adler 1982, ch. 5). In recent decades, however, Tepoztecans have diversified their economic activity so that, for example, the celebration of the barrio fiesta is no longer tied—for everyone—to the agricultural cycle in any meaningful way. Moreover, the rhythms of bureaucratic reproduction and change have become significant to more people; Tepoztecans today rely on public schools, they interact with a whole slew of government agencies, the municipality now pays for full-time employees, and so on. These changes have produced incoherence in Tepoztecan intimate culture: the elements of local culture are no longer mutually referential. This breakdown in coherence also signals changes in the intimate culture itself, which could, ultimately, evolve into separate (peasant, proletarian, and bureaucratic) intimate cultures.

In principle one may expect two extreme poles of "coherence" in regional culture: the culture of the dominant class (and of the localities where that dominant class has a very strong presence), and the culture of classes communicatively separate from that class. I call the relatively incoherent space between these two poles of coherence the "space of *mestizaje.*"[23]

The term *mestizaje* usually refers to the process of racial mixture between Spaniards and Indians, and to the genesis of a particular racial and ethnic type of person, the *mestizo*. In this context, however, I am using the term *mestizaje* in its deculturational sense. Mestizaje is the process wherein communities are extracted from their cultures of origin without being assimilated into the dominant culture. This is a process that entails fracturing the cultural coherence of a subordinate intimate culture. It also entails undermining the conditions for the creation of a new, independent, coherent culture. Because the mesticized groups are subordinate cultures in continuous interaction with the regional elites, they tend to adopt or to react against the culture of the regional elites, yet they lack the power to guarantee their own cultural reproduction.[24] "Coherence" is thus a dimension that we must study and explain in its regional and historical context. How, for example, are coherence and incoherence produced? What are the realms of greatest coherence and incoherence in the various levels of regional culture?

The spatial organization of dominant coherence, subordinate incoherence and subordinate coherence is the major parameter with which one can define and determine a core/periphery structure in the hierarchical organization of regional culture. If we view relatively coherent intimate cultures as cultural "cores" and the relatively less coherent transformations of those cultures as "peripheries," then cultural core/periphery structures would look very different from economic ones. In Morelos, for example, one can distinguish a petit-bourgeois core, several peasant cores, and several working-class cores. If we look at the dynamic relations between these cores and the cultural peripheries (uprooted peasant migrants, unemployed children of workers, and so on) we might conclude that, from the perspective of the regional political economy, peasant cultural cores are residual, working-class cores are emergent, and petit-bourgeois cores are dominant.

Regional Culture, Hegemony, and the State

The preceding argument has attempted to ground our understanding of regional cultural differentiation. I have argued that there exists a spatial dimension of cultural differentiation that allows us to understand cultural fragmentation as something other than a complete lack of cultural unity or identity. I have also implied that the processes of systematic differentiation and articulation are constantly crystallized in ideologies about place within the regional society and within the state. The state's "imagined community" allots places in both the political and the mythological dimension and so is always a starting or ending point in localist ideology. The nation-state is the level at which hegemony is attained and the terms of hegemony are constructed.

Marx understood that capitalism was a transnational system and that the proletariat would one day be a "world class." Since Marx's time, "world systems theory" has stressed the *interdependence* of capitalist accumulation on a world scale and the nation-state. From a regional-cultural point of view, this has at least two fundamental implications: "the market" is a form of transnational communication, insofar as commodities are *signs;* capital, on the other hand, imposes specific logics of production and social relations of production, and therefore it contributes to the creation of intimate cultures that may transcend national boundaries. On this transnational plane, however, nation-states are still in charge of providing an ordered space for capital, because they are still in control of the interactional frames for transclass communication: the legal encoding of social relations and the disciplinary systems of education and control (Althusser's [1971] "ideological apparatuses of the state," Foucault's disciplinary institutions). Hegemony is achieved, first and foremost, at the level of the state;[25] as capitalism develops, the hegemonic systems of different states, insofar as they are capitalist states, should tend to develop certain similarities.

Powers operating at a suprastate level create transnational power regions. These power regions involve two or more hegemonic systems that are being combined or juggled by transnational capital. This space, which combines two hegemonic systems, may, in some cases, be an emergent regional culture; this would involve building on the common elements in the hegemonic systems involved. The emergent regional culture depends on the differences between two or more states for different aspects of its reproduction. It is therefore important to remember the distinction between power-region, which is a region organized by the power of a dominant class, and hegemony, which is an institutionalized structure of interactional frames, localist ideologies, and intimate cultures which allow for consensus around a particular regime. Hegemony is a negotiated product that involves the interests of all the elites in a national space. As such, its terms may be sufficiently abstract to protect the specific needs of transnational elites. However, the basic "paradox of geographical scale" remains: "[T]he geographical paradox becomes, in world systems analysis, a surface manifestation of a basic antinom in the capitalist world-economy: classes *für sich* organized at the state scale, and classes *an sich* defined globally" (Taylor, 1987:287).

"Classes for themselves" occur at the state level because hegemony is organized at that level. For all of these reasons, the state is always a crucial cultural space of reference for regional cultural analysis. The cultures of social relations that are established in any cultural region always rely upon or conflict with the system established at the level of the state. The aforementioned localist *indigenismo* of Tepoztlán's elites during the nineteenth century, for example, can be understood as a negotiation of the place of the community in its regional context via an appeal to hegemony (this time through the national mythology) as a form of defense against the power of the regional elite. The regional elite, in its turn, attempted to use hegemony (this time through the national legal system) to undermine the basis of Tepoztecan autonomy by appropriating Tepoztecan communal lands. The "diffuseness" of hegemony is to some extent dispelled before our eyes when we see it in this spatially dissected light.

Conclusions

To this day, spatial analyses of culture have been greatly hindered by the opposition between behaviorists and culturalists. Behaviorists have been blind to representation and meaning, and so the analysis of ideology and culture has been lost on them. Culturalists, on the other hand, have tended to focus on culture from the perspective of actors, seeing hegemony as a "lived dominance." However, the only way to go beyond descriptions of lived dominance and into the systemic contradictions of a hegemonic order is by analyzing hegemony as a spatial order; it therefore requires taking a systemic and an actor-centered view simultaneously. Otherwise, spatial analyses of culture will never go very far beyond examining the repertoire of spatial tropes present in any particular intimate culture.

This chapter summarizes crucial aspects of a perspective that guides my thinking throughout this book. In it I have attempted precisely this combination in order to elaborate a political economy of regional culture. In the process I have invented, reinvented, or revamped several concepts: intimate culture, the culture of social relations, localist ideology, coherence, and mestizaje. On some levels, these concepts have a lot in common with other formulations. A reader may point to the similarities between intimate culture and mechanical solidarity; localist ideology is similar to ethnicity, and mestizaje to deculturation; coherence is a preexisting concept that has merely been revamped for the analysis of intimate culture. However, the formulations that produced these other concepts (mechanical solidarity, ethnicity, and so forth) were not developed for analyzing the spatial system of mediating structures that really makes up hegemony. I couldn't just use, say, the notions of mechanical and organic solidarity—which in any case are not identical to the opposition between intimate culture and the culture of social relations—because they were designed to classify types of society and forms of collective consciousness and representation; I preferred not to use acculturation, deculturation, and transculturation because these concepts were not geared to the analysis of ongoing regional dynamics.

By creating new concepts I have highlighted the theoretical problems involved in understanding regional culture. My ultimate purpose is not to promote a new vocabulary (although I have found this new vocabulary quite useful); it is to instate the mode of analysis that I have proposed. This mode of analysis focuses on culture in space by juxtaposing several kinds of relations between cultural production and spatial systems and by analyzing the tensions and contradictions between these relations. Three major dimensions of the analysis have been the economy of sign transmission and distribution, the regional political economy of class and its implications for the spatial analysis of meaning, and the ways in which dominant discourses help organize social space. When we juxtapose all of this we finally begin to understand the places from which cultural understandings are produced. We also begin to understand some of the systemic contradictions in various (national) hegemonic orders. In subsequent chapters I use the approach that I have outlined here to describe culture and ideology in Morelos and the Huasteca.

2

Introduction to the Regional Ethnography of Morelos and the Huasteca

In this chapter I will move from general considerations on national and regional culture to the description and analysis of culture and cultural interaction in two regions. The study of culture in these regions is designed to accomplish several purposes simultaneously. First, the description is an exercise in regional cultural methods and theories. Second, it contributes to our substantive knowledge of the formation of these two regions and of the kinds of class cultures that have been produced in those regional spaces. Third, the description of these two regional cultures opens the possibility of reexamining Mexican national culture in terms that must include the conclusions reached about culture in two extremely different regions. The regional ethnography is subdivided in two sections: one on regional culture and regional-cultural dynamics through "localist ideologies" in Morelos, and the other on the same topics in the Huasteca.

My initial working hypothesis was that I would detect the nature of regional-cultural organization by comparing culture in localities that occupied distinct rungs and niches in the regional political economy as defined with techniques from regional analysis, and that the contrast between cultural content and cultural organization in these two regions would help me to think about the question of national culture. Because of this, I planned a field research project in which I would interview a fixed number of people in four localities of each region. These localities were to be chosen according to their position in the regional-political economy.

Although this kind of multilocal study is indeed technically ambitious and cannot be carried out with the same canons of ethnographic description that one might expect from a community study, in the case of Morelos, at least, I benefitted from the fact that the region has been amply studied by anthropologists and that I myself had done a significant amount of fieldwork there on another occasion. Because of this I concentrated my Morelos field research on Cuernavaca. Regional cities are the main missing element in Morelos' ethnography and historiography. Fieldwork in Cuernavaca was perhaps the most difficult part of the general project, both because of the dimensions of the city (greater Cuernavaca has more than half a million inhabitants) and because of the very nature of Morelos as a cultural region. As we shall see, the history of Morelos' elites has made Cuernavaca an especially "amorphous" cultural center. In addition, I did my interviews on Cuernavaca at a time when I was teaching in Mexico City, so that I did not base myself there permanently, but commuted for interviews instead. This circumstance prolonged the research process. Work in Cuernavaca lasted almost a full year (April 1983–March 1984).

On the other hand, because of the relative scarcity of preexisting secondary sources, my work in the Huasteca felt both more novel and more conventional than in Cuernavaca—novel because the area is still insufficiently studied, conventional because my work involved more "participant observation." I stayed in the Huasteca with my family for approximately six months (July to December 1984), and then made occasional visits during the whole of 1985. Thus, the material for this study was gathered before the economic changes that have occurred in Mexico since 1988. Because the Huasteca is still a poorly ethnographed region, I personally "covered" the different levels of the regional system I had proposed: I worked in the regional city of Ciudad Valles, in the core rancho of Piedras Chinas, in the pueblos of Tamuin and Axtla, and in the peripheral hamlet of Tanchahuil. In the Huasteca I also benefitted from the work of several students, who did intensive work in the town of Axtla and more superficial explorations in Tanchahuil, Tenexo (peripheral hamlets), and Tanquian (another market town). Before beginning my period of intensive fieldwork, I had carried out a three-week expedition gathering folklore with three assistants. Reminiscent perhaps of the old diffusionist techniques, we traveled through many of the towns and villages of the Huasteca Potosina, Veracruzana, Hidalguense, and Tamaulipeca, and collected over one hundred stories, life histories, and myths in thirty-five localities across the whole range of central place types. The material that I collected in my interviews is mainly oral history (legends, myths, regional history, local history, family history, and life histories). I also discussed problems in local, regional, national, and class culture with many of my ethnographic acquaintances. Alongside of these interviews, which allowed me to begin to put together elements of different kinds of local, class, and ethnic cultures, I gathered other sorts of materials that were sometimes helpful; regional newspapers were often very interesting for the development of a "big picture" of regional cultures, as were some of the novels and memoirs on the regions and, most importantly, the observation of different kinds of family and local rituals and political events. The material I gathered was designed to capitalize on the fact that I was an anthropologist working in my own society, so I systematically sacrificed intricacy of description for breadth of perspective. To give the reader a quantitative impression of my work, I interviewed (often several times) a little over sixty people in the Huasteca—in addition to my initial corpus of one hundred much more superficial interviews—and had access to about one hundred interviews from my students, whose work I credit whenever I am citing it. In Cuernavaca I interviewed approximately forty people and benefitted greatly from my past work and from works synthesized in published and unpublished dissertations on the region.

I shall discuss here some of the general features of Morelos and the Huasteca Potosina, especially as they fit into the larger problem of Mexican national culture and Mexican nationalist ideology, linking regional cultural description to my overarching aim, that is, the re-presentation of the question of Mexican national culture. At the same time, the topic of national culture receives little or no attention in the analyses of the regional cultures themselves and so must be touched upon here.

The Huasteca and Morelos in Mexico: Relevance for a Reproblematization of Mexican National Culture

I decided to choose Morelos and the Huasteca Potosina because of meaningful contrasts in their regional organizations. Morelos is, very nearly, an economically and administratively self-contained region. It is a small state whose boundaries roughly coincide with two twin nodal regions. These regions center on the cities of Cuautla and Cuernavaca, the latter being the capital of the state. The Huasteca, on the other hand, is a vast economic region that has been splintered into several of the states of the Mexican federation, the most important being Veracruz, Hidalgo, and San Luis Potosí. There are smaller portions of the Huasteca in the states of Puebla, Tamaulipas, and Querétaro. There is no Huastecan capital, and no state whose capital is in the Huasteca (see map 1).

The Huasteca has a much stronger, more autonomous regional elite than does Morelos. Because Morelos borders the Federal District, its riches have traditionally been controlled from Mexico City: Morelos has

MAP 1

GULF OF MEXICO

HUASTECA
POTOSINA

SAN LUIS POTOSI ⊙   ●TAMPICO

N

PACIFIC OCEAN

MEXICO CITY ●

MORELOS

been articulated as a hegemonic region by a class (first of hacendados, now of industrialists) that is foreign to the region. On the other hand, the Huasteca's expanse and isolation has made for the existence of a powerful agricultural class of rancheros native to the region. In sum, Morelos is a region with a weak economic base for self-determination, yet it is a state that must produce an ideology of self-identification; the Huasteca is a region with an economy that is in large part controlled by the local elites, yet the region has been made administratively dependent on elites that are foreign to the region.

In addition to these contrasts in the relation between regional power and regionalism in the two regions, the Huasteca and Morelos provide other important contrasts: Morelos' population has been effectively concentrated in nucleated towns and villages since the late sixteenth and early seventeenth centuries. These villages were placed from very early on in a regional organization of production wherein some areas were destined for plantation economies and others were utilized mainly as a reserve of cheap seasonal peasant labor.

The long-term stability of the settlement patterns and of the core/periphery organization in Morelos—which have only been transformed with the industrialization of the region since the late fifties—contrasts with the characteristics of the Huasteca, whose internal core/periphery organization has been transformed importantly since the construction of the San Luis-Tampico railroad at turn of the century and, especially, since the construction of roads (beginning in the mid-1930s, but becoming especially important since the late 1950s). Before the Revolution, the Huasteca was more an hacienda than a plantation economy. This meant that the importance of a rural proletariat was much less and that the exploitation of Indian peasants was carried out mostly through systems of sharecropping and renting. In addition, the Huasteca is more of a rural region, in the sense that it has traditionally maintained an important number of small and dispersed rural hamlets (either in the form of ranches or of peasant hamlets), many of which have been distant from the political order of towns and pueblos during extended periods of time. Finally, the Huasteca is a multiethnic region, with an Indian peasantry and a mestizo elite, whereas Morelos has been peopled preponderantly by mestizos even as far back as the 1850s. The transition in the Huasteca from a predominantly hacienda system to a rancho system[1] has not meant an immediate erosion of complex relations of "race" and "caste" between the dominant Mestizo classes and the Indian peasants and workers.

How have Huastecan and Morelos history and culture been incorporated into "national" history and culture, and what are the effects of this integration on symbolic production within the regions? How has the strategic location of each region been used to construct regionalist or localist ideologies? What particular symbols are chosen to construct these different levels of identity? How does the logic of symbols fabricated and used for localism, regionalism, and nationalism relate to the dynamics of regional culture? These are some of the questions to be addressed here.

The description provided will be used to point out the different kinds of spaces that exist in the two regions for the development of localist ideologies, as well as the problems that the regions present for the construction of a national identity. The ways in which the culture and history of these two regions are connected to official versions of Mexican national culture and history will also illuminate the nature of local cultures in Morelos and the Huasteca. Finally, the exercise effectively introduces the regional ethnographies that follow, for it demonstrates the fallacies involved in constructing images of national culture via a unitary cultural interpretation of national history through the medium of regional cultural ethnography.

The Eagle Stopped in the Huasteca: An Economy of Peripheral Symbols

Before arriving in Mexico City, the [Aztec] eagle stopped in San Pedro Coyutla, which used to be a part of Pánuco and Pueblo Viejo.

It is a legend that they had no homes, that they lived only with arrows and were like pilgrims. Those people were following that bird here to form their city.

Over in Coyutla a Toltec, an Indian woman, saw where the eagle posed itself and realized that that place was to be Tenochtitlan, was to be Mexico City. That's why I tell you that the government has really tried to better Coyutla, because they found the old maps of San Pedro Coyutla.

The woman saw the eagle stop and that the people were coming, there were lots of people. They were the so-called "piráminas" [I don't know what don José meant by this, for he was well aware of the name Aztec or Mexican] who did not have a city and were following the bird, such that wherever it stopped, there they would build their city. Then the woman scared the bird away because she was afraid of it, and it flew and the "piráminas" followed it until they found it upon a cactus in Lake Texcoco. And there is Mexico, the capital. But the capital would have been here, and that's why the government has tried so hard [to better the conditions of Coyutla], because the Great Tenochtitlan was to be in Coyutla, but the Indian woman scared the eagle. That's what's in the papers that the government has been searching for in all the old archives; they found the map in San Pedro Coyutla.[2] (Story narrated by don José Argüelles, healer in the Huasteca Veracruzana)

There are several striking elements in this story, which has variants that are told in many villages of the Huasteca. First, there is the sense that the region was an alternate location for the heart of power: the Mexican eagle stopped in the Huasteca. Second, the region was left abandoned once power was established in Mexico City. San Pedro Coyutla is an unknown little village. Finally, the story stresses a recent revalorization of the locality. The government has searched out—and found—some of the valuable documents that reveal the real worth of the village, and has since become interested in giving material aid.

There can be no doubt about the fact that the Huasteca is a region that has remained forgotten by the national government. The impressive archaeological ruins of the region are unknown to most Mexicans.[3] The history and ethnography of the region have, until recently, attracted little attention. The culture has not been emphasized as being prototypical of "Mexico."

On the other hand, despite the silence about the region from "national society," the Huasteca has always shown itself to be a center of power and culture in its own right. Before the modernization of transportation during this century, regional commerce was organized around the Pánuco River and its navigable tributaries; regional produce was exported out through Tampico. Like Yucatán, the Huasteca could orient itself exclusively to foreign markets. In the nineteenth century this potential for regional autonomy was recognized; it resulted in the political fragmentation of the Huasteca and its inclusion in several states, with capital elites that were in every case non-Huastecan. However, administrative fragmentation and formal political subsumption to other regional elites did not fully succeed in incorporating the region to central power: regional *caciquismo,* which is a form of local autonomy, was endemic to the Huasteca well into the 1960s, and caciquismo is still a force that must be taken into consideration at local levels.

Economic and political autonomy from Mexico's urban centers meant the development of histories substantially different from Mexican "national" history, most particularly as it has been construed in postrevolutionary regimes. The form and content, even the dates, of the major social movements of the Huasteca are often different from those of "the nation." The region's dominant social groups have been relatively independent from the national ruling classes; they have at times developed their own cultural ideals. The region's Indians have not (yet) been selected to play the role of "exemplary Indians" in nationalist ideologies. And, most important, the internal logic of social relations, which is dominated by relations of caste and of racism, has not been adopted as the dominant ideology of stratification.

This is not to say that the culture and history of the Huasteca are unrelated to "national" culture and history. On the contrary, national events and ideologies have always affected the region, but they have done so in specific and original ways. For instance, the "Mexican" Revolution provoked a revolution in the Huasteca. However, the kind of leadership provided by the ranchero class was entirely different (in both the style of the charismatic leaders and the never too explicit motives of the revolt) from the official accounts of the revolutionary struggle.[4]

So, for example, the regional cacique Gonzalo Santos is known to have claimed that the problem with the Revolution in the Huasteca was that "there was no enemy." One of my interviews with an old revolutionary soldier in Valles affords a remarkable example of the perceived nature of Revolutionary factionalism in the Huasteca:

> CL: [After Zacarías's minute description of military confrontations between *carrancistas* and *villistas* in the Huasteca] But, don Zacarías, why were Villa and Carranza fighting?
>
> Zacarías: What? [Don Zacarías was hard of hearing]
>
> CL: Why did Villa and Carranza fight?
>
> Zacarías's Wife: [Shouting] WHY DID VILLA AND CARRANZA FIGHT?
>
> Zacarías: Why did they fight? [He thinks a little] Because, you see, Villa and Carranza did not like each other. They were enemies.

This is perhaps, at least from the Huastecan point of view, the ultimate truth about factionalism during the Revolution. There was no ideological difference between the major leaders: the Lárragas and the Santos were mortal enemies, despite the fact that both were "Carrancistas"; Cedillo was allied to Villa for part of his career, worked independently for another, and finally found alliance with Obregón. Personal enmity, clashes of interest between strongmen or strong families, were the leitmotiv of the Revolution. Alliances were made according to personal proximity to these leaders, not by political program. The people that voluntarily went to the Revolution seem (from the interviews, there is no good historiography of this yet) to have been either close associates and dependents of the ranchero leaders, or homeless wanderers with nothing to lose. I have no evidence of Indians participating voluntarily in the different revolutionary factions.[5]

In sum, the Huastecan Revolution does not coincide with the official, or even the dominant academic, characterizations of the motives, leadership, and participants of the "Mexican" Revolution. And much the same can be said for most other social movements of the Huasteca. In fact, if we periodize twentieth-century Huastecan political and economic history, we will find many coincidences with major "national" dates: 1940, 1960, 1976, and so on. These dates are important in the Huasteca because they are important in the relations among the Huasteca, the federal government, and the national economy. However, the actual processes that they inaugurate are different from what these periods represent for "national history": the period of modernizing stability known as the "Mexican Miracle" (roughly 1940–1965) coincided in the Huasteca with the "traditionalist" stability granted by the sturdy *cacicazgo* of Gonzalo Santos, who sought—among other things—to avoid the industrialization of his region. The 1960s ended Santos's absolutist control over the region and the federal government attempted to undermine the economic base for ranchero caciquismo by building roads, placing federal industries, and imposing a major irrigation project upon the region. This sort of federal intervention for the dissolution of regional power was a characteristic of the decades from the thirties to the sixties in most other regions of the country. The expropriation of Gargaleote, Gonzalo Santos's main ranch, was like the symbolic arrival of Cardenismo to the Huasteca, only it came forty years later. In fact, the recent governmental interest in the Huasteca, noted in the legend of the eagle, is, on one level, an attempt to terminate the political and economic hegemony of the regional ranchero class. It is an attempt to synchronize Huastecan culture and history to "national culture," with, in fact, no recognition of what Huastecan culture and history has been.

The Great and Untapped Huasteca

Huastecan culture, Huastecan history, has not yet been immortalized in textbook or mural. Yet the specificity of the Huasteca as a region in itself has been recognized. The region gets portrayed, from the earliest accounts to this day, as a vast, unexplored, unexploited region.[6] It is seen as quintessentially Mexican because it represents the great, dormant, untapped, Mexico. It is a part of Mexico's reserve of physical and cultural wealth. The rugged terrain, the hot and humid climate, the bold and open mestizos, and the culturally rich and colorful Indians are the themes in this self-interested Central Mexican interpretation of the Huasteca as untapped periphery.

In the last instance, this interpretation of the Huasteca as periphery is an attempt to reorder the social organization of the region, an attempt to control the region from without, an attempt to "integrate" (i.e., appropriate) the region to national society. To define the region as rich periphery is, of course, to stress that it belongs to you, that it is within your reach and potential control and that it does not have an internal political and social organization that is worth respecting.

The portrayal of the Huasteca as a frontier that is open to national exploitation has its parallel in the ranchero portrayal of the region as having been unpopulated at the beginning of the century. These images are in fact contested. The characterization of the Huasteca as untapped periphery, as frontier, stresses that it is a "public" region, in the sense that all Mexicans are free to go there and exploit it as they will. The sense of "public" as equivalent to access here is an ideological tool of domination that includes silencing the region's traditions and organizations. In sum, the oblivion in which Huastecan culture and history has been thrust has its counterpoint in the inclusion of the region as part of the rich background, the reserve wealth, of the nation. This ideology guarantees that the region will not be included in national society in its own terms, but shall always be controlled or remain forgotten.

The Hidden Value of Local Culture

The Huasteca's legitimate claim to cultural and historical specificity vis-à-vis "national" culture and history has been resolved in nationalist ideology by the construction of an ideology which could be dubbed "of frontierization." Through this ideology of frontierization, the region's culturally constituted political and social demands are muted in the same breath that the region's potential for future growth is stressed. We began the description of this ideology, however, with a story—that of the Huastecan eagle—which synthesized some aspects of the *Huastecan* perception of this peripheralization. In what follows I shall continue to explore the ways in which this situation vis-à-vis the nation is perceived and exploited.

The portrayal of the Huasteca as frontier has, on occasion, been contested. These conflicts are a reflection of—and are themselves—what we call "regionalism." At the same time, regionalism is only one response to symbolic peripheralization. Another, related though antithetical, response is to accept and exploit the image of wealth and freedom involved in the peripheral imagery. This kind of exploitation is potentially very much linked to regionalism, in that it underlines the region's cultural distinctiveness: the secret value of the region is itself an alternate truth to the truth of The Center. At the same time, this peripheralist ideology should not in itself be confused with regionalism, because it is not allied to any kind of political assertion of autonomy. Regionalists and peripheralists coincide in the recognition of secret regional wealth, but whereas regionalists link this recognition to a specific form of politics, peripheralists utilize this ideology for personal benefit.[7]

The quest for these regional secrets is a significant pastime: rancheros and agriculturalists seek and greatly respect traditional forms of knowledge on agriculture and livestock. It is believed—and I do not discredit this—that "traditional" Huastecan people (every cattleman should have at least one on his payroll) can predict rainfall through their observation of the behavior of animals. They know what little plants and animals can be chewed or swallowed to cure different diseases or even just to keep healthy and alive. They are a source of wisdom on local sentiment, and some of the Indian healers can see into one's body and soul with their "mirrors," a kind of black stone used for diagnosis. Regional culture is full of secrets that solve riddles that science and other forms of non-Huastecan cultural production cannot explain.

These mechanisms perhaps help clarify several striking phenomena on the Huastecan cultural landscape. There is the example of Domingo (popularly known as "Beto") Ramón, the famous healer from the municipio of Axtla.[8] Beto Ramón is a Nahua native of a small *ejido*, Ahuacatitla, in Axtla. He has apparently studied the herb lore of the region and is a "botanical doctor" (by this he means that he cures only medically recognized diseases, and not folk illnesses such as *mal de ojo, empacho, mollera caida,* and *susto*). However, Beto Ramón is not an ordinary folk healer. He has built an exotic emporium, including a chapel and a medicine factory, at Ahuacatitla, where he lives and sees his patients. He gets bus loads of patients from as far as Monterrey, Guadalajara, Mexico City, and even the United States. He has become one of the richest men in the region. Axtla has two hotels that were built to house his patients. These patients must cross a river on a metal raft and take a bus up a dirt track for several kilometers to arrive at his clinic.

A good part of Beto Ramón's success must be attributed to his identification with precisely the kind of alternate peripheral value that the Huasteca is associated with. Patients who find no hope in conventional doctors eagerly discover a well-developed alternate truth in the Huasteca. Beto Ramón's emporium amidst the lush vegetation of the remote Huasteca stands as a tribute to the alter-truths that the Huasteca opposes to "national," and even "Western," culture.

The theme of a developed alternate culture reappears continuously in the discourse of the local intelligentsia. The periphery becomes the center because in fact it *is* the real center of its inhabitants' lives. Oralia Gutiérrez,[9] a woman who has organized many cultural activities in the region, including the archaeological museum of the region, believes that the pre-Columbian Huasteca was Atlantis, the city of advanced culture that disappeared. The region, for her, is the point of origin of all Mexican (sometimes of world) civilization. The Huasteca is the place of The Truth that is continually being trodden upon and menaced with destruction by the politicians and their economic interest groups, by the powerful and ignorant cattle ranchers, and by self-interested national intellectuals such as archaeologists, medical doctors, agronomers, and veterinarians.

What is most striking here is not so much that someone believes, traces and tracks this assortment of clues that lead to the hidden greatness of the Huasteca, it is the fact that this person is perhaps the most active cultural figure in town; Oralia is in or behind practically every cultural event in Ciudad Valles and has almost singlehandedly created a museum. Her work cannot be lightly dismissed. Oralia is living proof of the lack of importance that national government has allotted to the region, her struggle to obtain just recognition for the region's culture—though intuitively stated by way of making the region central to the world—is a latent theme in Huastecan regional culture.

In other words: (a) Huastecan culture and history have little place in official renderings of national culture and history; (b) this lack of place—which is a result of the real autonomy of Huastecan society vis-à-vis the national capital—has been countered in nationalist discourse with the construction of an ideology of frontierization; (c) this ideology of frontierization is locally countered with an ideology of hidden values and alternate truths harbored in the region; and (d) these hidden values and truths can be channelized politically into different forms of regionalist social movements and economically into the exploitation of "otherness" for personal gain.

Examples of this abound. I shall mention only two more that I consider to be of special interest. Belief in hidden treasure is a phenomenon that has been noted by a few anthropologists and that has received some theoretical attention (cf. Foster 1948, Schryer n.d.). The argument has centered on the point of whether the belief does or does not support the hypothesis of Limited Good. I am interested in another aspect of the problem. I have known several people who seek hidden treasure: the treasures of the Capablancas, rebels of San Luis from the time of independence, and of wealthy rancheros that were buried during the Revolution; riches offered by the Devil in exchange for one's soul. The striking point about these hidden treasures is not so much that they are believed to be the only (diabolical or not) means to prosperity, but that they enforce the notion of the land as containing and hiding wealth. Knowledge of the region potentially yields profit.

Most rancheros recognize that studying outside the region is by no means enough to manage adequately a Huastecan ranch. Several members of the younger generation of rancheros who came to administer their ranches after studying in universities confirmed this opinion: the land, the climate, the marketing conditions of the region made many technological ventures unfeasible. The most innovative cattle rancher of the region has had important successes in breeding cattle because he has mixed popular observations with sophisticated scientific methods.[10] Local knowledge is valuable and cultivated. Hidden treasure is a culmination of this ideology, for treasure hunts involve a combination of topographic and historical erudition. At the same time, to go on quests for hidden treasure, or to think about searching, calls for deepening one's familiarity with the region. One must adapt oneself to its history.

The final example of the ideological spaces created for regional identity is the relatively well-known case of "el Lord," Mister Edward James. Mister James was an extravagant Scottish nobleman and a great supporter of radical intellectuals, especially of the surrealists.[11] He was interested in botany and traveled extensively in Mexico collecting plants and animals. On one of his trips he met Plutarco, a Yaqui Indian who worked as telegraphist in Cuernavaca. Plutarco eventually became his administrator and has now inherited his Mexican properties. When "el Lord" reached Xilitla, in the Huasteca, he marveled at its natural beauty and acquired a ranch that had been the property of General Castillo, Xilitla's revolutionary *caudillo*. At this spot Mr. James erected a kind of surrealistic castle of antifunctional architecture which, he claimed, served the purpose of confusing the archaeologists of the future (and I'm sure it will). In the middle of the jungle, amid limpid pools of water, there are monumental cement columns (in a kind of Gothic/Arabesque style) that sustain nothing, stairways that lead nowhere, buildings meant only for the jungle to inhabit. And the beauty of this statement of man-constructing-for-nature-to-devour is that it proves again, in the most

mystifying manner, that the region is a center of something for somebody. Although the eccentric ways of Mr. James (including his alleged
hatred of baths and manicure and his love of ferocious animals) may be
understood by Huastecans more as lunacy than as "art," his show of
money in that particular place contributes to the glory of the region.
Moreover, the subordination of the resources of an arch-Western million-
aire to Huastecan nature is a statement that is intuitively understood (I
think): "el Lord's" investment of money into jungle (instead of jungle
into money) and his association with a Yaqui Indian are statements
about the ultimate "truth" of the Huasteca vis-à-vis the West. This is
understood, even if it is not shared (for the rancheros it is an economically unsound extravagance; for the peasants it is a mystifying caprice).
There is a will in Mr. James's constructions to preserve the Huasteca
from the kind of commercial exploitation to which it is being submitted.
The same will can be recognized in the pilgrims that are cured by Beto
Ramón, in the rancheros that consult local savants, in the regional intellectuals' rendering of Huastecan ancient history.

The Huasteca is assimilable to national culture only as vast periphery,
never in its own terms. Yet this characterization of the region as periphery, this ideological attempt (conscious or not) to ignore the history and
culture of the region, provokes the continual rediscovery of the importance of the alternate truths present in local tradition. Thus, as in the
myth of the eagle, the Huasteca is continually recast by local intellectuals, rancheros, peasants, merchants, and foreigners as an alternate
center of culture. The commercial and political exploitation of these
alternatives result in different brands of localist ideologies.

Regionalism Without a Regional
Elite: Morelos Regionalism and
Morelos in National Culture

When I did fieldwork on politics in Tepoztlán (1977–78) I was struck
by coincidences of periods and dates, which seemed to characterize the
relation between local, regional, and national history. At the time I
noted it as a curiosity; today I believe that Morelos' culture and history
has served as a fundamental piece of raw material for the construction of
notions about "national history" and "national culture."

There are several reasons why this should be so. First of all, Morelos is
a distinct economic and administrative region; it has, therefore, an "otherness" with regard to Mexico City, which allows it to be construed as the
quintessential "rural Mexico." More importantly, Morelos is a region
that has been constructed by the Mexico City elites. The core/periphery
organization of the region—which has been maintained to some extent

even after industrialization—was carried out by Mexico City hacendados, politicians, and industrialists. The proximity of Morelos to Mexico City has made control of the region from Mexico City relatively easy
and absolutely indispensable; this is the ultimate reason for the coincidence in periods and dates with "national history."

At the same time, Morelos has been particularly useful for the construction of a national image of the Mexican countryside because of
Zapatismo, Morelos' regional revolutionary movement. In contradistinction with the Huasteca (and probably with most other Mexican regions),
Morelos' Revolution was led by the peasantry and had a class-based
peasant ideology. Although we shall go into the reasons for the emergence of a regionalist movement organized around class strife later, it is
important to point out here that Zapatismo was transformed into the
official rendering of the social strife that was at the base of the Revolution, particularly since Cárdenas's regime in the 1930s.

With the adoption of Morelos' Revolution as the quintessential
Mexican Revolution came the implicit endorsement of Morelos' late
nineteenth century as the fundamental Porfiriato. This process of trans-
forming Morelos' history into national history was, of course, aided by
the continuous presence of national figures in Morelos from the time of
Moctezuma: Morelos was his vacation spot; it was the estate of Hernán
Cortés, the summer palace of Maximilian, the national capital of Juan
Alvarez, the vacation spot of President Calles. At the same time,
Morelos has been a mestizo region since at least the mid-nineteenth
century, much the same as Mexico is supposed to be a mestizo nation.

Because of the postrevolutionary politics of Zapatismo, Morelos is
the state that was first granted ejido land, and where agrarian reform was
carried out most extensively; it is therefore the "showcase" region of the
"revolutionary" governments of this century. Since the 1940s Morelos
has also become the seat of industrial development and so appears as a
model of social development: from a hardy, nationalist, mestizo, revolutionary peasantry to a state-educated nationalist proletariat. Finally, perhaps for all of these reasons, Morelos has been one of the most—if not
the most—researched regions in the country. There is more anthropological and historical information available for ready use in the construction
of "national history" and "national culture" than there has been for most
regions, and social scientists have (perhaps unwittingly) contributed to
an identification of Morelos history with "Mexican rural history" by
insisting on utilizing their studies as "case material" for issues of national
import—for example, the relation between "the peasantry" and the
state, the social psychology of "the Mexican peasant," folk culture in
"Mexican villages," and so on.

Morelense Regionalism as Class Strife

Morelos' history and culture offer an easy choice for the construction of an image of rural Mexican history and rural Mexican culture. Instead of being the "great untapped periphery," Morelos is the continuously tapped, and well-known, periphery. Where the Huasteca gets cast as "national potential," Morelos becomes "national tradition." This process, which is partly caused by the lack of a regional hegemonic class, culminates with the cooptation of Zapatismo into government in 1920 and its symbolic utilization as quintessence of the Mexican Revolution under Cárdenas and his successors. In this sense, Morelos' regionalism is simply an affirmation of Mexican nationalism that cannot occupy an oppositional space vis-à-vis the centralist cultural "truths." Local knowledge, local discoveries, become national property ipso facto. I will not present many examples of Morelos' regionalism and nationalism here in order to avoid redundancy with the chapters that follow; however, it is important to have a clear general understanding of the spaces for Morelos' regional identity and their relation to the construction of national identity.

In apparent contradiction of the ideology of Morelos' regionalism as a form of Mexican nationalism, there is a sense in which Morelos' regionalism has been a pure form of class struggle: because of the weakness— sometimes nonexistence—of a regional hegemonic elite, regionalism in Morelos could never be utilized by a dominant class as it has in the Huasteca. The assertion of regional culture in Morelos was therefore a symbol of unity between members of a class—the peasantry—in opposition to members of other classes that are, *en passant,* associated with Mexico City and national culture. This feature of Morelos' regionalism is what has made its cooptation into "national culture" so important.

At the same time, this form of class struggle/regionalism in Morelos is characteristic only of the peasantry, and not of the emergent working classes, for whom a Morelos' regional culture has scarcely any meaning. Because of this, and given the fact that Morelos has been transformed in the past decades into a predominantly urban economy, Morelos' peasant-based regionalism is every day more of a museum piece for manipulation by the regional petit-bourgeois classes of tourist promoters and middle-level politicians. These local and regional upper classes appropriate the residual forms of peasant regionalism into a regionalist discourse and thereby profit from the coopting hand that the federation has put forth to Morelos.

Let me summarize: (a) Morelos is an economic and political region that lacks an indigenous regional elite because of its proximity to and importance for the Mexico City elites; (b) because of these elites' direct control over the region, Morelos becomes a good candidate to play the role of "exemplary peasant" in "national history" and of "rural culture" in "national culture"; (c) at the same time, the lack of a local hegemonic class means that Morelos' regionalism can in fact be equivalent to the struggle of the peasantry against the elites, which is what it became during power void produced by Maderismo in 1910; (d) this last feature gives a double intention in the appropriation of Morelos' culture into "national culture": Morelos is a useful example of an obedient region, but only if its peasantry is economically coopted and peasant regionalism is transformed into a veiled form of nationalism (instead of a veiled form of class struggle); (e) this process of incorporation and cooptation of Morelos' culture into national culture is eased along with the industrialization of the region, since the cutting edge of Morelos' peasant regionalism is taken away because of the peasant's increasingly marginal position, and peasant regionalism is therefore opened to commercial and political exploitation by local elites.

Morelos and the Huasteca in the Study of Regional and National Culture

I have argued that the study of Morelos and of the Huasteca is important for several reasons. First of all, it demands a differential treatment of regional culture within this essay, in that the organizing principles behind the historical constitution of these regions as cultural regions are variegated; second, the actual descriptive results will point the way to a better understanding of the relationship between regional cultural organization, local and regional ideology, national ideology, and national culture (if this last notion can be usefully redefined). The problems that I have presented in this introduction, which should be thought of as contributions to an analysis of the spaces available for regional identity in two regional cultures, and their implications for the construction of national identity will be the ending point of part 1. In the chapters that follow I will backtrack into the discussion of the organization of Morelos and the Huasteca as regional cultures. Next I shall discuss some of the main intimate cultures in the regions and their interrelations in a system of regional power. Finally, I shall systematize forms of localist ideologies that are important at different levels of regional cultural organization and regional cultural transformation. This discussion, which in fact includes the bulk of the field material that I shall present in this book, is the indispensable first step for reframing the regional and national culture question.

Section 1

Regional Culture
in Morelos

3

Cultural Hegemony in Morelos

General Background

Morelos is both an economic and a political nodal region. Since colonial times at least it has had an economy that has revolved around the lowland production of sugar (and other cash crops), with a relatively simple core/periphery structure wherein marginal highland zones supplied seasonal labor and agricultural resources to lowland, commercially exploited, areas (cf. Warman 1976, de la Peña 1980).

Politically, Morelos has always received recognition of its regional wholeness: during the colonial period most of what today is Morelos was staked off as the estate of Hernán Cortés and his descendants, who had control over the appointment of all civil officials.[1] After independence the two major subregions of Morelos—the region dominated by Cuautla and the one centered on Cuernavaca—were each political and military districts of the state of Mexico.[2] Since 1869 the region has been a state in the Mexican Federation,[3] and in 1894 Cuernavaca was made the seat of a bishopric whose boundaries exactly coincide with those of the state.

Popular wisdom has it that, consonant with the nodal economic and political region that is Morelos, there is a regional culture. Some of the major characteristics of this culture would be (to cite only the historical museum at Cuernavaca): the typical Morelense peasant culture, which finds its cultural climax in Zapatismo; the legacies of lowland hacienda culture; "Indian" Morelos (centered on a very narrow set of communities, cf. Lomnitz-Adler 1979, Dakin and Rieski 1975) and the cultural legacy of urban Morelos, especially Cuernavaca. Closely inspected, however, the regional integration of a Morelos culture is dubious. A cultural region implies systematic internal cultural diversity, organized around the hegemony of a dominant class. When a region has a weak dominant group, it tends to be culturally disarticulated. There will most certainly be culture there—that is not what is at stake—but the cultures involved will be weakly linked with one another. The differences between local cultures in these contexts will not form a part of an interrelated totality.

Morelos' proximity to Mexico City has fettered the development of a regional economic and political elite. The pinnacle of economic and political power has always been directly controlled from Mexico City, and this has provoked weakness in the cultural impact of the regional dominant group. In this chapter I shall present the nature of and limits to regional cultural hegemony in Morelos by discussing, first, the general history of the conformation of the Morelos region and, second, the relation between the political integration of Morelos and cultural hegemony.

The Economic Region

The state of Morelos has been compared to a bowl that is slightly tilted towards the southeast (Lewis 1951:3). The center of the bowl is crosscut by a low internal range that goes south from Tepoztlán down to the Cerro de Jojutla, in the municipality of Jojutla (see maps 2 and 3). This range divides the basin into two large subtropical and tropical valleys: the Plán de Amilpas and the Cañada de Cuernavaca. The Cañada de Cuernavaca is rougher terrain than the Amilpas, though both valleys have a fair amount of irrigation[4] and are ideal for commercial crops such as sugar, rice, cotton, and greens.[5] The external rims of the state are almost all mountainous lands that are not adequate for mechanized agriculture and have no irrigation facilities. In the past these marginal areas were used mostly for subsistence agriculture, for providing firewood and charcoal, and for grazing cattle in the fallow lands. However, because of the ever-easier access from Mexico City, this area has been increasingly utilized for labor-intensive seasonal cash crops, especially tomatoes and sorghum.[6]

The main urban centers of the region are located within the two valleys: Cuernavaca and Cuautla, but also Jojutla, Zacatepec, and Yautepec. Although many of these towns (Cuautla, Jojutla, Yautepec) grew in intimate relation to their rich agricultural hinterlands, Cuernavaca's importance has stemmed more from its strategic location in the transport route from Mexico City to Acapulco than from its participation in the commercialization of local agriculture.[7] The produce of Morelos' rich lands have traditionally been concentrated in these regional cities and thence exported to the Federal District.[8] The increasingly good coverage of the state by roads has allowed a corresponding increase of direct control over agricultural produce by the main Mexico

MAP 2

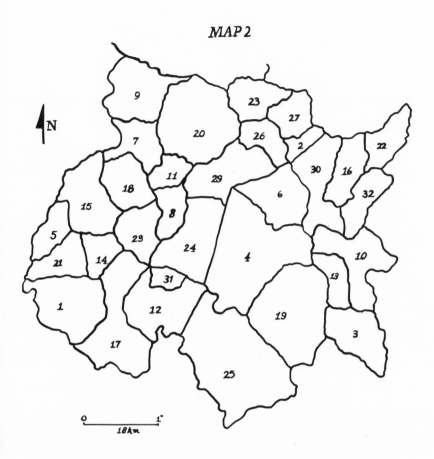

MORELOS, MUNICIPAL BOUNDARIES 1980

1. AMACUZAC
2. ATLATLAHUCAN
3. AXOCHIAPAN
4. AYALA
5. COATLAN DEL RIO
6. CUAUTLA
7. CUERNAVACA
8. EMILIANO ZAPATA
9. HUITZILAC
10. JANTETELCO
11. JIUTEPEC

12. JOJUTLA
13. JONACATEPEC
14. MAZATEPEC
15. MIACATLAN
16. OCUITUCO
17. PUENTE DE IXTLA
18. TEMIXCO
19. TEPALCINGO
20. TEPOZTLAN
21. TETECALA

22. TETELA DEL VOLCAN
23. TLALNEPANTLA
24. TLALTIZAPAN
25. TLAQUILTENANGO
26. TLAYACAPAN
27. TOTOLAPAN
28. XOCHITEPEC
29. YAUTEPEC
30. YECAPIXTLA
31. ZACATEPEC
32. ZACUALPAN

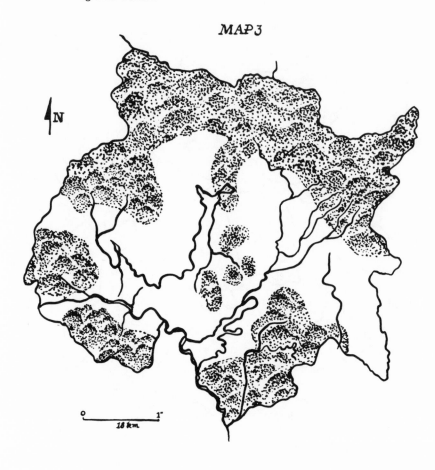

MAP 3

MORELOS,

RIVERS AND SELECTED CONTOURS

 MOUNTAINOUS ZONES

 MAJOR RIVERS

City merchants of La Merced (today the Central de Abastos) and the Mercado de Jamaica. Thus the orientation of commerce and the sources of wealth of the regional elites have changed somewhat.[9]

The marginal lands of Morelos, its economic periphery, have traditionally been devoted in considerable proportion to subsistence production. Map 4 shows the traditional (1940) core/periphery structure of agrarian Morelos, and map 5 shows the geographical overlap between this organization and the locus of industry and commerce. The agricultural periphery can be divided into several different zones. The north, northeast, and northwest zones correspond to the Sierra del Ajusco and cover all of the northern municipios of the state (Tetela, northern Yecapixtla and Ocuituco, Tlalnepantla, Tlayacapan, Atlatlahucan, Totolapan, Tepoztlán, Huitzilac, and northern Cuernavaca). This zone has important extensions of coniferous forest and of *texcales* (lava fields); arable land is rich but scarce. Like the whole of the periphery, all agriculture here is seasonal. The south-southwest is a different ecological area, corresponding to the mountains of Guerrero and to a chain that divides Morelos from the state of Mexico (small portions of the municipios of Cuernavaca, Temixco, Miacatlán, most of Amacuzac, small portions of Puente de Ixtla and Jojutla, important parts of Tepalcingo and Axochiapan), this west-south ring is drier and less fertile than the northern periphery. It has no recourse to the exploitation of the woods and has traditionally been used for cattle grazing or, in some parts, for seasonal farming. The eastern rim of the state has sections that are close to the ecology of the north (parts of Zacualpan) and that are like the south (parts of Jantetelco and Axochiapan).

Today the occupations of this population are varied. Although the periphery still maintains to some degree its traditional role of reserve labor (cf. de la Peña 1980), the workings of this have changed considerably. Until this century the regional core relied on the use of seasonal peripheral peasant labor in the lowland plantations (cf. Lewis 1951, de la Peña 1980, Warman 1976); but the continuity of this phenomenon in this century has been somewhat overstated. Although highlanders still seek permanent and seasonal work outside their villages—in the lowlands and in Mexico City—the importance of this labor supply for the lowlands is rather slim, compared to that of the seasonal labor that comes from the much vaster, poorer, periphery that is the state of Guerrero and Oaxaca.

The Revolution greatly diminished the population of the state of Morelos. There was a great amount of killing, hunger, and disease. There were also streams of migrants from the main cities and towns to Mexico City. The cities of Cuernavaca, Cuautla, and Jojutla were completely uninhabited in 1918, which accounts, in part at least, for the exaggerated decrease in population reflected in the 1921 census. The people who came back usually did so as of 1922 and even into the 1930s. The temporary absence of people in Morelos made for good conditions for people from Guerrero, and migration from that state became important at that time. The importance of the influx from Guerrero grew with

MAP 4

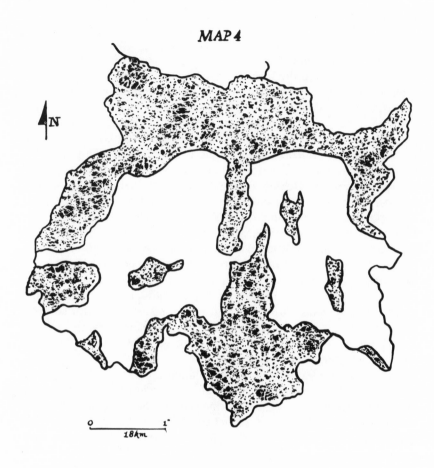

MORELOS, CORE/PERIPHERY STRUCTURE

1940

 AGRICULTURAL PERIPHERY

AGRICULTURAL CORE

MAP 5

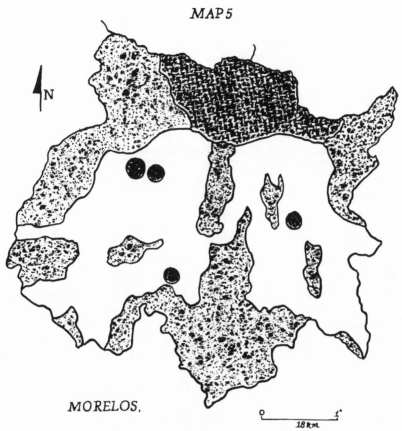

MORELOS,

CORE/PERIPHERY STRUCTURE

1980

0 _____ 1°
18 km

AGRICULTURAL PERIPHERY

AGRICULTURAL CORE

AGRICULTURAL PERIPHERY
REORIENTED TOWARDS MEXICO CITY

INDUSTRIAL CORE

the establishment of a centralized sugar industry, by the construction of the huge cooperative mill in Zacatepec in 1938. Before this, sugar production in Morelos had been decentralized in about two dozen smaller sugar factories. The cutting of the cane was therefore also decentralized and much of the labor came from the Morelos periphery. Along with centralization of production came centralization of the organization of cane production, which meant mass recruitment in Guerrero.

The relative prosperity of the Morelos peasants has also been a factor in the dependence of agro-industry on Guerrero's peasants. The importance of migratory labor for agriculture grew in the 1950s with the introduction of tomatoes in the periphery. Migration to the cities became important with the industrialization of Cuernavaca, beginning in the early 1950s but especially since the mid-1960s. Today in the core and industrial municipios (Cuautla, Cuernavaca, E. Zapata, Jiutepec, Jojutla, Temixco, Yautepec, and Zacatepec) 8 percent of the permanent population is from Guerrero and Oaxaca; in the core agricultural municipios (Amacuzac, Ayala, Coatlán del Río, Mazatepec, Jonacatepec, Miacatlán, Puente de Ixtla, Tetecala, Tlaltizapán, Tlaquiltenango, and Xochitepec) and in the peripheral municipios (Zacualpan, Yecapixtla, Totolapan, Tlayacapan, Tlalnepantla, Tetela del Volcán, Tepoztlán, Tepalcingo, Ocuituco, Jantetelco, Huitzilac, Axochiapan, and Atlatlahucan) the corresponding figures are 4.9 percent and 1.2 percent. On the other hand, the agricultural core and periphery both receive seasonal migrant labor from Oaxaca and Guerrero (the so-called *oaxacos*). There has been no quantification of the size of these migrations, which are most important in the lowlands at the time of cane-cutting (between November and April) and in the highlands for the tomato crop (between August and October).

Morelos' periphery still supplies labor to the core, but its conditions of export have generally been more favorable than those of Guerrero's:[10] Morelos' greater wealth and proximity to the center has meant that peasants have had more access to education, and so to many of the first industrial jobs, as well as to some of the more desirable positions in the services. The peasant economies of the periphery are now not always supplemented by labor as rural proletarians: sometimes family income is increased by help from children who are bureaucrats, or the peasants themselves are seasonal or part-time industrial workers. This is especially true in the municipios that are close to the industrial centers, such as Tepoztlán, Huitzilac, Jiutepec, Temixco, Cuernavaca, and Cuautla.

One might sum up the historical transformations of Morelos' core/periphery structure as follows. The region was originally created through the interests of an hacendado class that organized a regional division of labor and of land use wherein the natural tendency for water to concentrate in the basin was reinforced through artificial irrigation in order to create a regional core of cashcropping, mainly sugar production, and a periphery dedicated both to peasant subsistence under several forms of land tenure and to subsidizing hacienda production through the production of firewood and grazing lands for hacienda mules and oxen.

This initial core/periphery organization was transformed in some important aspects with the collapse of the hacienda during the Revolution (especially since 1913–14). The period that ensued was characterized by the peasantification of the core through agrarian reform, which was extensive in Morelos as early as 1929. However, the substitution of the hacienda as the major force shaping the region did not revolutionize the old core/periphery organization of land use, although it did temporarily diminish the use of peripheral seasonal labor in the core, mainly because of the depopulation of the periphery. This is because the sugar mills and the governmental organizations for agricultural credit (in coordination with the ejidos) continued to control most of the land use decisions, especially since the formation of the Zacatepec sugar cooperative in 1938.

The third period begins around 1950 and it is characterized by the industrialization of the core, the commercialization of much of peripheral agriculture, and the growth of the service sector, particularly around tourism. To a certain extent, this new organization undermines the old definition of the Morelos region itself; the reorientation of peripheral agricultural production directly to the Mexico City market and the proximity of Mexico City for buying consumer goods has meant that parts of the old northern periphery are now in fact oriented directly to Mexico City, without the commercial mediation of Cuernavaca or Cuautla. On the other hand, most of the current economic organization was built around the old core/periphery organization; industrial parks were located in Cuernavaca and Cuautla, and the growth of industry and services is generally concentrated in the old regional core. In addition, because of the utilization of the original spatial organization of the economy, the structure of commerce and the general organization of the central-place hierarchy were maintained, although the difference in concentration of services between the different kinds of central places was exacerbated.[11]

The original regional division of labor was well suited to the needs of the industries that established themselves around Cuernavaca in the late 1950s and 1960s. During this time, there was scarcity in the supply of specialized labor; skilled industrial workers lived mostly in Tlaxcala, Puebla, and Mexico City and were unwilling to move to Cuernavaca. The geographical position of Cuernavaca and transport efficiency to and from Mexico City were incentives for creating industries in Morelos' core, but labor had to come from the periphery. Peasants were transformed first into construction workers and then into industrial workers. When industry expanded further, especially since the construction of an industrial park on the outskirts of Cuernavaca (CIVAC), peripheral labor became supplemented with workers from outside Morelos (cf. Arias and Bazán 1977).

The transformation of Morelos' regional economy from its agricultural base to an industrial and service base thus initially reinforced the old core/periphery structure. However, the modernization of transport to and from the state has transformed agricultural production and the market orientation of much of the periphery, especially the northern zones.[12] Since the 1960s there has been a tendency towards the disintegration of Morelos as an economic region. The industrial and commercial core are dependent on the decentralization of Mexico City industry and bureaucracy and of tourism and weekend homes, and large portions of peripheral agriculture have become commercially oriented peasant landholdings whose produce is oriented directly to the Mexico City market. Significant portions of the old agricultural core are being destined to housing for tourists and for the location of industry and industrial neighborhoods: "Cuernavaca" is now an urban zone that encompasses much of the old agricultural municipios of Temixco, Jiutepec, and Emiliano Zapata. There is a certain tendency for Cuernavaca to collide with Cuautla on an east-west plane of urban expansion that includes also the town of Yautepec. In sum, the modern economic evolution of Morelos can be conceptualized in three stages: an initial (1870–1910) period of regional organization where the economic core revolved around the commercial produce of haciendas;[13] a second period (1914–50) of peasantification of the core in terms of land tenure, reorganization of agroindustry around federal investment, and growth of the tourist industry in Cuernavaca; and a third period (1950–86) of industrialization, commercialization of peripheral agriculture, and vast urban expansion.

The Weakness of the Regional Elite

It is apparent, from the preceding argument, that the Morelos region has been nodally integrated for most of its modern history. However, I shall argue that, despite this integration, Morelos has never consolidated a powerful regional elite. This datum, which I will trace in its local political manifestations, is crucial for understanding the nature of Morelos as a regional culture.

The historical weakness of Morelos' elites is entirely attributable to the region's position in Mexican political and economic geography.

Morelos is a tropical, relatively well-watered region between the temperate and cold regions of the Federal District and the scalding, dry mountains of Guerrero. The produce and climate of Morelos have been valuable to the elites in Mexico City since pre-Columbian times. In addition, its position in the commercial transport route between Mexico and Acapulco, in the political-revolutionary route between the Guerrero mountains and Mexico City, and in the work/labor-supply route for the Guerrerenses explains much of the region's development.

The state of Guerrero is a vast mountainous zone that is, even today, poorly communicated with Mexico City. At the same time, the Guerrero mountains must be traversed to arrive at Acapulco, a port of key importance since colonial times.[14] Guerrero's topography allowed for the creation of settlements that thrived on the margins of central government control. It was a region where maroons settled (cf. Aguirre Beltrán 1972); Indian communities could subsist relatively uninhibited by the state or even by the Church (cf. Ruiz de Alarcón 1984). The people of Guerrero have traditionally lived without the presence of the federal government, and, perhaps for this reason, "machismo" and violence are extreme there. For these and other reasons, Guerrero has been a crucial point for guerrilla warfare, rebellion, and revolution in the history of Mexico; it is far enough from the center to sustain armed movements for extended periods of time. At the same time, the mountains are close to some of the nation's key areas: the port of Acapulco, the internal valleys of Iguala and Chilpancingo, and Morelos.

Morelos' history has been deeply affected by its proximity to and mediation between Mexico City and Guerrero. Its climate and culture are closer to those of Guerrero, but economic and political interaction with Mexico City have meant that Morelos is a region "with government." Morelos' people have always been closely monitored by the federal government in Mexico City; Morelos' economy has always been controlled or influenced by people from Mexico City. The capital city of Cuernavaca has served as a kind of summer residence to national level dignitaries since Hernán Cortés, including Maximilian and all postrevolutionary presidents. All of Morelos' governors have been named by national presidents, and usually without much trouble from the regional elites.[15] The federal government has always shown less tolerance for rebellions in Morelos than for those of Guerrero. How else can one explain the incendiary campaigns against the Zapatistas? Were there not Zapatista and Zapatista-like rebellions in other regions? The key importance of Zapatismo and the violence with which the movement was finally suppressed lies precisely in its proximity to Mexico City.[16] Direct federal intervention is a theme that runs across the entire political history of Morelos.

During the Porfiriato the axis of the Morelos economy and government was the hacienda. The hacienda was the core of Morelos' economy, and yet it was not controlled by the regional elite. There were over thirty haciendas in Morelos, all of which were owned by upper-crust Porfirian families that lived in Mexico City (cf. Von Mentz 1984, Melville 1979). Regional elites were essentially local landholders with moderate-sized ranches[17] that also monopolized local commerce. Their power rested in their position as money-lenders to the local population, and also as contractors of local labor. They controlled municipal presidencies, never the governorships. They had cordial but subservient dealings with hacienda owners and administrators. They were necessary for any government to take into account, but they could not themselves take hold of government.

Morelos' major cities were quite similar to one another, and Cuernavaca stood out very little from the commercial centers of Cuautla and Jojutla. Local politicians here were more important because they tapped a greater web of commerce. Perhaps some of them were richer and more refined than their counterparts in the peripheral cabeceras. They were an elite that could travel a bit more than the local elites of the villages. They could perhaps wrangle more favors from the state government and move about to Mexico City with greater leisure. However, it is impossible to say that this elite had a crucial importance for most of the regional population.

The state's first governors were major political and military figures that had no significant links to Morelos' economy. Their role was the pacification of the region. As political strife in Mexico dwindled, however, the governorship fell into the hands of the Mexico City hacienda-owning families. Political power in the municipios was kept by the local caciques. The pact between these local politicians and the hacendado class characterized state politics in the middle and late Porfiriato. Local politicians aspired only to local power over their municipios.[18]

The proof of the weakness of Morelos' autochthonous Porfirian elites is in the Revolution itself. Zapatismo arose as a result of the political crisis that Maderismo produced. Peasants organized and claimed, first, their rights to control the governorship in lieu of a wealthy and unpopular hacendado family and, next, their right to obtain lands that had been alienated from the towns by the haciendas since independence.[19] What is peculiar about the Zapatista revolt in contrast to the other regional revolutionary movements, is the lack of leadership by the local elites. The cacique class fled to Mexico City, was butchered, or collaborated with the different occupying armies. It showed little capacity for leadership. This contrasts with the active role of regional elites in the revolutionary leadership of most other Mexican regions, and implies a lack of ascendancy of the elite over the population. Patron-client ties between the peasantry and the elite were weak. The elites could not produce a project of their own. They were unable to occupy the void left by the reactionary hacendado class. In sum, the first period of hegemonic regional organization of Morelos is characterized by the existence of elites that only had power at the local and municipal levels. These elites did not articulate Morelos as an economic or political region, and they lacked an orchestrated regional political project.

The Revolution was a period in which political rule was fragile. Parts of Morelos were controlled by different armies, while others were temporarily abandoned. The decrees and policies of the different armies seemed to have allowed some stability in a few sectors,[20] but by and large they were obeyed only to humor the factions in power. In 1920, after the assassination of Zapata and the military defeat of Zapatismo, the remnants of Zapata's movement supported Obregón's coup and thereby entered government. From 1920 to 1930 the state was usually run by military governors, most of whom were middle-ranking Zapatistas. However, these Zapatista governments did not rise to a real position of regional power, in part because they were closely surveyed by the federal government in Mexico City, and in part because their peasant project meant the elimination of a regional hegemonic class. The old elites were impoverished and often had to begin accumulating again from scratch (cf. Lewis 1951; de la Peña 1980).[21] The new cacicazgos taken up by Zapatista officials in the 1920s were given no room for expansion, and the most important leaders were made officials of the regular army and then transferred to other regions (as in the case of Genovevo de la O, who was the most important military leader after Zapata's death). The degree of local autonomy from the state government during this period was relatively great (cf. Lomnitz-Adler 1982), despite the fact that Morelos was under direct federal military control until 1930. However, due to a lack of resources the position of the state during this period was analogous to that of the municipios that have been described by Roberto Varela (1984): there was no room for local democracy, no resources to build on, no possibility to expand into greater (internal) domains. In this sense, the Revolution meant the strengthening of the local level power structures at the expense of regional integration, while, at the same time, local power structures could not be a basis of very important accumulation of resources because of agrarian reform and capital scarcity.

Agrarian reform in Morelos was carried out as of the early 1920s and was practically completed by 1929 (González Herrera and Embriz Osorio 1984). Most of the sugar factories were destroyed in 1914, and what was left of them was pillaged by revolutionary generals and sometimes transferred to haciendas outside the region.[22] There was no room for the recreation of the old hacienda class, but for the moment there was no internal basis for the consolidation of a regional elite either. Warman (1976) has described the repeasantization of production in eastern Morelos during this period. The land was distributed mostly among peasants,[23] and the capital was taken out of the system altogether, at least until the construction of the Zacatepec mill in 1938. Although the local landholding classes were, by and large, untouched by agrarian reform, still they did not have the necessary capital to integrate the region economically or to control it politically.

In many cabeceras the 1920s was a decade of conflict between revolutionary leaders and economic elites. Most of Morelos' villages had armed caudillos that wished to prolong their internal political power.[24] The haciendas and hacienda society were agonizing: a power void existed in the regional economy.

By 1930 the economic situation of Morelos was more clearly defined (agrarian reform and tourist development) and local and subregional caudillos were neutralized. After years of military interim governors, the state constitution was reinstated, elections were held, and Vicente Estrada Cajigal, a general born in Cuernavaca[25] who had passed the Revolution in Michoacán as friend and collaborator of general Pascual Ortiz Rubio, was elected governor. Through his association with president Ortiz Rubio, Estrada Cajigal had dealings with the all-powerful ex-president Plutarco Elias Calles.

The reinstallation of constitutional government in Morelos in 1930 marks the beginning of change for the state. Since the rise of Zapatismo, Morelos had been portrayed in Mexico City as a lawless region. There had even been a proposition in the National Congress of dissolving the state of Morelos and turning it into a territory, governed directly by the national government (López González 1968). However, the Calles-controlled regimes decided otherwise. They gave great impulse to Cuernavaca as a tourist center. They built a highway from Mexico to Acapulco crossing Cuernavaca. Cuernavaca was perhaps the first tourist center in modern Mexican history. Beaches were not yet accessible, and Cuernavaca was quaint and had good weather, several fine hotels, and a gambling casino.[26]

Nevertheless, the power of Morelos' first postrevolutionary constitutional governor, Vicente Estrada Cajigal, was ultimately based on his proximity to ex-president Calles. Estrada Cajigal was unable to prolong his power after the end of his term. In part this was due to Calles's own political bent: Calles named Refugio Bustamante, a country bumpkin, noble-hearted but certainly not controllable by anyone but Calles, governor.[27] Estrada Cajigal's possibilities of extending his regional power came to a definite end with the exile of president Calles. Cárdenas, the new national strongman, did not support Calles (or Estrada Cajigal's) projects for Morelos. He closed down the Casino de la Selva, which was the biggest tourist investment in the state, and decided to buttress Zapatismo, to which end he built the mill at Zacatepec and made it into a cooperative for peasants of the Jojutla region.

Where was regional power at the time? The peasants had their land. But they had it through the ejido system, which was even then a way in which the federal government could control the peasantry without the mediation of traditional local politicians. The sugar industry was in the hands of a cooperative,[28] which proved to be an arena for conflict between local peasants and the federal institutions that ran the management of the mill. In these confrontations the federal government has always had the upper hand. The attempts at creating local businesses (a regional bank, the introduction of new crops such as grapes, the building of tourist facilities, a few minor sugar mills) were carried out in partnerships with national politicians. As fate would have it, these politicians' power usually ran out before the projects came to fruition.

When the 1940s came around and a period of intense capitalist expansion was promoted at the national level, Morelos still had no bourgeoisie with any kind of real control over the region. The capital investments that entered Morelos—slowly in the 1940s, quickening in the 1950s, and reaching a peak in the 1960s and early 1970s—did not need to bargain very much with that elite.

Perhaps the biggest moneymakers in Cuernavaca became the people involved in real estate. Here the locals had advantages over the Mexico City crowd because several families owned fair-sized ranches that were transformed into urban property. But even in this the Morelos elite was not entirely successful. Some of the most prominent people in real estate and commerce in the postrevolutionary period have been migrant families from Guerrero. In the case of real estate, the Estrada family (not to be confused with Estrada Cajigal) was able to obtain property of most of the outskirts of Cuernavaca. When the city grew, this property became extremely valuable. Other important businesses in real estate have meant wealth for those governors and presidents involved (through the appropriation of communal or ejido lands), but rarely for the local elites.

In the 1950s investments in Morelos began growing in importance, but so did federal control over governors. In this period, presidents began imposing outsiders to the state government. Governors since the 1950s have tended to leave Cuernavaca after the end of their terms. The stable elements of the bureaucracy are permanent Morelos residents. However, these people can rarely ascend to the most important posts in the state. They are indispensable for any governor to have on his staff, while at the same time the main posts are allotted to close political allies that come from Mexico City.

On the economic front, it is equally true that the rich are not in control of the major aspects of the economy. All industry is owned—and usually managed—by either Mexico City or transnational capital. Rural land is mostly in the ejido regime. The elites are left only with control over local commerce, and even this is limited because of the proximity of Mexico City. The attempt to create a professional class of Morelenses that could oust competition from Mexico City has failed. The state university is only seventy kilometers away from the national university in Mexico City. The best students still tend to go to the national university, and training at the Universidad de Morelos is so poor that people with a Morelos degree usually get jobs as assistants or helpers of professionals trained elsewhere.

There is a sense, then, in which Morelos is very weak as a hegemonic region. The main forces shaping regional organization have always been based in Mexico City. At the same time, however, Morelos is an internally differentiated and articulated politico-administrative, economic, ecological, and historical region. As such it has a regional culture: Morelos is not merely a homogeneous zone of the Mexico City regional culture because it has been internally organized into mutually dependent zones (be it hacienda production or industrialization or political administration). Because of this, Morelos is clearly distinct in its problems and characteristics from the surrounding regions: the Valley of Toluca, the mountains of Guerrero, the valleys of Mexico and Puebla. But part of its distinction is precisely the economic, political, and cultural weakness of its core. On the other hand, because Morelos is a state, the weak Morelos elites have the institutional guarantee (and obligation) of a certain degree of regional cultural integration via the production of regionalist ideology.

Political Integration, Economic Disintegration, and Cultural Hegemony

Until this point I have shown that, although Morelos is an internally differentiated social space, its internal cultural differentiation did not entail the dominance of a regional class and, furthermore, the regional dominant class has grown out of the relatively unimportant economic spaces left untouched by the national bourgeoisie: local commerce, some local landholding, some of the local service industries, and most of the state bureaucratic apparatus.

This last institution, the state apparatus, has been an important locus of regional integration and is the only power source that gives Morelos' local elites a role in the construction of regional hegemony. The very existence of a state coincident with the economic region of Morelos implies recognition on behalf of the national elites of an autochthonous regional leadership, so that the regional elites look upon the state government as a legacy of their own. For these reasons it is important to understand the workings of the Morelos state apparatus in relation to the conformation of regional hegemony.

I have already mentioned that the governors of Morelos and the municipal presidents of Cuernavaca apparently are appointed only with presidential approval. In addition to this, the official party (PRI) has developed a tendency to name governors whose most important virtues are loyalty to the party and to the president, regardless of their local political appeal. One might in fact argue that the party tends to choose candidates *without* a strong local standing, in that "loyalty to the party" implies precisely a proven willingness to abandon one's social following in order to go wherever the party wills. This fact has meant that in Morelos, for the past thirty years at least, governors have had a weak internal popularity base and have had to bring their top-standing officials in from Mexico City.[29] The Cuernavaca elite has had to be content with second-string positions or, if they are too important for this, with unofficial advisory positions. The nature of the political spaces left over to the regional and local elites is, however, somewhat different from that which characterized the Porfiriato.

Municipal Power Revisited

Municipal power and municipal administrative structures are the best known and best studied aspects of Morelos' politics. This is due to the preponderance of anthropological studies in the region; however there is a critique to be made of the municipality-centered view of politics that has emanated from these studies. There would appear to be something about the municipio that makes it seem to the ethnographer the "natural" locus of community politics. There is much to be learned, however, from taking a state perspective on municipal politics.

Municipios have a political seat, the *cabecera,* which is meant to coincide with the most important locality of the municipio. The main offices of the municipio are the municipal president, the *regidores,* and the *síndico.* Together these officers form the *cabildo,* which is the main decision-making unit. All of the cabildo is elected for three-year terms.[30] There is no reelection to the same post. In addition to members of the cabildo, the municipio has a few officials who are not elected. The most important is the municipal secretary, who must know how to read and write and who often acts as counselor to the municipal president in matters bureaucratic. There are also municipal tax collectors, policemen, and garbage collectors.

The localities outside of the cabecera are represented by *ayudantes,* local politicians named by the municipal president. The ayudantes carry through the orders of the municipality and serve as law enforcers, but they are also expected to take local complaints to the cabecera.

Varela (1984) has shown that there is systematic variation in municipal political function according to the size and resources of the municipio. He distinguishes three kinds of local level politics. The first pertains to localities that have almost no internal class differentiation; these are peripheral communities that are rarely cabeceras.[31] From Varela's anticultural point of view, politics in these places might be described as "much ado about nothing" insofar as there are no great resources to be gained or lost; however, politicking still seems to be important to the villagers who take part in them (politics, as Geertz has repeatedly shown, is not only about controlling resources). There is communal democracy, but no important resources for power and social change.

The second kind of locality in Varela's model is the average poor peripheral cabecera and municipio. In Morelos this kind of municipality gets very few governmental resources while at the same time they are within the range of the governor's interest. According to Varela, this interest on behalf of government, when added to lack of local resources, makes, perhaps, for the worst kind of political immobility. There is no democracy because the main municipal positions are controlled from the outside, and there is nothing important to politic about because there are no resources.

The third kind of municipio is relatively large and wealthy. Here the municipal presidency is strongly contested, and it is important for a governor to impose his candidate. Although there is little room for democracy in these municipios, there are important spaces for politics because the cabildo has the resources with which to carry out public works and with which to affect the local population in significant ways.

To this typology one would have to add the very biggest and richest municipios of Morelos, especially Cuautla and Cuernavaca. In Cuernavaca the municipal president can usually not be named without consent from the national president. This means that there is room for friction between Cuernavaca's municipal presidents and Morelos' governors. The case of Cuernavaca is complicated by the fact that it is the capital of both the municipio and the state, and many public works of the state government directly compete with those of the municipality.

A view from the center of state government can add dimensions to

Varela's description of local level politics. From the point of view of the state politicians with which I spoke, including a wide variation of posts, from ex-governor, to ex-municipal president of Cuernavaca, to senator, to bureaucrat in the state government, there is no such thing as a municipio that is of no interest to the governor. This is because even the poorest municipal presidency is contested by more than one local family. In addition, most municipal presidencies, including most of the very poorest peripheral municipios, seem to be lucrative for members of the cabildo. Granted that this has not always been the case, and that perhaps fifteen or twenty years ago there were a few municipal presidents who ended their term in worse economic shape than when they started, but that seems not to be the case in any municipio of the state today, and was probably rare even during the state's poorest years. Municipal presidencies are seen as political and economic prizes in the context of state politics.

The major moment in municipal politics is the time of the selection of the PRI's candidate for the municipal presidency.[32] All municipios recognize this to be the key decision and the scene for the most important factionalism. Different factions speak with the governor and with whatever contacts they have in the state bureaucracy and in the state offices of the PRI. The contacts of the different factions are crucial in this period. Factions without contacts will try to stir up as much popular support as possible in an attempt to intimidate the governor and keep him from making an unpopular choice.

The state offices of the PRI, although ultimately dependent on the governor, have their own rules of operation. The leaders of the party's sectors (labor, peasantry, and the "popular sector") are weighty politicians in their own right and have traditional spheres of influence. Some municipios, for example, "belong" to the peasant sector (CNC), others to the labor sector (CTM), and yet others to the popular sector (CNOP). These sector leaders also have their say in the legislative elections, in that senators and representatives also have sector affiliation (and are expected to dress the part; the "sectors" are the official state image of civil society; leaders of the CNC must therefore dress or speak "like peasants" or ranchers, and the same logic applies to the other sectors).

I do not have very good information on the workings of these sectors or on the bases for their weight vis-à-vis the governor and other political figures. State leaders of the sectors have close relations to the national leaders and thereby get concessions from the different levels of the executive branch and from Congress, but they must also submit to the governor's designs. Those of us who have written monographs on local-level politics in Morelos (e.g., Krotz 1974, Lomnitz-Adler 1982, Arias and Bazán 1979, de la Peña 1980, Varela 1984, and Warman 1976) have thus far paid insufficient attention to the extreme complexities of politics above the municipal level. Everyone knows that municipal presidents are imposed by governors, and there are cases where suspicions about municipal presidencies being sold by the governor to the best bidder are well founded. But, undoubtedly, the web of relevant relations and institutions that are ultimately involved in the selection of municipal presidents is complex, and although the governor does the choosing, he must bear in mind a certain overall picture composed of the totality of municipal presidents in the state, the senators and representatives, the members of his staff, and the officials of the sectors. Thus the amply documented tendency for governors to name unpopular candidates for municipal presidents cannot be explained exclusively—as I did (1982)—by the will of the governor to maintain extremely dependent and mediatized municipal presidents. The governors' decisions also involve the interests of what we might call the "political court" of Cuernavaca (made up to the main influential sectors at the state level), which is an arena that has as of yet been invisible to the ethnographers of the region.

The existence and importance of this court in the selection of municipal candidates is undoubtable, and one of the effects of the pressures of this court on municipal politics is that unpopular candidates are frequently selected. The effect of selecting unpopular candidates is most certainly the weakening of the office of municipal president and of the municipio in general. Political tradition establishes that the popular (and unselected by the governor) factions get spaces in the cabildo, which usually makes for a cabildo of enemies who have great difficulties in agreeing and in engaging in concerted action. This situation ultimately fortifies the position of the state vis-à-vis the municipio and heightens the *deus ex machina* effect of the governors' occasional direct interventions in the municipio (cf. Lomnitz-Adler 1982).

The most extreme example of this has come to light under the much debated policy of Lauro Ortega, the current governor.[33] Lauro Ortega has invented a municipal ritual that he named "Juntas de Fortalecimiento Municipal." These *juntas* are day-long sessions in which the governor and his secretaries go to a municipio and discuss in a public assembly all of the municipio's problems. There is a list of speakers, all of whom read one-page speeches stating a concrete need of the municipio: a school, a factory, a fruit-canning machine, a land problem. Lauro Ortega listens to each speech, and at the end of each he calls out loud to the relevant secretary and says, while the secretary furiously takes notes, something like, "I give 80 million pesos for the construction of this school. Write a check out to these people for them to buy material. The bulldozers should be here in the morning." Unfortunately, the checks often bounce. Some politicians privately claim that the sessions of "For-talecimiento Municipal" have probably entailed paying more money than the government has.

What is culturally interesting about these juntas is the appeal of the style of decisionmaking. The town is seen as having lived with ancestral problems which townsfolk themselves cannot resolve; according to this myth, the problems of this town never reach the ears of the people in power. So the governor must physically go to hear and see the problem and give it immediate solution. Perhaps Lauro Ortega is as demented as his opposers claim. Until his time, all governors were aware of their real limits and took care to make only exemplary miracles, while Ortega has decided to multiply the bread and the fishes on a daily basis. The "bounc-ing of the checks" could signal the end of the belief in the governors' control over manna.

Politically, Morelos can thus be described as a region wherein the upper bureaucratic echelons—chosen by national-level, Mexico City politicians—have the power to appoint key officers at the local level. These key officers are often locally unpopular, and so municipal auton-omy is undermined. On the other hand, the local links of the state bureaucracy are relatively weak, which is why central power is some-times represented as being divorced from—or ignorant of—local prob-lems. These political phenomena are linked to the economic issues dis-cussed in the first part of this chapter. The weakness of the regional economic groups helps explain the issue of the political articulation of the region.

These general comments on the workings of Morelos state govern-ment (which by no means substitute for a reading of the numerous, already cited studies on local politics) are an indispensable point of reference for understanding the hegemonic organization of the Morelos region and the spatial organization of culture that I shall discuss in the following chapters. The pressures that local factions exert on state gov-ernment officials are culturally framed in regionalist and localist terms; the ideologies that legitimate a governor's actions across the Morelos administrative region are also based on interpretations of local and re-gional cultures. The political space that I have outlined is a basic grid for the ideological appropriation, transformation, and use of local, class, and regional culture.

4

The Cultural Region

A Problematization from the Core

In the chapters that follow, I shall discuss the nature and organization of Morelos' regional culture by making particular emphasis on the transformations into "intimate cultures" of two major class cultures: a peasant class culture and a petit-bourgeois/petite-bureaucratique (pardon the neologism) class culture. The emergence of intimate cultures that belong to a proletarian class culture will be discussed along with considerations of the ways in which incoherence is produced for intimate cultures of peasant class culture. In this chapter I have set out to problematize Morelos' regional culture from Morelos' regional core. The problem that I am posing is: in what sense are Morelos' intimate cultures interrelated in a system of *regional* hegemony?

The first element that is indispensable to the comprehension of Morelos as a cultural region is that Morelos elites do not wield an overbearing power over the regional populace except through the superiority of their patterns of consumption (i.e., except through "distinction"). They are neither major owners of the means of production nor do they control the state apparatus. Because the local elites do not independently control the local subordinate classes, they cannot simply create their own cultural styles and expect them to sustain their status as upper classes. The Cuernavacan elites cannot invent their own cultural system of social distinction. Instead, they latch on to the idiom of social difference that comes to them through the media and the example of Mexico City and elsewhere. This is—culturally—why this class has to be considered a petite bourgeoisie.

On the other hand, because these regional elites do partake in the control of the state bureaucracy, and because the existence of the state of Morelos entails a project of regional culture (through state schools and the university, through its museums and cultural activities, through the local radio stations and newspapers), Morelos' elites have been given a way of providing a regional idiom of social difference that their economic position does not warrant in and of itself. The ambiguous situation of the local elites in the conformation of regional hegemony is most perceptible in Cuernavaca, the economic and political core of Morelos. In this chapter I discuss in general terms some of the intimate cultures of Cuernavaca. This discussion limits ethnographic presentation to the minimum necessary for understanding that the core of Morelos can hardly be said to produce a culture that is conformed in the dialectics of hegemony between local dominant and subordinate classes. On the contrary, I argue that the upper classes are fragmented in two intimate cultures: that of the middle bureaucracy, which has attempted to create for itself a position of brokerage through control of the state political apparatus or through an appeal to this control via an ideology of re-gional culture ("regionalism"), and that of the local bourgeoisie, whose importance stems from its wealth.

So the two strategies of regional hegemony, which are at times com-plementary and at times at odds with each other, consist in (a) the absorption of the entire Morelos region into a fully capitalist Mexican economy in which a superiority of means of consumption is the primary determinant of social position, and (b) the inscription of the entire Morelos region into a political system that can be controlled only through the mediation of regional politicians. These processes of re-gional hegemony, and the problems of regional culture created by them, can be well understood with reference to the Morelos regional core, and particularly Cuernavaca, which is the seat of the regional economic and political elites.

Cuernavaca

The physical characteristics of Cuernavaca provide clues about the discontinuities in hegemonic cultural projects in Morelos' core. The extremely erratic urban design of the city is a testimony to the lack of an elite with sufficient hold over the city to enforce a continuous project of urban expansion. It is not that there never were plans made for an orderly expansion of the city; rather, the interests of each regime domi-nate during a limited number of years and are forgotten as soon as a new governor or municipal president reaches office.[1]

One could carry out an archaeology of governmental projects that is more often than not tied to the different politicians' interests: the urban development of different zones, the planning of the web of traffic, the creation of new commercial zones, and the like. The most striking element is the lack of continuity between projects and the urban problems that have ensued. Cuernavaca is a city with a severe water shortage, with severe traffic problems, with severe housing problems.

The aspect of culture that I shall explore here, in the analysis of the core of the Morelos region is that which appears as a non-culture, as a "lack of culture" to both insiders and outsiders. The illusion of a "lack of culture" is produced by particular forms of what I have called "incoherence" that are nonetheless compounded into a cultural organization, which I shall call "Cuernavacan baroque," that seems perpetually transitory and therefore "acultural."

The specific characteristics of incoherence in Cuernavacan culture must be understood in terms of (a) the enormous growth and expansion of the city, (b) the slim role of local elites in this economic expansion, (c) the existence of hegemony produced through the power of extralocal groups and classes, and (d) the absorption of Cuernavaca's new population into a relatively stable political economy. "Incoherence" in Cuernavaca is reflected in the abundance of personal and small-group belief systems that have very limited possibilities of expanding into and controlling public spheres of cultural manifestation; in a concomitant tendency for erosion in the strength and tenability of some of these beliefs (which are characteristically either peasant in origin or of an old, small-town, petit-bourgeois elite); and in the transformation of some of these beliefs into world views (the construction of new coherence) on the part of some individuals and groups, but still in the context of lack of control over the public sphere. Structurally speaking, what we have in Cuernavaca is a great diversity of cultural groups whose systems of internal reproduction are threatened or completely shattered because they have been thrust into a new environment that they cannot easily control (urban Cuernavaca is really only forty years old), and because that new environment is centerless in that the public space is not controlled by any local group. In this sense, Cuernavaca could be said to be one of Mexico's first "postmodern" cities, except that here the postmodern effect (pastiche; lack of a coherent, overarching cultural project; decenteredness) is not so much produced by the overabundance of media (although some of this exists today) as by migration to an economic pole that is controlled from without.

I call this society "baroque" because it is stratified and pluralistic, yet the positions of the social hierarchy are not created or controlled by the local elite. This means that the local elite is not a hegemonic class and, because of this, cultural diversity is endemic. We have, therefore, both the diversity and the hierarchy of a baroque; however, it is a "dependent" baroque, because the whole organization of the local hierarchy is outside local control, and so the "higher" and "lower" classes are not directly interdependent. Each of the local intimate cultures thus suggests the existence of a social whole which cannot be found within the limits of the city. It is a kind of peripheral postmodernism.

A great many symbols in Cuernavaca are, then, characteristic of particular groups or even private to some families, and therefore continually contested, corroded, and recreated. This is the reason why a city such as this appears "cultureless." However, a few examples of Cuernavacan "private" symbols will suffice to bring culture history back into the picture.

Types of Neighborhoods

If we describe Cuernavaca by the kinds of settlements that compose it, we can arrive at an initial typology of classes in the city. This is a useful starting point for an analysis of cultural interaction in the core.

1. There is the "old Cuernavaca"—today merely the downtown area—that concentrates much of the city's commerce, but also maintains some of the "old" Cuernavacan society: *vecindades* (tenements) of the traditional urban poor and some of the dwellings of old-time merchants and teachers who were once the city's middle class.

2. There are the little villages that used to surround Cuernavaca and that have been engulfed by the city. These places—Amatitlán, Tlaltenango, Acapantzingo, San Antón, Chapultepec, Chipitlán, Chamilpa—were once peasant villages. In fact, the ejido grants that were allotted to these villages after the Revolution have become an integral part of the problem of Cuernavaca's expansion, because ejido land cannot (officially) be bought and sold and must be formally expropriated for conversion into urban land. To this date, these villages still maintain a stratum of old village inhabitants, some of whom are still part-time peasants on minuscule fractions of plowable land. At the same time, many of these villages house the local middle classes and the weekend homes of Mexico City people. (In 1984 Cuernavaca's population more than doubled on the weekends.) The old villages are the most "picturesque" parts of town and, as such, they tend to attract the higher classes, thereby pulling up the prices of local land and making selling attractive to the old inhabitants.

3. There have been several middle- and working-class housing projects. The first were carried out by Textiles Morelos (one of the earliest industrial investments in Cuernavaca) at Teopanzolco. Since then complexes have been built for different sectors of the bureaucracy—teachers, electrical workers—and for the workers of CIVAC (the industrial park

at the edge of the city), along with projects funded by workers' housing programs such as INFONAVIT in different parts of the city.

4. The illegally occupied working-class barrio has a relatively short history. It started appearing in Cuernavaca in the late 1950s but has never stopped growing. These settlements (which include the colonias of Rubén Jaramillo, Otilio Montaño, La Lagunilla, and others) have complex political histories, for they all originated as land invasions organized by different political groups and impresarios. They are therefore the loci of intense political competition for the organization of followings and, generally, are areas open to the competition of different kinds of groups for proselytization. Protestant churches, for example, seem to have been most successful in these districts (as have the Catholic reforms carried out by the radical bishop of Cuernavaca, yielding the famous *comunidades cristianas de base*).

5. The "residential" district for the local well-to-do and for the Mexico City weekenders also has complex histories that often involve expansion into communal and ejido land.

These five settlement types undergo variations and transitions. So, for example, some of the working-class housing projects have become "residential neighborhoods" (a Mexican euphemism for middle- and upper-class neighborhoods) after the zones have been provided with utility services. Likewise, the "invaded" settlements have tended eventually to become legalized and urbanized and in this way become settlements for a more established working class. Finally, there is a tendency for the Cuernavaca elite to reestablish itself in the residential neighborhoods where Mexico City weekend homes predominate, which has the effect of making this elite spatially diffuse and therefore difficult to locate and count.

Despite these and other complexities which are generally related to a mode and logic of urban expansion, the conceptualization of the city as divided into those five main types of class-based settlements is a useful point of departure for a discussion of intimate cultures and of the culture of social relations in the core.

Peasants in Cities[2]

There are two major modes of peasant cultural existence in Cuernavaca: as migrants who live in sprawling shanty towns and are employed in the factories or the services, and as dwellers of peasant villages that have been engulfed by the city. The two transformations of peasant culture that ensue from these situations are distinct from each other. As we have seen, the city of Cuernavaca has expanded greatly and it has engulfed several villages of the municipio which had (some still have)

ejido or communal lands and which were until the 1940s peasant villages: Chapultepec, San Antón, Tlaltenango, Acapantzingo, Chamilpa,
Amatitlán, Chipitlán. Some of the peasant population of these villages is
still present in them, and some of these old families play an important
part in the development of local communal culture. Each of these villages still has its church, most of which are zealously guarded by the
"old" (peasant) inhabitants of these communities against the modernizing influence of the Church (especially under the leftist bishop Méndez
Arcéo). Village fiestas are still organized in each of these villages, usually with a mayordomia system which is sustained not by the personal
contribution of the mayordomo but rather through a system of money
collection in which old-timers and newcomers contribute economically
to a celebration that is primarily organized by the old villagers.

Side by side with this conservation of communal control over the local
church are the landholding organizations that still exist in most of these
barrios. The old families of these villages have control of the village
documents that attest to property of communal lands (in the cases of
villages which retained their communal lands, such as Tlaltenango and
Chamilpa) or to their ejido titles (in the cases of Chapultepec, Acapantzingo, San Antón, and Amatitlán).[3] As Cuernavaca grew, these peasant
families complemented work on the ever-diminishing fractions of agricultural land with urban employment, especially in the construction industry during the 1940s through the 1960s and to an ever greater extent in
industry and the professions for the younger generation. The result of
this transitional stage between peasantry and proletarianization—a state
that, let it be said in passing, only occurred thanks to the process of
repeasantification through ejido grants in the 1920s—is culturally complex, and the forces in favor of maintaining a "traditional" (in fact not
very traditional) peasant culture in these barrios may not yield easily or
immediately to those of a proletarianized culture. Peasant interests in
urban land, which has become extremely expensive in each and every
one of the peasant barrios, is a force in favor of the maintenance of a
local barrio culture. In addition, these "peasant" families are particularly well placed to articulate their peasantness with proletarianization in
a profitable way. They are in a big city and so can take advantage of
some of the comforts of urban life. Their children can study in Mexico
City without incurring extreme expense. They may even work in Mexico
City or Cuernavaca without severing ties with their homes. On the other
hand, because of the convenience of staying at their traditional homes
and sites, "peasants" in these villages retain their kinship ties with the
four or five kin groups of the villages and so become immediately constituted into the best organized local groups, which is again a factor in the
maintenance of peasant culture in the city. The fact that a level of

community is maintained in these barrios allows for the reproduction—albeit in the form of a subordinate discourse—of local culture.

So, for example, José Roca, one of my ethnographic acquaintances of this particular group, told me stories of religious mystery and terror that are typical of Morelos peasants: stories of the *llorona* or of apparitions of the devil with bags of gold. He also told of some of the miracles performed by the Virgin (de la Natividad) of Tlaltenango, his village. And then he told me a story which his elders told him but which he claimed not to believe:

> Once they took the image of San Jerónimo [from the local chapel] to Mexico City for repair, and when they sanded the paint from his arms the statue bled. I do not think that this was so, because I don't think that there are apparitions of saints and virgins these days. The apparitions that supposedly occur now are ways of making money; there were many miracles and apparitions in the times of Christ, but now that things are going in such a bad direction I doubt that they can appear.

Despite the seemingly categorical rejection by José of modern apparitions, he then proceeded to ask me whether I believed in them, whether I thought it possible that San Jerónimo bled when he was repaired, because perhaps I knew more than he and could tell him what to believe.

This example shows, I think, the way in which Roca's peasant ideology is subordinated to hegemonic legitimation. He unashamedly believes in witchcraft (and of a kind that is local and peasant in origin) because a doctor once admitted to him that in fact there were women who bewitched men; he openly recognizes that there were miracles and apparitions in the times of Christ because the Church recognizes that this is true; but he reserves judgment about the veracity of a local miracle in which he and his friends believe because his community is in and of itself insufficient to legitimate a belief outside of this small community itself. This is an example of what I mean by Cuernavacan baroque, the existence of a rich and private group culture which is not backed as a coherent system by the local hegemony, but which is not substituted by a hegemonic coherent culture. Cuernavacan baroque is, therefore, a system in which hegemony is very incomplete. Alternate and potentially incompatible senses of reality coexist in the urban space. Cultures like this urban peasant culture are not cultures of resistance that were created in a dialectic with the local elite. Although the existence of this "baroque" order can, as we shall see, facilitate or provoke urban movements of resistance, these local cultures often simply "open up" to the pressures exerted by the general hegemony. This aperture to dominant ideologies decreases the local culture's coherence (and, therefore, the efficacy of its cultural symbols is undermined) and contributes to an "incoherent" baroque wherein the culture of the whole city is formulaic, hierarchical and full of intricacy. Yet the intricate details are not microcosms of the structure which they rest upon. Urban peasant culture is not a direct product of the "architecture" of Cuernavacan cultural relations in and of themselves.

Another important feature of this engulfed and transformed peasant culture is that, because of its partial coherence and because neither the hegemonic state nor the emergent proletarian cultures have fully substituted local coherence, it lends itself to occasional periods of "closure," or of affirmation of local coherence. These affirmations of local coherence—resistance—can occur either through local movements of self defense (for example, around the defense of communal or ejido land, or around the defense of the local church) or through foreign "prophetic" leaders who ally themselves with these local cultures and proclaim their viability as regional cultural alternatives. An example of this latter form of local organization is the perception of Zapata in this peasant context:

> Afterwards [after Cortes's establishment of mills at Atlacomulco and Tlaltenango and his organization of the countryside] came Zapata's Revolution, and the story changed. Zapata began defending the people that worked the land. He was the foreman [*capataz*] or horse trainer [*caballerango*] of a rich man, of one of those Spaniards, he was a foreman and so he saw how they treated the peons until he could stand it no longer: he saw so much that he couldn't withstand it, and he began planning revolt with other men from this state. Then a Spaniard, a patron, tried to hit a peon, and that was when the revolt [*la bola*] began: all of the peasants were already in agreement, they were only waiting for a provocation, and that was the movement that the Indians, my forefathers, created.

In this interpretation of the outbreak of the Revolution I am interested only in pointing out that Zapata is perceived as a foreman—that is, not directly as an oppressed peasant or an Indian—who saw oppression and could not stand it. His legitimation of the peasant cause through revolt and revolution is, I think, an example of the way in which this relatively engulfed or incoherent peasant culture is organizable through the proposition of an alternate hegemonic order from the outside; thence its inclination to messianic movements and occasional revolt.

Another example of "closure," of affirmation of communitas and of the validity of local culture over hegemonic culture is the relationship between Tlaltenango, its church and the official Church. Frictions between local peasant villages and the Church also occurred in several other of the engulfed communities of Cuernavaca. In the early sixties

Bishop Sergio Méndez Arceo decided to revamp the cathedral of Cuernavaca by removing the baroque altars and saints from the inside and saving instead some beautiful seventeenth-century murals of the martyrs of Japan. The remodeling of the cathedral caused quite an uproar among the traditional Catholics of Cuernavaca.[4] The cathedral was left bare of saints. It has today only a cross without Jesus at the center and some words of the Lord cast in bronze. In the years that followed the redecoration of the cathedral, the Church began a more or less concerted campaign in Cuernavaca against the local saints and in favor of Christ (a campaign that is not without parallels to Protestant influence in the region). What follows is an example from Tlaltenango:

CL: Does Tlaltenango have its own priest?

JR: Yes. He lives here. About a month or so ago they robbed the Holy Virgin [*la santisíma virgen*] of her crown. It was a crown that, we know here, had some worth. But the Father says that he does not care so much, and that it is not worth looking hard for the criminals because it was not very valuable, he says the only thing of value that was stolen was the cup for communion. A few Sundays ago I asked him, "Father, is there any news on the Virgin's crown?" and he says, "Look José, the police is looking actively, but it says in the papers that what we should do is not to give valuable donations to the virgin." And I said "Why? If we give the virgin things, it is we that are doing the giving. If I give twenty pesos out of my own pocket, and someone else gives another twenty that's our business, and we will buy her a crown." They [the priests] tore down our great remembrance [*recuerdo*], because, I tell you, I am from here and I remember it since I was little. They took from us part of the two altars to San Jose and the Sacred Heart. . . . Once Father Luis called me and said: "Look José, I want you to tear down the *sagrario* that is in [the altar to] San José." And I said, "Yes Father," thinking that the priest had come to an agreement with the whole village. I went there with my uncle and between us we removed the *sagrario*. Father Luis then said to me, "José, I want you to bring down the altar, we are going to rebuild it in another way." And I said, "Father, I am from this town and I say that you won't tear anything down, and that to tear any of this down you have to call a meeting of the village and have them tell you to go ahead, if you don't do this you will have enemies in the village and something bad might happen to you." He did not hear me and kept on working. Some time later he had troubles with the people in town and was almost killed by gunfire. If the police hadn't intervened, something would have happened to that priest.

     Since the bishop was rebuilding the Cathedral [of Cuernavaca] they also wanted to do that here. But other towns did not allow this to happen. . . . I don't like any of that [the way they rebuilt the Cathedral] because they left the Cathedral like an exhibition hall. We don't want them to bother our temple. . . . It is our patrimony, we defend it.

I shall later discuss the history and reasons for the peasant culture of control over village churches. I simply wish to point here to the fact that this engulfed peasant culture maintains its communal boundary through land, kinship, religion, and culture, and that, nevertheless, it feeds into larger interests in Cuernavacan culture; the fiestas of the peasant *barrios* (no longer villages) are an important part of Cuernavacan cultural life, the physiognomy of the *barrios* is one of Cuernavaca's attractions,[5] the politics of land tenure with these villages are an important aspect of local politics, and so the culture of these urban peasants continually comes to the fore. Yet this peasant culture does not correspond to the dominant forms of urban production or livelihood; it is a peasant village culture that has been revamped for a new urban context.

The second sort of peasant culture in Cuernavaca is from the peasant migrants in the city. This culture is more complex and difficult to typify because we have peasant migrants from several parts of the country, and there are different generations of migrants involved, different patterns of settlement, and different economic niches occupied by peasants. For these reasons, I shall provide only some considerations about the general situation stemming from my interviews of people from several barrios. Many of these considerations are, however, also informed by writings and experiences in other, more intensely studied urban centers of Mexico, whose situations I found applicable in Cuernavaca. I cannot stress too much the fact that this whole regional cultural synthesis is tentative and, because of its very magnitude, I have not been able to amass facts enough for full accounts or "ethnographic proof" of each of my points. This will be especially patent in the descriptions of Cuernavaca's vast working classes.

In the interviews that I gathered from both managerial sources and working-class migrants, there appears to be a certain tendency in Cuernavaca (as, I think, in most of urban Mexico) for migrants to maintain important social ties with their native communities. Part of this tendency is cemented by the organization of work in large portions of both the "formal" and "informal" sectors. Workers in the services and independent workers tend to hire people whom they trust, and these ties of trust are most frequently found between close kin and between *paisanos* (people from the same village) who form networks which occupy specific working niches. So, for example, several industries in

CIVAC have conglomerates of workers who come from a single pueblo or a small set of neighboring Guerrero villages.[6] The factor of union control also reproduces this syndrome in the formal sector, where union leaders fill vacancies with their kin or with people from their villages of origin in order to retain internal control over the union.

In addition to this factor of peasant cohesion in the organization of work, there is the other, already well-known phenomenon of solidary links between migrants at the level of housing. Barrios and vecindades are often composed of several clusters of migrants from different localities. These arguments, which have been developed since the seventies by several anthropologists (see L. Lomnitz 1975, Cornelius 1975, Arizpe 1978), seem to apply in barrio organization and occupation groups in Cuernavaca. If we historicize the picture for Cuernavaca somewhat, we could portray the following situation.

Peasant migrants in Cuernavaca came in several "waves." The first important wave came right after the Revolution, which had caused local population to dwindle and therefore provided room for the accommodation of new urban dwellers. This wave was composed mainly of migrants from Guerrero, and these migrants tended to insert themselves in commerce and the services and have often acquired wealth and good "standing" in the city. For example, the sale of cheese, milk, and some meat products in Cuernavaca is largely controlled by one of these Guerrero families. Another of these large families has become important in local real estate. Many others went into small commerce and trades such as baking, and shoemaking. It is important to stress that this first wave of migration did not insert itself into industry, for it occurred before the industrialization of Cuernavaca. Outside of Cuernavaca, Guerrero migrants of this generation also peopled rural villages and some received ejido grants or bought small plots of rural property. Because of the expansion of Cuernavaca since the 1940s, the children of this generation of migrants tended to move up in the social ladder, assimilate, and become what is today a young generation of Cuernavaquenses of mixed (Cuernavaca and Guerrero) origin.

The second wave of migration occurred in the 1950s and especially since the 1960s. These migrants came to occupy the relatively well-paid positions that were opening up in industry. When the first factories in Cuernavaca opened, there was a positive scarcity of labor. In Textiles Morelos, for example, an ex-manager informed me that they hired local peasants from the Jiutepec-Tejalpa-Tepoztlán region to become construction workers and then trained them for industry. There was scarcity of trained labor for the industries and a reluctance to move to Cuernavaca from the industrialized regions of Puebla, Tlaxcala, and Mexico City. The new factories thus set up training programs for their employees and the people from Guerrero and other regions began flowing in. Among the local workers it is often recognized that migrants from Guerrero and Oaxaca work harder than native-born Cuernavaquenses due, no doubt, to the harsh working conditions in the Guerrero and Oaxaca countryside and also to the migrant condition, which is characterized by an impulse to accumulate, often in order to pull one's entire family out of its rural setting or else to buy land back in one's village and return as a prosperous peasant.

This generation of migrants is also the one that has occupied new urban settings outside of the old Cuernavaca. Some of these urban settings have been created in the form of *fraccionamientos* (private land that is urbanized or semiurbanized and sold). Other areas have been created through invasions of private or ejido lands in political movements that often entail political or economic clientelism between invaders and specific leaders (sometimes party leaders, sometimes government bureaucrats, ejido leaders, and so on). This second wave of migrants can be internally divided into the early migrants (up to the early seventies) who tended to find jobs rather easily, and the later ones, who often have both more family links in the city and more difficulties in placing themselves in the labor market. The difficulties in job placement are especially patent for the children of this wave of migrants. The migrants of this "wave" show much concern for problems of drug addiction and delinquency in their barrios and for their children. In these barrios, the most important of which are Lagunilla, Ruben Jaramillo, and Otilio Montaño, there is also a veritable competition between different organizations for the faith and following of these displaced, culturally incoherent generations. Fundamentalist Protestant sects flourish there, but so do political parties and Catholic organizations.

The barren, dirt-track, cinder-block *barriadas* that show so many external signs of improvisation are the loci of the transformation of peasant culture into one of several alternatives, ranging from urban-peasant transitory cultures of migrants who hope to return to their villages as peasants to emergent ties with the formal sector through factory employment or through the education and placement of children in the bureaucracy, and to family atomization. Culturally, the most important processes in this sector are those of (a) retrenchment of peasant ideals through "transitory" migration, (b) adoption of petit-bourgeois culture and ideals through the mobility by education of the younger generations, and (c) proletarianization. The "non-culture" of atomization pervades the whole of these peasant-in-city habitats, and is identified by locals in the syndromes of drug addiction, delinquency, and lack of respect toward elders and especially toward one's parents. These three cultural transformations of peasants are, once again, central to the creation of Cuernavacan baroque, for they tend toward internal coherence, yet they do not become entrenched in a single coherent cultural formula because of the intense mobility of the sector.

Emergent Forms of Proletarian Cultures

In what sense are Morelos' intimate cultures interrelated in a system of regional hegemony? The core is a particularly apt place from which to ask this question, because in it we can observe the regional elites and their relations to several of the regional subordinate classes. I began this problematization by discussing some of the general features of peasant culture in Cuernavaca. The brief sketch provided above (which shall be developed later) shows three major "transformations" of Morelos peasant culture in the urban core context: the transformation of peasant culture into a specific type of political position in a generation of upwardly mobile peasants whose lands have been engulfed by the city; the transformation of peasant culture into the ideal in terms of which an apparently transitory proletarian or lumpenproletarian existence is justified; and the transformation of peasant culture into a peculiar brand of proletarianized or lumpenproletarianized individualism.

This discussion of peasant cultural transformations in Cuernavaca leads directly into the question of emergent forms of proletarian culture, of which perhaps the last two transformations of peasant culture mentioned above could be specific forms. Cuernavaca was the setting of intense union activity in the late seventies, at the time of the national upsurge of "independent" unions that were unaffiliated with state-controlled labor confederations. This union activity, which culminated in an unprecedented series of long strikes in several of Cuernavaca's major factories (notably Datsun, Yacsa, and Textiles Morelos), reflects a certain degree of social consolidation of the local proletariat, and not only a specific national conjuncture.

This social consolidation was helped along by the construction of working-class neighborhoods, a process inaugurated by Textiles Morelos in the early sixties and followed by working class compounds in CIVAC and for workers of several state industries, and by the ever-growing preconditions that are necessary to get a job in a factory, as one worker related:

When I got a job at Textiles Morelos [in 1955] they told me, "just bring your *cartilla*" [proof of military service]. I got my job with nothing but my cartilla. Today you need a junior high school certificate, the cartilla, a clearance from the police, and a medical certificate. In other words, it is complicated now; there are many prerequisites for getting a factory job, and you need to go to many government offices to get them: to the ministry of health, to the military zone where you did your service, to the school where you studied. . . . This means that today the peasant who comes to work in the city can only get these jobs if he's got the papers, and for that he's got to know his way around, he's got to "be with it." But a peasant that has no papers doesn't get in. It is interesting though that in a short time he [the peasant] will get a job on a construction, and then he begins to walk the streets with a job. His needs force him to adapt to the city.

At the moment, however, it is hard to tell whether the ways of life of this class are in fact reproducing transgenerationally and becoming consolidated in families and neighborhoods, or whether participating in the formal labor sector is but a generational phenomenon of transition between a migrant peasantry and professional and service sectors of the petite bourgeoisie and bureaucracy. However this may be, it is certain that a well-developed proletarian class ideology has emerged in sectors of the Cuernavacan proletariat and that the proletariat seems to be developing an intimate culture of its own. Some of the salient features of this culture are: (a) a reorganization of family relations, wherein the patriarchal peasant family structure is functionally revamped (with an ideology of continuity) into a context where the transmission of social relations and cultural capital are more important than the inheritance of property; (b) relations of neighborhood and barrio membership which are economically and socially important, often through the mediation of the church; and (c) at the same time, a national identification that is as strong as local identity, insofar as the relationship with the factory and the workplace is perceived as being dependent on national, not local, economic, juridical, and political conditions.

So, for example, Chavita—who already told us about the documents you need to enter factory work—migrated with his parents and siblings to Cuernavaca in the early fifties. He and his three brothers got jobs at Textiles Morelos, one of Cuernavaca's largest industries, and they all bought into the company's housing project at Teopanzolco. This neighborhood has been strongly shaped both by its relationship to industry and by the Church's leftward-leaning comunidades de base.

Chavita describes his impressions of his job thirty-five years ago:

I remember when I first arrived at the factory. For me it was a beautiful thing to enter a place where something is produced; and also to have a sure income. That is what one always is looking for: not to live with the anxiety of knowing that next week you will have no work.

Moreover, Chavita has no longing for the peasant life; he knows the hardships that his fellow workers suffered in the villages of Guerrero and Oaxaca:

> I had a compadre [from Guerrero] who came here. I once went to his village with him and, truly, you can't live there: there are just a bunch of real skinny turkeys in this town that's all dusty because there's no water. There's no place to work there but the fields; and people just collect *guamúchiles* and *nanchis* to sell [two fruits—guamúchil is a pod—that grow semiwild and command very low prices in local markets; they are really only semicommercial products, since there is practically no demand for them in urban centers]; and maybe someone has a goat to make some cheeses with. My friend lived in this town with four children until he could live there no longer and [seventeen years ago] he came here.

Thanks to the conflicts between management and his union and to the influence of a new priest, Chavita grew conscious of the contradictions between the interests of capital and those of labor, and he participated actively in a long strike that paralyzed the industry ("he who struggles against this class system is a good Christian"). Later, the leaders of the independent union movement were fired, intimidated, or thrown in jail. Chava himself was fired after twenty-four years of being a worker. However, thanks to the union movement's already quite sophisticated leadership, he and the other ten activist workers who were fired got large compensations. With their money, the fired workers tried to form a carpentry cooperative, which failed.

> The majority of the *compañeros* that were fired along with me are still around; they've already spent all of their [compensation] money. They didn't invest, they didn't buy anything. I believe that this too is caused by the factory: the factory makes you useless. In the factory they tell you: "don't think, just work!" So you work. You don't think in there; in the factories you are not allowed to think, you are only allowed to work. There are others who do your thinking for you. But I learned to be a carpenter, and I am still a carpenter.

Along with his brothers and sisters, Chavita has been active in union movements and in urban popular movements that have been organized against price increases in public transportation. The Church's comunidades de base are at the center of his activities in the city and in his neighborhood. His family—brothers and sisters—have always helped one another and have all participated actively in the comunidades de base. Chavita attributes this family solidarity to the fact that his parents never owned anything: "There is nothing to divide us, nothing to fight over: no inheritance."

However, Chavita's children are no longer factory workers. One daughter is a nurse, another a psychologist; one son drives a delivery truck, and the other has a taxicab. So his family is diversifying from the point of view of kind of activity and income. Not only that, the neighborhood—which was wholly built out of the paychecks of the workers—has also gone up economically, it has become more heterogeneous. Finally, the situation of the Church in the neighborhood has also changed. Bishop Méndez Arceo, who promoted the comunidades de base, was replaced in 1983 by a conservative bishop who began shuffling all of the leftist priests around. When I interviewed Chava, it was not yet clear whether the Church would still be a center for community activism.

Although Chava's (and many others') commitment runs very deep, it is not clear whether this working-class orientation will reproduce generationally. The changes in the spaces for the social reproduction of the working classes, the suppression of union activity in factories (mostly through firing, but also through coercion), and the transformations of the local church are all obstacles to the consolidation of this particular intimate culture, which has church, neighborhood, and union meetings as its major public spaces. Although the importance of family relations seems—from all of my interviews—to be crucial for the Cuernavacan working classes, the extension of social relations outward, toward the neighborhood, the union, or the church, and the construction of a relatively coherent system, is problematical.

An example of this is the neighborhood of Jiquilpan, which began as a small middle-class settlement on a hilltop, and then grew into a predominantly poor area. On the top of the hill is an enormous church, which is presided by Father Domingo Sedano, a conservative priest who was born in Cuernavaca.[7] Father Sedano explained the history of Jiquilpan to me, and then said, "This church is a white elephant. The people of this parish are very heterogeneous, very disperse. There is not a good nucleus of Christians here, as there is in older settlements like Acapantzingo." On the other hand, Father Sedano wants to provide his parish with a place of worship that is equally inviting to the rich and the poor:

[Liberation theologists] say that they have opted for the poor. But it is not a simple option for the poor, it is for Marxism; and that is a good pose for youngsters and hotheads, or for older people who want to receive a cut or that seek political power. But behind it all there is a certain ambition, a certain envy, so that most of those Marxist leaders end up rich. This has been a big problem that has divided the Church . . . and this business of removing the images of saints has disoriented and disgusted many people. We have lost many people. Many no longer go to church—they became disoriented and resentful—and many others have become Protestants. In Morelos we have lost many people because of our imprudence.

Thus, Father Sedano's role in his community is to offer the solace of the Church to its inhabitants, but not to organize or support neighborhood political action, as the priest in Chavita's neighborhood did. Moreover, Jiquilpan's people work in many different areas and so do not share a factory experience or a factory history in the way Teopanzolco does; neither do they share a history of politically organized land invasions the way other neighborhoods do. The result is that the proletarianized cultures of Jiquilpan do not seem to be getting constituted into a coherent intimate culture.

The national orientation of proletarian culture is key to the general point of this chapter. The most developed forms of emergent proletarian cultures are nationally, not regionally, oriented. Factories belong to national branches of industries. They grow and dwindle because of factors that are almost entirely extraregional; unions are affiliated to national confederations that are controlled by national political parties. More importantly, perhaps, the rights to which workers aspire are intrinsically dependent on the national state: minimum wages, access to better systems of social security, public schooling, federal housing, and the like.

As we have seen, workers today are people who have had a considerable amount of formal education, and they need to know some of the ropes of government bureaucracy even to enter industry. Once they have entered, they may, as Chavita did, end up knowing quite a lot about government legislation and about the way in which government operates. Thus, the national orientation of the working classes has made it easy for a worker's children to attempt to climb socially through education. In these cases, state culture is embraced as a mechanism for advancement, and the content of state culture can be manipulated to one's advantage. (Although it may perhaps be the case that with the current economic crisis, working-class culture in Cuernavaca will hold on to its local production of symbolic values and cultivate itself—instead of state ideology—as possibilities of mobility and betterment through the state appear ever more distant.)

The culture of Cuernavacan working classes can therefore be thought of as a culture in intimate relationship with a logic of expansion and contraction of elites that are not Cuernavaca's elites. In this sense, the working class contributes to the constitution of Cuernavacan baroque, for it has a pouchlike existence within the city. This suggests another way in which Cuernavacan baroque can be described. It is like a ghettoization of an entire city. Bounded groups that tend to produce intimate cultures of their own are but weakly articulated among themselves because in fact each group maintains relations of power that are predominantly extralocal in nature. Yet, as I have hinted above, the economic crisis of Mexico has tended in some cases to diminish the boundaries between groups and classes and to create articulations between "ghettos." In the past years, for example, strikes and other typically working-class manifestations have almost disappeared. They have been substituted for to some degree by popular movements against the city government and the governor for improvement of urban services, especially for the decline of transport costs, the legalization of shantytown properties, the construction of schools, and the extension of urban services. The economic crisis has tended to diminish the importance of extraregional resources in the region, and so has directed attention to local and regional institutions and power holders.

Petit-Bourgeois Transformations

In the nineteenth century, and until the 1950s, Cuernavaca was a city whose livelihood stemmed essentially from commerce (both regional trade and tourism), the state bureaucracy, and a few services, such as education, medicine, and law. The old inhabitants of the city are therefore strongly influenced by a petit-bourgeois cultural tradition that has, in a certain sense, been reinforced by the social mobility that characterized the poorer classes of the city until the crisis of the 1980s. Even the first unions of the city reflect petit-bourgeois predominance over the town. They were the bakers union, the waiters union, and the construction-workers union. Until 1960 most of the city's working classes were occupied in the hotel and restaurant business, in small shops, and in construction. The only industries of any importance were alcohol factories, which existed since at least the early nineteenth century. The physiognomy of Cuernavaca reflected this preindustrial character: the city was peaceful and quaint, with a wonderful climate and vegetation. Few buildings of any import were constructed after independence, reflecting the lack of dynamism of the local elite. The hub of the city was its commerce and its hotels.

The history of stores in downtown Cuernavaca was reconstructed for me by Valentín López, the regional historian and *cronista* of Cuernavaca. There was a periodical market that opened on Tuesdays and Fridays and was three times shifted in the past forty years in order to cater to its growing clientele and importance (it has been a daily market since the sixties). Aside from this marketplace, most commerce was on Guerrero, although there were other streets that had particular specialties, such as butchering and leather working. In this famous street there was a large pharmacy, a large hardware store, a clothing store, two or three cafes, a few shoe stores, a dry-goods store, and a liquor store. There was a single cinema in the center of town, which in the fifties also offered wrestling and boxing; moveable dining set-ups around the central kiosk and around the market; brothels in the periphery; hotels on the peripheries and in the center; the cathedral and several churches, a graveyard, and the seat of the bishopric; three schools, the governor's palace (once the palace of Cortés, today a museum); and the municipal presidency. That about sums up the spaces of public life.

It seems likely that the local Cuernavaca elite had a relatively coherent, self-sustained, intimate culture during the long period in which Cuernavaca was but a largish commercial and bureaucratic center. Evidence of the nature of this petit-bourgeois society is chiefly to be found in novels and travel books of the mid-nineteenth and early twentieth centuries.[8] It is also retrievable in interviews with "old Cuernavacan" inhabitants. As in the case of the peasant cultures I have discussed, an extended treatment of this material is provided below, in chapters on localist ideologies of these classes. The argument I wish to make here, however, regards the transformation of Cuernavacan elite (petit-bourgeois) culture from an initial point in which there existed what one could call a "Cuernavacan high society," to the social fragmentation of the elite and its bifurcate conversion to non-localist petite bourgeoisie and into a regionalist petty bureaucracy.

Returning to the development of the local elites, which I shall hereafter call the "petite bourgeoisie," I pointed out that there was an original state of community among this class in Cuernavaca. This community was consolidated through a shared public and institutional life; the elites went to Cuernavaca's well-known private schools. They went to mass at the same churches and at the same hours, they strolled in the square, and went to the same clubs and cafes. The most readily available information about the culture of the local elite before the Revolution is political. The Cuernavacan elite was conservative (contrasting with the liberal predisposition of most of the rest of Morelos), proclerical, and socially close to the bishopric, whose facilities were in fact donated by the local elites. Yet even the question of elite political culture is obscure for the prerevolutionary period. We know little of their relations with the state governors or of their bargaining position with them; one can only know for a fact that governors were more influenced by hacendado interests than by those of the local petite bourgeoisie, and that this class in many cases was an ally to the hacendado class and rested content with control over their small economic province.

However all of this may have been, the Revolution introduced important transformations in Cuernavaca's elite, since most of the old Cuernavacan "society" migrated to Mexico City before 1914, and many members of these families became permanently established in Mexico. This dislocation of what was already a politically weak elite provoked the beginning of the cultural disarray of that class. The importance of organization around the Church diminished after the Revolution. Education for children became more diversified, and participation in social clubs and cafes became ever more diverse. Finally, the industrialization of the city, beginning in the 1950s, finished diffusing Cuernavacan "society."

Because of the petite bourgeoisie's lack of control over the destiny of its own city, its reaction to the expansion of Cuernavaca, and to the abolition of its control over public spaces has been to maintain private social groupings, especially in the form of social clubs like the Rotarians and the Lions, and characteristic meeting places, such as the downtown cafes. On the other hand, Cuernavaca's elites often send their children to the university in Mexico City, where they are liable to find jobs and get married. This fluidity of movement between Cuernavaca and Mexico City, combined with the elite's limited dominance over the economic and social life of the city, has oriented the petite bourgeoisie towards "national culture" and "national society." Superiority and distinction are defined by the center: the brand of your car, studying in Mexico City universities, going to nightclubs and restaurants that were made for Mexico City tourists.

Up until the 1950s, the whole of Cuernavaca would meet on Thursday and Saturday evenings to walk around the kiosk in the central plaza. People from all classes ate at the stands, and young men and women circled the kiosk in opposite directions, the women batting their eyelashes and giggling, the boys laughing a little too loudly and smoking (if their parents were not present). Several phenomena undermined elite participation in these and other public ceremonies. Industrialization is one, but there is also the effect of the creation of Cuernavaca's "secret city": the fortified weekend homes of politicians, businessmen, artists, and intellectuals. As an ethnographic acquaintance said: "Cuernavaca is the cemetery of the elephants; great men come here to die." The tremendous expansion of tourism set the local elite's social sights outside of the local provincial tradition. Instead, they fixed on the new discotheques, bars, restaurants, and clubs, and the Cuernavacan "youth" began partaking of the cosmopolitan mores of the wealthy Mexican and American tourist. Strolls around the square, the public celebration of national holidays and the like have become pastimes of the lower classes.

Finally, the invasion of the city by people from outside Cuernavaca also made the elites entrench themselves. Walls began going up around their houses, and public routines became more diversified. In the past years the walls around houses have been ever heightened thanks to the high criminality that has emerged. As a friend pointed out, an archaeologist of Cuernavaca looking back at the period would have to put dates on the different heights of the walls around Cuernavacan houses, and (s)he would do well to baptize the periods with the names of the governors that have presided over public (dis)order: Bejarano I, Bejarano II, Ortega I, Ortega II, Ortega III, and so forth. The access to wealth has overriden all pretense to regional power, and the (nationally controlled) quasitotemic idiom of commodity consumption (cf. Sahlins 1976) has been entirely adopted by this class. In other words, the Cuernavacan petite bourgeoisie does not negotiate its social and cultural position through symbolic production in the context of regional social relations of production; it negotiates its position through its capacity to obtain— through its local sources of accumulation—goods and a lifestyle that places it in a specific position within a national ideology of class.

On the other hand, there are some professions within the petite bour- geoisie that do require an effort in the symbolic fabrication of social position. This is especially the case of the local bureaucracy. This sector of the local elite has had to produce an ideology of self-legitimation in terms of its position within the region, and in terms of Morelos' position within Mexico.

The Morelos bureaucracy has grown in the context of the national incorporation of Zapatismo into government, and in the context of the transformation of Morelos from a peasant to an urban and industrial economy. In the years following the Revolution (until 1940) local and regional politics were in fact extracted from the control of the regional petite bourgeoisie because of the fact that regionalist discourse had been effectively appropriated by Zapatismo and converted into an ideology of class strife. This situation began changing with the cooptation and re- placement of the main Zapatista leaders by the federal government, and culminated with the reactivation and expansion of an urban economy. These two factors combined have reopened an economic niche for the local bureaucrats, yet in order to occupy the position of regional political class, this sector has had to develop a regionalist ideology and an inti- mate culture that contrasts with that of the rest of the petite bourgeoi- sie's abandonment of itself to the class culture and ideology of the na- tional bourgeoisie.

State Culture and Personal Interest: The Culture of Social Relations

I have argued that Cuernavaca does not have an indigenous class that successfully dominates the city. There is no local class that can be called hegemonic, and subordinate classes are not all interrelated to a system of regional hegemony. Instead of this I have suggested the utility of the notion of a Cuernavacan baroque culture, which can be thought of as a tendency to ghettoize intimate cultures that are not hegemonically inter- related by the local elite. Two characteristics of this baroque are cultural heterogeneity and an urban elite that is culturally dependent on its consumption of external values. The fact that Cuernavaca's classes have distinct cultural understandings—which are mutually challenged and undermined—makes observers remark that the city "lacks a culture." The result is a tension between the erosion of intimate cultures caused by their apparently limited applicability, and the closure of intimate cultures as a response to the lack of cultural and social alternatives offered by the city.

An inescapable implication of this argument is that the description of culture in Cuernavaca demands recognition of the presence of a culture that is external to the region and hegemonic to it. This culture has its material backing in the presence of institutions that are not controlled by the local elites: federal institutions; state institutions that are manned by a governing elite that is imposed from Mexico City; factories that are manned by a governing elite that is imposed from Mexico City; factories that are owned by capital foreign to the city; schools; television; national unions; national associations of producers; and so on. These institutions represent what I have called "state culture," in the sense that it is the culture spread by the national state as the material operationalization of Mexico's dominant political and economic project (state culture is thus not to be confused with the intimate culture of the elites that have created this project).

The institutions that propagate state culture create the conditions of "Cuernavacan baroque." The public spaces of Cuernavaca, the urban development of the city, have been—to a large extent—created for national and transnational industries and for the development of tourism and weekend homes. Along with these developments have come government offices and services: the electric company, the telephone company, federal public schools. The compounded effect of all of this is an "impersonalization" of the public sphere, insofar as it is not locally controlled, and the "ghettoization" of the city that we have thus far described.

The "impersonal" streets and squares of Cuernavaca are, nevertheless, governed by a culture of the "impersonal," a culture that allows people to interact (or to avoid each other) in coded ways. This culture—which was initially studied in the United States by Erving Goffman, and which has been taken up recently in France by anthropologists like Colette Pétonnet, who has undertaken the study of "the city" by way of an analysis of behavior in impersonal areas—is partially transmitted by the media and the whole institutional apparatus of the state. However, state institutions also produce a culture that mixes this ideological repertoire with a set of practices and understandings that are not formally included in them. The way state schools operate, for example, is as distinctive of state culture as the formal content of primary education;

the way state-controlled unions operate is typically distinct from unionist legislation.

State culture is thus characterizable in terms of a particular relationship between an ideology about the relationship between and nature of the classes that compose Mexico and a set of characteristic institutional practices. These practices are almost as uniform as the highly controlled ideologies that legitimate them. This is partially due to the fact that the spaces for action within state and national institutions are internally similar. Schoolteachers all confront similar work conditions and similar informal (but centrally controlled) rules for action, promotion, and survival; local unions must affiliate with larger movements in order for their demands to have repercussions, and in so doing the unions must accept a few external conditions. In what remains of this section I shall note some of the characteristics of state culture in order to show why the importance of state culture in Cuernavaca tends to undermine the consolidation of a distinct regional culture. I shall briefly discuss the characteristics of success within state institutions, and the ways in which state power depends on direct control of communal spaces of the different intimate cultures.

There are a few aspects of state culture that must be noted. First, state culture is not produced in the home. Second, it is a culture that is experienced differently by those who have continuous institutional contact with it than by those who have access mainly to its ideologically purest facets, such as the media and the law. Third, it is a culture that is based on institutions that everyone has to deal with to some degree and at some point in their lives. Fourth, it is a culture that is itself a specific mode of the "culture of social relations" and learning this hegemonic culture of class relations is one of its main demands. Fifth, state culture redefines the nature of the different intimate cultures that it recognizes and then organizes them into a coherent and interdependent image of "national society."

There are certain common elements in the culture that emanate from practical contact with national institutions: (1) any decision for change in structure or organization must proceed from the center; (2) the dispositions from the center are carried through by middlemen (bureaucrats) who have motives for action that are distinct from those of the national ideology; (3) these motives and motivations may or may not be seen as extending to the entire edifice of government; some people perceive no difference in the levels of "corruption" (that is in placing personal interest over public interest) of a lower bureaucrat and that of the president, while others think of the president as a pure soul surrounded by ill-intentioned advisors; and (4) these motives are seen as egotistical yet perfectly comprehensible; they consist in supporting the private life and group of the bureaucrat over the abstract nation that national culture purportedly represents. In other words, the formal adoption of state ideology about the nature of national society is rewarded by the personal benefits handed out in state institutions to its members. Personal gain and national interest are wedded in state culture; they are related among themselves in the same way that statist ideology is related to state institutional practice.

If we accept the general implications of this idea, we will come to understand yet another dimension of global cultural incoherence in Cuernavaca. The importance of state culture there, its predominant role in the local economy, and its control over the state bureaucratic apparatus have fomented the development of "nationalism," which is in fact a culture of personal interest in which the spaces for collective political action of the intimate cultures are ideologically packaged in statist ideology and exchanged for personal benefit. The effects of the preponderance of the Mexican "corporativist" state in Cuernavaca are the undermining of internally interrelated intimate cultures in exchange for a nationally controlled representation of those intimate cultures plus personal gain.

The intimate cultures that I have sketched out in this chapter have a tense relationship with this abstract "nationalism," insofar as they continually create their own forms of identification that stand against the statist culture. The culture of Cuernavaca's peasants can either be nationalist tourism-fodder or the basis of strong communal identity that is not so easily commercialized. Cuernavaca's proletarians can attempt to create communities that oppose the state. The local bureaucracy can contest the predominance of Mexico City and, together with the local bourgeoisie, they can try to achieve greater control over Cuernavaca's public life. These dialectics between statist ideology and the local intimate cultures are the bases of Cuernavacan baroque.

Conclusion

If we look for the organization of regional culture in the core we will find several transformations of peasant class culture, an emergent proletarian culture and transformations of a petit bourgeois class culture. This latter class was dissolved as a social group with the Revolution and, especially, with industrialization and economic diversification. Today, the public spaces of the city are controlled by federally imposed governors and economic projects of development that result from alliances between these governors and specific Mexico City and international investors. This situation has provoked the subsumption of local petit bourgeois culture to the culture of the national bourgeoisie, as seen by the media and the information (formal and informal) available to the local elites. The class segment that does produce a culture that has pretensions to a specifically regional constitution—the Cuernavacan bureaucracy—has developed and thrived as the weak beneficiary of the conflict between the regional peasantry and the national bourgeoisie and state classes.

On the other hand, Cuernavaca's peasant and proletarian cultures are not in any crucial way dependent on or even opposed to the local elite. Their permanence and development in the city depend on factors controlled from without the city and the region, and the relevance of their intimate cultures for life in the city is therefore always partial. This fact, the difficulties in developing intimate cultures that are pertinent to several spheres of action within the city, makes for the prevalence of cultural "incoherence" in Cuernavaca, an incoherence that is erroneously interpreted as a "lack" of culture.

Instead of lack of culture, however, it is necessary to recognize the fact that what we have is a series of intimate cultures, transformations of three class cultures (peasant, proletarian, and petit bourgeois), that are weakly interlinked by power relations. Each intimate culture has a relatively coherent internal repertoire that it can draw upon in specific contexts, while at the same time none of these repertoires can be easily sustained and reproduced in the present Cuernavacan urban context. I use the term *baroque* because the lack of coherence between intimate cultures and their lack of interrelation through direct forms of power do not stop the different intimate cultures from being hierarchically arranged into dominant and subordinate through all of their affiliations with national culture. Cuernavaca contains many more resources than those controlled by Cuernavacan elites. Cuernavacan elites therefore ally themselves to a hegemonic project that is not in their control. Hierarchy remains, but a locally controlled, locally all-encompassing hegemonic culture dissolves.

5

Central Places and
Regional Cultural
Organization

Regional hegemony in contemporary Morelos cannot be analyzed without reference to the region's relations with the state and with foreign capital. However, this does not alter the fact that Morelos is an internally differentiated space in which different classes have carved out their niches. The interrelations between these localized classes are the fundamental reference for understanding regional culture. In this chapter I discuss the regional organization of class. The purpose of the discussion is to provide a spatial framework in which to place Morelos' intimate cultures and the "flow of mestizaje" in the region. There is a certain aridity involved in constructing a typology of localities like the one I present here; however, I hope that this does not distract readers from the meaning of the exercise. Only by examining the localization of classes within a region can we specify the processes of regional cultural differentiation and change.

The first part of this chapter is devoted to a discussion of types of localities in Morelos. Localities will be classified according to three main criteria: position in the marketing hierarchy, position in the core/ periphery structure, and position in the political-administrative structure. These three aspects of regional organization are interrelated. Marketing centers tend to be more important in the core of an economic region, administrative centers tend to be placed in important marketing centers, and so on. Nevertheless, it is useful to keep them distinct, because the region's core/periphery structure will point us in the direction of the spatial organization of production. The central place hierarchy will point us in the direction of commercialization and types of localities, and the administrative structure will point us toward regional politics.

The discussion of kinds of localities and zones within Morelos allows a presentation of the spatial dimensions of intimate cultures in Morelos. I will present a general picture of the regional organization of Morelos' culture, as well as an outline of the transformations that Morelos' regional culture has undergone in the past thirty years.

Types of Central Places

Morelos' core/periphery organization has been changing drastically since the transformation of the state from an economy based primarily on agriculture to a predominantly industrial and tertiary economy. Because this change is recent, beginning in the 1950s but really acquiring significance as of the mid-1960s, the cultural consequences of the former core/periphery structure are still strong and must be understood. The discussion provided in this section will thus make continual reference to two distinct periods of regional economic organization (reflected especially in changes in the core/periphery structure): the period before 1960—which can be seen as having a surprising degree of continuity back to the colonial period—and the period since 1960. There are many continuities between these two periods, especially from the point of view of the organization of the old agricultural periphery, yet the distinction between the industrial and preindustrial organization of the region is a necessary point of departure.

The period before 1960 is characterized by the division of agricultural resources between a relatively flat, fertile, and well-watered core, and a rugged, unwatered, and often stony or forested periphery. Some municipios occupy predominantly peripheral lands (Huitzilac, Tepoztlán, Tlayacapan, Tlalnepantla, Totolapan, Atlatlahucan, Yecapixtla, Ocuituco, Tetela, Zacualpan, Jantetelco, Axochiapan); others occupy predominantly core areas, although practically every municipio has some core and some marginal lands, making for enclaves of peasant and capitalist agriculture in practically every municipio.[1] Spatial economic organization of this period was also characterized by the commercial domain of the regional cities over the agricultural periphery, a tendency that has been somewhat mitigated in the northern periphery by easy and direct access to Mexico City, as well as by the growth of commerce in the peripheries themselves.

In Morelos, the population has been highly nucleated in comparison to many other Mexican regions.[2] Population in the region was concentrated in villages or haciendas, isolated peasants houses are and were rare at least since 1900.[3] The smallest nucleated settlements, what I call *hamlets,*[4] had populations ranging roughly from two hundred to eight hundred inhabitants. The nature of commerce in these hamlets has suffered its most important change since the introduction of dirt roads and trucks, as of the 1940s, but most importantly since the 1960s.[5] Those hamlets did not have periodical markets, and generally depended on their cabecera's weekly markets for buying most supplies, as well as for services such as mail, courts, church,[6] and official business. Hamlets generally have one or several small stores, usually the room of a house, that sell small quantities of goods which are required at the spur of the moment. From my unsystematic observations, I include the following goods: candles, light bulbs (when there is electricity), candies, soft drinks, beer, liquor (usually aguardiente or other non-brand distillates), some canned food and perhaps coffee, sugar, and maize. The main business of these stores is the sale of soft drinks and liquor. Shopkeeping is never the sole occupation of the family and, on the contrary, stores are usually run by women, the elderly, and children. The male owners of the stores have either agriculture or transportation as their main business.

The next type of settlement in the marketing hierarchy is the village. The population of the village typically ranges from around one to eight thousand inhabitants. All municipios have at least one village—their cabecera—but some have more. Villages have periodical markets, once or twice a week. They also have permanent stores, not only of the kind found in hamlets (characteristic of the outskirts of villages) but also stores that have their own buildings, and that are often run directly by productive males as their principal source of income. Until about thirty years ago, all villages had a general store, in which one could buy no end of products, from agricultural appliances (machetes, digging sticks, parts of plows) to sewing equipment, packaged food and dry goods, gifts, fabric, and sometimes even some ready-made clothes. These stores can sometimes still be found[7] but the general tendency has been to substitute the general store with several more specialized shops: the *papelería,* the *ferretería,* the *mercería, abarrotes,*[8] and liquor stores. Other kinds of commerce sometimes found in villages are the pool room, the bar, the pulquería,[9] the brothel,[10] the pharmacy,[11] the feedlot where fertilizers and animal food are sold, the doctor and veterinarian, and hotels for traveling salesmen.[12]

Villages also concentrate some services and government offices, although the kind and number depend on whether or not the location is a municipal cabecera. Minimally, a village will have a church, police, and a judge; often they will have offices of the electricity, water, and telephone companies, a public telephone, a post office, registrars for buying and selling property and for marriage, birth, and death certificates.

The next highest level is that of the central market town. Until 1950 it might be said that this was the highest level in the Morelos marketing hierarchy, since there were only minor differences between the kinds of marketing and services one could carry out in the towns of Yautepec, Jojutla, Jonacatepec, Cuautla, and Cuernavaca. Since the industrialization of the state and the concentration of bureaucratic and industrial elites in Cuernavaca and, to a lesser extent, in Cuautla, these two towns can be classed as regional cities.

The central market towns have permanent markets and what one might call "commercial districts" in the center, where articles such as cloth, clothing, shoes, and furniture are sold to locals and to people from the villages and hamlets. Market towns also concentrate more entertainment than villages, with large concentrations of bars, several movie theaters, wrestling and boxing, red-light districts, and restaurants.[13] Market towns in Morelos will also have garages for car trouble and one or two car lots. In addition, medical services—both state and private—align their supply facilities with the central-place hierarchy. Hospitals are a rarity in villages, and government hospitals offer surgery only in market towns and regional cities. Tractors and agricultural machinery can be bought in these towns, and some state offices, such as agricultural credit banks, the district judge, the state representatives and senators, operate at this level. The population of these towns is from ten to fifty thousand.[14] Market towns traditionally centralized much of the produce of the periphery and exported to Mexico City markets. I have no systematic data for this, but it is my impression that the importance of warehouses for food at this level has nearly disappeared since the major expansion of marketeers from Mexico's Central de Abastos market.[15]

The final level of the central place hierarchy is the regional city. This level includes only two sites, Cuernavaca and Cuautla. These cities have high schools and technical education for teachers, nurses, and technicians. Cuernavaca has a state university.[16] They have a much wider range of specialists and technicians in medicine, and law, and they house engineers, architects, and members of most professions. Generally one might say that these cities distinguish themselves from the market towns more on the basis of their services than their commerce. Regional cities operate commercially much the same as market towns in both retail and wholesale.[17] In the case of Cuernavaca, the degree of services is augmented by the fact that it is the seat of state government, and therefore hosts all state offices and services.

This rather simple central-place hierarchy must be imagined as operating within a specific core/periphery structure. Until industrialization, this structure could be envisaged quite simply as the dichotomy between rich and marginal agriculture.[18] The position of the different central place types within this core/periphery structure is crucial for classifying localities in Morelos; for example, hamlets in the core were made up almost exclusively of day laborers (*jornaleros*) before agrarian reform, whereas peripheral hamlets relied on combining seasonal agriculture with seasonal wage labor. The picture was of a predominantly peasant versus a predominantly rural-proletarian society. Likewise, peripheral villages had a more numerous peasantry—and therefore greater local autonomy—than core villages. Market towns and regional cities have always been in the core and therefore present no complications for this analysis.

The structure and logic of the core/periphery organization of Morelos changes somewhat with industrialization and with the development of tourism. In most cases, industries have been located at towns with a preexisting infrastructure (i.e., central market towns); and the most important industrial developments have been in the Cuernavaca and Cuautla areas.

The other major case of industrialization is that of agroindustry: sugar and rice. In the case of rice, mills were set up in the early 1900s in the major towns of Cuautla, Jonacatepec, Jojutla, and Cuernavaca. The sugar industry is different. Sugar mills were constructed inside the haciendas that produced cane since the sixteenth century. In the late 1800s sugar factories began acquiring some independence from cane production in southern Morelos (cf. Crespo and Vega, in press); but the process was drastically accelerated by the postrevolutionary reorganization of the industry, and by the construction of the Emiliano Zapata mill at Zacatepec in 1938. There are no numerical data for this, but my impression is that when the sugar industry was decentralized, there was greater use of labor from the peripheral villages of Morelos. Today the tendency has been to convert Morelos' core "peasants" into a kind of land-renter and for labor to come from Guerrero, Morelos' great periphery.

Industry, of course, changes the logic of spatial organization entirely, since the factors of production that are taken into account—accessibility of labor, transportation facilities, proximity to natural resources—may be found in the agricultural peripheries or the core. In the case of Morelos, however, the decisions on industrial location have usually heightened the old core/periphery divisions.[19]

The relationship between the location of the tourist industry, on the other hand, does subvert the old core/periphery structure to some degree. In the 1930s tourism in Morelos concentrated in Cuernavaca, and so merely added commercial textures to the region's capital; however, starting in the 1950s, a great number of Morelos market towns, villages, and even hamlets have attracted tourism. Much of this tourism is in the form of weekend homes. This has meant new kinds of jobs in both the agricultural core and the periphery since, from the perspective of tourism, this is an irrelevant dichotomy. Today many villages have full- or part-time construction workers, gardeners, and watchmen. Tourism has also played an important role in bringing urban services—such as telephones, electricity, and paved roads—to towns that might not have them otherwise.

Another major change in the core/periphery structure has occurred with agrarian reform. Because Morelos was the site of Zapatismo, it was allowed extensive agrarian reform in the core, which is not the case in most of Mexico. In the first instance, this produced a peripheralization of the old core. Core hamlets became peasant villages (cf. Fromm and Maccoby 1970, Romanucci-Ross 1973, Rounds 1977); core villages regained their agrarian base. The "recorification" of these places has been a complex and uneven process. Some of the new ejidatarios were transformed into minuscule landlords whose main labor was used in either wage earning or petty bourgeois activity; this is the case of many of the cane-growers for the Zacatepec cooperative, but also of those who rent ejido lands for cash or share (cf. Singelman et al. 1979). It could be said that since agrarian reform, the core was redefined according to access to relatively high-paying wage employment. Land became a kind of fallback or security for the new core population, whereas it remained the central source of income in the periphery.

This peculiar economic logic—ruled on the one hand by productivity of soils and on the other by agrarian reform and proximity to urban labor markets—has produced a hybrid culture. We shall follow the form and logic of this culture in Morelos through its central-place hierarchy and core/periphery structure, but we must be conscious of the fact that centralization and peripheralization are movements that are ever present in Morelos' twentieth-century history. It is an inevitable consequence of proximity to Mexico City's politics and problems.[20]

Localities, Class Composition, and Intimate Cultures

In this section I shall discuss some of the structural implications of the description above in order to provide a model for understanding intimate cultures in the Morelos region. Figures 1–3 show class composition in different types of localities during three periods of Morelos' core/periphery structure. Figure 1 is of the agricultural period before agrarian reform, figure 2 is of the agricultural period after agrarian reform, and figure 3 is of the industrial period.

In order to clarify the use of my distinction between class culture and intimate culture, readers should note the existence of the same classes in several different settlement types. Intimate cultures are the cultures of

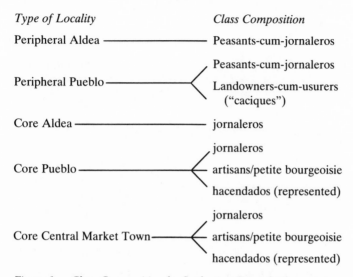

Figure 1.   Class Composition by Settlement Type: Settlements Before Agrarian Reform

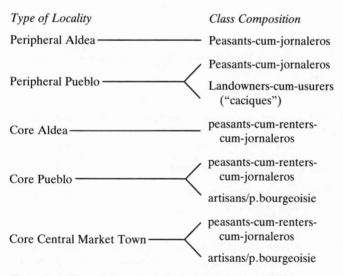

Figure 2.   Class Composition by Settlement Type: Settlements After Agrarian Reform

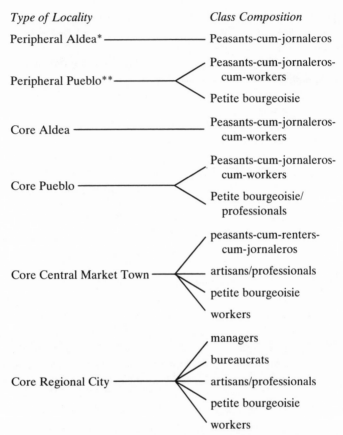

*During this period, aldeas are commercially more independent from pueblos, and pueblos from market towns, than in prior periods.

**The growth of the petite bourgeoisie in pueblos and the access to a greater variety of jobs in and outside pueblos on behalf of the peasantry undermines caciquismo in the period.

Figure 3.   Class Composition by Settlement Type: Settlements since Industrialization

the classes *in their specific localized contexts;* so, for example, in the Morelos case, the figures suggest the existence of distinct peasant intimate cultures in almost every level of the system.[21] I expect peasant class culture to vary in each of the different types of localities precisely because of the different forms of class interaction and class domination that characterize the locality types. Returning to my peasant examples, peasants of peripheral hamlets of the agricultural periods did not have continuous face-to-face relations with the peripheral cacique class, whereas peasants of the peripheral villages did. These distinct interactional contexts provoked many differences in these two forms of peasant culture. In the villages, peasants participated in community rituals that included problems of alliance with the local caciques and that were often financed by the local elite, whereas these forms of ritual were not typical of peasant hamlets.[22]

An implication of this line of reasoning is that we can discuss the relation between class culture and intimate culture in terms of the specific forms of power relations that characterize different types of localities in the regional political economy. So, for example, there would appear to be two main peasant intimate cultures implicit in figure 1: peripheral-hamlet peasant intimate culture, and peripheral-village peasant intimate culture. Peasant culture in the hamlets would have had the structural characteristic of a local culture in which domestic units and extradomestic family ties are the main social and political local institutions. Relations of power and dependence were established with people outside the hamlets: caciques from the municipal cabeceras or administrators of haciendas who bought local surplus products or hired seasonal wage labor. Hamlet intimate culture was therefore characterized by a sharp ideological division between life in and outside of the community. These are places where, sometimes even today, when outsiders arrive, all the doors are closed, and fear and suspicion set in. The situation is altogether different in the peripheral villages, where relations of class exploitation and patronage occurred within the village itself. The social heterogeneity of these localities and the larger population of the villages also allowed for a more elaborate ritual cycle in which alliances with different classes and political groups were established (cf. de la Peña 1980; Lomnitz-Adler 1982).

If we turn to the class culture of the petite bourgeoisie of the preagrarian reform period (figure 1), we have three major transformations: the petite bourgeoisie of the peripheral villages (which are called here "caciques"), of the core villages, and of central market towns. In this case, the most important cultural difference is between core and periphery. The petite bourgeoisie of the periphery were the largest local landowners, the owners of permanent commerce, the most important source of local credit, and the local political elite. Because they were few in number (due to the conditions of agriculture in the periphery) and because of the physical absence of the hacendado class or of its administrative representatives, the petite bourgeoisie of the periphery became a class with independent power over municipal and local politics.

This was at times the situation of the petite bourgeoisie in core villages or market towns. Here the petite bourgeoisie was more numerous, due to the greater importance of commerce in these zones and, more importantly, this class was in direct contact with the representatives of the hacienda, who were the main source of work, credit, and patronage for the local lower classes. For this reason, the petite bourgeoisie of the core was often not a powerful cacique class, for it did not control municipal politics or even local social life in the monopolistic forms that were characteristic of the periphery.

The next important class culture is that of the *jornaleros* (day-laborers), which can be analyzed in two main transformations: jornaleros of core hamlets (which were often ranchos and haciendas) and jornaleros of core villages. Information for this class in this period is much scarcer than it is for the Morelos peripheral peasantry, and so a reconstruction of the differences between these two intimate cultures for the period is difficult. Nonetheless, I believe that in most cases the difference in class culture of the (core) hamlet and village jornaleros was not as linked to control over communal life, as it was in the case of hamlet and village peasants. Core hamlets were often directly administered by haciendas and so entirely out of jornalero control. Instead the main difference could have been a greater peasant communal conscience in the core villages, and a greater culture of dependence on the hacendados in the hamlets, whose inhabitants were often *peones acasillados* (day laborers who lived on hacienda lands).[23] The reason for this rather counterintuitive conclusion is that core villages tended to have some remnants of communal lands from the colonial period. Ideals of peasant independence lived on in villages, whereas hamlets were too much in the center of hacienda activity.

Finally, there remains the hacendado class. Although this class spent most of the year in their Mexico City mansions, its cultural influence in the region was very significant. Morelos' haciendas had *cascos* (the main buildings of the property, which often included a colonial-style seignorial mansion, a sugar factory, a chapel, gardens, stables, and servants' quarters) which stood for the true centers of enlightened Mexican capitalism. In these mansions, the hacendados entertained each other and also invited local notables: the pharmacist, the wealthy merchant, the *jefe político*.[24] Also, the hacendados cultivated rural pastimes like *charrería* (an elaborate, horse-centered, set of activities that include ornate *charro* costumes, high-quality horses, and elaborate racing and lasso contests known as *charreadas* or *jaripéos*); de la Peña (1980) has documented that they also contributed to local and regional village fiestas, so that, on the one hand, hacendados boasted their wealth and their technological innovation[25] while, on the other, they cultivated a kind of genteel ethos.

This hacendado culture was the exemplary center of power and culture in Morelos until the destruction of the haciendas during the Revolution, and, as such, it had very deep influence in the regional culture. So, for example, during the political turmoil of the late 1850s and '60s the state was infested with bandits known as *plateados* (from *plata:* silver). These plateados, who became legendary figures in regional folklore and the subject of several novels, appropriated the hacendado's charisma. They too cultivated horsemanship and despised the barefoot villager. Their ornate, silver-studded saddles and charro costumes were what inspired their silvery name. On the other hand, the influence of the hacendado power aesthetics is also clearly present in the figures of both Emiliano and Eufemio Zapata, who were elegant charros and not barefoot "Indians."

The image of a kind of enlightened rural nobility—with its combination of landed wealth, capitalist investment, and deep historical roots in the land—has also been appropriated by high-level officials and the new post-hacienda rich. The emperor Maximilian took up the image of the charro for himself and cultivated it with special fervor in his Cuernavaca house, where he is said to have had a romantic liaison with *la india bonita* (the beautiful Indian señorita). In more recent times, several of Morelos' governors have built and fixed up ranches in which they entertain their important guests and prove their ties to the land, and some of the biggest tourism ventures have revamped hacienda cascos and made them into hotels, or else they have tried to recreate Morelos' feudal grandeur in modern imitations. So, *malgré la revolution,* the cultural model of the hacienda, has served many different people even to this day.

Figure 2 reflects the changes in intimate cultures brought on by agrarian reform. If we compare it to figure 1, we note that there are no substantial changes in class composition in peripheral settlements. All remains much the same there, except for the actual balance of power between the classes. Because of agrarian reform, the independence of hamlet and village peasants vis-à-vis municipal caciques and core entrepreneurs increased greatly. Peasant control over communal institutions was much greater, and forms of class strife substituted forms of patronage in many peripheral villages, especially from about 1920 to 1945. However, as the political force of Zapatismo diminished in the state government, and as demographic growth provoked land scarcity, power relations were again recast into their former place, and the petite bourgeoisie of peripheral villages regained its position as local caciques.

The situation was altogether different in the core, however, where a massive process of repeasantification occurred. Haciendas were destroyed during the Revolution, and their reconstitution became impossible with agrarian reform. This caused hamlet and village jornaleros to

"re-turn" into (or become) peasants. The culture of this repeasantification of hamlets has been best described by Fromm and Maccoby (1970)
and Romanucci-Ross (1973), and the implications of repeasantification
for class analysis in the core has been discussed by Singelman et al.
(1979). It is clear from Fromm and Maccoby's account that the transition from peon to peasant was culturally not at all simple. But the
complexities of the problem are even greater when we consider that the
core remained the locus of commercial agriculture in this period. In the
case of the sugar industry in particular, this meant that central planning
above the level of the peasant household remained indispensable, so
that "peasants" of the sugar-growing regions became a kind of hybrid of
peasant, renter, and wage laborer.

In core villages, the situation of peasants is much the same. During
this period core villages became somewhat more similar to the old peripheral villages, in the sense that the local petite bourgeoisie achieved
more power than it formerly had, and sometimes became a "cacique"
class of sorts. Limitations on the power of core caciques now came from
competition with the regional political class rather than from the power
of an extralocal economic group. There can be no question that the core
petite bourgeoisie was politically strengthened by agrarian reform.

Figure 3 presents class composition in settlements since industrialization. The changes involved in this transition are multiple and complex.
In the periphery we have, as a first observation, the transformation of
the general terms of dependence between core and periphery. Peripheral hamlets achieve a large degree of commercial independence from
peripheral village thanks to the new road systems; peripheral villages
depend less on regional market towns and cities due to the increasing
real proximity of Mexico City. Furthermore, peripheral dependence on
the core for seasonal employment changes during this period, for agricultural employment in the core is predominantly taken by Guerrero and
Oaxaca migrants, and urban employment becomes possible for sectors
of the periphery.

This situation of ready access and increased work opportunities in the
agricultural periphery also has important effects for the political structure of the periphery, and during this period the petite bourgeoisie
declined as caciques, and they were converted into a class without monopolistic hold over local resources. These situations imply important
changes in the intimate cultures of hamlet and village peasants, as well
as in village petit-bourgeois culture. For the latter, the change is from
the cultivation of a local culture which was used in the intense social
relations of that class in relations of dominance or patronage vis-à-vis
local peasants to the cultivation of money for a position in a more open
regional economy. For the peasants, the change is towards a more direct

participation in the regional working-class sectors and for a transformation of the political alliances implicit in "traditional" peasant culture
(which often takes the form of "rescuing traditions" without the old
political implications of those traditions).

In the core the main cultural event is the emergence of a working
class and the expansion of the petite bourgeoisie and professional
classes. We also have the emergence of a new level of regional organization: the regional city. Regional cities offer a truly urban set of services
and goods: hospitals, universities, bureaucracies, shopping malls, automobiles. At the same time, the relation between regional cities and
agricultural peripheries is of a kind of detachment that did not exist
between the old central market towns and the agricultural core and
periphery. The social detachment between the new industrial core and
the agricultural periphery has also been the setting of the emergence of
the new "petite bureaucracie," which has had the task of reinventing
Morelos' regional culture.

Conclusion: Power, Hegemony, and Flows of Mestizaje

In the structural transformations of class cultures that we have discussed, we see processes of cultural change that involve four main classes:
the peasantry, the petite bourgeoisie, the rural proletariat, and the urban
or modern proletariat. These processes of change can be properly understood only in terms of their regional expression in intimate culture. In the
case of the peasantry, the flow of mestizaje runs from an original situation
in which two major forms of peasant intimate culture coexisted: hamlet
and village peasant life. After agrarian reform, peripheral-village peasant
life was exported to core villages, and core hamlets adopted a new form of
peasant intimate culture. The expansion of peasant culture into the core
after agrarian reform is part of twentieth-century Morelos' culture history. In the third period of industrialization, we have the erosion of the old
peripheral village peasant culture (which, we will remember, was always
ritually most elaborate), this erosion is due to the "opening up" of these
localities and to the decline of the local cacique class. This transformation
in the periphery implies deep changes in the meaning of peasant "traditions" and has also meant the decrease of coherence for peripheral peasant culture.

At the same time, the peasantification of the core is a process that
ends in this period, and an ever greater proportion of repeasantified
village inhabitants participate in the emergent working classes and in the
service sectors. The petite bourgeoisie of the region is also transformed
in important ways during this period. There is the decline of the periph-

eral caciques, the extraregional orientation of the urban petite bourgeoisie, and the emergence of the petite bureaucracie. Finally, during the period of industrialization, the old jornalero class, which had been transformed into a new quasipeasantry, is revitalized in the form of migrant labor from outside of the state. At the same time, an urban working class emerges out of a migrant peasantry from Morelos and elsewhere. Sectors of this new working class can still be analyzed as transformations of peasant culture.

On the other hand, throughout this history of local changes in class and class composition, some extinct or endangered class cultures continue to haunt regional cultural production. One example of this is Morelos' hacienda culture, which still stands as the most elaborate example of a regionally based elite culture. The phantasmagoria of hacienda culture runs through the whole history of cultural change in the region. When the whole Mexican polity was collapsing in the late 1850s, the plateados appropriated the values of the hacienda and became a Mexican, gutsy version of "robber barons." Then, just a few years later, in his effort to consolidate a Mexican aristocracy, the emperor Maximilian took up this imagery. During the Revolution, Zapata worked with the hacendado image in order to construct his own persona, which succeeded in rising so high above "his" troops. Finally, in the contemporary period, when the regional identity of the elites is so questionable, the fallen banner of the hacendado has been taken up by industrialists and governors and it has been presented for the consumption of presidents, special guests, tourists, and even, on occasion, peasants and workers.

In the next three chapters, I shall explore the spaces for the construction of coherence in some of the intimate cultures that have emerged in Morelos.

6

Rural Cultures in Morelos

Transformations of Peasant Class Culture

In contemporary Morelos, peasants occupy four distinct settlement types: peripheral and core hamlets, and peripheral and core villages. The peasants in Morelos' agricultural core are historically distinguishable from those of the periphery because they have undergone a process of repeasantification since the agrarian reform. Because of their distinct historical conformation, it is worth giving separate treatment to the peasant cultures of the economic core and periphery.

I shall discuss peripheral and core peasant cultures in terms of the peasant ideology of community and social relations and of what occurs when the material possibility of maintaining these communities is undermined. In a sense, then, this chapter presents a discussion of peasant culture in a community context, and of what happens to the peasant constructions of self once this context is transformed or extinguished. The discussion begins by sketching out peasant culture in the periphery during periods when communal peasant ideals were operating in practice. Much of the argument on the nature of this peasant communal culture is a recapitulation of cultural arguments of earlier authors. Once some general aspects of peasant community ideology are established, I go on to show the elements of this peasant culture that have been maintained in (core) contexts of community demolition. Through this latter exercise I hope to show that the apparent "culturelessness" of the urban poor can be better understood in terms of peasant cultural understandings operating outside agrarian communities.

When Redfield described the peasant (peripheral-village) culture of Tepoztlán, he did so in terms of (a) an elaborate ritual cycle that symbolically integrated the constituent segments of the municipio (the barrios and hamlets) and (b) rituals that stood for the relationship of the village with its agricultural subsistence base. Redfield also characterized peasant culture in terms of a tension between local culture as the tardy assimilation of urban literate culture, and a folk tradition of local heroes, from the pre-Columbian Tepoztecatl to Emiliano Zapata, who stood for village independence and might. About twenty years after this synthesis of Tepoztecan culture, Lewis restudied Tepoztlán in an effort to show the relevance of political-economic analysis for an adequate understanding of peasant cultures.

At the deepest level, it is perhaps ascertainable that Lewis's most important difference with Redfield was his suspicion of the supposed import of a solidarity of village, barrio, and even family. For Lewis, the struggle for wealth, domination, or survival was so important that it undermined the collective cultural order. In this sense, Lewis's political critique of Redfield can be read as another instance of Sahlins's opposition between cultural and practical reason and, as such, it can be relatively easily discarded (as, for example, in Bock 1980, Lomnitz-Adler 1982, or Ingham 1986).

However, another reading of Lewis's critique is also possible. One could say that Lewis was describing a specific culture of atomization, factionalism, and conflict, whose implications undermined, or at least problematized, village, barrio, and family as privileged loci of local culture. In other words, a culturalist reading of Lewis would point us in the direction of discovering a peasant culture with a weak institutional basis for the community's reproduction, with relatively unimportant or irrelevant collective manifestations and relatively disarticulated levels of collective organization, without recourse to the kind of vulgar materialist explanation of these characteristics that Lewis often lapsed into.

It is in this frame of reference—in relation to the tensions between a communal culture and the atomization of the peasantry—that a description of Morelos' peasant intimate cultures is most profitable. There are two ways of discovering the elements of this tension: one is a historical analysis of the cultural disarticulation of the peasant community in a process of increasing atomization that is the result of the reorganization of the regional economy and the proletarianization or "semi-proletarianization" of the peasantry. The other is based on a synchronic analysis of the tensions between community and individual or family in the context of a peasant *tradition*. The first section of this chapter is devoted to the description of "traditional" peasant community ideology (including tensions between individual needs and this community ideology) as it occurred during a period of "closure" in the regional political economy; the second section is devoted to the description of peasant culture when it is unharnessed from the peasant community in core urban contexts and in processes of aperture of the peasant periphery.

Communal Peasant Culture in Morelos

The first thing about peasant rituals in Morelos is that they signal membership in and interaction between communities. In Morelos, as we have already shown, there was a period of peasantification between 1914, the year of the definite collapse of the hacienda system, and (roughly) 1950, when the growth of the urban capitalist sector reoriented agricultural production and the organization of labor in the region. This historical period is one in which peasant ideals of community are *de facto* dominating the landscape, and so it is a good point in time to analyze communal peasant culture.

The consolidation of peasant community culture during this period of contraction in the regional economy is reflected in the importance of ritual. At that time there was an elaborate set of well-tended and well-attended rituals (cf. Redfield 1930) at the level of the family, the neighbors, the barrios, the village, the municipio, the Morelos region, and the Central Mexican region. The municipal level of ritual (which in the peasant periphery usually fully encompassed the category of "village") was enforced by the relatively frequent monopoly over the periodic markets in the cabeceras, and by the centralization of local political decisions and governmental services there (civil registry, judges, schools, doctors); for these same reasons, the municipal cabecera was an important space for the selection of marriage partners and compadres. The closure of peasant communities during the period between the Revolution and 1950 can be observed in these rituals. Most noticeable in this respect is the village appropriation of the Church.

Most rituals in peasant Morelos (and Mexico, for that matter) were internally dichotomized into a church celebration and a profane fiesta. This is true of rituals around the "life cycle," the agricultural cycle, and the religious calendar. De la Peña (1980) has shown that these two aspects of ritual—sacred and profane, church and village—were, in colonial times, a simultaneous ritualization of peasant communitas and of regional integration through the Church. The peasant community (and factionalism between communities) was ritualized in the context of Church surveillance and of an alliance with the Church.

This situation changed somewhat during the nineteenth century, particularly with the triumph of liberalism, in that the Church was to some extent discredited in its function of integrator of hegemonic culture. However, during the nineteenth century the role of the Church was to a certain degree maintained through the material support offered by hacendados to the celebration of village patron-saints' days. The Revolution inaugurated a period of peasant closure because of the peasantification of the core, which explains the tendency for local appropriation of both sacred and profane aspects of peasant rituals. Villagers and families of the "peasant period" in modern Morelos history appropriated the local churches (and their saints), so that the opposition between the secular and religious elements of the fiesta tended to imply only the distinction between the village (centered around the physical edifice of the village church) and whatever social group was carrying out the fiesta. The local church became a symbol of the local village, and not necessarily of its alliance with a supraregional state.

The cultural effects of this local appropriation of the churches—attributable on the one hand to the severing of State/Church relations and on the other to the decline of haciendas—were the (momentary) legitimation of peasant knowledge, of the "traditional" peasant interpretation of the world. This period therefore marks a moment of great potential coherence in peasant culture, for peasant theories of good and evil, sickness and disease, and right and wrong are legitimated by a Church that is very much in peasant control, and only incipiently challenged by a state and a bourgeoisie which are still weak and resourceless.

The nature of this "full" peasant culture, whose specific historicity in Morelos has not always been stressed,[1] can best be explored through certain of its ideological expressions. This is because, to my knowledge, the "peasant period" was too short and conflict-ridden for peasants to actually take full control of social reproduction, even in most peripheral villages.

Probably the most synthetic, internally coherent, way of bringing together the principles of peasant community culture is by an analysis of the culture of power and its metaphoric interrelations with the culture of sexual relations and the relations between the sexes. Ingham (1970) and I (1982) have shown that there exists a discourse—epitomized by the "hot/cold" classifications of food (cf. Lewis 1951, Friedlander 1975), but also running through local conceptions of illness, politics, sexual relations, and economic relations—that metaphorically connects all of these diverse domains.

The ideological principle common to these forms of popular wisdom would appear to be that social forces are thought to be of two basic kinds, one aggressive or exploitative and one passive or exploitable. These two forces are neutralized when they are adequately combined, and the most common cultural *ideal* is the neutralization of these forces in order to obtain reciprocity in the economic sphere, a combination between hot and cold in food, *respeto* (respect) in social interaction, distance between a peasant existence and state politics, and a familial existence with a sharply defined division of economic, social, and emotional labor between men and women.

So, for example, when I did fieldwork in Tepoztlán (1977), people often thought of politicians as lusty (*calientes*, or hot), exploitative, mean machos (*cabrones*). Any disinterested person stupid enough to follow them was a *pendejo* (a stupid fool) who would get "screwed" (*jodido, chingado*). In other words, sexual intercourse serves as a metaphor of exploitation in much the same way as it helps people think about the properties of foods and diseases.[2]

This ideological complex helps explain several intriguing aspects of Morelos peasant culture: the apparently contradictory quality of peasant politics wherein the major political manifestations are individual "apathy" and collective revolt, for example. An understanding of this ideology also helps explain attitudes towards male and female homosexuality, and cultural ideals of social interaction between men (female homosexuality being relatively unproblematized, whereas male homosexuality is a metaphor of exploitation: the "male" party in homosexual intercourse is an extremely "hot," exploitative person, while the "female" party is "cold," exploited and looked down upon). The ideal male relationship is respeto, a category that implies mutual recognition of potency or virility and mutual agreement to direct that potency elsewhere.

The cultural ideal of a peasant community is, then, peasant production in a village of "respectable" men with their families. No unfamilial existence is desirable. There is sharp division of labor inside the family, and an integration of families into barrios (or hamlets) through kinship (the "barrio families" that I have noted elsewhere, 1982) and neighborhood. Barrios and hamlets are integrated into villages and municipios through identification. Interestingly enough, this cultural organization is not alien to that described by Redfield in his own, arcane, way.

However, as Lewis was quick to note, this peasant ideology was rarely fully realized, and has only been dominant in Morelos for short and easily distinguished historical periods. Peasant cultural ideals become actual cultural practice only in the specific context of a stagnated, stable regional system; and even so they often entail intense political struggles with the local cacique classes.[3] More importantly, perhaps, the political-economic limitations for the feasibility of the Morelos peasant cultural ideal have produced cultural results that appear to negate these cultural ideals term for term. I will approach this problem historically and spatially, for both of these dimensions are indispensable for an understanding of Morelos regional culture.

Fragmentation of Coherence and the Spatial Transformations of Peasant Class Culture

It seems obvious enough that the Morelos peasant cultural ideal of reciprocity, family integration and communal life is only materially realizable in specific historical and regional circumstances. The proletarianization of male labor potentially (though not necessarily) upsets the relevance of community political and ritual relations; the proletarianization of women most definitely upsets many of the patriarchal family ideals. Direct capital investment in peasant communities modifies the nature of village communitas as well as the content of local ritual and culture. The modernization of the Church, which in Morelos occurred mostly during the tenure of Bishop Sergio Méndez Arcéo, who belongs to the "theology of liberation" faction of the Church, has often meant a loss of communal control over ritual and the ritual cycle; direct federal and state investment in villages has limited political autonomy, and so on. The ideals of what I have been calling here the "peasant period" have thus been fragmented spatially into several different kinds of communal and family practices which can be profitably understood within the spatial dimension of regional transformation.

It is my thesis that most of the rural cultures of Morelos, and indeed some of the urban intimate cultures as well, are transformations of this peasant culture. In order to understand the nature of these transformations we must turn away from the relatively pure forms of peasant ideology that emerged in the periphery during the "peasant period" and look instead to the rural culture of villages in the regional core and to the culture of urban migrants in cities. For these purposes, the works of Fromm and Maccoby (1970) and Romanucci-Ross (1973) in Chiconcuac and the studies of Lewis (1964 and 1969) on the so-called "culture of poverty" of Tepoztecan migrants are invaluable.

In their socio-psychoanalytic study of Chiconcuac, an ex-hacienda (core hamlet) that was repeasantized during the ejido grants of the 1920s, Fromm, Maccoby, and Romanucci-Ross portray a culture with several salient elements: (a) strong incidence of matrifocal families; (b) relatively poor level of village cultural activities (which is explicitly contrasted with the findings of Redfield and Lewis in Tepoztlán, but could just as well be contrasted with ritual cycles across the whole Morelos periphery); and (c) a pervasive "machismo," associated with extremely high incidence of adult male alcoholism and with what Fromm and Maccoby call an "authoritarian, unproductive, sadomasochistic personality."

In Lewis's studies of the "culture of poverty," which we shall read here not in their vulgar materialistic dimensions, but rather as telling cultural accounts of the lives of migrants written by a meticulous ethnographer, the salient cultural characteristics of Tepoztecan ("Aztecan") migrants to Mexico City are: (a) increasing matrifocality and dissolution of the traditional monogamous patriarchal family; (b) exacerbation of machismo and polygamy; and (c) disappearance of communal rituals and organizations (reflected in the last instance in the fact that Lewis had to privilege the study of families over that of communities in order to study the cultural phenomenon of "poverty").

Yet the image of dissolution, of anomie, of disruption of cultural order, that emerges from the accounts of the "culture of poverty" of Lewis and of Fromm and Maccoby are misleading; they do not sufficiently emphasize the relationship between the particular forms of cultural dissolution and the peasant cultural ideology that explains the specific acts and choices made by peasants when the community has disappeared. So, for example, why should a heightened sense of machismo be the result of the frustration of peasant communal and family ideals? Why should factional politics, patron-client relationships, and *compadrazgo* survive the dissolution of the peasant community? Why should the family remain, in Lewis's terms (1969:17), "a natural unity of study" for cultural anthropology in Mexican cities?

Peasant Culture in Non-Peasant Spaces

In Morelos we can observe transformations of the peasant culture I have summarily described at several levels of the regional system: in the core hamlets and villages, where capital investment and proletarianization place severe limits on communal organization, and in urban neighborhoods of migrants. The cultural transformations that I shall analyze are all about the workings of the peasant ideological complex in transformed social contexts.

The dissolution of the village (peasant village or hamlet) as the main point of reference for economic reproduction implies that the ideal relationship of respeto (respect) between men is not easily enforced. Respeto is a relationship that is established in the context of (projected) long-term relationships wherein both parties feel independent from each other, yet at the same time recognize the importance of collaboration. Thus the exploitative tendencies that are inherent to the cultural conception of "males" become curbed within a system in which male dominance is satisfied within the home, and companionship between equals is emphasized in communal contexts.

The proletarianization of the peasantry undermines the patriarchal family and the male ideological need for power gets liberated from—or frustrated out of—the familial domain; instead it is expressed in the continuous competition between men for resources and status. In this sense Morelos' "mesticized" ("incoherent") culture is one where the position of men is unstable and always viewed as transformable through good business deals, patronage, and jobs. In the sexual and familial sphere, however, the heightened "machismo" that is liberated out of peasant culture is a reflection of the fact that men have difficulties in asserting authority over wives, and especially over their children, and so seek the satisfactions of manhood in polygyny or other conventional signs of manliness.

This point of view also helps explain one aspect of urban machismo that is often noted but has rarely been analyzed. The specific form that urban polygyny most commonly takes in Mexico is the so-called *casa chica*. This institution involves not merely having a fixed lover or lovers, but actually establishing one or more parallel families, whose existence is ideally kept entirely separate from the male's primary or legal family. This form of machismo therefore does not merely involve having sex with many women, it entails having *children* with many women—in other words, having alternate families. Through this mechanism, men can guarantee being longed for and sought after as husbands and fathers, since they can play one family off against the other.

At the same time, the liberation of an exploitative ideology about the nature of things (synthesized in the "hot/cold" dichotomy) from the rules of complementarity that kept it in harmony legitimate a culture of personal gain. Exploitative and exploitable people are seen as existing freely in the world and as naturally attracting one another: because exploiters and sufferers are uncontrolled, one must do what accommodates one's interest the most, at least in the anonymous realms of the public.

This ideology of personal gain is probably what led people like Oscar Lewis into believing that the culture of these urban groups is like a Pavlovian response to the duress of material survival, a "culture of poverty." In fact this is not at all the case; the ideology that legitimates personal gain in the public spheres is constituted in terms of the peasant culture I have described. Moreover, this description of the logic of transformation of the Morelos peasant culture into a specific kind of proletarian culture is still incomplete; the tendencies toward heightened machismo, which are a result of the breakdown in the peasant ideology of balance (between hot and cold, male and female, in reciprocal economic exchange, in political participation), do not get unequivocally constituted into a project for cultural reproduction. On the contrary, the ideals of family unity and communitas are frequently maintained at least at the level of family culture and ritual. This fact is perhaps also useful in the explanation of the emerging importance of nationalism (as the figuration of the kinds of imagined communities posited by Anderson) within these groups. The nostalgia for the (supposedly) anxiety-free culture of the peasant, where religion, family, and work are integrated into a coherent symbolic system, pervades the mesticized cultures of the Morelos regional core. Families give great importance to familial rituals, and especially to those rituals that define the place of their individual members in "society" (examples of this are the importance attributed to a girl's fifteenth birthday, but also to baptism, marriage, confirmation, and to the celebration of all of the days that commemorate kinds of relationships: Mothers' Day, Father's Day, Dia del Compadre, Teacher's Day, Children's Day, and so on).

One might say, then, that the "mesticized" peasant culture of the Morelos core—the ideology of legitimized personal gain, of aggressive male behavior, the vulnerability of conjugal bonds and parental authority—in certain senses reinforces peasant ideas about the self. It reproduces the notion of a world that is divided into passive and aggressive forces, and so many proletarianized peasants pine for community and reciprocity and reconstruct families, neighborhoods, and churches out of those ideals. Peasant cultural attitudes in the core are therefore ideologically manipulable by alternate propositions for communitas (such as those posed by the Church, disembodied from a peasant community, by Protestants, and by the State and political parties). Peasant cultures of the core are more amenable to changing forms of political participation than peripheral peasant cultures.

I have showed that ideologies of exploitation (in several metaphorical senses: economic exploitation, sexual exploitation, "social" exploitation) result from the rupture between peasant notions of self and peasant contexts of social reproduction; this has helped to describe the specific forms that this exploitative culture takes, and it has distanced us from an acultural understanding of the so-called "culture of poverty." At the same time, exploitative ideology and the ideology of legitimate personal gain is amenable to the general conditions of capitalism in Mexico. The rupture of the community and its substitution by a *desire* for community therefore facilitate the manipulation of this group both as a potential consumer of market goods and as a consumer of ideologies.

Coherence and Incoherence: Flows of Mestizaje and the Cultural Core/Periphery Structure

I have been describing Morelos' intimate cultures in terms of transformations in two basic class cultures: peasant culture and petit-bourgeois culture. These two classes, which formed the most important poles of local urban and rural culture in preindustrial Morelos, have been transformed by the process of industrialization in the state. In the last few chapters I have attempted to show that (a) there has been a systematic spatial dimension in the transformations of the two main "coherent" poles of Morelos culture, and (b) that the process of disarticulating the coherence of peasant and petit-bourgeois cultures has not meant shedding peasant, petit-bourgeois, or even hacendado ideologies, whose relocation in distinct spatial contexts of economic and political relations helps explain the characteristics of the emergent coherent cultures: that of the (culturally fragmented) urban and rural proletariat, and that of the (fragmented) members of the "middle sectors."

In these conclusions I shall synthesize my discussion of intimate cultures by focussing on the regional dimension of cultural transformation in Morelos, its implications for the different intimate cultures in terms of their internal coherence, and thence their position within regional hegemonic culture. The regional and historical localization of coherence and incoherence in Morelos' intimate cultures is indispensable for an understanding of the spaces where myth is created about these different cultures in the culture of social relations, as well as the production of myth that is internal to the intimate cultures. In this sense, these conclusions form a bridge between the preceding discussion of regional cultural organization and the presentation of localist ideologies that will occupy the remaining two chapters of the Morelos section.

The Cultural Core/Periphery Structure

There are two useful ways of defining a core/periphery structure in Morelos regional culture: one is through the nature of the links with the regional hegemonic culture, another is by proximity to any of the coherent class-cultural poles of regional culture. The first strategy would lead us to define a single core/periphery structure, whence the regional core is occupied by an absentee state culture, a relatively weak petite bourgeoisie, and the classes which are internally most fragmented and so subscribe most directly to the aspirations of this petit-bourgeois class (such as the most upwardly mobile sectors of the working classes and the most prosperous peasants). The inner core would be the classes that are in continual interaction with the regional elites and have little control over public spaces of class reproduction (and so are "incoherent"). This is the case in Cuernavaca of much of the working class and the "marginal" or "informal" urban sectors. An inner periphery can be discerned in the classes with intense interaction with the regional hegemonic

classes and with greater control over public spaces of communal reproduction; this is the case, for example, of the "peasant" culture inside
Cuernavaca, but it is also the case of the working classes that have
gained control of their communal spaces, for example, through independently controlled unions, control over their barrios and churches, and
the like; some of the more stable elements of the rural proletariat also
come into this category, as in the cases of peasant communities that are
dependent on the Zacatepec or Oacalco sugar mills. The cultural periphery would then be constituted by the intimate cultures with a relatively
large degree of control over their public and reproductive spheres and
with relatively infrequent interaction with the regional elites, such that
an internally coherent, and to some degree autochthonous, culture is
produced. This is the case of the peripheral peasant villages in the state,
and especially of the peasant hamlets of the economic periphery.

In addition to this core/periphery organization one is forced to add a
category of transient people, constituted by persons split from their
communities and not incorporated into new communities. Lewis's ethnographies occasionally suggest that this class of persons may feed into
the hegemonic culture, since the dissolution of peasant communal existence can be internalized as an ideological premium on personal gain (a
liberation from the strictures of the community). However, these people
often attempt to retain ties with their communities of origin, or else to
create their own, new communities, but they can also remain marginalized from all communal levels of the system.

The second way of conceiving the Morelos cultural core/periphery
structure is in relation to proximity to poles of cultural coherence.[4] In
this case we would have three main cores: the *dominant* core around the
regional petit-bourgeois elites, the *residual* core around peasant communities, and the *emergent* core around an urban proletariat. In the peripheries of each of these cores we would have the following intimate cultures: at the periphery of the (dominant) bourgeois core is the upwardly
mobile proletariat and artisan classes, the rich peasant/rancher class,
and a proportion of the "informal sector." At the periphery of the (residual) peasant core we would have the semiproletariat and seasonal migrants that aim to return to their communities, the rural proletariat that
aspires to repeasantification, and the "peasants" of the economic core.
Finally, the (emergent) proletarian core's periphery is ambiguously
shared with the bourgeois and peasant cultural peripheries. It is made up
of rural proletarians who begin to orient themselves to a working-class
culture, and of city dwellers whose ties with the countryside are ever
weakening.

These two ways of defining the regional core/periphery structure are
mutually complementary and of equal analytical import. The first division

points to the organization of regional culture from the point of view of regional power; the second perspective helps to understand the spatial logic of hegemony, and the processes of cultural change in their regional and historical dimensions. It is in the space of contention between the (relatively) coherent class-cultural cores of this second Morelos core/periphery structure that localist ideologies emerge; and it is only in this context that localist ideologies (nationalism, regionalism, villagism, peasantism, petit-bourgeoisism, workerism, and other group-isms) can be analyzed.

7

The Localist Ideology of
a Vulnerable Elite

In prerevolutionary Morelos, Mexico City elites controlled most of the productive apparatus as well as the higher rungs of the state bureaucracy. This direct control helps explain the conformation of a regional peasant identity such as has been described by Womack, Warman, and others. During the period which immediately followed the Revolution, Mexico City slowly regained control of the different levels of the state apparatus, but much of the regional economy fell back into peasant and local cacique control. Since industrialization, the national and international bourgeoisie have placed their investments in industry and have controlled agricultural production mainly through the market. In this most recent period the regional elites have come to the fore as a kind of incarnation of the cultural ideal of a (Mexico City-centered) cultural hegemony. Their struggle for regional power involves the construction of social difference through consumption and on control over the state bureaucracy. In order to attain both of these aims, the regional elite needs to lean on the national state and use its expertise and its local resources to attempt "joint ventures" in both the economic and the political sphere. In this chapter I explore the politics of the intimate culture of the regional elites through the study of some of the more salient aspects of its localist ideologies.

In an interview I held with an ex-governor, we spoke of Cuernavaca's cultural heterogeneity. Said the governor:

> You will find this lack of unity in all aspects of the city. Of course you will. Cuernavaca has become a heterogeneous population. Cuernavaca is saved

because of its climate, the light, the sun, the scenery; but from a sociological and cultural perspective I don't think the city has any salvation whatsoever. It is going towards a definitive ruin, because it is becoming impersonal, and that is most painful.

A much younger Morelense politician/professional said,

None of the governors that I can remember [since the early sixties] had any kind of transcendence in the state. None has acquaintances or any of the social attributes that a governor should have: that he be known to a compadre or by the lady in the corner store, that he be known in the municipios and be invited frequently to luncheons, that he be known in the state congress and by the chamber of commerce and industry. . . . Never.

The people from Morelos who are in politics are easily cast aside and very mobile. But we Morelenses are not united. . . . We have never demanded that Morelenses occupy the important posts. Why? because every individual is out for his own benefit [*cada quien trabaja para su santo*].[1]

Morelos' regional core is dependent on a periodically shifting, external source of power, the federal government, and on a managerial class that is paid by non-local firms. This dependence on a shifting external source has provoked, as we have seen, Cuernavaca's privatization: what the governor called the depersonalization of Cuernavaca, what the bureaucrat referred to as Morelense individualism, what I called Cuernavacan baroque. This individualism at the elite level in the core is in a way a flight from the formation of an elite localist ideology; the localist phrases which I got from the governor and bureaucrat, and from many others, show this clearly. Instead of producing an ideology about the nature of a bounded intimate culture, we have in Morelos the wholesale adoption by the elites of the place assigned to them in a national culture of social relations.

This process of renouncing an actively produced collective identity, this conjunctural elimination of localism, can best be spotted in the spaces of elite myth. Roland Barthes (1957) defined myth as stolen language, the decontextualization of action in order to transform it into unstated evidence which favors another's interest. The analysis of the position of the Morelos elite in regional hegemony can be perceived in its myth-production and in its participation in nonregional myths.

Morelos' elites have produced and appropriated for themselves a set of myths about the region which ultimately tend towards legitimating their position as a regional elite. This is undeniable. So, for example, the museum at Cuernavaca devotes disproportionate attention to "Indian Morelos," with pictures and models of ethnic culture from the towns of

Tetelcingo, Tepoztlán and Hueyapan. This presentation of Indian Morelos is complemented by a somewhat less conspicuous presentation of
mestizo peasant Morelos, a thatched hut with assorted modern and
traditional artifacts, including a rundown TV set. The controlled image
of the Indian and peasant and its displacement to the context of a regionalist ideology (as well as to the promotion of tourism) are thus
present in the politics of the regional elite.

The obverse of elite appropriation of regional culture for its own
purposes can be seen in the ways in which peasant and Indian cultures
are effectively "muted" in interactive contexts between elites and peasants. This process has been aptly illustrated by Díaz Cruz (1984) with
material from a taped political meeting between Ana Laura Ortega (the
current governor's daughter) and ejido representatives from the Indian
town of Tetelcingo.[2] Says Díaz Cruz:

> [Government officials] all have the same idea: if Tetelcincas have any
> significance for them, it is as individuals needy of their help. And they
> expect the Tetelcincans to feel the same way. Ana Laura [the governor's
> daughter] has expressed it more aptly: [the following are sentences taken
> from the political meeting which is transcribed in its entirety] "I repeat,
> my role and my interest is to solve the whole village" [*pueblo*]. And she
> does so under a very peculiar notion of democracy, "in which we shall all
> participate collectively." Ana Laura then imposes her decision: "All right,
> we will then write this petition to the governor; do all of you agree, or is
> there someone that disagrees?" In addition she does not allow any criti-
> cism to be leveled against her: "if I desire to work with you the least I can
> ask is that you also work . . . and that you not contradict me." Finally,
> Ana Laura concludes that "[we shall] forget the criteria of childishness and
> foolishness [which in her opinion has pervaded in the town], we will see
> things truthfully, things as they should be." (p. 95)

This process of imposing Ana Laura's perspective on the community was
preceded by the following meaningful warning:

> And I ask the people of this village, what do you think I came for? To lose
> time? I could be sitting in Cocoyoc [an expensive nearby resort], drinking
> soft drinks and guarding myself from the rain, instead of working up a
> sweat [*sobándome el lomo*] with you. That's obvious, isn't it? So, then, if I
> wish to work with you, the least I can ask is for you to do the same, and for
> you not to contradict [or reproach] me. (p. 91)

So the Morelos elites do appropriate intimate cultures of the region
through mythification (the official representations of peasant and Indian
culture) and its concomitant "muteness" (the one-sided "dialogue" between governor's daughter and peasants). However, this appropriation

of regional culture is in fact limited in context and importance. It is crucial for state governors, representatives, technicians, and municipal presidents, but it is only of subsidiary importance in non-political contexts. This is because petit-bourgeois mythology of regional intimate cultures is only a fragment of a greater appropriation of the region by the state and the national and international bourgeoisie. I shall illustrate this again with political material from the ex-governor:

> It seems that now the situation [of lack of municipal resources] is changing, and they are giving the municipio the resources that legitimately belong to it. . . . It seems that now the municipios are receiving an important portion of the property taxes, on top of large percentages of the federal aid that used to be destined to the state government. These are aspects of the "pact for decentralization"—or should I say "centralization"? For it is a curious thing, what happens in Mexico; when we "decentralize" is when we centralize the most. . . . The more federalist, the more centralist.

What is this power that centralizes by decentralizing? How does it pertain to the regional elites of Morelos, and how does it affect their intimate culture and its politicization through localist ideology?

At the level of power relations, decentralization means dispensing with the independent power of the regional elites, bureaucratizing the regional elites, making them administrators instead of owners. At the level of culture, this bureaucratization, this divestment of regional power, is manifested in the weakness of localist ideology, in group identification through patterns of consumption, not through power of domination. At the level of myth this makes the regional elite's situation appropriable by the federal government and bourgeoisie. The myth that ensues is the myth of democracy, the myth of decentralization, which implies the existence of native leadership without granting it any real autonomy. The Morelos state bureaucratic organization is a reproduction of that of the federal government; the state is the federation writ small. Morelos' history is national history writ small. The governor is like the president; the regional elite is like the national elite. Only in fact it isn't.

In this regard, the mythmaking of the regional elites occupies a space that is defined by the designs of the national state; the regional elite has been allowed to share in the control of the regional state apparatus, and that is a position it could scarcely have attained on its own. This situation can be analyzed through the ideas of Cuernavacan government-related intellectuals.

There is in Morelos a small group of intellectuals whose ostensible function is to organize cultural activities and write speeches for politicians or articles in regional newspapers. This group of individuals serves as a kind of source of reference for politicians and political institutions of the state. It is a function that has very limited institutional space. The state university has no social science or humanities degrees; however, the university does sponsor some cultural activities that involve the regional intellectuals. There is also the Dirección de Investigaciones Históricas y Actividades Culturales of the state government, the municipal archives, and the state high schools. Regional newspapers are either parts of national chains or are coopted by the state government or local merchants,[3] except in the case of *El Corréo del Sur,* which is critical of the government and has had close ties to the Church.

Because of the positions of this intelligentsia vis-à-vis the regional elite, the localist discourse of this group is more directly involved with the creation of independent regional power than is characteristic of the elite discourse itself. I shall discuss material from three cases here: one from interviews with one of the best-known regional intellectuals, and two from local dilettantes who nonetheless occupy positions in the production of a regionalist ideology.

I shall begin with one of the "dilettantes," whom I would rather not blame excessively for their intellectual dilly-dallyings, in that the kind of financial and institutional support that Morelos provides for cultural activities can hardly sustain much more intellectual weight. The example is meant to illustrate the participation of elites in the national (essentially centralist) myth in which Morelos is presented as Mexico writ small:[4]

The engineer, Mr. Hernández (a pseudonym), worked at one of Morelos' cultural institutions during my field work. I had a few long chats with him when I began working in Cuernavaca. In my first conversation with Hernández he spoke of his passion for the state and for Mexico, and of how he had walked across most of Morelos.[5] Hernández was very interested in my book on Tepoztlán because "Tepoztlán has the purest Nahuatl in Mexico." Hernández thus began speaking of Nahuatl philosophy and of the importance of Nahuatl for Mexican culture. He then revealed to me one of his long-term projects, which he claims is gaining acceptance in the government: the reconstruction of Cuernavaca's ancient center. Hernández believes that it is possible to reconstruct central Cuernavaca on the basis of the only plausible and self-evident hypothesis (there are no remains of central pre-Hispanic Cuernavaca): like Tenochtlitlán/Mexico City, the transition Cuauhnahuac/Cuernavaca entailed the destruction of Cuauhnahuac's ceremonial center and its transformation into a central plaza. Inside this ceremonial center (so runs the hypothesis) what could there be but an ensemble of pyramids identical to the ones in Mexico City, only smaller? Hernández proposes to rebuild a model of central Tenochtitlan in central Cuernavaca, and thereby to recuperate the "roots of our spirit."

This case may seem to the reader to be abnormal, yet Hernández's particularly audacious bricolage is not, it seems to me, completely fortuitous. The elimination of an autochthonous elite, the undermining of Morelos as a cultural region, makes it fertile ground for the retrojection of "national history" into the regional void that is left over. This construction of regional history via the importation of national history—especially to the regional core—has the additional advantage of lending transcendence to regional history as a kind of perfect embodiment or quintessence of "national history." The myth of Morelos as a reproduction of Mexico legitimates the maintenance of a (weak) regional elite at the same time that it sustains the integration of the region to national order. It is thus no coincidence that the elite ideology that Morelos is Mexico writ small has a national counterpart in the fact (which I argued above) that Morelos history has been a kind of model of "national history." Since the official appropriation and nationalization of Zapatismo, Morelos has served as a paradigm of "rurality" in national history. This strategy has been useful not only because of the importance of Zapatismo in postrevolutionary ideology, but also because Morelos has always (even in pre-Columbian times) been controlled by Mexico City. It is a region without a political elite of its own. "Mexican history" and Mexico City serve as paradigm for the Morelos elite because the local reproduction of a "national" phenomenon legitimates the existence of a regional elite, a regional bureaucracy, a regional state.

The second example of the position and role of intellectuals in Morelos' regionalism is an event that affected "Mr. Valdez," who is doubtless one of the most knowledgeable people on Cuernavacan and Morelos' history. He is often consulted in ceremonial events such as anniversaries of the foundation of the city, birth and death dates of local heroes, and anniversaries of battles. Valdez responds to this function by specializing further in Morelos and Cuernavaca, thereby increasing his worth as a source of empirical knowledge on the region. Valdez has also written a fair number of historical works that have been published locally. The periodizations in these works are all political. His history is a history of political figures and events, with very little economic or social history. Because of the value of Valdez as a source of local knowledge, he has also gained some political weight.

Valdez once made a statement that the official party's candidate for governor was not born and had never lived in Morelos. The result of this statement was a six-year banishment of Valdez from public service, and—worse yet—he was (unofficially) declared persona non grata in the state university. His private law practice was also sabotaged. Valdez was finally forced to look for a job in Mexico City and to commute during the whole regnum of that governor. This example illustrates the place and importance of local history for the regional state elites: a memory of local events, dates, families, and people is always important in the fabrication of governors' speeches, in scheduling commemorations, in making up guest lists for commemorations, in constructing cinematographic representations of the past, and so on. Valdez's prominence stems in large part from these needs.

The third, and final, example shows the forms of mythification available to the regional intelligentsia, as well as the tensions in the use of this ideological power. These involve, simply, the conflict that exists between placing these myths at the service of a weak regional bourgeois or bureaucratic elite or in utilizing them in a struggle for increasing power of different regional sectors, such as the peasantry or the workers. The example comes from several conversations with José Fuentes (a pseudonym, again), a local intellectual who produced the following impression on me:

> [From my field notes] The people in the state government are personally acquainted with many of the important people of the villages of Morelos [such as the two old peasants who were in Fuentes's office during our first interview]. Many of them are specialists (if not professionals) in history, they know corridos of historical figures, and they like to talk about them. They live within a temporal perspective which includes dramatis personae that are alien to most people. . . .
>
> My opinion of Fuentes is that he is a dilettante who knows a lot of people [i.e., has contacts]. He combs his hair back to mark the fact that he is a poet. He studied, but never finished, philosophy at the UNAM, he has participated in countless research projects that he has not finished, and he writes poems on Rubén Jaramillo and El Tepotécatl. In this sense he incarnates Cuernavacan culture: costrumbrista poetry with social content, whose major finality is . . . to allow public administrators to show people like me—or bureaucrats from Bellas Artes or the Ministry of Education—that they are "doing something."

Despite these impressions, Fuentes's discourse proved to be quite interesting. Fuentes lives in a tension between the fact that his production is remunerated by the state government and by his private belief in his allegiance to the popular causes and (thence) in the intrinsically revolutionary value of his work. This tension finds its best expression in Fuentes's theories of the origin of knowledge.

The primary characteristic of these theories is that knowledge and discovery are *systematically* disassociated from social recognition and fame. So, for example, the true creators of the Renaissance were the (unacknowledged) Etruscans, "who were the real *chingones*" (virile big-shots). The Aztecs, too, were nothing; the real savants were the Toltecs and the Mayas. The proof of this is that Soviet scientists (who, predict-ably, are more *chingón* than U.S. scientists) come to Mexico every year to study the science of the Mayas in order to learn from them. The ancient Egyptians were nothing, the people who knew their stuff were the unknown builders of the sphinx and the pyramids at Cheops.

Several elements are important in this ideology. First is a mechanism for delegitimating dominant groups and official histories. Dominant eth-nic groups and classes are portrayed as appropriators of knowledge and culture they did not really produce. Second, this "theory of the origin of knowledge" becomes a revalorization of Fuentes's own marginal posi-tion and a revalorization of the culture of dominated intimate cultures as well. This revalorization of Fuentes's own culture (to the detriment of dominantly accepted cultural contributions) takes on a particular form here. First of all, it preserves the dominant parameters with which superi-ority or greatness is measured. Second, it proves itself superior to domi-nant culture along a wealth of mutually unconnected lines. Third, it explains its own cultural subordination in terms of a lack of *desire* to dominate. These characteristics are the reason why this ideology is not intrinsically a subversion of the hegemonic cultural order.

Let me illustrate these points. (1) Fuentes retains the hegemonic parameters of superiority or greatness. Fuentes's use of the word *chingón* to measure Toltecs against Aztecs is a key here. Virility is the main metaphor of superiority, and (as in the case of the urbanized peasants) sexual intercourse is the metaphor of power relations. Thus Fuentes's use of his knowledge in the seduction of women is a major theme in his conversation, and the empirical proof of the worth of his knowledge is that it allows him to sleep with women of higher classes and to exploit people of those classes. So, Fuentes told me of how he had been asked to sing his Morelense songs at a bourgeois party and how later he slept with the wife of a "rich Jew" who had attended. Also, Fuentes is proud of his macho exploits as ethnographer: "I drank with him, and when he was very drunk I got him to talk about what Jaramillo's brother did when he died."

(2) Fuentes finds evidence of his own superiority (and that of other non-dominant cultures) in many unconnected places. This is an impor-tant point, since it has to do with the production of coherence in a subordinate, incoherent, intimate culture. The proof of the superiority of alternate-to-dominant knowledge is not derived from the systematic superiority of subordinate to dominant theories; it is based on the empiri-cal observation of the fertility and potency of native theories, generally in spaces that are not satisfactorily occupied by dominant culture (curing

cancer, satisfying women's sexual desires, producing arts and crafts). So the constructor of cultural coherence in mesticized culture attempts to essentialize dominant culture through a characterization of a few of its available samples, and to show the comparative wealth of an entirely unsystematic corpus of alternate knowledge, whose only common theme is its perceived otherness.

(3) Inferiority is explained in terms of a lack of will to dominate. This is integrally related to the themes of virility, fertility and versatility which I have discussed. Socially recognized domination is not desired because a more profound kind of domination already exists: "I was making a clay jug on a wheel in Puebla and little by little I was surrounded by gringos who were astonished at my work. When I finished—it was very good work—I squished the jug in front of all of them."

This gesture is, it seems to me, typical of this aspect of Fuentes's localism. He has the real power, the real fertility, "the art," which the rich gringos lack and desire, but he is not interested in exchanging it for access to what the gringos have (money). He claims to be content with his own fertility, but he does not resist flaunting his "superiority" and his spite.

This last element of Fuentes's localism is, I think, the one that guarantees that his ideology does not actually help conform a coherent intimate culture outside the intellectual's head. In fact what we have in the case of Fuentes is his personal use of a mythified alternate culture for the purpose of promoting himself. So, for example, his knowledge of Zapatistas and corridos are what get him a job in the government cultural agency; he sings in a theater with a revolutionary's rifle strapped to his back, but his audience is middle class; he makes clay pots at fairs that are for gringos.

In this sense, Fuentes is a good example of the political space of elite localism. He appropriates different intimate cultures in a myth of regional potency whose final aim is to legitimize (a) the need for experts on regional culture and (b) his own importance. The fact that the government hired Fuentes is thus not as gratuitous or as self-destructive as it could seem. Fuentes is playing the tense political game of broadening the independent power base of regional power without actually subverting the established order.

Morelos' existence as a state in the federation and its coopted position in official nationalist discourse gives local middle- and upper-class groups a space (albeit small) in the government apparatus as well as an opportunity to enlarge that space by broadening and specifying the content of regionalism. Thus, the cultural heterogeneity and the "impersonalization" of parts of the region are countered by the production of myths about local Morelos cultures, most particularly peasant culture. Morelos' regionalist intellectuals therefore usually range among (a) connecting national history to local history; (b) constructing a bricolage of apparently coherent "otherness" with which to oppose, subdue, or seduce outside influences in the region; and (c) constructing genealogies of local power for the region's political groups.

8

Peasant Localism as "Regionalism"

Peasant and State in Morelos

The weaknesses of the regionalist discourse of Morelos' elite and its virtual absence in the working class have as their counterpoint a peasant regionalism. Because Morelos peasants have had much in common—a history of struggle over land, a common mestizo identification, long-time subjection to the same policies, social movements—Morelos' peasants have, by and large, a common regional identity.

This commonality was, of course, especially apparent during the Zapatista Revolution, when a national crisis left a severe power void in the region. Womack (1969) believes this regionalism to be one of Zapatismo's major political limitations, and he is doubtlessly correct; but the alternate question is to ask how it is that the Zapatista movement was able to achieve regional dimensions. A lot of ink has been spilled on the topic of the political participation of peasants, on whether they are like "sacks of potatoes" or not, on whether they are revolutionary or not. In Morelos, peasants successfully organized into a regional movement that turned "national" because of Morelos' proximity to Mexico City. What were the conditions that allowed Morelos peasants to do this? The lack of a local regionalist elite, combined with the cultural homogenization of the peasantry, produced a kind of regional identification and understanding. It might be said that Morelos' proximity to Mexico City allowed for the existence of a radicalized peasant regionalism that perhaps did not exist in any other regional revolutionary movement of the period.

Catherine Heau (1984) concludes an interesting essay on the *corrido* folk songs of nineteenth-century and revolutionary Morelos with the affirmation that:

> In the case of Zapatismo not all is explained by the socio-historical causes that are always invoked: the concentration of rural property, the expansion and modernization of the haciendas, the poverty of the peasants, the 1907 recession, etc. Other parts of Mexico had similar conditions but did not produce peasant uprisings of the magnitude of Zapatismo. The rapid radicalization of the people of Morelos is also explained by their strong sense of cultural identity, which implied a common memory (the Siege of Cuautla, resistance against the French invaders), many shared emblems and symbols (for example the places of pilgrimage) and, above all, common interests and hopes tied to the land as a medium for reproduction and social subsistence. (p. 273)

Heau shows that the corridos were sung throughout the region, especially during the regional fairs that commercially and symbolically articulated the region (cf. Bonfil 1971) and on market days in the pueblos. In the corridos, Heau finds expression of a culture of peasant egalitarianism and a peasant-based morality that, according to Salvador Rueda (1984) can also be found in the common law that was created during the Revolution in Zapatista camps.

The view of Morelos as a peasant, culturally uniform region ignores the place and importance of local and regional elites; it emphasizes only the community/hacienda dichotomy.[1] In addition, this view of peasant culture makes no effort to differentiate between kinds of peasant localities. However, Heau and Rueda are certainly correct in observing the existence of a regional peasant culture (that may not always have been as egalitarian as they claim), articulated through a regional system of religious pilgrimage, marketing, and identification in the struggle for land and livelihood.

What is this peasant regionalism? What is peasant localism in Morelos? Throughout the many works based on oral histories in Morelos[2] one can trace a localist discourse related to (a) local and municipal lands, (b) *barrio,* village, municipal and regional shrines, (c) regional polity, (d) national polity. Probably the best single source for studying those ideologies is still *Pedro Martínez* (Lewis 1964). Pedro Martínez was a politically active peasant from Tepoztlán ("Azteca"), who had been a Zapatista in his youth, participated in factional (class) struggle for local power after the Revolution, was temporarily exiled to Mexico City, returned to local politics and peasant agriculture, and converted to Protestantism.

It is interesting to note the place that "Azteca" plays in Pedro Martínez's life history, for it is ever present, yet relatively unelaborated as an independent localist discourse. Azteca always comes up in the context of the struggle for land (which, during extended periods of Martínez's life, is equivalent to livelihood) and in the struggle for justice (because justice is dispensed by the municipal government). In both cases, Azteca is understood to be a part—though not a replica—of an overarching system of justice which includes the state government, the national president, and a few other national organizations (the Liga de Comunidades Agrarias, the CROM, the PRI). The ideology of justice that was so important to Pedro Martínez and many other peasants is about the internal control over village and municipio. The struggle for land has both a context of intracommunity strife and of village and municipal communal identification.

Lewis always insisted on a view of peasant community life that was ridden by conflict, treason, and suspicion. He also produced ample evidence to back this view. In *Pedro Martínez* the struggle for justice is by no means limited to the confrontation between the poor peasants and the local "caciques"; it is also prominently about confrontations that are regularly taken to the local court, about intrafamily relations and difficulties between neighbors. Pedro Martínez's description of his return to Tepoztlán after the Revolution illustrates this. Pedro complains that the villagers who stayed in the village during the Revolution stole goods from the houses of neighbors who had left for the struggle or emigrated. There is no question of those neighbors returning what they had taken from their fellow community members. Other examples of this kind of intracommunity suspicion and exploitation abound in *Pedro Martínez* and in *Life in a Mexican Village*. The camaraderie, reciprocity, and egalitarianism in intracommunity peasant relations has been romantically overstated.[3]

This does not imply that ideologies about equality, camaraderie and community do not exist. These ideologies about peasant community and reciprocity are expressed in the struggle for control over municipal politics and in the defense of communal and ejido lands from "foreign" invasion ("foreign" invasions include conflicts between villages and private holders—haciendas in the old days—and conflicts between villages). The localist ideologies that ensue are discourses about peasant rights to livelihood and about caring for the patrimony of their children's livelihood.

In combination with this aspect of localism, which is about the "natural law" of family and the familial metaphors behind the idea of community, is an ideology about the intrinsically moral character of peasant production. The peasant has a right to a plot of land not only because he deserves to live, but also due to the unexploitative nature of peasant production (the peasant produces what he consumes). In this sense, there is a kind of natural righteousness in peasant localist ideology, for (ideally) there is no exploitation of individuals in peasant production. Peasants live "off the sweat of their brow," and so can look down upon forms of livelihood that appear to be exploitative and non-agricultural.

Finally, peasant localism is also an ideology of kinship and inheritance. Peasants have a right to a *particular* strip of land because their forefathers had titles to it. This aspect of peasant localism had political importance during Zapatismo and during the agrarian reform. Zapata's Plán de Ayala asked for the restitution of communal lands. Peasant communities often insist—when they are allotted ejido grants—on the fact that the land is being returned to them. Originally, this discourse referred to returning property that had been communal in colonial times, but when ejido distribution surpassed those limits, an ideology of ancestral rights appeared and some peasants began conceiving all of Morelos as being originally theirs.

Thus the ideology of kinship and inheritance is at the very base of peasant community localism (and peasant reproduction); it forms a kind of "natural law" here. This point is crucial in the reconciliation of the atomistic view presented by Lewis, where a kind of Hobbesian "poverty" reigns, and the numerous and important manifestations of collectivism which have been romantically misinterpreted as an all-pervasive solidarity and trust between peasants.

The ideology of justice within the community, reflected in the frequency with which family and interpersonal disputes are taken to local authority in peasant communities of Morelos, is an appeal to this natural law of kinship, inheritance, and access to making a living unexploitatively by working the land. When this justice is broken by the local authorities, peasants go to the state and federal governments to demand the reinstitution of justice in their pueblos, and state and federal governments are expected to defend (usually for a fee) this original right.

This is the basic logic of peasant community localism. One might notice, *en passant,* that it helps explain the importance of coparenthood as a mechanism for avoiding competition or exploitation by extending a kinship ideology to other people. Pedro Martínez asks his best friend's wife to be his son's godmother in order to avoid having an affair with her. The power of caciques or employers is also made more beneficent by compadrazgo.

If community localism is based on an ideology of the morality of peasant production plus the right of inheritance through kinship (the metaphor of the *family*), peasant regionalism is based on the morality of peasant production plus the metaphor of the *community.* In this particular form of regionalism, Morelos is seen as a set of quasifamilies (communities with their inherited right to land) that are interrelated through alliance. This alliance can be actually based on exchange of women through exogamy, but it is above all a metaphor of matrimonial alliance, expressed through religious pilgrimages within the region and marketing interdependence between villages. Nearby villages often have yearly pilgrimages between them, and the region as a whole participates in the yearly fairs (described by Bonfil 1971) and pilgrimages to Chalma— outside the western margins of Morelos—and to the Basilica of Guadalupe in Mexico City.

The villagers who do not participate in this sort of religious regional community tend to maintain the metaphor of regional identification as a community nonetheless. The fact that there are frictions and ancestral hatreds between communities in Morelos in no way hinders this metaphor, for internal conflict and hatred are an integral part of these peasant communities as well.

Finally, a nationalist ideology is also present in these localist discourses, but usually only insofar as the federation respects the principles of communal right and justice. The rights to working land for self-sustenance, the rights to access to land because of ancestral inheritance, are considered to be Mexican rights. Nationalism is also important to the degree in which (a) the president is seen as the last court of appeal for "justice," (b) the hacendados and other economically important non-peasants can be characterized as foreign (*gachupines* or *gringos*), (c) the experience of migration to the United States and exposure to non-Mexican habits in tourism or the media are points of reference.

In these final remarks on peasant localism I attempt to place these ideologies in the historical periodization of regional culture that I have been developing here. Localist community ideology has been important since colonial times. This is a point well taken by Warman in his use of the colonial phrase ". . . *Y venimos a contradecir*" as title and leitmotiv of his historical description of eastern Morelos. Evidently, there has even been some expansion in the importance of this kind of peasant localism, especially during the period of peasantification produced by agrarian reform. Old haciendas such as Miacatlán, Santa Rosa Treinta, Oacalco, or Chiconcuac became peasant villages in their own right. On the other hand, regional identification such as we have described it here may be more of a prerevolutionary phenomenon, a product of the hacienda's role in the integration of a regional rural economy.

In the recent reorganization of the regional economy, however, the contexts and contents of localism have changed somewhat. I have already discussed the emergence of an urban-peasant localism, complete with the vindication of local church and saint; this is but one of the new contexts of peasant localism. Another case, also centered around local control over church and ritual is that of the villages of Atlatláhucan, Jumiltepec, and Santa Rosa Treinta, all of which ousted—after strong internal strife—their priests and are now served by an excommunicated priest of the region. This kind of revolt against centralized Church control over local shrines has occurred with less violence in other localities.

Yet another context of localism is that which I described (1982) for Tepoztlán, where communal land and water have been at the center of ideological conflict over the growing importance of tourism and weekend homes. In towns that receive an influx of migrants (well-to-do Mexico City dwellers and poor Guerrero migrants) localism has served to delimit a relatively privileged group of "old" inhabitants from the newcomers. So, for example, one of my acquaintances migrated from Guerrero to work in Cuernavaca and established himself in the suburban peasant village of Chamilpa. My acquaintance felt unwelcome at Chamilpa because all of the communal decisions, including matters concerning children's schools and other governmental services, were managed exclusively by Chamilpeños, on the grounds that they were the legitimate members of the community. This situation finally caused him to move into a neighborhood with a migrant majority, where he feels more at home. Many of Morelos' rural villages now have neighborhoods of Guerrerenses. These migrants are often considered to be thieves and so are marginalized, via localist ideology, from communal decisions.

In this new regional economic organization, peasant regionalism has also taken on a new significance. It is now the ideology that buttresses peasant local interests within a complex system of lobbying that prominently includes the interests of workers and capitalists. This brand of regionalism has retained a fair amount of regional political weight. I have already mentioned, for example, that Morelos' representatives to the Federal Congress usually come from the "peasant sector" of the party. This success is due, no doubt, to the ideological importance of Zapatismo in the legitimation of the regional state. However, peasant regionalism has also served rather effectively to legitimate peasant self-defense of communal and ejido lands, even against the state government itself. For example, Pedro Martínez describes a negotiation between his faction and the state governor about deposing a municipal president: "That's when I learnt the saying 'When the people [*pueblo* means people and village] arise, there is no law.' So the people put him [the municipal president] there, now the people will take him away" (p. 122). In this same spirit of taking the law into communal hands, I have described Tepoztecan peasants confronting government-backed hotel industries and the federal light and water companies. Peasants of eastern Morelos confronted the draft during World War II (see Ramírez 1974). Cane-growing peasants joined Jaramillo against the government-run sugar mill. In sum, there is a long tradition of peasant localism and regionalism wherein the family, the neighborhood, the community, and the region (a "league of communities") are all metaphorically interconnected. In this ideology—which is buttressed by real social connections that may exist among people of these different levels—"the Other" is the foreigner who comes to the region in an attempt to take over land; or it can also be the person that is unlinked to this genealogy of land-linked peasants. In this sense, family and land are or can be tied to "ethnicity," and this ethnicity in Morelos is defined as being "Mexican."

This identification of Mexicanness with being "of the land," or "of the family" (of the race) is, of course, politically potent, and it has made Morelos' peasants into a potentially threatening force for governors and for outside investors.[4] On the other hand, the predominance of claims to control over *land* have, at times, limited the political influence of the peasants and allowed for coalitions between peasants and urban politicians who respect community claims over land. This facilitates the mythification of peasant culture and its transformation (by the regional elites) into official regionalism and nationalism.

Intimate cultures in Morelos revolve around three coherent poles: a pole of peasant coherence, a pole of petit-bourgeois coherence, and a pole of proletarian coherence. Spatially speaking, these poles are located in peripheral villages and hamlets, and in some urban neighborhoods of the regional cities. The petit-bourgeois pole operates largely within a national idiom of social distinction; however, there are members of that class—the people who engage in local politics—who must face inwardly, towards the region, in an attempt to broaden the spaces for a native political elite and for a native bureaucracy. The proletariat in Morelos moves between the peasant and the petit-bourgeois poles. Some proletarians see their situation as transitory, either because they hope to return to their home towns as wealthy peasants or because they hope to move upward in the social scale. They hope the incoherence caused by proletarianization is only temporary and situational. There is, however, a proletarian culture that has been consolidating over the past few decades in which family, neighborhood, education, and union take on a new meaning.

Given the regional debility of the petite bourgeoisie and the fact that the proletarian classes of Cuernavaca do not yet have a strong regional organization, Morelos regionalism has always been politically threatening, in that it can easily lapse into class strife, especially between peasants and urban investors and politicians. Because of this, Morelos elites have sought mutually convenient alliances with Mexico City elites, wherein Morelos' historical grandeur is at once recognized and coopted.

The culture of social relations that has emerged in the region is formed in the relation between the different transformations of intimate cultures and the market and in their political interrelations. The interplay between intimate cultures and different localist ideologies is crucial for the definition of the regional political sphere. So, for example, a peasant may attempt to subdue the harshness of capital-labor relations by asking his employer to be godfather to his child. In her turn, the employer may be willing to accept this relationship, figuring that it will make her worker more trustworthy; she will be positively happy to accept the relationship if she wishes to gain political legitimacy as a member of the community.

In the areas where politicians are not personally known to the public, regional bureaucrats may represent this cultural identification with the people by the use of particular outfits that are associated with the countryside (for example, a *guayabera* shirt or a *sombrero*). When people seek to establish their economic position, they probably wear suits or other urbane outfits that link them to a national system of economic and educational stratification. The culture of social relations is created in frames that are constructed either in relation to a system of distinction dependent on a national system of hegemony, or in relation to the politics of regional identity in regional space.

Section 2

Regional Culture in the Huasteca Potosina

9

The Huasteca as a
Hegemonic Region

The region that I discuss in this section is a large subregion of the Huasteca (see map 6). This subregion, called the Huasteca Potosina, has its own centers of power, which nodally integrate it. Power is mainly in the hands of a ranchero/merchant class that resides in most of the municipal cabeceras of the region, and especially in the regional city of Ciudad Valles and the main agricultural centers and market towns (e.g., Tamuín, Axtla, and Tamazunchale).

The Huasteca Potosina is a part of a larger economic and ethnohistorical region, the Huasteca, which is the tropical and semitropical drainage basin of the Pánuco River. However, the Huasteca Potosina belongs politically to the state of San Luis Potosí, whose capital (which is also called San Luis Potosí) is in a very different economic and cultural region. This means that the politics of Huastecan regional culture are quite complex, for on the one hand the Huastecan element is underlined vis-à-vis the San Luis elites and, on the other, the Potosino element can serve to differentiate this regional culture from that of the other Huastecan regions.

Ecology and Agricultural
Production

The Huasteca is an ecological region that spans parts of several states, the most important of which are Veracruz, Hidalgo, and San Luis Potosí, but also covering portions of Puebla, Queretaro, and Tamaulipas. On the whole, the region can be divided into three types of zones: the high

153

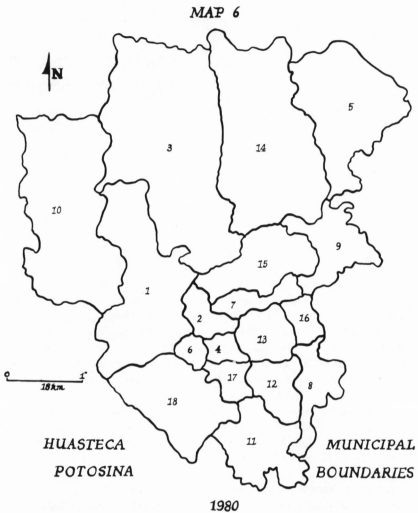

MAP 6

N

18km

HUASTECA
POTOSINA

MUNICIPAL
BOUNDARIES

1980

1. AQUISMON
2. CIUDAD SANTOS (TANCANHUITZ)
3. CIUDAD VALLES
4. COXCATLAN
5. EBANO
6. HUEHUETLAN
7. SAN ANTONIO
8. SAN MARTIN CHALCHICUAUTLA
9. SAN VICENTE TANCUAYALAB

10. TAMASOPO
11. TAMAZUNCHALE
12. TAMPACAN
13. TAMPAMOLON
14. TAMUIN
15. TANLAJAS
16. TANQUIAN
17. VILLA TERRAZAS (AXTLA)
18. XILITLA

mountains of the Sierra Madre Oriental, where vegetation changes from coniferous to tropical forest; the low mountains with their internal valleys; and the coastal plains.[1]

Each of the main political subdivisions of the Huasteca has one or more major market towns or regional cities at its core. The Huasteca Potosina has Ciudad Valles and Tamazunchale, the Huasteca Hidalguense has Huejutla, and the Huasteca Veracruzana has Tantoyuca, Tuxpan, and (since more recent times) Poza Rica. All of these subregions have Tampico as their main economic capital, although the predominance of Tampico over the whole of the Huasteca has diminished somewhat since the decline of riverine and railroad transport.

The Huasteca Potosina (which I shall henceforth call Huasteca, and specify places when I am referring to the pan-Huastecan region) gravitates commercially around Ciudad Valles, especially since the construction of the Tampico-San Luis railroad towards the end of the last century. Above the commercial level represented by Ciudad Valles, which is to say for important business or specialized services, the Huastecans go to Tampico and, to a lesser degree, to San Luis (the state capital) and eventually also to Mexico City and to the Texas border (especially Brownsville and McAllen).[2]

The Huasteca Potosina is subdivided into eighteen municipios: Ciudad Valles, Tamuín, San Vicente, Tanquián, Tamasopo, Aquismón, Xilitla, Tamazunchale, Ebano, Axtla de Terrazas, San Martín Chalchicuautla, Tancanhuitz de Santos, Coxcatlán, Huehuetlán, San Antonio, Tanlajás, Tampacán, and Tampamolón.[3] The municipios of Valles, Tamuín, Ebano, San Vicente, Tampamolón and Tanquián are located primarily in the coastal plain, which is used mostly for cattle and sugar-cane production. The municipios of Tancanhuitz, Huehuetlán, Tanlajás, and San Antonio are in the low mountains. The valleys formed in that small range (see maps 7 and 8) are appropriate for cattle ranching, but the mountainsides are used for the production of corn, sugarcane for *piloncillo* (a kind of hardened molasses), and some citrus fruits. This zone has a sizable Indian population of Huastecans and Nahuas.

The mountainous or hilly municipios of Tamazunchale, Xilitla, Axtla, San Martín, Tampacán, and Coxcatlán have recently been transformed into important citrus-growing areas. The more pronounced mountainous parts are utilized much the same as in the Tancanhuitz zone, although there is more coffee grown here. The low portions of all these municipios are used for cattle and for sugar cane.

The Huasteca is a prosperous agricultural and cattle-growing region. Until recently, it was the main provider for the Mexico City meat market.[4] In 1960, however, President López Mateos proposed the construction of a huge irrigation project, known as Pujal-Coy, which implied,

MAP 7

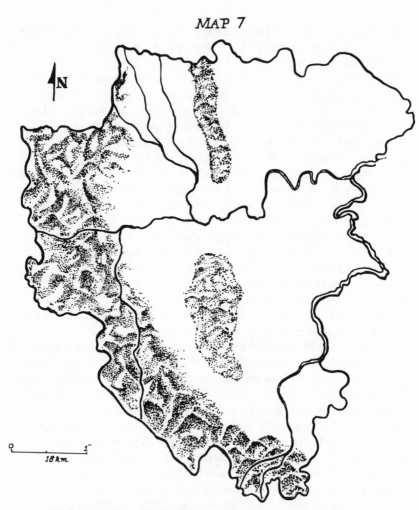

HUASTECA POTOSINA,

RIVERS AND SELECTED CONTOURS

   MOUNTAINOUS ZONES

———   MAJOR RIVERS

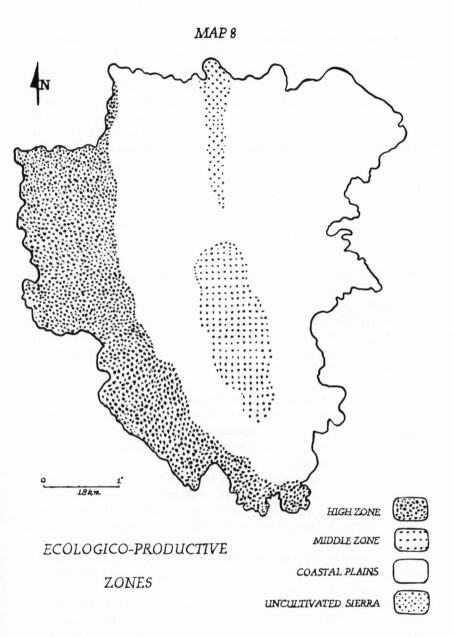

MAP 8

N

o_____1'
18 km.

ECOLOGICO-PRODUCTIVE

ZONES

HIGH ZONE

MIDDLE ZONE

COASTAL PLAINS

UNCULTIVATED SIERRA

among many other consequences, the expropriation of approximately 280,000 hectares of privately held ranchero land in the region. The Pujal-Coy project, and the expropriation of land, have not yet been, and may never be, fully realized, yet the project's impact on cattle production has been considerable, for it has provoked a decline in capital investments from the insecure ranchero class. The Pujal-Coy project has also become translated in a reactivation of land reform in parts of the region, thereby accelerating the decline of cattle production; as we shall see, cattle ranching is not a preferred activity for peasants.[5]

In addition to the Pujal-Coy project, the growth of the sugar industry has also meant a decline in the importance of livestock. Sugar production in the region has existed since the sixteenth century. In the major ranches and haciendas of the region sugar was processed in small *trapiches* or in the minuscule family mills (*moliendas*) that can still be seen today. Sugar was made into *piloncillo* (sugar cakes). Some was exported out of the region by train to San Luis or by river to Tampico, and some was sold locally and used as sweetener or converted into aguardiente (a product much used in local consumption) and in the pay allotted to Indian and mestizo day-laborers. There were also a few sugar mills built at the turn of the century, at Rascón, Aguabuena, and Buenavista, in the municipios of Valles and Tamasopo, and at Ganal, on the banks of the Moctezuma River.

With the Revolution the mills of the region stopped working. In the subsequent period, a fair amount of investment by U.S. citizens in the municipio of Tamasopo picked up the sugar industry there, centered especially at the mill at Aguabuena. However, most of the regional production of cane seems to have been destined to the family trapiche production of piloncillo.

In 1961 the federal government built the Plan de Ayala mill at Ciudad Valles, and cane production began displacing some cattle ranching there. Since then mills have been constructed at El Naranjo near the state border with Tamaulipas, at Acamba, and at Rascón (the Plan de San Luis). There is also a mill at El Higo, Veracruz, that is near the eastern fringes of the zone, and there were plans, postponed since the 1982 economic crisis, for building a mill at Tanquian, in the heart of the cattle region.

Sugar cane for piloncillo is still an important crop, but almost exclusively for the Indian populations. Piloncillo used to be produced in almost all ranches and haciendas: today it characterizes agriculture in the remote and marginal lands of the region. The sugar mills have a certain radius beyond which it is uneconomic to transport cane. In addition, the sugar planted by the Indians for piloncillo is low grade, has no irrigation, and is often not artificially fertilized. Production of piloncillo is compatible with peasant household production, and therefore Indians have withstood tremendous depreciations of piloncillo and have ousted commercial piloncillo producers from the market.[6] Piloncillo is bought primarily by the tequila factories of Jalisco, but also by medium-sized rum and brandy producers such as Ron Potosí, whose factory has been located in Valles since 1955, and by small and medium-sized aguardiente producers of the region.[7]

In sum, the major agricultural export crops of the Huasteca are cattle, sugar, citrus fruits, coffee, and piloncillo. Cattle ranching is important throughout the region, although it is particularly prominent in the municipios of Tamuín, Valles, Ebano, San Vicente, Aquismón, and Tampamolón; sugar is grown for the mills in the municipios of Tamasopo, Valles, and Aquismón, and it is planted for piloncillo in all of the municipios with hilly and Indian peasant communities (especially Tanlajás, San Antonio, Tancanhuitz, Tampamolón, Aquismón, Tamazunchale, and Huehuetlán). Citrus fruits are also grown in the relatively cool and moist hilly "middle" zones, most particularly at Axtla, Coxcatlán, Xilitla, Huehuetlán, and Tamazunchale. The importance of coffee in the region has dwindled in the past forty years, and most especially in the past decade; however, this crop is still grown in the cooler, mountainous zones of the municipios of Aquismón, Xilitla, and Tamazunchale, and there are still some remnants of coffee production in the sierra of Tancanhuitz. Citrus fruits, coffee, and cattle ranching compete to some degree in the hillier municipios, whereas in the flat coastal plains the main options are between cattle and sugar, with some new options in tropical fruits, particularly papayas.

There are two major sorts of peasant agricultural products: maize[8] and piloncillo.[9] These two products are often complemented by the typical cash crops of the region, most particularly coffee and citrus fruits (but also cattle for the richer peasants).

Transformations in the Core/ Periphery Structure and Kinds of Central Places

The central-place hierarchy in the Huasteca is very different from that of Morelos. Population density for the area as a whole is much lower.[10] The Huasteca is still a predominantly agricultural region, such that its major towns—with the recent partial exception of Ciudad Valles—are commercial, not industrial. In addition, it would seem that the colonial policy of concentration of Indians was not as firmly carried out in there as it was in Morelos. Many of the settlements of the Huasteca are of recent creation (cf. Schryer 1980); much of the area was a kind of frontier until very recently. Some ranches and congregations would appear to have their origins in the second half of the nineteenth century,[11] and many more appear during the present century. The nature of the Huastecan agrarian economy has required the existence of small units of production that are far from the main population centers. Cattle ranching demands the presence of a few peones *in situ*. In sum, the presence, until quite recently, of an agricultural frontier in the Huasteca, the economic logic of cattle ranching, and the apparent lack of strict colonial government in the region all help explain a relatively dispersed settlement pattern. Before getting into the details of this pattern, however, I will highlight some aspects of the organization and transformation of the economic core/periphery structure.

Because of the low population density of the Huasteca, and because of the region's poor transport conditions for marketing products outwards, the nineteenth and early twentieth-century core/periphery structure of the region must be conceptualized in terms of (a) access to capital investment, and (b) transport facilities. In contradistinction with the case of Morelos, there has been no *stable* division of land use into a rich agricultural core and a labor providing agricultural periphery.

The Huasteca is a lush and well-watered region. However, until the massive introduction of cane for sugar in the 1960s irrigation was not a major factor in the organization of production. This is in part because the main crops of the region, cattle and coffee, do not require irrigation. In part the situation is also a result of much land availability for the dominant classes and relative capital scarcity. The economy that stemmed from these conditions was one in which the local elite of hacendados and rancheros monopolized most of the land, thereby creating (artificial) land scarcity for the Indian population, which was obligated to enrich the regional elite either through sharecropping, renting, or wage labor.[12]

Within this logic of production and land use, which was kept intact through a system of impartible inheritance in the elite classes known as the *condueñazgo* system (cf. Márquez 1977, Santos 1986), the core/periphery structure can be conceived of as having depended upon the kinds of production to which surfaces of land were destined. The value of a piece of land within a ranch was related to its proximity to the rivers. Transportation was, in this logic, a major factor in determining whether a piece of land was suitable or not for commercial exploitation, the more so because land near the riverbanks tends to be more productive. Márquez has described the ample use of sharecropping by rancheros and hacendados of the region at the turn of the century. The regional elite could not, by and large, aspire to capitalize its property directly, and so was content with exploiting day laborers, sharecroppers, and renters in order to obtain a comfortable living.[13]

After the Revolution this system began to be transformed. Some of the lands which had belonged to the antirevolutionary porfirista rancheros and hacendados were distributed among peasants, particularly as an incentive for their military support in Cedillo's campaign against the Cristeros.[14] In addition, in order to avoid vulnerability to agrarian reform, and partially also due to the urbanization of parts of the ranchero class, the system of condueñazgos came to an end and properties were fractioned. Due to the initiation of this process of fragmentation of large properties, and to their conversion into ejidos and ranchos manned by smaller family units, lands that had been tropical forests were opened to agricultural exploitation and to cattle ranching. This situation provoked a certain amount of migration into the region and allowed for a large rate of internal growth within an agricultural economy.

The tendency to divide land into relatively smaller fractions, united with the greater access to the region provided by the Pan-American highway (1935) and its sequels (the highway to Tampico, built in the 1940s, and to San Luis in the 1960s, and the development of a system of roads, often gravel but generally passable, within the region in the past decades) made for a kind of "corification" of the whole region, in the sense that most of the ranches began depending mainly on wage labor for the production of export products.[15] Although there are different kinds and qualities of land in the region, there is no systematic differentiation of land use comparable to that which was implanted in Morelos: all lands—except for the truly steep mountainous terrains, which only Indians cultivate—are apt for commercial exploitation, and the main criterion for the kind of use to which land is put is still capital availability.

Because of this, it is possible to speak of a periphery in the Huasteca that is composed of agriculturalists with low capital investments. These are principally made up of the old Indian communities (of which there are 107 in the region), a great majority of the Indian and mestizo ejidos (of which there were 214 in 1970),[16] and some of the less cared-for ranches. These peripheral zones in the Huasteca do provide some services to the dominant projects of the core, although they are not exactly the same as those provided by the old landless Indian population that was tied to the ranch or hacienda. The peripheral zones provide the core agricultural and livestock areas with a cheap labor supply, which is clearly more important for citrus fruits, coffee, and sugar cane than for cattle ranching, which occupies significant numbers of people only for clearing fields; even this has been substantially reduced by availability of specialized agricultural machinery. But these relatively densely populated peripheries of peasant production also provide the regional elites with a market for commercial goods and a supply of artificially cheap products that can be commercialized at substantial gains by the elite.

This is particularly the case of the production of piloncillo, which is very important throughout the "middle" and "high" zones, and also of coffee production and, more recently, of Indian citrus production. Because peasants have very little access to trucks and warehouses, and because they cannot provide any kind of credit to large-scale buyers, they are easily exploited by merchants who concentrate their produce, stock it in warehouses, and sell at enormous gains. This kind of business, which might be aptly described as living off the Indians, is and has been an important business for sectors of the ranchero class in most Indian municipios.

In sum, the current core/periphery structure of the Huasteca must be understood in relation to the system of production (including the availability of capital investments), and not as an inert, continually renewed, geographical division between highlands and lowlands. Within this core/periphery structure, the capitalized producers benefit from the cheap labor of the peasant periphery;[17] other portions of the regional dominant class also benefit from buying and selling to peasants. In many villages and townships the same ranchero families buy Indian commercial produce and sell Indian consumer goods, the prototype of this activity being the seller of aquardiente liquor and the buyer of piloncillo.

Now that these general aspects of Huastecan spatial organization are understood, we can turn to the settlement pattern of the region. The lowest level in the central-place hierarchy is the rancho. This kind of settlement consists of anywhere from one to twenty or thirty families. The livelihood of these families is—or was until recently—organized around one or two ranches. Until the 1920s these ranchos housed the extended family of the owner and the families of his *peones de confianza* (trusted workers). In the old core/periphery organization of the region, the ranchos were in some senses at the center of the region's social life. As of the beginning of the century, however, with the construction of roads, and especially with the growing concentration of services in the towns (electricity, plumbing, education, entertainment, and medicine), rancho owners have tended to move into these municipal cabeceras, and the ranchos have become—in most cases—places in which only the peones and their families live.

The next level in the hierarchy is the comunidad. In terms of size and the characteristics of commerce, this level is very similar to the hamlet in Morelos; the difference lies in the history of the two kinds of places. There are two major kinds of comunidades in the Huasteca. The first are the Indian communities that retained their land during the Porfiriato and then had their holdings confirmed by the Ministry of Agrarian Reform. These are comunidades in the strictest juridical sense. Their origin is in the common buying of a plot of land, or in colonial endowments to the community.[18] In this kind of community, settlement patterns are often extremely dispersed, to the degree that community membership cannot always be predicted by proximity to a nucleus of population, but only according to the community to which the land belongs.[19] The comunidades are usually serviced commercially by the municipal cabecera closest to them. People from the comunidades "descend" to the market towns every week for the periodical markets. Within the comunidades there are often one or two minuscule stores that sell soft drinks, aguardiente, beer, perhaps a few candies, perhaps a little corn. These stores also function as intermediary buyers of local cash crops, especially piloncillo, but because their position as intermediaries depends entirely on the mestizo merchants who own pickup trucks and warehouses, their margin of profit is slim indeed.[20] Recently, some comunidades have been allowed to harbor small, communally run, government CONASUPO stores, where basic products, such as corn and beans, are sold at state subsidized rates.

The other kind of comunidad-like settlement is the ejido of relatively recent creation. Land reform in the region was carried out in three major epochs: during and after the Cristero Revolt (c. 1928), during Cárdenas's regime (1934–40), and in the presidencies of Echeverría (1970–76) and López Portillo (1976–82). Until this last period, most of the ejidos created corresponded to already existing Indian communities or some well-populated mestizo ranches. Since the Echeverría reforms, many of the ejidos created have been related to the Pujal-Coy irrigation project, which has entailed importing peasants from outside the Huasteca and mixing Indians with mestizos into settlements that are often nucleated and, to some extent, urbanized.

In both cases (traditional comunidad and relatively recent ejido), however, these kinds of settlements, which I shall refer to generically as comunidades[21] have similar kinds of services and commerce. There are no periodic markets; there are one or several small part-time stores, whose major business is usually selling soft drinks, beer, and aguardiente, and also sometimes buying local products to resell to the mestizo merchant elites, locally referred to as *coyotes*. In piloncillo-making comunidades, coyotes come once or twice a week on fixed days to pick up piloncillo, and Indians who are not in a rush for cash will sell directly to them. During the harvest of other commercial goods, such as oranges or coffee, coyotes also come around to collect produce at cheap rates.

Many comunidades now have schools, although they often reach only into the third or fourth grade. Some comunidades have boarding schools for Indians from faraway places;[22] these schools are bilingual and are run by the Instituto Nacional Indigenista. A few comunidades have small clinics, as part of a governmental program for "marginalized communities" (IMSS-COPLAMAR), and most of the major ones have recently built chapels in which the priests occasionally offer mass.

The next level in the central-place hierarchy is the village. This level is quite similar to its counterpart in Morelos, the main difference being that there are relatively few villages in the Huasteca. All municipios have a village for their cabecera, but there are hardly any villages that are not cabeceras.[23] Villages all have periodic markets of varying importance; they all have schools (although high schools are still rare) and a few permanent stores, several bars, a church with a priest, and usually the services of the municipal government. Population in Huastecan villages ranges from about one thousand to seven thousand inhabitants.

The boundary between the village and the market town (which would tentatively be the next level up) is somewhat more difficult to establish in the Huasteca than in Morelos because of the greater scarcity of towns and because of the difficulty in distinguishing between the larger villages and the market towns. Villages that are situated in important crossroads, with abundant ranching in the hinterlands, become something like central market towns. In the past years these places began offering banking services and especially large periodic markets; however, few of them have important permanent commercial facilities, and only Tamuín has industries worth mentioning (a Nestlé factory). Towns like Tancanhuitz and Aquismón have a commercial elite that trades with the abundant Indian population. Towns like Tamuín, Tanquián, and Axtla have commercial facilities to accommodate some of the needs of their prosperous ranchero elites. One finds important permanent commerce only in the towns of Tamazunchale and Valles, which, until about twenty years ago (when Valles began industrializing), could both have indisputably been considered central market towns. Today, perhaps only Tamazunchale fully fits the category, for it not only has a permanent market, (though, like all towns in the Huasteca, including Valles, it still has its weekly market) but also several banks, a medium-sized hospital, a high school, furniture stores, shoe and clothes stores, record and book stores, and restaurants and hotels. There is a sense, however, in which it cannot be said that Tamazunchale is anything but a large village, in that inhabitants from most villages will go directly to Valles for commercial needs that are unfulfilled locally. The commercial importance of Tamazunchale rests on the densely populated hinterlands of the municipio and on its key location on the Pan-American Highway.

In sum, the only settlement that is clearly of a different nature than the villages is Ciudad Valles, which I shall classify as a regional city. I shall therefore abandon the distinction between village and market town in the Huasteca and speak only of important or unimportant villages. Valles, on the other hand, concentrates far and away the most state services in the region. It has two hospitals and several medical specialists; it was the first locality to have secondary schooling, and now houses a kind of junior college that is part of the State University of San Luis; it has a commercial district of about four or five full blocks, including two department stores and many specialized stores. It is also the seat of some industry. The Ron Potosí factory was established in the city in 1956, after the original site at El Pujal was destroyed in a flood; the Fibracel factory—which has been responsible for true ecocide in the region—was established in the late fifties; the also very polluting Plan de Ayala sugar mill was built in 1960; and two cement factories were built in the late sixties.

The kinds of relations between these types of central places do vary somewhat according to the population density characteristic of the different productive subzones of the Huasteca. So, for example, the ratio of comunidades to villages is highest in the peripheral municipios where peasant production is most important (villages of this kind, such as Tancanhuitz or Coxcatlán, service as many as twenty comunidades each, although the surface of these municipios is relatively small), and lowest in the cattle herding municipios (Valles services about thirty comunidades, distributed over a surface fifteen times larger than that of Tancanhuitz; Tamuín services less than twenty such comunidades in over twelve times the surface). The number and distribution of ranchos in this space is more difficult to ascertain, both for reasons of available information and because variance seems to be of a more random order.

Class Domination in the Huasteca

Despite the changes in the organization of regional space that I have just described, the Huasteca is more of a cultural region than Morelos. The region has consistently been dominated by an elite that has created and attempted to maintain its own intimate culture and patterned forms of cultural relations between the classes and ethnic groups of the region.

This class is, of course, the ranchero class. Each municipio of the Huasteca has one or several major families of rancheros: the González, the Castellanos, the Esper, and the Ocejos in Valles; the Santos, the Romeros, the Balderas, and the Castrillóns in Tamuín; the Terrazas, Jonguitudes, and Pérez in Axtla; the Santos and Martells in Tampamolón; the Ortas and Lárragas in Tanlajás and San Antonio; the Pérez and Heverts in Tamazunchale; the Riveras in San Martín; the González in San Vicente; and several others (a partial guide can be found in Santos's autobiography).

Today anyone with twenty or thirty hectares can be considered to be a ranchero, but prominent rancheros will own anywhere between fifty and two or three thousand hectares, in addition to the fact that many rancheros rent land from ejidos. This class has exercised political and economic control over the municipios and the Huastecan political districts since the nineteenth century. Since the Revolution, Huastecan rancheros have had very significant positions of power and influence at the state government level.

The ranchero class has effectively articulated the Huasteca as an economic, political, and cultural region. This is because this class depends on all of the major features of the regional core/periphery structures; it makes its primary wealth from the land (even people whose fortunes have been built on commerce, such as the Spanish, Italian, and Lebanese migrants of the turn of the century, invest heavily in ranches and tend to turn into a ranchero class). Commercial wealth is partially to be gained through the exploitation of the Indian peasant logic of production; and control over land and commerce must be upheld by control over local governments. In other words, the arenas that are crucially important for the reproduction of the ranchero class involve the central aspects of the economic and political life of the whole of the inhabitants of the region.[24]

In addition to these aspects of the regional dominant class's "objective" interests in its articulations with all of the region's classes and groups, the hegemony of the rancheros is enforced by the meaning which the ranchero life has for members of this class. To a large extent the rancheros are socially and culturally oriented towards their own system of values; rancheros need not pay very much personal attention to their ranches, though their ranches and their cattle are a source of personal pride. It is common for a ranchero to drive in his pickup truck to the ranch around ten in the morning to see that all is well and then go back home. Afternoons and evenings are spent in an intense and often expensive social life. In Valles ranchero men go to the Café España, while in the smaller towns social centers gravitate around the houses of prominent rancheros or bars that centralize gossip around the game of dominoes. In these gossip sessions information is exchanged on the prices of different products in the market; on technological innovations that are relevant for the production of cattle and cash crops; on pieces of property that are for sale; on political movements in the region; on relations with the cowboys and peones; on who is going out with whom. In addition to the economic and political value of these reunions, this lifestyle is immensely valued and meaningful to the rancheros. It constitutes one of the main satisfactions of the ranchero life.

Ranchero families of the Huasteca form, to a surprising degree, a socially cohesive group. There have traditionally been effective means of gossip and information flows between the ranchero families: rancheros of different municipios intermarried at least since the nineteenth century, and do so to a surprising degree even today, despite the fact that most young men of the ranchero class leave the region for extended periods to study in Mexico City or San Luis. Another means of intraregional elite communications are the fairs. Each municipal cabecera has a fair that usually lasts for about a week. These fairs are sponsored largely by the ranchero class. In addition to their significance for regional marketing (some fairs exhibit cattle and other local produce for major buyers; all fairs concentrate a wealth of products that are significant especially for the day laborers and peasants), their most important function from the point of view of the rancheros is social. At night there are cockfights where ranchero families of the municipio match their birds against *partidos* of other municipios. Here the rancheros prove their abilities as rancheros and Huastecans; they have a good time, and they also show off their wealth.[25] During these cockfights the rancheros of the region meet, bet, drink, gossip, close business deals, court political allies, and defy political or personal enemies. There are also "family nights" at the cockfights, where rancheros take their wives or official girlfriends, or meet elegant girlfriends-to-be. All of these mechanisms of cultural communion and local and interregional gossip have the effect of conforming a social class that has a great potential for political mobilization, economic agreement, and concerted action.

Another crucial aspect of the power of the rancheros in the Huasteca is more historical than structural. The Huastecan region has successfully been controlled politically by a set of caciques that are very much identified with ranchero culture. Most important in this sense is the figure of Gonzalo N. Santos, who personally dominated regional politics from the mid-twenties to the late sixties.[26] *Santos* and *santismo* in the Huasteca provided the ranchero class with several elements that were important for their prolonged control over the region. When Gonzalo Santos was governor of San Luis, he violently freed the region from cattle thieving and made conditions for cattle production possible; Santos also defended the rancheros from agrarian reform for many years and, perhaps most important, he defended the region against industrialization. In fact, the industrialization of the region has been mainly carried out by the federal government in an attempt to undermine the regional power of the ranchero class: major federal investments, including the first sugar mill at Valles and the Pujal-Coy project, were carried out by President López Matéos in 1960 as a thrust against Santos's political influence.

For these historical reasons, the rancheros of the region have some political experience in presenting and defending their internal control over the region and regional hegemony and, although it may be a losing battle for them (at least to the degree in which industrialization of the region is inevitable, or to the degree in which the government is forced to go through with the Pujal-Coy irrigation project), the rancheros have successfully maintained their key position in the region so far.

10

Class Culture and Intimate Cultures of the Huasteca

To a certain extent, it is useful to understand the Huastecan cultural region in terms of two kinds of zones that correspond to the major kinds of productive complexes of the region: the ranching zone, where the dominant forms of class relations have been between rancheros and their cowboys (which is above all the cattle ranching area of the *planicie costera,* but also occurs as a productive complex throughout the region), and the zone in which dominant forms of class relations are between a ranching/commercial elite and an Indian peasantry from the comunidades (the piloncillo/coffee/citrus producing area).

Intimate Cultures of Rancheros and Peones de Confianza

The cattle ranching area of the coastal plain (most of the municipios of Tamuín, Valles, San Vicente, and Tanquián) has the lowest population density of the Huasteca and is characterized by a large number of ranchos and relatively few comunidades; most comunidades of this zone are ejidos of recent creation. The ranchos are composed of predominantly mestizo[1] populations, which means that this area is characterized by cultural and power relations predominantly between mestizos.

One striking element in the cultural organization of this area is that the culture of the villages is seen as being directly related to that of their rancho hinterlands. For example, in the case of a rancho in San Vicente that I was able to study, the peones of the rancho knew the members of all of the main families of the municipio, both of the ranches and the cabecera. On market day one can see the people of the ranches intermingle with relatives and acquaintances from the cabecera. The cabecera is not hostile territory for them. The differentiation between inhabitants of ranchos and of villages is superficially like that of country bumpkin to urbanite; however, the "urban" population of these villages has intense dealings with the ranchos, which are by and large the main source of wealth for the families of the villages as well, such that the people of the villages can usually not afford to pretend ignorance on matters rural and, moreover, must show competence in the rancho mode of life.

This is a key cultural characteristic of ranchero hegemony in the region; rancheros must know the country, its ways and its people, and be able to compete in certain realms of cultural knowledge that are recognized as important by all classes. For example, they must know how to defend themselves both physically and verbally; they must "speak like men," drink like men, know how to ride a horse and how to shoot a gun. Urban wives of rancheros, on the other hand, may or may not cultivate ranchero culture. Some of these women represent the rich rancheros' links to civilization and (national) high society, whereas others reinforce the men's ties to the land.[2]

This mode of cultural domination means that, in a sense, the ranchero elite bases its domination on an ideology of equality with their mestizo subordinates (who have traditionally been the *peones de confianza* and cowboys of the ranches). Rancheros are superior to these peones not because they are essentially different from them, but because they are better, more distilled, versions of the same. A report of the sumptuous wedding of a very wealthy ranchero from Tamazunchale can exemplify this.

Mr. Bull gave the groom a new van, which is a kind of modern ranchero equivalent of a horse. These vehicles are driven mainly by men, and cherished by them. He gave a new car to the bride (a car is more urban and more feminine, or, rather, it is sexually unmarked), and he also gave them a new furnished house and a one-month trip to Europe. The wedding was held at San Martín, the town of the bride's family. The bride arrived at church riding in a black, horse-pulled carriage. She wore a champagne-colored dress made out of cloth from Toledo, Spain. Behind the coach, there was a group of finely dressed *mariáchis* (Mexican musicians) brought in from Salvatierra, Guanajuato, and behind them were five men dressed as charros in very fine horses. The groom arrived at the church mounted on a spotted steed. He wore a black charro suit and a white hat, and his father also dressed as a black charro. The mariáchis sang the mass, and then the party moved to Tamazunchale's Lions Club, where the feast was held. About half of the club was filled with people from Tamazunchale (the groom's family) while the other half were mainly from San Martín (the bride's family). Vast quantities of food were served: *zacahuillis* (a delicious Huastecan tamale dish), *carnitas, chicharrones,* and goat *barbacóa.* The music to dance by was executed by "The Panther's Show," a local band that emulates the latest Mexico City hits. In other words, Mr. Bull consistently struck a balance between urban and ranchero symbols: a (manly) ranchero car and a (more feminine) city car; mariáchis in the church and Panther's Show in the saloon; zacahuillis on the plate, and Buchanan's on the rocks.

The identification between rancheros and cowboys contrasts with ranchero ideas about Indians and about their relations to them. Many rancheros (and mestizos who participate in the ranchero hegemonic ideology) believe that Indians are a different kind of being. The terms *sin razón* versus *de razón* ("without reason" and "reasoning," respectively) are still utilized in the region, although they are no longer the only terms in which the relation between mestizos and Indians are cast. The white elites of the region consider the Indians to be racially inferior and generally do not cultivate Indian cultural attributes in the way that they do cultivate competence in peon-cowboy culture. Even during the relatively recent times when rancheros tended to speak "their" Indians' languages (Huasteco or Nahuatl), and to know their customs, this knowledge was valued on the count that it allowed communication and control over the Indians, and not in the sense that it was knowledge to be assimilated to one's own personal customs.

In an interview I had with Gaston Santos, who must have been roughly forty-five years old, he told me,

> when I was a boy the Huasteca was a much less populated region than it is today, and there were only Indians and gente de razón. I remember when I was little that there were people that we called *arrazonados* because they were Indians who could speak Spanish. But in those times there were really only Indians and whites.
> The Indians were and are marginal economically, socially, and culturally. They live in the sierra and have had no impact on the history of the region. Families like my own dominated the region. Among these families the Santos family was the most important. Why? Because we were richer, whiter, and more intelligent [*más ricos, más blancos, y más inteligentes*].

Indians are often seen as childish, sometimes as beastly. Knowledge of Indian ways by much of the ranchero elite is often remarkably scanty, especially by the rancheros who have not built their fortunes on the commercial exploitation of Indians.[3] I have seen ranchero families from Axtla salute Indians who, because of their attire, were obviously Huastecans with the Nahuatl *Yahui.* In gossip sessions at the Valles cafes

I have heard stories comparing the workmanship of Huastecos and Nahuas; some of the concepts uttered there have absolutely no relation to the facts that I was able to observe in Indian communities at San Antonio and Tampamolón.[4] In sum, the rancheros of the cattle-ranching zone share an ideology of superiority with the mestizo peones of the ranchos. In this shared cultural code, there are certain values that legitimate the economic and political superiority of some mestizos over others in terms of an egalitarian ideology of male assertiveness. This common ideology between mestizos contrasts on the one hand with the ideology of domination that exists between rancheros and Indians, and on the other with the ideology of free-market exploitation of labor that has begun invading the region, particularly since the 1960s.

In this sense, it could be said that the ranchero intimate culture and mestizo cowboy intimate culture are transformations of a single class-ethnic culture in which class domination is explained in terms of individual prowess and hereditary family traits. On this last point, the metaphor of cattle breeding provides a conceptual solution for the problem of hierarchy between equals. The main problem in the cultural identification between rancheros and cowboys is class difference and class injustice. The ranchero class attempts to explain its predominance in individual terms (rancheros are super-cowboys), yet the problem of higher and lower birth, and the extreme importance of family, obstruct this egalitarian, self-made-man ideology. The cattle-breeding metaphor bridges this contradiction by making prowess, boldness, and intelligence hereditary.

Evidently, this ideology of supposed equality is not always to the liking of the peones and cowboys, especially when there is a breakdown in the traditional ties of patronage with the rancheros. So, for example, in the rancho that I worked in, my main ethnographic acquaintances were a family of peones. Don Juan, the patriarch of the family, sees himself as a kind of brother to the sisters who owned the ranch; he feels that it is his place to be by them even if their children, who are taking control of the ranch, do not respond to this loyalty. Don Juan's elder son, however, is of a different turn of mind. In his opinion the rancheros have always exploited his family and have never given them their due. The son does not see the ranchero's superiority in terms of either prowess or fate; he sees it only in terms of their historically renewed voracity and in terms of the governmental support that they receive. The breakdown of patronage between rancheros and peones, and the increasing predominance of ordinary wage-labor relations tend to produce an image of class difference and class struggle between these two classes, despite ranchero attempts to maintain cultural identification with the subordinate rural mestizo classes.

The tendency to substitute cultural identification between rancheros and their mestizo workers has been exacerbated by the fact that the villages of the region have been growing, especiallly at the expense of ranchos. Much of their growth is due to the concentration of services in the villages, and the ease of access to many ranchos provided by improvement in roads. The movement from the ranches to the villages was inaugurated by the rancho owners at the turn of the century, and thereby initiated the severing of social ties between owners and workers. With the introduction of roads, beginning in the late 1930s but really picking up since the late fifties, peones and peasants began following suit. This, of course, has had a snowball effect on commerce and services. The general tendency is, I believe, for many of the ranchos to disappear as settlements and remain only as work places, which eventually can only contribute to the emergence of class-cultural distinctions between rancheros and mestizo day laborers.

The process wherein the rancho has become a work place has also allowed for a new trend in the use of women as markers of social difference; whereas the ranchero women of the older generations also cultivated and reinforced the family's identification with the culture of the cowboys, the wealthy women of the younger generation are often completely severed from the rancho culture and are oriented to local high society and to the consumption of high status goods from the outside. This trend also reinforces the already highly separated spheres of interaction of ranchero men and their wives. Men's talk includes the rancho, which is now becoming of little interest to the women.

In other words, the tendency for ranchers and their peones to form a single localized cultural complex is being substituted by a tendency towards social and cultural polarization between these two classes. The end of the rancho as a settlement, the physical distance between rancheros and mestizo peones and cowboys, the opening up of the countryside through a system of roads, have all contributed to the cultural proletarianization of the peones (their disidentification with the rancheros) as well as to the embourgeoisement of the ranchero class (a growing will to be "urban" in consumer and cultural patterns).

Intimate Cultures in the Villages

Villages are composed primarily of the following economic groups: the ranchero/commercial elite; the professional class; the small-scale merchants of the market; servants; peones who work in nearby ranches; peasants who farm nearby plots; and craftsmen (mainly bakers, auto mechanics, carpenters, and construction workers). This population can be divided historically into a relatively new population of rural poor (village peones and peasants) and the oldtimers, mostly rancheros, merchants, craftsmen, and servants.

Villages are the main social and cultural loci of the regional ranchero class. They are also seats of municipal political government which, in the Huasteca, has had a somewhat greater degree of autonomy from the national state—and even from the state government—than municipios have enjoyed in Morelos. Evidently this autonomy is lived as caciquismo; it is autonomy based on the real control of municipal affairs by a few interconnected ranchero families. Rancheros predominate over municipal politics, the organization of major fiestas, decisions on urbanization, schooling policies, and law and order.[5]

The culture of the villages' lower classes is still tied to a large degree to that of their masters, although this trend has slowly begun to change with the growth of the villages and the loosening of the ranchero's monopolic hold over subsistence in the region. Rancheros of today are sometimes surprised at the "lack of loyalty" of some of their servants and cowboys. This lack of loyalty would have been unthinkable a few years back, when employers outside of the ranchero class were scarce for a landless laborer. However, patron-client ties are still important in many, many cases.

For example, Gonzalo Santos's son Gastón became a movie actor and played some leading roles in Mexican cowboy films. When these films were first shown in Tamuín, in the early sixties, some of the peones, who were attending the cinema for the first time, pulled out their guns when Gastón seemed to be in danger and shouted at the screen, "¡Cuidado patrón! ¡Cuidado! ¡Por la espalda!" ("Look out boss, look out behind you!). The whole town referred to Gaston and Gonzalo Santos as "patrón," and Gonzalo's family participated as godparents and guests of honor in innumerable weddings, baptisms and feasts.

In a sense it could be said that the traditional village poor, the servants, cowboys, handymen, and sharecroppers of the rancheros, have a culture that especially glorifies ranchero culture. This is the class in which a man's greatest pride was the quality of his horse (often conferred to him by his patron); it is the class that has produced all those songs about horses and the dexterity of cowboys. The traditional village poor are clients of the ranchero-subsidized priests; they are voters in the ranchero-rigged elections. They organize cockfights and horse races, always made on a smaller scale than those of the real rancheros. When they run into money, they buy the outward signs of ranchero progress: a pickup truck, pointed boots, a good hat, a good horse, and a two-story house.

The village-based class that finds least common ground with the rancheros is often the professional and commercial class, where the ideal of leisure and prosperity can rarely be wedded in the same fashion, and where an ideology of personal valor and knowledge of the countryside is substituted, to some degree, by an identification with urban Mexico and its ideals of cultural distinction through literacy, competence, politeness, and other values perpetated by the national educational and bureaucratic system.

On the other hand, this orientation towards "national culture" does not necessarily imply a different attitude towards the Indian population. So, for example, an acquaintance who is a town doctor said that the people whom she likes to treat the most are the poor and that, in fact, they are the ones that give her the most—for they bring her bread, eggs, oranges, bananas, chickens, cooked food, ornaments, and other gifts. The rich rancheros, on the other hand, are more demanding and despotic and, because they are used to paying for every whim, they see the doctor as just one more servant. In other words, this doctor created ties of patronage and loyalty with her Indian patients, much the same way that rancheros sometimes have done with their Indian protégés.[6] Schoolteachers have also been able to create alliances with the local poor and the Indians in ways that diverge from the culture of social relations that is propagated by rancheros. So, for example, several of Axtla's schoolteachers had close political ties with Indian agrarian authorities and, because of these ties, they had a strong following in local factional politics.

However, this class of merchants and professionals can rarely obtain too much cultural or political weight in Huastecan villages. Their capital depends, in the last instance, on being favored by the local rancheros, and there are not sufficient numbers of professionals for them really to command a cultural life of their own. The result is that these representatives of "national culture" are subordinate to the ranchero elites, and sometimes intermarried with them. The mantle of kinship, real or "fictitious," cloaks potential political and cultural difference between the hegemonic ranchero culture and the contesting culture of the professional and merchant (petit bourgeois) representatives of "national culture." The maintenance of ranching as the main source of wealth has promoted a full identification between merchants, professionals, and ranchers, for any successful merchant or professional will seek to own land and thereby enter the club of the rancheros.

Returning to my examples from Axtla, in the period of my field research, the town was divided into two main factions. One was made up of the old families of rich rancheros that had had political control over the town during most of the century. The opposition faction grew around a conflict between teachers in the junior high school; this faction was led by several schoolteachers, a nouveau-riche ranchero family that was not part of the main ranchero clique, and a rich local merchant. For its internal workings, this faction depended on the rich ranchero and merchant, because only they could round up the necessary resources for the faction to become a serious contender for local political office. Because of this dependence, the faction's candidate for municipal president was the wealthy merchant; the schoolteachers involved in this faction became known as able mobilizers of people, but they never got out from under the tutelage of the local rich.

Intimate Cultures in the Rancho

In its origins, the rancho almost invariably was inhabited (even if part-time) by the ranchero. This provides the origin of the cultural identification between rancheros and their Mestizo dependents. But there are additional subtleties in the ties between rancheros and peones in the old ranching system, and they are all based on the fact that both ranchero and peon were equally tied to the ranch. The ranchero class was "tied" to the ranch not only in a sentimental and cultural sense, but, just as crucially, in the sense that the sum total of a ranchero's power and prestige depended on his ranch. The ranchero class has traditionally had little formal education and is not too polished in the manners and etiquette of Mexican urban elites; rancheros have therefore been a relatively immobile class. One of the key reasons why ranchero families in the Huasteca led the Revolution was their lack of economic and social mobility. Once the collapse of the old regime was evident, rancheros had no choice but to arm themselves and defend (or expand) their property or migrate and move down in the social ladder.

In contradistinction to the Morelos regional elites of hacendados (or to some of the hacendados of the Huasteca), who were usually educated, with capital in addition to their haciendas and luxurious homes in Mexico City, the rancheros of the Huasteca were tied to their land. When they heard of the Revolution, their situation must have been much as Gonzalo Santos is said to have described: an almost completely idyllic life of machista leisure, "playing conquian at the bar, with plenty of food and Indians and women to serve them." And, although it is no doubt true that there was factionalism between ranchero families for political supremacy in the region, even the rancheros who benefitted from Porfirio Díaz's policies (which was not the case of the Santos family in 1910) had either to fight or be willing to lose their local predominance.

In the old-style ranchos, peones and rancheros were both "of the land." Don Juan, the father of my friend at the Piedras Chinas ranch, was adopted into the household of the Juárez family, owners of the ranch. In his role as *"hijo de crianza"* (or *criado,* adopted quasi-son, quasi-servant), Juan was a kind of particularly loyal servant. He had to ask the permission of his patron to marry and to establish an independent household. Upon the death of the patron, the ranch was left to the three daughters, whom don Juan considers to be his "sisters," although he recognizes, not without some bitterness, that he has never received anything from them. Even the plot on which his house is built is theirs. Two of the sisters have died recently and the ranch is faced with the inevitability of a new partition among sons and nephews. These sons have not been raised on the ranch and feel no loyalty or attachments to Juan and his family. Possibly they will throw him out of his house when the last of the sisters dies.

Pepe, don Juan's son, has a small store in Tamuín and has built a small house for his parents there, but don Juan refuses to move. "I was born and raised here. I will die here, or at least I will wait for the last sister to die, if she is to die before me." Rancheros in traditional rancho culture are of the land. Don Juan feels that he owes loyalty to the ranch and to his patrons (and the memory of his patrons). Of course, because the traditional ranching system has been eroding in the past decades, his view is no longer being reciprocated by the heirs of his patrons, much in the same way that his children do not feel the same attachment and loyalty to the ranch or to the Juárez family.

Rancho culture cannot be understood without some kind of treatment of kinship. Ranchos are units that are run by small numbers of families, and often these families are interrelated. Rancho families are usually patriarchal, and residence upon marriage is preferably virilocal, most often patrilocal. Rancho households are usually a *solar* (or patio) in which there are a compound of wattle and mud houses. These buildings house a grand family, made up of a couple, their unmarried sons and daughters, and one or several married sons with their families. Upon the death of the parents it is often the case that brothers divide the solar and produce grand families of their own.

The major house of the rancho, that of the owners, often housed people like don Juan, adopted children-cum-servants that were eventually allowed to create families of their own in the vicinity of the major rancho house. The existence of the peones in their houses depended entirely on their loyalty to the rancheros, because all property was of the ranchero.[7]

The peones of a ranch are often allowed to farm within the boundaries of the property. In the olden days, before agrarian reform, many of these peones and cowboys had steady plots in which they were sharecroppers. Today, long-term sharecropping agreements are rare, for they facilitate legitimate claims for ejido grants; the modern modalities of farming access for peones are renting land on yearly contractual bases or borrowing plots that have lain fallow for many years and working them for one or two years (in this second system, the peones do the hard work of the clearing in exchange for growing corn for a year or two).

Because peones are a landless class, inheritance is not such a strong problem for them; I have the impression that rivalry between brothers in the rancho is not as severe as it tends to be among peasants, or among ranch owners for that matter. At Piedras Chinas my friends censured the ranchero family because the children were about ready to kill each other for the inheritance. This kind of disunity between brothers was not approved by the peones, who took it as a sign of excessive male assertiveness, ambition, and lack of unity. On the other hand, brothers are crucial for peones and rancheros alike, for they represent the capacity of a family to defend itself physically, politically, and economically.

Intimate Cultures of the Peasantry

The Huastecan peasantry can be ethnically divided into three groups: Nahua peasants (who populate the southern municipios of Tamazunchale, Axtla, San Martín, Coxcatlán, Tampacán, Xilitla, Tancanhuitz, and Tampamolón); Huasteco peasants (in the northern municipios of Valles, Aquismón, Tanlajás, San Antonio, Huehuetlán, Tancanhuitz, Coxcatlán, San Vicente, Tanquián, and Tampamolón); and mestizo peasants (who are most prominent in the municipios of Tamasopo, Valles, Tamuín, San Vicente, and Tanquián).[8] Mestizo peasants are a product of agrarian reform, and they form the peasant majority only in the municipios of the coastal plain. The mestizo peasant communities are either formed with ex-peones who received land (usually since the 1960s), or newcomers who were allotted land in the Pujal-Coy irrigation project. Huasteco or Nahua Indian peasants, on the other hand, have been the traditional peasantry of the region, although the number of Indian peasant communities also expanded with agrarian reform. These historical factors help explain the fact that Indian communities tend to be more consolidated as communities than mestizo ejidos, which are not only of more recent formation but also tend to group together people from a large number of ranchos, such that internal ties of kinship tend to be thinner than in the Indian communities and ejidos.

I did not carry out any intensive interviews in mestizo ejidos, and so can only make a superficial commentary on intimate cultures there; I did do work in a Huasteco Indian community, and some of my students worked in a Nahua community. From this material, one can derive some of the following general structural characteristics of these intimate cultures.

Indian peasant communities of the Huasteca are relatively "closed."

They are generally inhabited by a single class of peasants and are usually monoethnic (although there are some interethnic marriages among Huastecos, Nahuas, and mestizos). Class differences between members of these communities are only incipient; there are sometimes families that take part in the regional system of *coyotaje,* for example, by doing the job of contracting fellow Indians for rancheros, or by buying local products and reselling them to mestizo merchants. As far as I have been able to tell, these differences tend not to get transformed into a long-term class distinction. Differences of wealth within the community are most often related to amount of land available per family and to the position of the family in the domestic cycle. In both Nahua and Huastec communities, residence is preferentially virilocal (uxorilocal residence usually occurs when landless men marry women of wealthier families) and residential units tend to involve patrilineal grand-families that settle around the family plot. Sometimes, these plots have names associated with the families that own them, to the extent that in Tanchahuil (a Huastec community in the municipio of San Antonio) family plot names replace "official" last names within the community.

Most Indian communities of the region, then, are made up of a relatively small number of patrilineally related families that live in a dispersed settlement pattern, and are interrelated through marriage. The larger communities tend to be more closed in upon themselves than the smaller ones in the sense that they can be endogamous to a large degree, whereas the smaller Indian communities are perforce exogamous and so form close ties with their neighboring communities.

All of the communities that I know of have a well-developed system of communal work and of political—and sometimes religious—cargos. The system of communal work, usually called *faenas,* functions with surprising regularity (this is clearly not the case in any of the Morelos villages that I know about, where faenas are either occasional or have fallen into almost total desuetude): adult, most often married, men meet once or twice a week to carry out jobs such as mending roads, clearing and working communal plots whose produce goes to the local school, and working land to help finance one of the local religious fiestas. These faenas are important social occasions, which usually end in gossip sessions and drinking.

The internal system of cargos seems to vary somewhat between communities, but politically the most important post is usually that of the *juez* (judge), who is changed yearly in two ceremonies, one officiated by the municipal president (always of the village mestizo elite) on New Year's Day, and another ceremony inside the community. Other officials are the *juez segundo, juez tercero,* and a large number of *vocales;* there are also *mayordomos* of different local saints, although these tend not to be very important, for Indian communities did not have their own churches until very recently (fiestas of the patron saint were always located in the mestizo-dominated cabeceras); and the communal and ejido authorities. Many communities today have been converted to Protestantism, and so no longer have these fiestas. Protestant Indians are also wary of communal faenas because of their association with drinking. Unfortunately, I have no information on these Protestant communities.

This whole ordered system of authority—which is repeated also in the organization of the faenas and of the dances—contrasts markedly with the egalitarian nature of internal class relations. Positions of authority are valued, but they do not bring economic benefits (often they entail significant losses of time and money). The positions of internal authority, and the whole local representation of legitimated order, are an important ideological mechanism in the articulation between these peasant intimate cultures and those of the dominant ranchero elite. Members of these peasant communities have surprisingly few face-to-face dealings with the ranchero elites, in that the mestizos who venture inside the communities usually deal directly either with the local authorities or with the local Indian merchant. Moreover, the beliefs and values of these local cultures are sometimes completely at odds with dominant belief systems. This is most apparent in matters "religious" and "medicinal," but in fact occurs throughout many aspects of these cultures. The hierarchical organization of a local structure of authority, which sometimes reproduces an ideology about the place of God, Mestizos, government, and the communities in the world do not correspond to an economic differentiation within the community, but is rather an ideological system about internal cohesion and about the position of the community in the universe.

In other words, Indian peasant intimate cultures are relatively well closed off from direct ranchero intervention, if only because of the position of these communities in regional social space. They are mono-ethnic and articulated with mestizos only through the market, but most marketing occurs in the mestizo pueblos. At the same time, because they are clearly in a subordinate position, they conciliate the contradiction between internal equality and collective subordination with a hierarchical culture of authority. On the other hand, the strongly valued autonomy of many Indian families is often threatened by extreme poverty, and the Indian communities of the region do lose a lot of members through emigration. Many Indian families send their children to Indian boarding schools so that they will get better meals. Some of these Indian children go on to live outside of their families. The army was an especially common destination for young men in the communities studied, and domestic service was common for young women. Many of the young men and women who leave the community never come back to live there.

Finally, a word must be said about the situation of mestizo peasants. These mestizo communities tend to contrast with the structural situations described above on several important counts. First of all, the mestizo communities tend to keep important social ties with the local villages and market towns. Mestizos have tended not to elaborate a rich internal system of authority or of cultural difference, and tend instead to create communities that are satellites of the municipal cabeceras both ritually and politically. The population of these mestizo communities is usually more heterogeneous classwise than that of the Indian communities. Many ejido owners are also owners of private property. Often there are members of the main ranchero families in the ejidos (or at least renting land in these ejidos); there are complex relations of renting within these communities, and often elaborate factionalisms complete with local caciques that are tied to municipal level factionalisms. These peasant groups form an important part of the politically mobilizable groups in municipal politics; they tend to be organized by different party organizations, such as the Confederación Nacional Campesina (CNC), and as such are, once again, appendices of village intimate cultures. Tensions between mestizo peasant communities and villages have perhaps not been strong enough in the past to sever the intricate cultural links between these two kinds of settlements. The mestizo ejidos can therefore generally be conceived as a particular transformation or context of the ranchero/peon complex described above.

Emergent Intimate Cultures: The Proletariat, the Professional Class, and the Urbanized Petite Bourgeoisie

The argument that I have developed is based on the historically supported view that the three basic class cultures of the Huasteca are the ranchero class culture, the peon class culture and the (Indian) peasant class culture. Throughout the description, however, it has become evident that the organizational principles behind this tripartite division in classes and class cultures have been modified, sometimes substantially, during the last half century. Specifically, I have pointed out that the rancho as a settlement, and as the privileged locus of ranchero/peon relations has been corroded in the past decades; I have also pointed to the emergence of a mestizo peasant class and to the (restricted) emergence of an industrial working class. In this subsection I only formalize the nature of these transformations from the point of view of the emergence of new intimate cultures in the region.

The dissolution of the rancho as settlement, the concentration of the ranchero class in the villages and in Ciudad Valles (the regional city), and the concentration of urban—governmentally controlled—services in these villages have made to some degree for the embourgeoisement of the ranchero class. Although this process is only emergent, it is clearly observable, and it is reinforced with the growth of a bona fide petite bourgeoisie at the village level. This new class is made up especially of professionals who come to staff the growing number of urban services in the villages, and it has somewhat mixed allegiances to the state culture that I have already described for Morelos and to the local ranchero culture, which still effectively dominates much of Huastecan village life. I myself (being a representative of this professional class) often felt something of a fool with my "serious" urban professional values when I confronted the extremely social, leisurely lifestyle of the ranchero elite. I seemed to be like the silly "good little boy" of every classroom, furiously taking notes and asking questions while everyone else participated in their creative *desmadre* (a kind of antistructural pastime that could be characterized in terms of subordinating one's time to one's on-the-spot ideas and desires, a good ranchero's *raison d'être*).[9] The professional pride of the petite bourgeoisie and its characteristic "holier than thou" self-image is often corroded by the charismatic superiority of the ranchero lifestyle.

Nevertheless, in Cuidad Valles at least, some of the external values of the petite bourgeoisie have begun to gain a little influence in the ranchero class, especially in that section of the class that does not directly take charge of its ranches. If this class and its culture were to become the dominant class and intimate culture, it is foreseeable that this would be the end of a regionally hegemonic culture in the Huasteca, which would be in even a worse position than Morelos to sustain a regional culture, given the fact that there is no built-in space for a politico-bureaucratic regionalism here.

The emergence of a proletarian intimate culture in the Huasteca is only observable in Cuidad Valles, the village of Tamuín and at the sugar mills. In the case of the sugar workers, we have a legitimate proletariat that has been imported into the region because contractual relationships with the mills are controlled by the national union of sugar workers. This union has achieved positions of significant political strength in the areas in which it operates. For example, during my field work in Valles, the municipal president was a national leader of the sugar union. My impression of this incipient working class is that in fact it is not very closely connected to the ranchero/peon/peasant classes that are predominant in the region (I met workers who did not know that the Indians of the region were Huastecos and Nahuas), and that, instead, it is oriented outward, towards state culture and the culture of the media. This new proletarian class does occupy more or less homogenized spaces in the region, for there are working class districts in Valles and Tamuín, and housing projects of the sugar factories at El Naranjo, Tamasopo, and Rascón. In this sense the class has the capacity to produce an encapsulated intimate culture of its own, and it could be a seed for an emergent "Huastecan baroque."

Flows of Mestizaje

I have discussed intimate cultures of rancheros, Indian, and mestizo peasants; peones; the commercial bourgeoisie; and some aspects of the new working class. The structure of change in these intimate cultures, the production of incoherence in these intimate cultures, must be understood in the context of the political and economic interaction between them.

Important cases of interactions that tend to undermine the internal coherence of intimate cultures and produce mestizaje are the flow of seasonal labor from the comunidades to the ranchos; the flows from comunidades to regional cities in and outside of the region (mainly in Tampico, Valles, and Mexico City, but also to the United States and other Mexican regional centers); the migration of rancheros from their ranches to villages and regional cities; the flow of peones from the ranches to ejido communities; and of peones from ranches to urban employment in the region.

To understand the nature of these processes of mestizaje, we must place them in the context of the patterns of reproduction set out by the elderly of each intimate culture. We start from the premise that there are cultural ideals of reproduction within each of the intimate cultures described—even when these ideals coexist with a collective will to change. These reproductory ideals can be evidenced in the models of the "life cycle" proposed by powerful members of the intimate cultures. After all, no one's life is a cycle; however, members of intimate cultures attempt to organize the lives of their peers and children in terms of a determinate set of stages that will have as its outcome cultural reproduction: a cycle.

Mestizaje must be understood in terms of two kinds of processes, the acculturation of an individual, family or community from one intimate culture to another, and the corrosion of internal consistency between the elements that compose an intimate culture. For the first kind of mestizaje, which implies changing cultural allegiances, it is necessary to focus on the stages and transitions between stages that are perilous for the reproduction of intimate cultures. It is usually at these points, these weak links in the reproductive schemes of cultural conservatives, that people begin to abandon the reproductive scheme of their parents or peers.

In the case of the Indian comunidades the two sorts of processes of mestizaje are most likely to occur during young adulthood, before marriage and inheritance. The Indian community has very little hold on its members at this stage of the developmental cycle. Many young men have little work in the community and must seek employment outside, which entails the possibility of assimilation into another culture. If a young man goes to work out of his community and then marries out, he is likely to continue to work outside and may never claim his rights to land or to full community membership. If, on the other hand, the young man is married in the community when he migrates, or if he takes an Indian wife, then he may maintain his ties with his inheritance and the community even for a very extended period, returning only for the main holidays. However, these ties entail accepting much incoherence in that family's intimate culture, because allegiance to community culture is maintained almost schizophrenically in contexts that are entirely alien to the original cosmological principles of those communities.[10] So one can distinguish here two kinds of mestizaje, one that constitutes an attempt to break permanently with the Indian community, and one in which membership is maintained, although not lived continuously.

Upon analysis, these kinds of mestizaje produce radically different effects. Mestizaje through incoherence of a community's permanent population means the (theoretical) possibility of greater cultural manipulation by the members of that community. A community that has bilingual women or men who know the ways of, say, the intimate culture of peones and the culture of social relations between peones and rancheros, has the capacity to play with these new elements and attempt to realign its own cultural identification in different ways vis-à-vis regional and national culture. Communities with a fair degree of this kind of mestizaje will often show periods of de- and re-Indianization.[11]

On the other hand, the type of mestizaje wherein an individual member of an Indian community lives outside of the community but maintains ties that permit her/him and his/her family to return is a process in which the outsider may come to represent all of the good things that the outside world has to offer. This kind of mestizaje produces a tendency for prestigious consumption. When migrants come to their villages for a visit, they bring with them goods that are considered to be superior. They drink distillates with brand names; they may have a fancy tape recorder or radio, or bring in city clothes. This relationship between the mestizo-Indian and his/her community is different from the kind of mestizaje discussed above. Here the goods of another intimate culture are being flaunted as a way of legitimating the individual's strained ties to his/her intimate culture of origin. At the same time, the visitor's very presence in the community establishes the fact that there are at least some good points to the intimate culture. The visitor becomes a contact for the community to the outside world, a stepping-stone for more mestizaje, while at the same time (s)he is enforcing the importance of— or at least some aspects of—the intimate culture. These aspects will be reproduced in urban settings if in fact the migrants set up a little network of Indians where they work.[12]

Finally, the individuals who leave and do not come back simply enter the different mestizo groups of Mexican regions in a context where most of their past is of no practical use. The Indian communities that we studied produced all three kinds of flows.

The major process of mestizaje amongst the rancheros began with their migration towards urban centers, at first mainly to the cabeceras, then especially to Valles, and finally some to San Luis and Mexico City. This process must be understood in two reproductive contexts: the first is the education of children, the second the revaluation of the importance of the niceties of civilization for the ranchero's family.

Education has increasingly become recognized as an attribute of some importance to the ranchero class. However, education entails danger to the reproduction of this class. First of all, if a ranchero-child becomes truly interested in his or her profession, then they may never care directly for their ranch again. They may permanently move out of the region and cease reproducing the class culture. If, in addition, a young person studying at a university meets someone in the city and marries, there are strong possibilities for that couple to stay in the city and to keep weak links with the rancheros; the climate and life of the Huasteca are considered difficult for a city girl to bear.

Ranchero parents are aware of these difficulties, and some have attempted to curb these tendencies by encouraging children to enter professions that are useful in their ranches. Also there is some pressure for endogamy within the ranchero class. Many of the children of ranchero families come back to the Huasteca to seek a girlfriend to marry, or else move socially in a Huastecan circle in San Luis.

Regardless of these tactics, however, the tendency for rancheros of younger generations to become educated has undoubtedly presented a few difficulties for the reproduction of ranchero intimate culture and of ranchero domination in the region. The urbanization of the ranchero class has meant that their traditional macho attributes of strength, deftness, and prowess have been curbed somewhat, and that they often must put on shows of these attributes to which they are not at all suited. Thanks to this, the urbanized ranchero class is losing the cultural base of their patron-client ties with their ranch workers, a situation exacerbated by the fact that urbanized rancheros tend to care less about their physical property. Although selling one's ranch is still considered to be an emotionally difficult thing to do, this seems to be more common than it used to be, especially in the case of rancheros who live outside of the region.

Urbanization tends to weaken some of the bonds of loyalty and trust in the traditional culture of social relations that existed between rancheros and peones. It would surprise me very much if the current ranchero class could organize their workers to fight a revolution for them, the way rancheros did in 1910. The niceties of urban life tend to make the displays of masculine dominance more of a show and less of a day-to-day reality; if a ranchero is not careful, he will turn into a *catrín* (a city pretty-boy), and even if he is careful it is likely that his children will be catrines. The separation of the rancheros from their land tends to substitute the ranchero/peon culture of social relations with a capitalist/worker mode.[13]

Finally, the peon intimate culture of the ranchos tends to become mesticized into either a mestizo peasant culture of the kind described above (through agrarian reform), or into a proletarian rural day-laboring culture. In both cases, the cowboy and peon become conscious of the weakness of the ties with ranchero owners and so attempt to break free from this relationship either by gaining direct access to land through an ejido or by gaining income elsewhere. The workings of this process of mestizaje have relatively fewer implications of incoherence than the case of Indian mestizaje when the change is in the direction of peasantification, for most elements of the peon culture can be maintained there— including identification with the ranchero-dominated villages—without detriment to political and economic reproduction. If, on the one hand, migration is to a non-Huastecan city, the situation of this peon class is in several ways similar to that of the Indian peasants, because it implies the devalorization of all of the knowledge accumulated in peon intimate culture.

General Aspects of the Huastecan Culture of Social Relations

By way of conclusion I outline some of the elements of the Huastecan culture of social relations, for the organization of regional hegemony contrasts so with that which we have seen for Morelos.

The Huastecan culture of social relations can be understood in terms of the competition between two hegemonic projects: the still-dominant ranchero system of hegemony and the state culture, which has gained terrain through federal investment, roads, education, and mass communication. This second project involves the disintegration of the Huasteca as a hegemonically ordered regional culture (as we saw for the case of Morelos); the ranchero project, however, has in fact organized regional cultural space in the region for an extended historical period, and rancheros have successfully controlled most governmental institutions in the region.

Ranchero hegemony has meant the construction of a culture of social relations based on interrelating three main kinds of intimate cultures: ranchero intimate culture, peon and servant intimate culture, and Indian peasant intimate culture. The culture of social relations that hierarchically integrates these different intimate cultures is complex, especially because of the extreme cultural differences between the intimate cultures of the rancheros and those of the Indians; however, it is characterized by a clear-cut order of domination and command based on a classical liberal ideology that legitimates inequality between mestizos in terms of the personal prowess and intelligence of rancheros over peones, and a racist discrimination of Indians as being radically and culturally inferior.

I classify the ranchero culture of social relations as of liberal origin because it bases the legitimacy of domination on *individual characteristics* of members of the dominant and subordinate Mestizo classes, and because it provides a *racist* (not a caste) rationale for domination of Indians. However, this vision of Darwinian genetic superiority is only the rancheros' self-explanation of their situation. Rancheros also allow and foster paternalistic and hierarchical relationships with Indians and Indian communities. These paternalistic relations are no longer part of the ranchero dog-eat-dog liberalism; instead, they frame Indian subordination within a view of social interdependence. Thus the Huastecan culture of social relations has at its core an individualistic ideology, but rancheros have also permitted—and sometimes even encouraged—the prolongation of castelike relations with the Indians.

The culture of social relations that stems from this can also be contrasted to what I have described as Cuernavacan baroque: the society is culturally divided in two (mestizos and Indians), and these two main cultures are in a clear-cut relationship of domination/subordination. Cuernavacan baroque was the product of a hierarchical society without a local dominant class; Huastecan culture of social relations is based on a racially legitimated subordination of Indians and an individually legitimated superiority over other mestizos, and a paternalistic ideology of complementarity between Indians and mestizos. At the same time, I should underline that this perspective on the culture of social relations is that of the dominant ranchero class. I shall explore the ways in which the other classes conceive of their place in Huastecan society in the following chapters.

11

Ranchero Localist Ideology

In this and the remaining chapters of this section I shall present localist ideologies in the main Huastecan intimate cultures. My purpose is to show the ways in which different coherent models of local cultures are constructed. I have thus far outlined cultural interaction in the Huasteca in terms of the formation of "intimate cultures" and their articulation into a regional culture by way of the creation of a "culture of social relations." I have also attempted to point to the process of regional cultural formation in terms of the creation of coherence and incoherence in different intimate cultures in a dynamic process of cultural change (mestizaje).

Localist ideologies are forms of cultural synthesis that involve the creation of cultural coherence. I am especially interested here in pointing out the different ways in which coherence between intimate culture and the culture of social relations can be attained and developed. I also seek to show the conceptual and institutional spaces in which these attempts towards cultural synthesis occur. The ultimate aim is to show a regional view of the spaces and possibilities for the creation and preservation of coherent cultural ideologies and programs of the different regional cultural groups. These chapters have the additional function of providing a clearer picture of the specific cultural elements, symbols, interpretations, and relationships that have thus far been described in rather abstract terms. Localist ideology is a privileged way into these issues because it synthesizes the politics of regional culture through the medium of cultural categories, rituals, and beliefs.

The spaces in which localist ideologies are produced must be understood in terms of the place allotted to the Huasteca in the ideology of national identity constructed by the "state culture." I have argued that Huastecan culture and history have been cast into a kind of "miscellaneous" category of great periphery or frontier. On the other hand, the center's lack of recognition of the main elements of Huastecan culture and history in fact provide a space for the assertion of precisely this culture and history as a kind of alternative within Mexican culture. In this chapter I discuss some of the ranchero localist ideologies that have emerged in this context. As in the case of Morelos, the ethnographic materials that I use for the discussion of localist ideologies come from particular individuals; what interests me in the analysis of these people's localist discourse is not so much that they be perfectly representative of their intimate culture's localism, for they are typical in some respects and idiosyncratic in others. I am most interested in understanding the kinds of cultural elements and the kinds of spaces and solutions to localism in different people's syntheses.

Gonzalo Santos and the Politics of Regional Symbols

The main figure in modern Huastecan political history has been, without a doubt, Gonzalo N. Santos. He has also been the leader who has used local culture and ideologies in the most original and effective ways. Santos provides insight not only into the nature of local, regional, and national ideology within the Huasteca, but also into the different possible cultural roots and forces of caciquismo.[1]

Gonzalo Santos was one of the younger sons of a prominent landholding family in the municipio of Tampamolón, in the cattle ranching zone of the region (see Santos 1986 and Márquez 1977).[2] However, due to the intense factionalism between the major ranchero clans, many of the important ranchero families of the Huasteca were unhappy with Porfirio Diaz.[3] According to Gastón Santos's version of the problem:

> Porfirio's problem was that he lived too long. If he had died ten years before, he would have passed on as Mexico's greatest president, the creator of a modern Mexican nation. But he lived too long, and wanted everything for himself and his friends. It is like the PRI: the governments that stemmed from the Revolution were great, but the party has lasted too long.

According to Gastón, people in the Huasteca (i.e., his family) were fed up with the Diaz regime because there were some ranchers and hacendados that had all of the political and some of the economic privileges.

For this reason, a class of wealthy rancheros, and even a few hacendados went up in arms.[4]

The whole Santos family—brothers and cousins, nephews and uncles—went up in arms under the leadership of Pedro Antonio Santos, the eldest brother, who was a prominent lawyer and Maderista in the capital of San Luis. At that time Gonzalo was only about fifteen; yet he joined the Revolution and went up in the ranks rather quickly. When the Revolution ended he was a colonel, and he was promoted to general during the Escobarista rebellion (1929). Pedro Antonio was murdered in 1913 and Samuel Santos, Gonzalo's elder brother, became the most prominent military figure of the family and remained so until he sided against Obregón in the de la Huerta rebellion. Samuel was spared thanks to Gonzalo's proximity to Obregón. From that point on, Gonzalo Santos was the indisputable head of the family, and he became a major national political figure and the head cacique of the Huasteca.

During most of the Revolution, however, the most important military figure in the Huasteca was a member of a rival ranchero family from nearby Tanlajás, Manuel Lárraga.[5] The Santos regiment fought mostly in areas other than the Huasteca, and so Lárraga remained in control of the region for most of this period. However, Lárraga made two major political errors in the aftermath of the Revolution: he sided with Carranza against Obregón in 1920, and with de la Huerta against Obregón and Calles in 1923. Gonzalo Santos himself was sent to quell Lárraga's rebellion in 1923, after which Lárraga was exiled to the United States and finally died in Tampico many years later.

Some of the stories that Santos told to his friends about the Revolution are worth reproducing here, in that they reveal the situation of the main Revolutionary leaders of the Huasteca:

> We Huastecans went to the Revolution out of boredom. Before the Revolution we had a good life. We lived out there in Tampamolón and did nothing other than play conquián or domino in the bars. We had a lot of Indians to serve us, and plenty of food all around. We went to the revolution for boredom. When we heard that there was shooting going on in the north, we decided to pick up our guns and go, but we weren't dissatisfied with don Porfirio.

> You know, the problem with the Revolution here was that there wasn't an enemy. It was hard. I had to go into some small village with a hundred men and the villagers would have to feed us, they would hate us. So what I used to do before going into town was to send six of my men ahead of us and into the bar. There they would start a brawl and then we would come in and save the townspeople from those ruthless outlaws. Then the people received us well, they gave us food, they even gave us their daughters and the women didn't want us to leave.

At the end of this story my friend asked Don Gonzalo, "But general, what about morality?" (¿Y la moral?). To which the general responded thoughtfully: "¿La moral? La moral es un arbol que da moras."[6]

This kind of story, which General Santos told his friends in the Huasteca, apparently contradicts the revolutionary ideals and sacrifices that Santos emphasizes in his published memoirs, where he speaks of patriotism, courage, and revolutionary ideals, of the struggle against Porfirista and Huertista "reactionaries," and of the revolutionary exploits of the anticlerical leaders. In fact, however, these two types of stories are complementary and not contradictory.

The narrative reproduced above is all about the internal situation of the Huasteca, where the revolutionary leadership came from—or was subordinated to—the elite ranchero classes (the Lárraga extended family, the Santos extended family, and even some hacendado families, like the Rodríguez Cabos). The liberal and anticlerical tradition of these families, many of which had supported Juárez against the French, and the ranchero culture of individual courage and dexterity with guns and horses were combined into a nationalist revolutionary ideology whose main formal characteristics were an anti-aristocratic posture; identification with the mestizo Mexican people without recourse to an ideology of state socialism; and valorization of self-made men and of the possibilities that Mexico provides for this form of freedom (which is also understood as a freedom to command, a freedom to create charismatic leadership, a freedom to do whatever one can get away with).

There is an illustration of this aspect of ranchero self-image in a passage of Santos's memoirs, where he tells of how he refused a quite substantial bribe from political opponents. He said to them:

> I want to tell you, I want you to know, in case you don't know, that I am a bandit. And we bandits are not for sale. Only honest people like you are for sale, so go on and look for someone honest to buy off because—I'll say it again—I am a bandit and I am not for sale. (1986:224)

Revolutionary ideals of nationalism and equality in an anticlerical, antiaristocratic (but also anticommunist, antimoralistic) mode were wedded to an ideology of freedom from the law: equality stemmed precisely from every man's right to assert dominance, regardless of birth. In this case, Santos is asserting that "revolutionary" liberty to dominate. He is not respecting the status quo by receiving a bribe; he is dominating it by overtly imposing his will. He is not a corrupt bureaucrat who is taking advantage of an assigned position; he is a willful and independent "bandit."

During Carranza's presidential period, the Santos were removed from power in the Huasteca by Manuel Lárraga, with whom the Santos had a standing feud.[7] This situation changed drastically, however, at the triumph of Obregón's faction with the Plan de Agua Prieta. By this time Gonzalo Santos was already in Mexico City, after having passed a brief stay at the docks at Tampico, where Samuel (his brother) was head of the port authority, and where it is said the family made a sizeable fortune. Gonzalo Santos arrived in Mexico City as a congressman, and soon became the leader of Obregón's majority faction in both houses. He also was able to achieve considerable influence in San Luis politics because Saturnino Cedillo, the cacique who controlled state military at the time, was also an enemy of Lárraga.[8]

In the years following 1922, Gonzalo Santos made a career as the main Obregonista leader in congress. He was a shrewd and ruthless politician. For example, it was he who proposed, defended and won the bill to reelect Obregón, despite the fact that it went against the most basic of Maderista principles: no reelection. Upon the assassination of Obregón, Santos played key roles in the creation of the Partido Nacional Revolucionario and in the assent of Calles to the position of Jefe Máximo. During Ortiz Rubio's regime, however, Gonzalo had frictions with Calles's sons and with Cedillo and so went to an honorable political exile as ambassador to Belgium. At this time, Gonzalo learned to speak French and English, and he also avoided participation in the conflict between Cárdenas and Calles.

In the meantime, Gonzalo consolidated his properties in the Huasteca. In 1922 he set up his new headquarters in Tamuín, the richest cattle ranching municipio of the region, and his famous ranches of Gargaleote and La Jarrilla grew immensely. According to one of my informants, in the 1950s Gargaleote had as many as 40,000 hectares; it as later broken up so that when it was expropriated in 1977 it had only a little over 7,000 hectares.

In regional politics, despite the already mentioned tensions, Gonzalo generally backed Cedillo except in his last suicidal coup against Cárdenas. For example, it is generally believed that Gonzalo Santos's strongmen were involved along with Cedillo's in the political massacre carried out in Valles (1937) against the followers of Aurelio Manrique, a radical opponent of Cedillo and candidate for the governorship. Cárdenas, who ended Gonzalo's exile in Belgium, also used Santos as a middleman between himself and Cedillo when relations between the two caudillos became strained.

After the frustrated rebellion of Cedillo (1939), Gonzalo seized power in San Luis. During this time several regional caciques were murdered, and some of these killings may be attributable to don Gonzalo. But don Gonzalo's prolonged political power was confirmed when Cárdenas selected Avila Camacho, a compadre and close associate of Gonzalo's, as his successor. Through this connection, Gonzalo Santos was named official candidate to the governorship of San Luis Potosí.

Gonzalo Santos's candidacy sparked intense protest in the city of San Luis, where his ruthlessness was well known, and where leaders from the Huasteca have always been looked down upon. The city of San Luis was an old mining capital, with long-standing quasi-aristocratic families. It was also a very Catholic, very conservative town. However, Avila Camacho ratified his choice, and Gonzalo Santos became governor. When he took power, he is said to have proclaimed, "If the imbecile Cedillo controlled San Luis for eighteen years, I will do that for at least twenty."

Gonzalo Santos's hold over San Luis state politics lasted from 1942 to 1959. During this period, Gonzalo maintained close relations with Mexico's presidents and is said to have entertained them frequently at his famous Cuernavaca mansion "El Alazán Tostado." Joaquín Guzmán, one of Gonzalo's closest Huastecan associates, thrice municipal president of Tamuín and once federal congressman, showed me pictures of Don Gonzalo with presidents Avila Camacho, Ruiz Cortines, and Diaz Ordaz at Cuernavaca. In his mansion he entertained much of Mexico's political elite. El negro Marcelino, the famous Huapango player from Valles, played music, and there were cockfights with roosters from Gonzalo's pens in La Jarrilla. Gonzalo Santos's memoirs also include photographs of Gonzalo with practically every postrevolutionary president except Echeverría and López Portillo, whom he detested.

During this period, Gonzalo named and controlled the governors and municipal presidents of the state. He also had close ties with most of the national government elite (the "revolutionary family"), and many of these figures acquired ranches in the Huasteca during this period. Jorge Pasquel—one of the main entrepreneurs of the Miguel Alemán period—acquired the enormous ranch of San Ricardo which is today a collectivized "model" ejido called Ponciano Arriaga; other well-known figures who acquired ranches in this period include the politicians Robles Martínez and Martínez Domínguez and the comedian Mario Moreno, "Cantinflas."

In the Huasteca, Gonzalo provided the ideal conditions for cattle ranching: he succeeded in stopping cattle thieves, who had been an impediment for ranchers until that time. Almost everyone in the Huasteca remembers with nostalgia the times when, thanks to santismo, there was no burglary or theft in the region. This internal peace was kept by a rural police force that had instructions to hang all cattle thieves and to shoot robbers on sight. Cattle ranchers also felt safe against agrarian reform: during the period of santismo there were no new ejido grants in the

Huasteca. The region remained almost exclusively agricultural, the only two industries that were established in this period were Fibracell (an ecologically devastating firm that is owned by the Banco Nacional de México and makes plywood) and Ron Potosí, a rum factory that buys piloncillo from the region's Indian communities.

On the political front, local caciquismos were maintained and enforced. Families close to Gonzalo were able to retain local power for an extended period. Successors to the municipal presidencies were named during meals in Tamuín, where Gonzalo would consult with his main municipal allies. The state and local police were entirely in the control of santismo.[9] Gonzalo Santos did not tolerate any opposition from parties or unions.

One of Gonzalo's major sources of internal opposition was from the Catholic Sinarquista Party. This party was particularly influential in San Luis Potosí, but it also had some hold in a few places in the Huasteca, especially Huehuetlán and, to a lesser extent, Valles. However, Gonzalo was able to make an alliance with the bishop at San Luis and with Padre Javier, the main priest of the Huasteca, and was able to keep the Sinarquists relatively quiet until 1960.

The end of Santos's hold over the state of San Luis came in 1959, when López Mateos made it clear that he did not support this cacicazgo. It is said that López Mateos's (alleged) hatred of Santos stemmed from Santos's role in the suppression of the Vasconcelista movement in Tampico, 1929. At that time, in a Mexico City riot, a leader of the Vasconcelista students, Germán del Campo, was assassinated, supposedly by Gonzalo Santos. He was also charged (and he admitted this murder in his memoirs) with the assassination of Fernando Capdeville, also a Vasconcelista student who was enamored of Gonzalo's first wife.[10] Lopez Mateos was a Vasconcelista in his youth, and so is said to have harbored hatred for the Huastecan cacique. But in his memoirs Santos says that he had a long-standing friendship with "Fito" López Matéos and expresses admiration for the man. It now appears that López Matéos may have removed Santos from the state government as a gesture to his San Luis allies, but that fact did not corrode his influence in the Huasteca. However this may be, he dislodged Santos from the state capital and began a campaign of integration of the Huasteca into national society.

Santos's local autocratic power was undermined by federal investment in the region: a sugar mill and a cement factory were built in Valles, and the road from San Luis to Valles was constructed. Most important, there were the plans for making the cattle-herding zone into an irrigated agricultural district, which implied the expropriation of some of the ranches and the transformation of the region into a peasant zone that would be strongly dependent on the federal government for land grants, for irrigation works, for credit, and for technical assistance. Gonzalo Santos and the rancheros of the Huasteca tenaciously fought against this project and successfully stopped its continuation when Diaz Ordaz, an old friend of don Gonzalo, was named president of Mexico. However the return of Diaz Ordaz did not mean the reinstatement of Gonzalo as overlord of San Luis; instead Gonzalo was made Secretary of the Merchant Marine for a brief period. When Echeverría came into power, Santos lost most of his remaining influence. The Pujal-Coy irrigation project was reinstated. During the first years of López Portillo's regnum, Gonzalo's main ranch, El Gargaleote, was expropriated. This expropriation was planned as a real piece of state theater. Although the expropriation had been settled with the family weeks in advance of its formal announcement, and the ranch was going to be paid for by the government, the federal government sent troops, even parachutists, to take Gargaleote by storm. The federal government had symbolically finished Mexico's last great cacique. Gonzalo Santos died in 1980. His colorful memoirs were published five years after his death.

Ranchero Regionalism in San Luis Politics

I have already noted the strong opposition to Gonzalo's candidacy in the city of San Luis. An important reason for this resentment was, of course, that Gonzalo was from the Huasteca and represented the interests of that region's dominant class of rancheros. In addition, the elite of the state capital was (and, to a lesser degree, still is) a tightly knit social and cultural group with which Santos had very little to do. From the Huastecan viewpoint this dominant San Luis group is a stuffy, pretentious, downtrodden aristocracy (*curros*); from the point of view of "the families" of San Luis, the Huastecans are uncouth and uncivilized ranchers, whose recently acquired money and power they despise.

Gonzalo confronted San Luis's hostility in a characteristically undiplomatic and effective way (he was not, remember, an honest citizen caught in the trappings of bureaucracy and petty legality); he simply decided to subjugate the capital and prove his dominance over it. During his governorship, Gonzalo had the kiosk of the main plaza of San Luis removed and sent down to Tampamolón, his dusty home town, as a public humiliation to the capital. It is said that when he was governor, Gonzalo Santos went to the Lonja, San Luis's aristocratic social club, and urinated in one of the ashtrays. Gonzalo flaunted Huastecan culture—music, cockfights, and filthy, open and aggressive language—in the face of uptight San Luis.

During the santista governorships of Salas and Alvarez, the most important political decisions in the state were dictated from Gonzalo's ranch in the Huasteca (El Gargaleote), so that people from the capital were forced to travel there if they wanted resolutions to any of their important problems. It is said that when Gonzalo went to the capital on business, the governor would get up and give him his chair. In addition, Gonzalo's famous maxim ("In this state, the only politician who is allowed to steal is me") must not have attracted too much popularity from the politicians of San Luis.

Gonzalo presented himself as a Huastecan regionalist vis-à-vis San Luis's weakened elites and the city's traditional petit bourgeois and professional classes, he presented himself as somewhat of a populist with regards to the altiplano's working class, in contrast with his open hostility to projects for industrialization in the Huasteca. He wanted a rural Huasteca.

Gonzalo confronted the elite's antipathy by reaffirming his ranchero upbringing and symbolically defiling the San Luis aristocracy. His attitude towards the professional classes and the petite bourgeoisie of San Luis, however, must be analyzed in a different light. Gonzalo's frictions with these classes was related to the very bases of caciquismo. The professional class was structurally opposed to caciquismo, for it was directly affected by it. In this sense, Gonzalo Santos had to confront a situation in all respects similar to that of Cedillo, who was also disliked in the state university (UASLP) and by many of the city's professionals. Ideologically, the middle-class opposition to Cedillo made fun of his alleged ignorance and of his peasant upbringing. When Cedillo erected a monument in honor of his brother Magdaleno, the students hung a *huarache* (peasant's sandal) around the statue's neck. Cedillo's cabinet and followers were generally ridiculed for "not wearing socks" and not knowing how to read.

Although the San Luis middle class's relation with Gonzalo Santos shared some of the same structural features, it adopted a different ideological idiom.[11] In Gonzalo's case, it was his ruthlessness, not his lack of education, that was at issue. Movements against don Gonzalo inevitably asked for the removal of Mano Negra (Gonzalo's main hired killer) from the state payroll and generally stressed the problem of political freedom and of Gonzalo's arbitrary control over the state and municipal bureaucracies.[12]

Gonzalo was always careful in his politics towards this middle class (which he despised). At some level he must have realized that there was a basic incompatibility between his form of rule and their livelihood; the middle classes did not easily give up their control over the state bureaucratic apparatus. The following dialogue between Gonzalo Santos and

Alfonso Oliva Purata, a young member of Valles high society, illustrates the kind of relation Gonzalo Santos had with students:

GS: Who's next, miss?
[GS's secretary shows him in.]

AOP: Good afternoon, don Gonzalo.

GS: Hi! How are don Ciro and your father?

AOP: Very well, don Gonzalo, thank you.

GS: What's up, hot-head?

AOP: I wanted to greet you and to talk.

GS: Well, here I am. How can I help you?

AOP: Well, don Gonzalo, you know that the youth of San Luis is ready for the politics that are coming up [elections], because they are politically disquieted and feel they have a right to participate in the struggle. . . .

GS: Of course! Well said! All of us Mexicans have that right, and we have to demand it. So far, so good. What else?

AOP: That we have decided to form an independent party which will include all of the students of San Luis Potosí, with delegations in each municipio and directing groups in the state capital.

GS: The party will, of course, be affiliated to the PRI [the official party]?

AOP: No, don Gonzalo, the party will be—as I said—independent. We want no tutelages and no party line.

GS: Stop right there and listen well to what I am going to tell you. So long as you don't become affiliated to the PRI, there will not be in the state of San Luis a single independent party. I will make sure of that, I will tolerate it from no one. Understood?

AOP: [trying to lighten up the tone] You see, don Gonzalo? One comes here to talk with you and you just get angry. I am not here on a personal mission; I represent a very large group of people. . . .

GS: [sarcastically] Don't frighten me!!!

AOP: In other words, we wanted to inform you of our activities, not to ask your permission. I . . . [Gonzalo cuts him off]

GS: You what? And what also of your group? Do you think I don't have guts? Or that a bunch of sniveling idiots are going to give me a shove? What do you know about politics? Fools! You only just read some shitty book or listen to any of those idiots your age of which there are so many—because, to go no further, I have one here, hee-hawing right in front of me—for you to feel like machitos and to begin stirring things up with your "political disquiet" and all that crap!

But I want to tell you, cabrón, in fact I'll scream it to you in case you turn out as deaf as your father: there will be no independent party in San Luis as long as I am Gonzalo N. Santos; I, and these things that hang from me [his testicles], will make sure of that!

Also don't start to think that I am going to make martyrs out of any of the sons of bitches in your group. You all have a lot to learn before that. . . . I'll just be pleased to make you clean the toilets of the penitentiary with your tongues. Now, with regard to you—and I am telling you this personally, so that you simmer your political "disquiet," since it seems that you are the most disquieted one—I am going to give you an easy choice: prison, banishment, or death ["encierro, destierro ó entierro"; these became known as Gonzalo's three "ierros"]. But I want a decision now, because I, like you, am also politically disquieted, and I want to serve you fast, so choose!

AOP: What should I choose for? Do whatever you want. I came here in all propriety to speak with you and you just mock me.

GS: Listen. Shut your trap and go to hell. Don't go looking for three-legged cats, because you'll find they have four. I won't screw you only because of my friendship with your grandfather. [AOP left the room and did not form his party].[13]

Although it would be precisely this petit-bourgeois group, under the leadership of the Nava brothers from San Luis, that would lead the movement against Gonzalo Santos in 1959, they may not have succeeded without the support that they enjoyed from president López Matéos.

The example cited above has many meaningful elements for an analysis of Gonzalo's relation with this protobureaucratic class. He had personal relations with many of the families involved (especially those from the Huasteca, as in the cited case); he had a total disrespect for their verbose appeal to ideals and principles, since his conception of politics was entirely in the realm of Realpolitik. He knew they were easily frightened with straightforward repressive measures (they had no experience in revolution, as he did). He did not respect the official language of courteousness that is used in "normal" Mexican political discourse, thus speaking "perfectly clearly" and disarming the ideologies behind the middle-class movements. Gonzalo's argumentative discourse forced the "friendly opposition" to state firmly their basic motivations or leave. In a way—although this interpretation is beyond that given by my middle-class informants, all of whom regard Gonzalo's discourse as a combina-

tion of immorality and cleverness—Gonzalo's regionalistic colloquial-
ism was an appeal to realism, to saying things as they actually are (in his
words, "not to look for three legged cats"). And the "way things are" is
that if you form a political group, you are after your own interests. This
is legitimate if your interests are compatible with mine, but if they are
not, you won't beat me by an appeal to ideology; you'll have to beat me
with power. In this sense, the middle classes were so weak that it wasn't
worth making them martyrs. Gonzalo's colloquial discourse—the regional sayings and the down-to-earth obscenities—was a way of accelerating contradictions in his own favor; it was a way of cutting budding
social movements short, and it was therefore used in the contexts where
Gonzalo had a stake in unmasking incipient opposition and setting
things clear while power was still on his side. At least this is true in his
use of regionalist discourse with competitors of his same level: the San
Luis elite and the petit-bourgeois opposition.

A crucial aspect of Santos's political use of Huastecan regional culture
was the way he legitimated speaking the "naked truth" through populism.
He confronted the middle-class politicians with this, as against the contorted political idiom of the central Mexican bureaucracy, and he also
used the technique at the national level, where popular culture is officially
respected.

One time don Gonzalo prepared a big political luncheon at El
Gargaleote. The guest of honor was the Minister of Hydraulic Works,
and the politicking was to be on the Pujal-Coy irrigation project. The
minister, who was a very tall man, was to arrive at Gonzalo's airstrip at
lunchtime, but was several hours late. By the time he finally arrived, the
guests were tired and hungry. Don Gonzalo (who, by that time, was
angry) greeted him:

"What's up, my *mazacoate?*"

The Minister gave Gonzalo a puzzled look.

"You don't know what a *mazacoate* is?"

"No, Don Gonzalo, what is it?"

"The mazacoate is the biggest snake in the Huasteca, and it's just like you:
big and frightening, but harmless. It doesn't do a thing."

Another anecdote: in a discussion of the feasibility of the Pujal-Coy
irrigation system, Gonzalo called the Minister of Agriculture a brute in
front of President Diaz Ordaz and others. "The man knows nothing
about animals (livestock) or people," he said, and then he put his hand
to his hip and began to pull out his gun. The minister said, "No, don

Gonzalo, [don't shoot]. I am unarmed." To which Gonzalo answered: "On top of it he is not a man. If he was he would carry a gun. Give him one!"

And yet another anecdote from the struggle over Pujal-Coy: The Minister of Hydraulics received a sack of meat and cheese and a sack of corn, courtesy of don Gonzalo. Some time later, Santos asked the minister, "How did you like my gifts?" And the minister answered, "Wonderful, don Gonzalo, the cheese and the meat were splendid!" "You see," Gonzalo retorted, "it's what I've been trying to tell you. The Huasteca is for cheese and meat, not for corn."

Santos thrived on the tactical uses of bold, frank, and open ranchero machismo in the otherwise extremely formal milieu of central Mexican government. The manly ideology of the authentic revolutionary, the frankness that a charismatic leader allows himself, the feeling of racial superiority over Indians, all of these came through and brought a certain fear and respect to Gonzalo even in the national arenas. At the presidential addresses that are delivered every September 1, Gonzalo was known to arrive and sit wherever he liked, regardless of the punctilious seating arrangements.

The Gonzalo Santos lore is enormous and entertaining (except to his victims). But what I wish to show through it is that Gonzalo successfully utilized ranchero culture in a national forum, to the extent that he was the master of the Huasteca, overlord of San Luis for over twenty years, and one of Mexico's most important politicians for most of his lifetime. It is interesting to note that in this task of dignifying (through fear and respect) his ranchero background in national government, Gonzalo succeeded where many others, including his predecessor Cedillo, failed. Whereas Cedillo's peasant origins were almost always a political handicap, Santos made ranchero culture into an asset. But Gonzalo's success stemmed in part from the fact that he came from a dominant class. He was not easily humbled; he was used to giving orders. Gonzalo cultivated Huastecan culture because it was the source and context of his particular kind of power, Cedillo never found a way of using his native culture to attain political advantages outside of his native peasant domain.

Manipulation of Symbols for Intraregional Power

The preceding analysis reveals the tensions between Huastecan intimate cultures, in that the ranchero class combines its own culture of individual superiority with populist elements that legitimate its hegemony. A few examples of manipulation are indispensable for a general discussion of ranchero localism as a program for regional hegemony.

The ranchero class as a whole cultivates its knowledge of the region. In the days that I spent with rancheros, gossip sessions on the particularities of the region's history were important (and not because of my presence). In this sense, Gonzalo Santos is once again a prototype, for he attempted to lead the ranchero class culturally into its own roots. He demanded ranchero pride in Huastecan culture, and gave it symbolic prevalence over the culture of central San Luis (culminating in the transfer of San Luis's kiosk to Tampamolón). He firmly established that there is a Huastecan way of doing things; that if an outsider came to the region, (s)he must become familiarized with the region's ways.[14] Knowledge of the region, of its geography, its history, its fauna, were attributes that legitimated local power.

A second facet of the cultivation of regional knowledge is its utility in managing intraregional relations with the Indians and peones. The conscious incorporation of Indian beliefs, customs, and traditions into the discourse and actions of the ranchero classes only occurs at specific political conjunctures. We shall see later that it is the regional intellectual groups that take on a more consistent and continuous preoccupation with the place of Indian culture in the region. In "normal," day-to-day, interethnic affairs, the rancheros ignore the Indians' ways and simply impose their own desires in their own terms; this is, after all, the ranchero's privilege as regional elite. These privileges even include—as we shall see—the downgrading of Indians through verbal abuse and economic exploitation. The contexts in which Indian culture has been consciously taken into account and manipulated by the rancheros are situations where the general terms of global interrelations between rancheros and Indians are renewed, or else they are situations that need exemplary shows of culturally legitimized ranchero domination.

In the first case, we have the examples of the roles played by ranchero elites in the renewal of Indian local authorities or the case of accepting and fomenting the presentation of Indian dances in important political occasions, such as the visit of a governor or a president. In both of these cases, the rancheros play with Indian subordination in Indian terms. Rancheros are placed in a caste position of legitimate power (I shall present details of this in the following chapter on Indian culture and ideology.) In other words, the context of renewal of relations between the Indians and the powers that be (renewal of Indian offices, Indian support to Mestizo political figures) allows for the presentation of ranchero/Indian relations in terms of a spiritual and economic division of labor between the two groups, despite the fact that this view runs contrary to the liberal tradition of individualism and individual and clan domination that is at the center of the ranchero's self-definition.

This kind of ranchero concession to and manipulation of Indian intimate cultures can be seen in specific political cleavages. Gonzalo Santos, who himself spoke Huasteco, offers two interesting examples. The first is his use of diabolical imagery and of an alleged pact with the Devil for the legitimation of his personal power and superiority. This aspect of Gonzalo's rule is not mentioned in his memoirs, but is there to be described in the region, where it is sometimes said that Gonzalo had a ring with the figure of the Devil on it, that he had a statue of the Devil at Gargaleote, that he had a pact with the Devil.

These sayings of popular lore were in fact actively supported by Gonzalo himself (being superstitious, he knew these images well[15]). The name of his ranch, El Gargaleote, is also interesting in this regard: Santos took the name from the infamous French counterguerrillas who operated under the orders of General Lepin and tortured Juaristas in the Huasteca during the French intervention (1862–67). Santos's family, like many of the region's rancheros, were Juaristas; but Gonzalo appropriated the position of the French and called his own (armed) followers his "gargaleotes." The most famous and important of them was known as El Mano Negra (black hand). Mano Negra wore a black glove and often dressed in black; he became an integral part of the image of Gonzalo Santos in the region and is a figure who comes up frequently when people speak of santismo. (I have heard Indians of Tanchahuil refer to the rural policemen that operated during Santos's cacicazgo as *manos negras*.)

The image of a killer-assistant dressed in black was probably taken from an Indian dance—one of the few that have become popular with mestizo cowboys and peones—known as the dance of the Huehues (elders), but known in mestizo towns also as *viejadas* or *parrandas*. These parrandas are done at carnival (especially in Indian towns) and during the Day of the Dead in mestizo towns, notably San Martín, San Vicente, Tanquián, El Higo, and Tantoyuca. They consist of a kind of square dance made up of two rows of dancers that face each other; one is of masked men dressed in the attire of the main kinds of professions in the region (in San Vicente I saw cowboys, oil-workers and licenciados), and the other is of male transvestites. These two rows furiously dance to the orders of a "captain," who has diabolical attributes and is sometimes identified as a devil, an assistant (known as *el látigo,* "the whip," or *el vaquero,* "the cowboy"), and a bull. The assistant is dressed in black, with a black mask, cowboy pants, a gun, and a whip. This figure is very similar to Mano Negra in both attire and position.

The diabolical associations of this dance are also important in other important aspects of its organization. Dancers are said to make a pledge to the dancing group to dance for seven years, and they must dance for exactly that period to "liberate" their "obligation." In the dances of the

Day of the Dead, the parranda sometimes ends at the edge of the cemetery, where some of the dancers enter into a state of convulsion and are "possessed" by the Devil. The Devil, the Devil's assistant, and the bull circle around, intermingle with, and run across the geometrically arranged male and "female" dancers. The image that emerges is of a carnivalesque farce of society (the dancers in the two rows) being driven and harangued by the Devil, who is a ranchero, complete with Mano Negra and cows.

In this example, we see Gonzalo Santos utilizing a traditional image of the Devil, and of life in the rancho, in order to mystify the real bases of his awe-inspiring personal power. Gonzalo used these elements of popular imagery in order to prove a principle which, to paraphrase his son Gastón, could be restated as follows:

> Indians of the Huasteca are marginal socially, culturally and economically. The Revolution, and all major social movements, were carried out by the ranchero class. Why? Because they are richer, whiter and more intelligent. And within that class, the Santos family was always the richest and the most intelligent.

The final example that I offer is less intricate, but shows the general principles behind ranchero manipulation of the intimate cultures of subordinate Huastecan groups. It is a conversation between Gonzalo Santos and President Calles at the outbreak of the Cristero movement:

> General Calles told me, "Take this flag with the Virgin of Guadalupe [which was captured in a battle against insurgents] and wave it in Congress, make for a lot of agitation in the House and say in your speech that this flag of the Virgin of Guadalupe is not the one that Miguel Hidalgo waved from the church of Atotonilco, that this flag was in fact painted by nuns, maybe even American nuns, throw yourself against them, fill them with threats, and tell them that the government will defend the Constitution with blood and fire until we exterminate them if we have to." I told Calles, "My general, I am going to keep this flag as a historical token, and instead I will have a flag made with the image of Christ and the words *Cristo Rey* underneath, because we are going to keep the virgin of Guadalupe for ourselves, we'll need her when we sic the agraristas on them and we'll just leave them [the rebels] with Christ. Remember general, during the Revolution, that the troops from the center of the country, for example those of Carrera Torres and Cedillo [he could have added Zapata] always had an image of the Virgin of Guadalupe on their hats, but no one, in none of the revolutionary regions ever put on a Niño de Atocha, or a Christ or Sacred Heart; they all carried the Virgin of Guadalupe in their hats, this not by the Huastecan or northern troops who used turkey feathers or leather straps, but by the troops from the religious Catholic [*mocho*]

regions." The general approved my idea. Alvarez himself had the painting of Christ made, with evil intentions by the way, since they painted a Christ with the face of a criminal, of a hypocritical Jesuit. (1986:310)

Evidently, this manipulation of popular religion eased the way for recruitment of Huastecan Indians (Gonzalo's "agraristas") through economic incentives (agrarian reform): the land, the virgin, and the supremo gobierno struck keys that were closer to the Indian's hearts than that of Christ, the priest, and the hacendado.

In the material that I have presented in this chapter, I hope to have shown some of the principles of ranchero self-identification, which I have described in terms of a particular understanding of a nineteenth-century liberal tradition, wedded to an ethos of courage, manliness, and knowledge of weapons, of the countryside, and of horses. In a word, ranchero self-image and self-legitimation is constructed upon liberalism wedded to a mode of production that required a *don de mando* (the gift of commanding). This ranchero ethos produces a particular form of egalitarian and "frank" or "open" discourse that was well manipulated in the defense of regional power and regional autonomy. It even served Gonzalo well in his quite considerable power at the national level. At the same time, rancheros have had to recognize tacitly the need to manipulate Indian (and, to a lesser degree, peon) culture in terms that are other than their own: the terms of caste deference for Indians, and the terms of a diabolical pact for lower-class mestizos. Moreover, ranchero "frankness" also contrasts with the mannerisms of Mexico City and San Luis elites. The ranchero egalitarian language and ethos can be manipulated in order to present ranchero regionalism as a grass-roots popular ideology, instead of as the ideology of the local dominant class. Rancheros are thereby creatively orchestrating relationships with quite a variety of groups. Although they have not been able to impose their views at the level of the national state, they have been able to gain respect for them at the regional level, where they continue to grow and to prosper.

12

Indian Localism

The material that follows is presented to illustrate the ways in which localist ideology operates in an Indian community. As in the case of the previous chapter, where I privileged the analysis of a single case, the material I present is mainly from several interviews I had with Juan Santos, a monolingual Huasteco speaker from the community of Tanchahuil. My interviews with Juan Santos were the richest cultural materials that I was able to obtain. I had hired Juan's son Cayetano as translator and had worked with him for several weeks before we interviewed him. I interviewed people in Tanchahuil for several weeks. Six months later, I was able to direct three more months of fieldwork by two students, Miguel Angel Riva Palacio and Adriana López, both of whom have provided interesting historical and economic data to contextualize this interview.[1] In the pages that follow, I present the substance of my interviews with Juan so that the reader may enter the rhythm of research in this setting. After a full presentation of these interviews, I provide a general conclusion on what this sort of material implies for Indian localist ideology and the relation between Indian intimate culture and the position of these cultures in regional hegemonic organization.

Tanchahuil is a Huastec-speaking community in the municipio of San Antonio. It has approximately 1,100 inhabitants in a dispersed settlement pattern. Most huts are built near the *parcelas* (farmland) of their owners, and because land is generally passed on only to males, there are usually small complexes of huts that correspond to patrilineally related grand families.

Cayetano and I arrived at Juan's hut, which was invisible from the main road. Juan and I were introduced, and the conversation began. I asked Juan whether he was born "here" (I meant Tanchahuil; Juan interpreted this to mean the spot where his house is). He answered yes, that he, his father, and his grandfather had all been born near where his house is. Juan's father was called Domingo Mushi' and his grandfather was Juan Mushi'. The last name Mushi' designated the hill that is behind their houses; Mushi' is the family place.

I asked how it was that Juan's father and grandfather had the last name Mushi' when his own was Santos. To this he answered that people had two names, the *nombre de registro* (legal name) and the name by which they are known in the community. His father's legal name was Antonio Santiago, but in the community he was Domingo Mushi'; Juan's legal name is Juan Santos, but he is known in the community as Lucas Mushi'; Cayetano is locally known as Isidro. . . . I asked Cayetano whether he preferred that I call him Isidro, as he was known in the community, but he preferred that I use his "real" (legal) name. Cayetano does not unambivalently like these customs, at least not in front of people like me.

I asked Juan why they had two names, and he answered first with the self-deprecation for which Indians are well known: "Because until now we had no education [*estudios*] we have this custom of two names. When we go to register our children in San Antonio [the cabecera], we do not already know what the child is to be called, so we invent a name at the spur of the moment and then later use the one that we really wanted." Juan also claimed that they register children with another name as a defense within the community, because people within the community usually do not know each other's "real (legal) name."[2]

I asked Juan whether his was the only family that used their place name as a last name, and he said that, quite to the contrary, most families had this. "In the hill called 'Itz [moon] there lives a man called Martín and his son Diego 'Itz. Another family is called Mantub [stone], another is C'oyol [made of izote]. Also in a hill called Cubat Acanlab [post] there lives the family of Miguel Meléndez and Martín González. This particular hill is called Mushi' because a long time ago a man lived here. [At this point Cayetano stopped translating because, he said, there was no Spanish word. I asked him to continue.] The man who brings wind, rain, and thunder. That man lived here before, when there were no people here. That man was called Maam.[3]

"Before it didn't rain. When Maam was here it didn't rain, it was always hot. Then Maam's [male] children told him to go to L'ejem [in this case, the sea, but a neighboring community is also called L'ejem] to bring clouds for rain. Before Maam used to work, and it never rained. That is why he went to raise a cloud in the sea. Since the day he went to the sea, he has never come back, because he never died. He stayed there to bring water for rain.

"That man [Maam] left the hill and never returned home. His children remained and died because of the water. It used to rain very much and the water rose to the sky. But that man never did return, although we see him in June and July [the rainy season] when there is thunder. We can work and he brings the water.

"When Maam went to bring the wind and the water he ordered his children to make a wooden box [*cajón*]. The children got into the crate and because of this they did not die. Some of them brought along a lunch [*poc'te'*], a lunch of toasted tortillas so that they would not turn sour. When the crate was reaching the sky, some men had found refuge under the ground, so one of the children in the crate was ordered to open the underground hole with a crowbar and all of those men died.

"Of the many children that had gotten into the crate, only one had taken his lunch, so all the children died but three. When the water went down, this man was so hungry that he ate some of the dead men raw. That man lives to this day, and his name is buzzard [*to't*], he eats the dead.

"Another person who also survived the flood withstood his hunger. He made a milpa and controlled his hunger all of the time of the sowing. But when the stalks grew and elotes sprang forth, he realized that there was nothing with which to heat the corn. So he made fire with three sticks [*bachipe*]. But those men did not withstand hunger well and they ate the corn half raw. The owner of the milpa [not the man who plowed, but a kind of god] put the corncobs in those people's anuses and they then stayed with an animal's name. They are squirrels [*o'te'*].

"There was a third survivor who also did not withstand his hunger. He picked up the dead fish that were on the ground and ate them raw. That man was also transformed into an animal, he is the raccoon. These are the only three animals that are people, all the others are animals. That's where this ends.

"Then men were born who worked on the milpa, but those men did not eat, they only smelled the food—the tortillas and the coffee—and were satiated by the smell. After smelling the food they left it behind, they threw it away. These men had three legs, but they did not last many years. They were called *lintzi'* because they had three feet and did not eat food. They were extinguished because they threw away the food.

"When those men died, we were born. We eat everything, we eat tortillas and don't throw away our food. We do not have a name, because we do not lose our food, we eat it.

"But now, with the years, things are changing. The years are passing. Now it is 1984, next it will be 1986, 1987, 1988, 1989, 1990, until we reach 2000. We don't know whether they will allow us to continue or whether there will be another people on that year and we shall all perish. Some people, the ones that go to church, those will still live. Those that don't go will die. Christ will say whether they will let us all live or whether we will all die, "el virgen" will also determine this. This is where this story ends.

"We respect Maam every year when we sow our milpas. Maam ordered that the milpa be "respected" [*cac'nal alilab* means a recognition, a gratefulness, to the milpa]. He said that the people who go to work in March would chop down the forest [*monte*], in April they would burn the fields, and in May they would plant. That is when they will make the *respetación* [ritual of respect, in this case to Maam]. They will make *bolimes* [a kind of giant tamal made with an entire chicken] and atole so that when Maam comes everything will be planted. Later on, when they clean the fields, when the first elotes come, when they first pick elotes, they will again remember Maam and make atole and cuiches, and pay their respects. They bring the elotes whole and put them under an arch, along with flowers, bolimes, aguardiente, and copal.[4] There they will remember Maam, he is the first to receive these offerings that they make here."

At this point I asked Juan whether in this first respetación to Maam they did not also honor San Isidro Labrador (May 15) and Juan said the following: "Isidro was a person who worked very hard; he did not rest a single day. He worked with the plow. One Sunday he was working when he realized that he was dragging some angels with the plow. Since then he became forever responsible [*encargado*] for work, and that is why to this day we remember and respect those days." Juan also said that Maam and Isidro's respetaciones were distinct and carried out on different days: Maam's exactly before planting, Isidro's on May 15. Both are very close together, "but one is for he who brings the water, and the other is for the patron of work."

I then asked Juan why in Huastecan dances all the women move in a circle. Juan answered that they did not do this in all the dances, but that they do so because there are people that say that the earth floats on water. "The women who dance in a circle are asking that when they die they be buried on the edges of the earth and that the men will stay inside, in the center."

I was not understanding all of this. I tried to question Juan but could not get any clearer. The next day I tried again by asking why the women were on the edges and the men in the center. "The women are like the posts in the house, they sustain the world. The men are inside, as if they were inside the house."[5]

In an attempt to understand the main elements of Huastecan ritual, I then asked Juan why the dancers of the rituals always drank heavily. He said, "The dancers drink because they are guarding themselves against the devil. They drink as an offering to the devil, so that the devil gets drunk and will not harm them further. The dancers also respect the devil so that he will not send sickness to their families. They place bolimes and aguardiente on a table at the house of the *o'tesh* [captain of the dance] before beginning; there are people who pray the rosary, or they bring in a *rezandero* to pray. They then eat the offering and dance a little outside. With this the fiesta does not fall ill [*no se enferma la fiesta*]. This is done in all the fiestas where there is dancing: July 24 (Santiago Apostol), September 15 (Miguel Hidalgo), September 28 (San Miguel), and from December 24 to December 31. They make the offering in the house of the o'tesh. The dancers must drink a lot for the devil to get drunk. If they do not make an offering at the beginning of the ceremony, then the devil dances in front of all the dancers, the men begin to quarrel and fall ill.

"All diseases are caused by the devil. Also witchcraft exists to cause disease. If a dancer does not in fact respect that which he is dancing to respect, for example if he does not carry a bottle of aguardiente, all the other dancers will notice that he is not respecting and they will wish him ill, he will be sick and if he is not cured he will die. He can be cured either by a doctor or a healer.

"There are persons that are sorcerers and they can do harm, but here in Tanchahuil there are none. Now there are none, but there used to be; someone bewitched [*brujeaba*] people. They are called witches [or sorcerers, *brujos*] because they bring earth from the cemetery, take it to where there is an enemy and leave it in the house. That person gets sick. At that point the witch speaks with the devil and asks him to persecute that person. To this day there is someone in Tampamolón who is a healer but also knows how to *brujear.* When he bewitches someone, that person dies if he cannot find medicine.

"For example, there is a man that lives up the hill. He never respected his dance. Now he is sick. He has been in bed for months, and he dreamed with the dancers all the time, until finally they brought the dancers to dance in his home, but even that was not enough for him to heal, because he never took his offering when he danced and with that he got sick. They have taken him to a doctor, but he has not healed. The people who made him fall ill were his companions from the dance. When they saw that he did not respect, they sent him the devil, and even though they themselves later tried to lift the spell, they did not succeed.

"When the dancers make an offering with bolimes, when they bring *el socio* ["the partner," a kind of middleman spirit], the dancers bring a violin and a guitar and place them under the table. Then the socio comes. Each dancer has his cup of aguardiente. One by one they pour aguardiente in each corner of the table; they drink whatever is left over. They must finish a liter of aguardiente in this fashion. Then they eat the bolimes and when they are through they begin to dance. El socio will ask God for their welfare. They ask God [through el socio] that they not fall ill, that they not fight amongst themselves, that they remain together."

At this point I remembered other parts of Mexico, where the devil is sometimes referred to as "el socio," and so I asked Juan whether el socio was the devil, to which he emphatically answered no, el socio is a go-between, a middleman. The following day I asked Juan whether the socio was a person or a spirit and he said he was a spirit. I asked him whether the spirit was an Indian; he said no. I asked him whether the spirit was a mestizo; he said yes. However, in some rituals an Indian plays the role of el socio.[6]

I then asked Juan whether the dancers were asked to dance in the name of the whole community, and he said no, that they dance for themselves and that they plead for the welfare of their group. It is interesting to note, however, that most dancing groups are made up of people from distinct neighborhoods, which means that they are usually patrilineally related. Membership to a dance tends to be hereditary, although there is no obligation that this be so. The use of copal incense in dances and respetaciones is to salute the souls and communicate with them. "Copal smoke communicates our sentiments to the souls, and we burn copal over the offerings and over the table before eating the food that we offer to the Dead or other respected beings."

This day's interview ended here. Juan, Cayetano, and I were excited and exhausted. I walked down the hill amid the brush and the cane fields and returned to my urban-middle-class headquarters in Valles. The following day we resumed. Juan had prepared new stories, but I began with questions from the interviews of the previous days.

"Maam made the first rain. Before Maam there was no one, when Maam went to the sea and made rain, the first people began working their milpas and they continue to do so to this day.

"There used to be a big tree that had no thorns. That tree had a fruit that had no thorns but that was not edible. At that time the people were very foolish [andaban muy tontos], they did not fight, they were foolish, they did not study, they were very serious, they did not fight. In each community some of those people remained to take care of the trees. When the tree gave its fruit, a man would cut it, peel it, and make rattles [sonajas]. That's where the name of this community comes from [Tancha-huil is a hispanization of Tam Tz'ahuil: Tam= locative; Tz'ahuil= rattle[7]].

"The community of L'ejem got its name because there used to be a lagoon there that was never dry." I asked Juan how it was that a man had stayed in each community to guard a tree, and he clarified. "A man *and a woman* stayed in every community to guard the sign of that community [the tree in Tanchahuil, the lagoon in L'ejem], of these couples sprang today's communities. Each couple was like a seed, from which sprang children, who in turn married and had more children and the community grew to what it is today.

"Tanchahuitz got its name because that's where San Miguel [the Patron Saint of Tancanhuitz] is, and we took many flowers to San Miguel since there were no other churches but the one in Tancanhuitz. Most people went to Mass over there, and they took flowers. Tancanhuitz means flowers." At this point I (maliciously) asked why the town's full name was Tancanhuitz *de Santos,* knowing that Gonzalo Santos's decision to rename the town after his brother Pedro Antonio did not suit the logic of Juan's origin myth. Juan thought a little and answered, "It is Tancanhuitz de Santos because we take flowers to the saints [*a los santos*]."

I asked Juan why the first inhabitants of the communities were foolish. "They were called foolish because they allowed people to take their chickens and pigs and for those people to eat them while they remained serious and did nothing to the pig and turkey thieves. That was because they didn't study, they had no study and did not know how to read or anything. Then there began the school and teachers came and people began to send their children there and people began to notice that the people were taking the animals—cows too—and they began to defend themselves because they already knew what money was. And now there are more schools and teachers and people don't allow a person to take their things just like that, without paying."

Because I knew from interviews with other people in Tanchahuil that until recently mestizos in the market towns often took Indian products and consumed them without paying, I asked whether the people that took the animals and food were from the comunidades or whether they were mestizos. "The people who took those things were mestizos. They came here to do that, but later on the owners of the houses would not let them in to take more things out. Schools arrived and people began to think that it was not good to allow them to steal chickens; those people came here only to rob and the people here were very foolish, they did not know how to speak Spanish. Mestizos don't like to work, they only like to steal pigs.

"At that time there was no road, and that's why they liked to steal. Because here the people liked to plant their milpas, also frijoles, and those people liked to take those corn cobs and beans. Later they opened up roads and those people left. At that time there were no pueblos [market towns, cabeceras] or municipal presidents with whom to complain. They [the mestizos] would take the pilón and the corn, they took all of that. Then the people would remain with nothing. Later there were municipal presidents and places where one could complain, and since then people began to work at ease [a gusto]. Today we go to work and we leave the house alone, when we come back we find everything that we left behind.

"When there was no road people would walk along a track to Santos;[8] there they would sell coffee, corn and beans. The people who went on Saturdays would stay until Sunday, which is the market day, and would return on Sunday at midnight. Well, those were the ones who didn't drink, because the ones who drank would pass out on the way back and did not arrive home until Monday.

"Since the roads were built we now go to several places for market: Tampamolón, Coxcatlán, even as far as Tanquián. Now it is not so hard to take the piloncillo out to the roads. Before we sold more coffee than pilón; later we planted more sugar cane and we stopped selling corn and beans. To this day we continue to work the sugar cane, but now it is easy to take the pilón to Santos. Before we would take it on horseback or on one's own back. They didn't used to pay by the kilo, but by dobles; coffee was sold by the fanega: 1 fanega was 50 cuartillos, 1 cuartillo was 3 dobles. They paid very little for the coffee, two pesos and 50 centavos. Almost everyone sold only coffee, that's what they did for their work. The people who dried their own coffee and ground it in morteras would sell their coffee by the pound."

I asked Juan whether he did not himself experience the time when people stole the things of the community. He said his grandfather had lived during that time, and he told Juan everything. His father also lived through this; he told Juan, who is about fifty, that they buried all that they had—plates, jugs, cups, metates—so that when the people arrived at their house they would find it empty. "There were many mountains, at that time there were almost only mountains, not like today when there are no more mountains."[9]

"During that time [what follows is a narration of the Revolution] when they stole things, they also took the people, they took the owners of the plates and forced them to work as peones for the mestizos, and they killed the little children on the roadside and left them hanging on trees. They killed the children and took the older people, men and women. Those mestizos lived in Tibtzen [municipio of Tampamolón], that's where they had their houses. They called their house cuartel [military barracks; Juan said the word in Spanish]. That's where they took the people's things, at that time there was no pueblo of Tampamolón. They hid the women there and they made them make their tortillas, and they would go out to rob some more. It was a cuartel that they had there, it was their house. Later on, the pueblos were formed and the mestizos left. The men that they took from the communities worked as peones, they had to skin the pigs that the mestizos stole, they were also forced to fight. The person who didn't want to go would be hung on a tree, and the people who went with them had to fight.

"They didn't take my father because he was hidden, he didn't go out of his house. He ate in the forest, where he took his metate [a utensil for grinding corn and whatever else needs grinding] and his plates. There in the forest they made their tortillas. When the mestizos left they returned to their houses. Then they brought back their metates and pots and began sleeping in their houses again because the mestizos had gone. There were very few people in Tanchahuil because many had been taken away and slaughtered, few remained.

"Those who remained suffered a lot because God sent them a punishment. It didn't rain a bit. Three years passed without rain, they couldn't work because there was no rain. Then they were hungry. They finished their corn and there was no food. They began eating little green reeds of corn and sugar cane, others ate only chiles, those we call *piquines* that grow in the forest. The punishment came because many of the dead were left on the roadside, because they were not buried. Those punishments came because many people died.

"The people who had been doing the killing were finished because the government was created and it did not allow people to remain fighting. People began working at ease. The people that remained went to church to confess, to say that they were safe and that nothing had happened to them. They asked God to allow them to work at ease and for those people that came to kill never to return. And to this day they do not allow anyone to fight. If someone fights they take him to jail and charge him fines, and they fight no more, they work at ease.[10]

"At that time there were no priests. There was only one who was in charge of all of the pueblos that had a church [the cabeceras[11]]. Not like today, when all of the comunidades have a church or chapel. Now we have Mass here as well. There are now priests that make the masses and they sometimes come to the comunidades."

Because Juan is very devout, I asked him whether he was not bothered by the fact that the priests speak in Spanish while Juan does not speak or understand it. He answered, "I am used to speaking Spanish in the Mass. God understands all of the languages that are spoken, Nahuatl, Huasteco, Spanish, and English, but He speaks Spanish. It is that way also with the priests, they can understand what you say to them in Huasteco or Nahuatl, although we cannot understand what they say in Spanish.

"The priests can understand Huasteco and Nahuatl because God can understand them. Later the priests have hired catechists who can speak

Spanish and Huasteco, those catechists helped to make the chapels and now we send our children to the *doctrina* [Sunday School]. Today there are many catechists who speak Spanish and many people speak in only one language with the priest.[12] It used to be the case that there were Spanish speakers only in Santos. Now Spanish has spread out and they speak Spanish everywhere. Before there were not too many of those people, they were in Santos and Coxcatlán and in Tampamolón (the cabeceras), but they have grown and grown and now there are many people who speak Spanish."

At this point I began reviewing with Juan some of the more opaque (to me) points in the interviews. I began again with why the women dance in a circle.

"In the dances the women are left on the outskirts of the earth so that it [the earth] has force. It is like the beams that give force to a house, that sustain it. That is why the women must remain on the edges of the earth and the men must remain inside, just as we are in this house now.

"Before there weren't many women, there were only men. Then they cut some ribs [Juan represented a longitudinal cut] from the man and they told that man to buy colored yarn [that Huastecan women use in their hair], dresses, rings, black skirts, and a blouse. When the sun rose the woman was there, all dressed up with the things that the man had bought: dresses, earrings and also the *petope* [the yarn headdress], and even to this day the women still wear it, although there are some that don't use it." When Juan was a boy almost all women wore their petopes. Today more women wear dresses because the other way is more expensive, one spends a lot buying yarn, medals and earrings. "Those women wear dresses because they are easier to make, and so they do not wear yarn, earrings, or medals."[13]

I then asked Juan to tell me more about the souls that communicate with copal. He does not know where the souls go, but many people say that the soul goes to heaven while the body remains buried. "When someone dies, people go to buy him new clothes and they are very well dressed when they are buried. When the soul is going to arrive to heaven it will not be punished if it went to Mass. Those who do not go to church are punished by God. They are thrown into the fire and left there, they are not taken out. If you do go to church you still get punished, but not very much: you get thrown into the fire but later they pull you out and give you no more punishments. Those souls get punished a little because they have behaved a little badly.

"On the Day of the Dead [probably the most important feast in the region] the souls come and visit their relatives. November 30 is the last day in which the souls remain on earth. On that day they go back to heaven. On the 30th, the Day of San Andrés, they make an offering, they make tamales and cut flowers again. On the Day of the Dead people make little paths with *cempoalxochitl* [the orange flower of the dead] that lead into their houses so that the souls may find their way to the offerings.

"During the whole month of November the souls are with us, and although we can't see them, they can see all that we do. They come to get the offerings that we make for them and they take them as a lunch. On November 30 they go back to heaven because they are there as if in a jail; all the souls return and are locked up there. The offerings one leaves for them must last them a full year in heaven. The door of heaven is opened on Saint Peter's Day (June 29) and the souls start coming to earth from that day on. The souls are with us from June 29 to November 30.

"We cannot see the souls, but they see us, and they see the offerings that we leave them. They cannot speak, but they see and they hear. If they want something, one dreams whatever it is that they want and one puts it in their offering for them to pick up. The soul finally leaves because it has gathered its offering; if there is no offering left, the soul departs with hunger and it will remain hungry in heaven."

Juan often dreams of his deceased wife and her wants. Once he dreamed that she was sitting on a stone; she was carrying a bag but said that she was hungry, that she had not eaten a thing. There were other souls that also had their bags and they gave her something to eat from them. Since Juan dreamed this he has made a special offering to his wife on the anniversaries of her death and leaves her extra food for her not to suffer.

Another day I asked Juan about the cargos and offices in Tanchahuil. Juan has been *segundo vocal del juez* and was charged with visiting all houses to announce meetings, to ask for money for communal ventures, and to organize the faenas (communal work that takes place several times a week). This cargo is also known as that of *alcale* (without a *d*), and there are always fifteen or eighteen of them. If they do not do their job the *juez,* who is the most important local political figure, reports them to the municipal president in San Antonio.

"The juez carries a rod that is adorned with colored ribbons. The rod is like a woman. They put red, white, and green ribbons on the rod, like the flag next to the Virgin of Guadalupe [he pointed to an image on his table]. The rod is the one that makes sure that nothing happens to the authorities. It is for the juez to have force or strength during the period in which he keeps the rod. We also respect the rod. This happens three times a year: in January, in June, and in December. We buy many aguardientes and bread and we all chip in for some bolimes. We also pray a rosary. They do all of this so that nothing happens to the local authorities, so that they don't get sick, since they have the cargo of juez.

Every year the ribbons are changed. The incoming juez puts the new ribbons, the old juez takes off the old ones.

"The rod is going to be like the mother of the judges. They say that the rod is like a mother because before a new judge is selected, the person that is going to be judge dreams of a very beautiful woman, and that he and the woman like [love] each other. She is very well dressed and has ribbons. Afterward, when there is a village meeting, she will be watching over the one who is to be judge, and when he is finally selected, he will again dream with this woman. In this dream he greets the woman, and this means that he already has the cargo of judge. This is why it is like a mother."

I have presented the interview with Juan at length in order that the reader have a clearer idea of some of the elements in Huastecan intimate culture. Without these general elements a discussion of the spaces and forms of localist ideology are senseless.

The Indian cultures of the Huasteca are, along with ranchero culture, the most autonomous, coherent, intimate cultures. At the same time they are at the very bottom rung in the social ladder. They are apparently impermeable to non-Indian culture, and yet they are subordinated to mestizos. How is this paradox resolved? In Juan's explanations there are several elements of localist ideology that are extremely important to point to. I shall focus here on the following: the ideology of the Hispanic God; the conversion of Tancanhuitz de Santos into a Huastec place name; the love of law and order over chaos; the role of *el socio* in ritual; and the ideology of parallel worlds (Indian and Mestizo) that are linked by God and government.

In Juan's stories, there are several oppositional spaces between communities that are buttressed by different ideologies: there is the distinction between Huastec communities; there is the distinction between Huastec communities and seminomadic, predatory mestizo groups; and there is the distinction between Indians and established mestizo and Spanish groups of the cabeceras. These are the most relevant groups, although people also recognize the existence of Nahuatl-speaking peasants and of a few sporadic English speakers (the priest in San Antonio is Irish, and there is a hospital there run by American nuns). These groups are all interconnected by God, the Church, and the government.

The creation myths presented by Juan all enforce the moral and historical priority of the Huastec community as a whole. The people who finally survive the floods and prosper in the modern era are agriculturalists. These peasants are the basis of humanity, and they must respect the forces that created this order: Maam and the Owner of the Milpa. The first women were also meant to wear petopes, earrings, medals, and black skirts. The first places were created by Huastec couples that guarded Huastec place names.

But in this latter element, we already have the basis for distinction within the Huastec community. Contemporary Huastecans are descendants of different couples that were in charge of different tutelary objects. This element brings forth the possibility of distinguishing between the character of the members of different communities. Not only does each community stand for a family, but the internal cohesiveness of each community can derive into socio-psychological differentiation between communities. For example, the people of the community of Tzep-Acab (4 cane) are—according to people from Tanchahuil—supposed to be "tough as canes." So, the names of the communities can serve as a rich source of metaphors for conceptualizing differences between communities.[14] The internal differentiation between communities is also ritually expressed in the patron-saint festivities. Although the existence of patron saints for Huastec communities appears to be recent in this region: people still regard the patron saint of the cabecera to be the most important, and in many cases Indian communities have the same patron as their cabeceras or the cabeceras closest to them. Tanchahuil, for example, shares San Miguel with Tancanhuitz, and most people will still prefer to go to Tancanhuitz to celebrate San Miguel.

The historical priority of the Huastecs over mestizos is reaffirmed in Juan's transformation of Tancanhuitz de Santos into a fully Huastec place name. The attempt by the ranchero elite, in this case by Gonzalo Santos, to revalue Huastecan topography by changing Indian names to names of ranchero heroes is resisted.[15]

Another aspect of the assertion of the priority of Huastecan culture can be found in the syncretistic interpretations of national heroes, including national presidents and dignitaries. The colors of the virgin symbolically tie Guadalupe to Miguel Hidalgo, who is celebrated as a saint, to the rod of the *juez,* to the municipal president (who presides over the changing of the rod every January 1), to the national flag, and to the official party. These associations can be seen as serving the government because of the Indian support that is mustered through this ideology, but they also allow the Indians to place national government and national history in terms of their own cultural interpretation. The importance of this kind of syncretism has not been sufficiently underlined in the literature. Anthropologists and historians are fascinated by the task of relating pre-Hispanic religion to Catholicism, where, in fact, the sociologically most important syncretism is between government (including official history) and religion (including cosmogony). It is no doubt true that there is, in Juan's story, syncretism between pre-Hispanic religion and

Catholicism. We even see the conservation of Maam, a pre-Hispanic Huastec deity, and of a cosmogony that does not stem from the Bible. This concoction is a part of the intimate culture of Tanchahuil. But the syncretism between this interpretation of the nature of things and the official (state) interpretation of some of the same events is what is crucial for the *coexistence* between the two intimate cultures. Huastecans must twist their interpretations to fit some key elements of "national culture" because they are subordinated to it. It is precisely the nature of this subordination that determines the key elements of this "syncretism." Government institutions that affect Huastecans—especially the schools and the municipal presidency—require the presence of Huastecans on the major national holidays and on the election campaigns of official candidates for governor or for president. The National Indian Institute (INI) needs to show "its" Indians when officials are on tour, and Indians are publicly displayed in exchange for the support that INI gives them (especially in INI-controlled bilingual schools, but also, in some places, by economic projects—cooperatives, technical assistance—run by INI).

This "syncretism" allows for coexistence among extremely diverse intimate cultures by way of creating a Huasteco-centered interpretation of the culture of social relations. Huastecans that share Juan's ideas need not slip into an alien frame of cultural interpretation when they are dealing in Mestizo terms and logic, they have constructed in their own intimate culture an interpretation of this logic that sidesteps the challenges to Huastecan culture that would appear to be implicit in the mere fact of political and commercial subordination.

Thus, Juan's discourse involves the idea that Huastec culture is permeable to the dominant cultures, while at the same time assimilation is considered to be impossible, and perhaps also undesirable. The most fundamental statement in this tenor is contained in Juan's remarkable insistence on the fact that God himself is a Spanish speaker. Let me say that when we got to this part in the interview I had Juan and Cayetano go over this idea with me several times and in several different forms so that I could be positive that this is what he meant. And sure enough, the idea is that God, and therefore priests, can understand Huasteco although Huastecans cannot understand Spanish. At the same time, the vulnerability, permeability, and inferiority of Huastecan culture occurs only before God and priests, for everyone recognizes that average mestizos cannot understand Huasteco. We are confronted with an ideology of a subordinate inclusion of Huastecan culture within a dominantly Hispanic order; but the inferiority and subordination are not directly vis-à-vis all mestizos. Mestizos have an advantage with God, the Church, and the dominant order because they identify with the language of this order; however, they are not invested with all of its powers. This is why we get an image of Huastecan and mestizo worlds as being parallel, of never touching, while at the same time the Huastecan world is recognizably subordinated to the dominant national order.

This idea is found again, in different form, in the generally positive feeling toward government as arbiter among Huastecans, and among Huastecans and mestizos. Juan's account of the Revolution is perfectly fused to the rest of his story of creation. Juan never even mentioned the word "Revolution" or made any attempt to place it in another kind of temporal frame. During that time, the mestizos preyed on the "foolish" and "serious" Huastecos because there was no government, because there were no pueblos, only communities, mountains, and villainous mestizos running amok. The Huastecos liked to work, the mestizos liked to steal. Finally, after the brutal plundering of the comunidades, order was reestablished. The pueblos were formed, and in them government was established. This government controlled the mestizo thieves and allowed Huastecans to work in peace. It has also had its share of responsibility in the education of the Indians, in that it has financed roads and schools. Thus, the Huastecans alone, without government, were victims of the mestizos; but the Spanish-speaking government controlled and placed the foundations for eliminating the forceful and violent appropriation of Indian goods and lives. The culmination of this view of Huastecan dependence on a Hispanic order is, of course, the idea of a Hispanic God. Another telling expression of the same phenomenon is the part played by el socio in the respetaciones. El socio is a mestizo spirit that places the request of the Huastecos before God. A fully unambiguous interpretation of this element is difficult, and perhaps undesirable. At the risk of sounding entirely Durkheimian, I suggest that the image of el socio and his relations with God and the Indians is parallel to the image of government and bureaucracy. Indian requests will be heard and attended to only if they are spoken for by a Mestizo intermediary, who receives payment in return for his services.

These brief considerations allow us to conclude that (1) Huastecan (Indian) localist ideologies defend two major kinds of public spaces: communal territory and control over internal government and religion. (2) Because the high degree of coherence of Huastecan intimate culture occurs in a context of subordination, localist ideology is expressed by way of assimilating the culture of social relations into intimate culture, which is what I called syncretism here. Intimate culture is so important to and different from hegemonic regional culture that people develop an ideology of inclusion within that dominant order that is phrased in terms of intimate culture. In a sense, then, in Tanchahuil there is no Huastec localist ideology vis-à-vis government and regional order because its only possible form would be a struggle for cultural autonomy, and this is a kind of political movement that has many risks for the population. (3) Huastec localist ideology vis-à-vis government, and sometimes with respect to the Church, entails the recognition of subordination in a context of a plural society; it is an ideology of alliance with government within the frame of respect for the community. If this respect is not maintained, there is the distinct potential for a truly autonomist ideology to emerge.

13

Local Intelligentsia and the Flow of Regional Symbols in Localist Ideologies

We have seen how Gonzalo Santos used the regional culture of social relations in his favor at the regional and the national level. We have also seen how he used intimate ranchero culture to consolidate his standing within the regional ranchero class and with his political allies abroad. At the same time, Indian localist ideology has been shown to work in an entirely different logic. The coherence of Huastecan intimate culture and the subordinate position of these groups has made for the development of syncretism between selected elements of the regional and national cultures of social relations. The elements of subordination in those cultures of social relations are assimilated into a coherent intimate culture, thus stifling the challenge to Indian community and culture. In both of these cases, the internal coherence of culture is stressed. Gonzalo Santos's ideology stresses the coherence among ranchero intimate culture, Huastecan culture of social relations, and the true world of social relations (thence his "frank" and "open" discourse). Juan Santos's ideology gave unfragmented coherence to sacred history and political relations.

In both these cases we can perceive the relations among communities, power relations, and cultural relations in regional space. However, the entire picture is not yet complete, for the cases above outline a tension that exists in the hegemony of the regional versus national culture of social relations. Although Gonzalo Santos used his hegemonic regional culture profitably in national politics, Indians distinguish local mestizos and national authorities and tend to ally themselves with the latter. Likewise, I have shown that there is an incipient trend toward proletarianization of the mestizo rural workers, which also entails shifting alliances away from the regional elites and towards "national culture." Specific classes and communities seek to liberate themselves from the regional culture of social relations and are inserted into the national circuit, or at least they seek to play off regional hegemony against national hegemony. This aspect of the relations among intimate culture, regional hegemony, and localist ideology is best analyzed through a description of the localist discourses produced by different kinds of regional intellectuals. In this final chapter I shall analyze the different spaces for, and kinds of, Huastecan intellectuals. Then I shall conclude this section with a general consideration of the spatial organization and dynamics of Huastecan regional culture.

Residual, Dominant, and Emergent Forms of Production and Epistemological Spaces of Cultural Synthesis

In relation to his interest in dominant, residual, and emergent social formations, Gramsci developed the notion of "traditional" and "organic" intellectuals. Traditional intellectuals are those who represent and synthesize classes and social groups that are residual, whereas organic intellectuals represent dominant and emergent social classes and groups. Therefore, the Italian peasantry had only traditional intellectuals (most were schoolteachers or priests, for the Church was the main source of traditional intellectuals in the early twentieth century); the bourgeoisie had its organic intellectuals in the universities and liberal parties and in some elements of the Church; and the emergent proletarian class was in the process of creating an organic intelligentsia, especially through the Communist Party (the so-called "New Prince").

In this study of regional culture I am forced to reconsider the problem of intellectual syntheses of different class and group interests, because, after all, I have shown that regional cultures can best be thought of as *localized* transformations of these class-cultures ("intimate cultures") and their articulations in a context of regional and national hegemony ("culture of social relations"). Intellectuals of different classes and cultural groups are vested with the task of producing "coherent" cultural syntheses of intimate culture and of their place in the culture of social relations. This is why when we look at cultural syntheses in regional spaces we must widen the base of Gramsci's typology, for what interests us here is not only whether a given "intellectual" is traditional or organic, but whether the intellectuals in question are synthesizing intimate culture for the internal use of their group, whether they are creating coherence about a group on external demand, or whether they are invested with both an internal and articulatory function.[1] Our interest is less in the outcome of class struggle vis-à-vis the control of the Mexican state than in the description of the ways culture is hierarchically organized in Mexican regional spaces, so that intellectuals, too, must be located in the spatial dialectics of cultural production.

In the Huasteca I have already shown that the residual forms of production are the relations among rancheros and mestizo peones and the relations among the commercial rancheros and the Indians. The renegotiated ties between a modernizing ranchero class and the Indian peasantry, peasant Indian production, and the relations between the modernized rancheros and permanent mestizo wage-labor are dominant. The industrial forms of production, led in this case by state-owned corporations (the sugar industry and the oil industry, but also by private enterprises such as Nestlé, Cementos Mexicanos, Fibracel, and Ron Potosí) are emergent. Here is also an emergent quasi-urban petite bourgeoisie of small-scale merchants, civil servants, and the salaried technician classes (teachers, social security workers, secretaries, doctors, lawyers, and the like). In the description that follows I will explore the different kinds of spaces occupied by Huastecan "intellectuals."

The Huasteca has very limited institutional space for an intelligentsia. The first high school in the region was built in the 1970s. Today there is a kind of junior college affiliated with the State University of San Luis that operates out of Valles. None of this is or has been enough to sustain a university trained intellectual class. Most of the people with sophisticated education are ranchers or businessmen who have sought out a profession before settling back in the Huasteca.[2]

There are two kinds of structural positions for intellectuals in the Huasteca. One is in the articulation of different levels of regional political organization, and the other is at the pinnacle of the internal organization of specific communities or intimate cultures. In the first position we have (a) cultural representatives of localities vis-à-vis the region (priests, teachers, non-professional intellectuals), (b) cultural representatives of the region vis-à-vis state and federal government and intellectuals, and (c) political representatives of localities and the region vis-à-vis state and federal politicians and investors. In the second position we have (a) major local cultural figures (local savants, curanderos, doctors, priests, rezanderos, schoolteachers), and (b) spokesmen for major local economic figures (men of commerce and rancheros).

Some intellectuals share a strong internal and articulatory function, whereas others are more strictly internal or mostly articulatory. I shall call the intellectuals that have both internal and articulatory legitimacy "organic"; the strictly internal intellectuals will be called "traditional" and the strictly articulatory intellectuals will be "provisional," insofar as their existence depends on an incipient external need for connections with groups and institutions that are internally weak or nonexistent.

Provisional Intellectuals, or "The Truth Is a Lie, and Much of What They Say Is False Is True"

I shall begin by analyzing the sorts of localist ideologies that emerge from a "provisional" intellectual that occupies the position of regional representative of Huastecan culture vis-à-vis the outside as well as representing "high" culture in Ciudad Valles.[3]

Oralia Gutiérrez has had a prominent role in the diffusion and in the creation of Huastecan culture. She has collected and put together an interesting archaeological collection and has written on Huastecan legends and traditions. She designed the coat of arms of Ciudad Valles and is always present in the organization of local cultural activities. Oralia was born in Valles and her father owned a ranch. She married a secondary-school teacher and auto mechanic and leads a humble existence in Valles.

One of my first errands when I arrived in Ciudad Valles was to visit the archaeological museum, see the collection, and pay my respects to its founder and keeper, Oralia Gutiérrez. Because she and I were the only people at the museum, I benefitted from a private tour and became acquainted with a remarkable person. Oralia personally collected many of the museum's pieces, and she is responsible for their display. She also opens, closes, and watches over the museum. All of this guaranteed that I saw the pieces the way they were meant to be seen.

I was first guided to a glass box full of clay animals. Among these animals Oralia identified a rhinoceros, an elephant, and a camel. Although the least ambiguous of these figures was "the camel," I noted to myself that I was being confronted with a new—or at least different— synthesis of Mesoamerican pre-Columbian history.

For Oralia the ancient Huastecans coexisted with animals that traveled freely on the Earth at a time prior to continental drift. The Huastecan lakes of the period were optimal for hippopotamuses (a long obsidian lance that she found was no doubt destined for hunting these beasts). Oralia unequivocally identified what each and every piece of the collection was. There was usually a vague resemblance between her interpretation and what the figures looked like to an untrained eye, and—if I may say so—anyone acquainted with archaeological interpretation is well accustomed to a rather loose fit between expert interpretation and one's own perceptions. As Oralia explained the pieces to me, impregnating them with her particular interpretation of regional history,

I realized the rorschachian potential of archaeology for revealing the wishes and desires that go into all origin myths.

The rhinoceros and the camel were only the beginning. Soon I was confronted with an "Etruscan" head, another from India, and several from Africa. The ancient Huasteca had received cultural influences from the whole of the Old World as well as—predictably—from outer space. Maltese Crosses appear in vases and carvings, "the very same that the Pope wears across his chest!"

Oralia's interpretation differs from that of European diffusionists in that she is not interested in showing the multiple influences on the Huasteca, but rather by proving the Huasteca's centrality for world, and especially for Mesoamerican, history. The Huasteca, it turns out, is none other than the lost city of Atlantis. Quetzalcoatl came from the Huasteca. (To my delight, Oralia explicitly dismissed the "farcical" story of "Tamoanchán" that was defended by F. Plancarte y Navarrete, an illustrious nineteenth-century bishop of Cuernavaca, who claimed that *Morelos* was the birthplace of Quetzalcoatl and the point of origin of culture in the Americas.) Even the symbol of the eagle and the serpent are Huastecan. The Huastecos influenced Teotihuacán via an immense settlement of one million "teotihuacanos" who lived in highland San Luis before the construction of Teotihuacan (archaeologists have refused to acknowledge this). The Huastecans also influenced Monte Albán, whose famous *danzantes* are Huastecans. Chichen Itza and the Toltecs received Huastecan influence through Quetzalcoatl. Professional archaeologists do not want to listen to the irrefutable evidence because it brings down their theories. "There are many mysteries in the history of the world. I have the feeling that the solution to these mysteries is here."

In other words, Oralia's is a quest for centrality, for showing that her life, her place of origin, is relevant to the history and thought of Mexico and the world. However, few people in Valles are interested in the treasure that is the region, and the response from the National Institute of Anthropology and History (INAH) and other national political and cultural authorities has been disappointing. They do not seem to care— or do not want to believe—that the Huasteca developed the first Mesoamerican maize, for example. (The stellar piece of Oralia's collection is "the creation of the third humans with corn." It is a piece that looks like a head coming out of a corncob or, to my untrained eye, like a woman with a headdress. Oralia feels that this piece links archaeology and mythology, and it proves that the origin myth told in the Mayan Popol Vuh is of Huastec origin.)[4] Oralia has collected over six thousand clay figurines that represent all of the different human physiognomies coexisting in the Huasteca. From these figurines Oralia has inferred interesting conclusions on ancient Huastecan scientific developments. There were no diseases in those times, for Huastecans had, and still have, an extremely developed knowledge of curative plants.

Oralia feels that she has been supported by the common people of Valles in her efforts at proving to the world the centrality of Huastecan facts, and in this she is right. However, she complains that professional archaeologists, who control the official truth about history, do not want to learn of these facts because they would have to change their theories. Instead they instinctively protect themselves by ignoring the facts: "What [they say] is true is a lie, and much of what they call lies is the truth."

Oralia uses the words "beautiful" and "pretty" in an interesting (or should I say "beautiful"?) way. They substitute for the more scientistic term "interesting." Oralia finds it "beautiful" that the Huastecans had advanced medicinal knowledge. It is also "beautiful" that once upon a time the wise Mayans populated the whole of the Gulf Coast. These facts are "beautiful" and not merely "interesting" or "fascinating" because the Huastecans are Oralia's heroes; they are the Huasteca's progenitors and represent, along with the natural resources of the region, the Huasteca's internal strength.[5] In this sense, Oralia's is a socially committed science, for the motivation behind her intellectual quest is the construction of a positive identity for the region, its deperipheralization ("there are many mysteries in this world, and I have the feeling that the solution to every one of them is here"). This is why things Huastecan are "beautiful" and not merely "interesting."

Oralia cannot leave without losing her social standing.[6] Because the Huasteca is the context of her life, and because Huastecan life has not found its recognition in the national state, Oralia has the task of showing—at least to herself, but sometimes to others—that the Huasteca is a center in itself, that it has its own culture, its own history, and that by ignoring this history, the rest of the world, and especially Mexico, is ignoring its own past.[7] On the other hand, Oralia also wishes to solve the problems of knowledge of the world, at least the ones she hears about, with the information and means that are accessible to her, which is why she finds in the Huasteca a body of solutions to the gamut of enigmas of universal and national history.

At least as interesting as the epistemological space for cultural synthesis available to Oralia is the fact that her kind of intellectual synthesis articulates well with some of the interests of the state and of varied sorts of politicians. So, for example, Oralia was allowed to design Valles' coat of arms. She also received a lot of local support for the construction of a museum, and President de la Madrid even held an interview with her on his campaign tour. The reasons for this are that politicians need specific symbols with which to address the Huastecan region, symbols that will give the region a place within the nation, symbols with which to spice speeches, tourist guides, and textbooks.

In other words, there is a confluence between the state's needs for local culture and the impulse to turn periphery into center. This need to turn periphery into center is felt only by people in articulatory positions within the regional culture, and especially in positions that articulate with groups outside of the region, for example, schoolteachers. People in nonarticulatory contexts have no need to turn the periphery into center because, from their point of view, they are not in the periphery at all. The impulse to turn periphery into center generates a search for empirical and philosophical materials that produces results that are useful to the politician, such as museums, books, and practical knowledge. At the same time, because the creative impulse that lies behind this type of intellectual is that of both external and internal recognition, the intellectuals find it important that their materials be used precisely by these politicians.[8]

Internal Intellectuals

I have already analyzed the epistemological spaces occupied by a provisional intellectual who has been invested with the function of representing regional culture to supraregional instances. I shall now present material of a traditional intellectual of the peasant class, don José Rivera, a healer in a small Nahua/Mestizo pueblo.

Don José Rivera lives in a traditional-style Huastecan hut, surrounded by brothers and nephews, among whom are some of his village's local elite. Over the door of the house is a small uprooted agave (of the kind they call *sávila*) wrapped in red ribbon with a Virgin of Guadalupe above. In the stone wall that surrounds the house there is, among the stones, a pre-Hispanic sculpture of a woman.

The main house has two rooms. The main room is for the public and it has two entrances that are always open. The centerpiece of the room is a big Huastecan-style altar that don José renews every year on the Day of the Dead. The wooden arch is wrapped in spirals of orange and blue plastic. The table behind the arch is overloaded with medicines, mostly herbal but also with some commercial pharmaceuticals. There are also vases for copal incense, cempoalxuchitl flowers, and candles, and books that show biblical scenes in black-and-white plates. Behind the table, on the wall, are images of various saints, with the Virgin of Guadalupe in the fore. All of the images are protected by a kind of net scissored from blue decorative paper, and adorned with gold paper flowers.

Next to the altar is don José's rocking chair, and behind it is a big wooden cross that is painted yellow. On the wall is an old picture of don

José's mother and sister, two very traditional-looking mestizo women, and next to that is one of the calendars that local merchants distribute every year, with color prints of shapely, half-naked women. Across from the altar are a line of chairs for visitors and patients, and that is all there is in the room. In the other room don José has his bed and a bed in which he sees patients. All of don José's clothes hang from nails on the wall and there are herbs, roots, and pieces of bark lying on the floor in the corner. The floors in both rooms are dirt, and chickens and dogs come and go as they please.

My brother, my assistants, and I stayed with don José for six hours. And that was the first and last time that I saw him. Don José was eighty-two then. He was born "with the century," in 1900. He sat in his rocking chair and began telling us stories, cures, legends, history, and tales of his life almost without room for interruption. This occurred on the second day of my first trip to the Huasteca.

José arrived to his house a little later than we did. At the time I had three assistants and my brother along with me because I was working for the Mexican Ministry of Education (CONAFE) on a project on oral tradition in the Huasteca. My assistants had already met don José on a previous trip. They introduced me to him and began reminding him of their last encounter, but it was pretty clear that he did not remember them at all. It later became apparent that he thought that we were there for a cure.

José began talking in his recitative mode, which included long pauses that were not meant to be interrupted. José began curing at the age of eighteen when he worked as a midwife (*partero*). His knowledge of herbs was not passed through apprenticeship; rather, he has learned the uses of plants through dreams. Once a year, in spring, he goes out to the country and dreams, and in these dreams the uses of the plants that surround him are revealed.

The interview he gave us shows how don José works to impose a certain logic and coherence on the wide variety of conflicting information and innovations that arrive to his village from the outside. Much of his work is to incorporate the new information and the new practices into a view that can exist and prosper in his dusty village. On the other hand, his situation differs somewhat from that of Juan Santos (Mushi') because there is not the radical ethnic divide between him and "national society." This means that he is more immediately affected by the ideological changes outside of his village, and so has to continually incorporate new information in his discourse. Moreover, because he interacts more fluidly with Spanish-speaking society, he can be a repository of "traditional" wisdom for them. That is, after all, the reason why we were visiting him in the first place.

José once cured some doctors who came to see him from the city of Poza Rica. They had earlier attempted to get cured with Western medicine, but it had been impossible. José detected that one of them was ill because of a woman whom he could not remove from his thoughts. José told him to take garlic and other herbs every Tuesday and Friday for seven weeks. On the seventh week the man was cured. "There are women who poison men with a potion that they put inside of an orange, and there are others who use a drug that causes one's 'member' [penis] to fall off. You don't feel a thing, but in the morning, when you go out to pee, you start looking and searching for your penis and you can't find it." José has restored several men's penises because "every potion has its antidote."

"A woman's virginity is reflected in her eyes. When a woman loses her shame [entrega su pudor] something in her look gets broken." Don José can detect this immediately. Don José believes in "pure love" and that it is desirable to marry out of the purity of one's love towards a woman.

"There are two elements that scientists cannot study because of their ephemeral qualities: air and growth. Oxygen is the food of the soul. Growth is undetectable. At the center of one's body, near the heart, is an organ called el gran simpático. El gran simpático controls the system of energy in the human body; it is like the center of a spider web, and it feeds on the sigh. This is why when the soul is not well one feels like one has a stone or rock on one's chest that one cannot remove. This oppression does not let us sigh. When we are cured, we sigh, el gran simpático is fed, and the pressure on the chest is gone. It is much the same with the soul and air: if we stop breathing the soul must leave the body to search for its food, and the body dies. Oxygen, the food of the soul, has no color or any definable density. The best way to describe it is that it is white and thin [blanco y menudito], but that is not very accurate.

"Life is composed of four stages: childhood, which is the only truly happy period since one plays with everything without worrying where it comes from; youth, where bitterness starts setting in because of the realization that one needs to work and that all things will one day end; maturity; and old age."

Don José was still in his recitative mode. He developed a set of themes which were bounded by pauses that we were not encouraged to interrupt. With each pause came a mental association with a new theme, from which he elaborated a new capsule.

"Noah built an ark and God told him to allow all who helped him to enter when the flood came. The construction of the ark was announced for one hundred years. No one helped Noah, and everyone but Noah died. The Last Judgment is coming in the year 2000. We have already received many signs of its approach, many signs that had already been announced in the Holy Scriptures. There is war in the Holy Land. There is a change in the world's climate, but the Earth will finally be destroyed through an earthquake. Four angels will lift the earth from the four cardinal points and they will shake it. We will all be destroyed.

"Jesus said 'The last shall be the first, and the first shall be the last.' This means that the last ones to die before the Final Judgment [i.e., us] will be the first to enter heaven, and the first to have died [the ancient ones] shall be the last.

"There are three bombs that can destroy the Earth and that are buried in the bottom of the ocean. In the time of the Giants, there came from Jupiter two brothers. At that time there was no fire on Earth. The names of these brothers were Primotheus and Simotheus (*Primoteo and Simoteo*). Simotheus went to an island and made fire with two sticks and gave this fire to mankind. In the meantime, the inhabitants of Jupiter wanted to send Pandora to the world. They were making sure that she not be endowed with curiosity, but they got careless and involuntarily gave her curiosity. Pandora came to the world with the job of not opening a box that would bring everyone unhappiness. Pandora buried the box in the sand—like the three bombs that are at the bottom of the sea—and she left it there for twenty years, but in the end she could not resist her curiosity. She opened the box, and from it came forth the insects that are disease.

"Another important piece of wisdom to keep in mind is that God delays, but He does not forget [*Dios tarda, pero no olvida*]. Saint Isabel wanted a son, and she prayed to God that she become pregnant. She had perfect conduct, but God just would not send her a son. One day, when Zachary (her husband) was in a church an angel appeared and told him that Isabel was pregnant and that the son should be named John the Baptist. Since Isabel was already eighty, Zachary doubted the word of the angel and was made dumb for nine months as punishment. The first words that Zachary was allowed to utter were at the birth of his son: 'His name will be John the Baptist.' God delays, but he does not forget.

"John the Baptist and Jesus Christ were first cousins because Isabel and Mary were sisters. John the Baptist, who was handsome and simpá-tico, was called by Salome, who wanted him for herself. Salome was the daughter of the king and as a prize for her dance (which John paid no attention to) she asked that John be decapitated and that his head be put on a gold platter in which she had placed fruits."

All of these episodes were illustrated by don José with pictures from a book that synthesizes the Bible and has old engravings of the different scenes. José showed us pictures of Samson, John the Baptist, and others.

He told us the story of Samson. (Stories of treacherous women are his favorites.)

He later began talking about pre-Columbian times. "The Chichimecs were the first inhabitants of Mexico." José has some Toltec stones that help him cure women in labor who have heart conditions. All of Jose's curing tradition stems from the Toltec, who were the ones (*los meros buenos*) who really knew how to cure.

José also sang the songs of his youth and proved their superiority over the songs of today. "Today even the schoolteachers do not know the meaning of some of the lyrics of the old songs. For example they do not know the meaning of *frenesí* [literally frenzy, but this is a word commonly used in romantic *boleros* exclusively in the sense of frenzied passion] or of *cautela* [caution]. *Frenesí* means that you love somebody such that you wish to marry that person. *Cautela* is a trap that a woman sets for you."

After about three hours of this recitation, José asked which of us was the sick one. We were all slightly embarrassed, because only at that point did we realize that all of this talk was just a preamble to the cure. Fortunately, my brother Alberto had a migraine headache. José asked Beto his age. Beto said he was twenty-two, and José said he looked more like forty-two, the implication being that history is the story of human degradation; but Beto is, by the standards of the nineties, tall and good looking. In his days, don José could pick up objects that no one can raise today. On sight José diagnosed that Beto had cavities (he did not make him open his mouth, though) and recommended that he go to the dentist; he also recommended a drug that they sell in the pharmacy, which in fact did relieve Beto's migraines. He then asked *el güero* (the fair-skinned one: Beto) and *el chino* (the curly-haired one: me) to go into the other room so that he could give Beto an adequate checkup. He made Beto lie in his bed, lifted his shirt, took his pulse, and felt his abdomen. When he began to touch Beto he changed from the discursive mode to which he had subjected us for hours to a very familiar, intimate, and slightly obscene tone that inspired confidence in us. He found Beto too skinny, with heartburn and cerebral anemia.

The anemia was caused (although he did not bother to hear from Beto whether this was in fact the case) by the fact that Beto had sex more than one time in a night. Semen is a cerebral liquid that travels down the spinal chord and goes into the body through the kidneys and from there to the testicles. The secret to manly strength is semen (*es la pura leche*), and one must take care of one's semen; if one spills too much, one gets thin and drawn, like Beto. José continued checking Alberto as he talked. In Beto's testicles he could see that he was a family man. In his stomach he felt nerves and told him to take *cafiaspirina* (caffeinated aspirin) along with an herb, and several other herbal and pharmaceutical remedies for the stomach and the head.

When he was finished with Beto, he asked me to lie down for a checkup. He found that I too had an acid stomach. He decided that both Beto and I were family men. He talked a lot about how one must take care of one's sexual habits. In this respect he had mixed messages. On the one hand, he spoke about how "*al pajarito hay que encontrarle un buen nidito*" (one must find a good "nest" for one's "bird"), but on the other, he seemed to share the philosophy that, barring extreme semen loss, sexual intercourse to unattached women was important.

Don José then spoke of pregnancy. The woman's womb has seven exits, and each child is born out of a different exit until the eighth, when the cycle is renewed. This is why two births are never the same. José told me not to use or occupy (*que no ocupara*) my wife until two months after our child was born, because if we did have sex before that her uterus would not fall back into place (I should say that, by this time, José knew as much about us as we did about him.) Young people these days are such savages that they even occupy their wives while they are pregnant. This should never be done.

José asked Beto whether he worked aside from studying, and then began rebuking him for allowing our parents to support him, as he was already old enough to work and support himself. Also, if he wanted to study, he should not have sex too often, because one needs a lot of brain power to study.

Don José then spoke of the importance of economy in the home. The economy is in the kitchen. A woman has to see that no food gets spoiled and that the maid isn't stealing anything. With the economy it is the kitchen first and then the trunks, and if one does not mind the chests everything will be stolen, and one will be left only with the key.

After finishing a long checkup with me, he told us to get dressed and said that now we would go get some of the plants that we needed for our cure. But before this, José gave me an *abrazo,* opened a small gourd, and gave me an old Mexican silver coin as a present and remembrance from him, because he liked me as a friend (*me caiste como un puro amigo*). Beto and I were stirred with emotion, and "*el abuelo*" (as he liked to be called) took us to his other house, a small hut in the back where he delivers babies.

He opened the house, which was closed with a padlock, and showed us first a bare room with nothing but a petate mat on the floor and a calendar on the wall. This was the delivery room. Then he opened the other room and it contained two full-sized, dull-black wooden coffins. Beto and I were a little shaken. I asked el abuelo what the coffins were for. He said that one of the coffins was for him; he did not want to cause anyone troubles on the day he died. The other coffin was for whoever needed it. "People always come to ask me for things!" He always helped in times of emergency. José also said that he often came into this room to rest and be on his own.

We then went out to the patio. The three o'clock Huastecan sun was adding to the dizziness I was feeling from the compounded effects of José. We began pulling some plants (*golondrina* and *malbón chino*) that were for Beto's and my cure. When we had finished, José walked us up to the neighborhood store and bought Beto the medicine he needed to combine with his herbs.

When we finally came back in to the altar room, our friends were exhausted and hungry from the wait, and it was clear that there was a different sort of relationship established between José and us. He got up, made us some coffee, and let in an Indian who had been sitting outside the doorstep for about three hours, awaiting his turn and listening. The man told José his problem: his three-year-old child was very weak. José gave him some syrup and the man left.

José then explained to us the uses of some of the medicine, and slipped back into his recitative mode. He told us about a gang of hustlers who used to operate in those parts and was known as the "mano negra"; he told us that he once confronted them, and they finally ended up killing each other. He told us of how he used to own two trapiches and had many Indians working for him (let it be said, in passing, that although José is white-skinned and a mestizo he speaks Nahuatl and has a strong Indian following, as in the case of the man who waited three hours for his advice; José's house is in the Indian style, and is not much more luxurious than most). José said one should never trust the peasants because they lead lives of fear and so they talk easily under pressure.

He said the Revolution began in his village in the year 1914 and lasted twenty years. He told us of how his aunt defended the virginity of her daughters by throwing lime powder in the eyes of the soldiers. He recited again how things would get worse and worse until the year 2000. He told us of how this drought (there had been a terrible drought for two years running in the Huasteca, but it rained the following year) was only the beginning of the end. He told us of how all the prices were rising, and of how one must save in times of abundance so that one can defend oneself in hard times. José insisted several times that in the old days the women "showed less but sold more" (wore less shapely clothes, but went to bed more often). He also told us a remarkable story that went with the adage *el bien con mal se paga* (a good deed is paid back with an evil one), but I will save that one for another book.

Six or seven hours had elapsed since we arrived at don José's. We were exhausted and hungry. I had a headache. What was all of this? How to explain it? Was this "useful information" for a study on regional culture? How is this discourse produced? What does it represent? Four years after meeting don José, I decided to include this interview in my work. José's teachings were, to me, mainly about the way knowledge is poorly distributed in regional and social space, and about how unconnected bits and pieces get reconnected into relatively coherent wholes that are effectively used to counsel, and even to cure, people. At the same time, don José made me think of the difficulties in summing up the thinking materials that peasants are confronted with, and the inherent weaknesses of José's position as an intellectual: the great space for cultural incoherence that José was continually bridging by compounding information that came to him from out of town with a cultural and historical interpretation that was consonant with his beliefs and experiences.

Don José recognizes—sometimes explicitly, and sometimes tacitly—his insertion in a series of traditions from which he derives information: the Toltec tradition, the biblical and Greco-Roman tradition, and the scientific tradition, to name the three most salient ones. And yet José depends on revelation for the construction of his own cures and knowledge. Once a year, he goes out to the country and "dreams" about remedies and cures. Although one might argue that this use of revelation is itself a part of the "Toltec" and "Christian" traditions, I believe that José systematically depends on his own intuitive syntheses ("revelation") because he has to combine so many disparate elements into a system that still makes sense both morally and intellectually.

At the same time, José is different from Oralia (and perhaps from many anthropologists) because he is a producer of coherence for local consumption, and so is not caught in the middle ground between local culture and the needs of an official bureaucratized apparatus. Because of this, the whole of don José's construct is in some aspects less fanciful and idiosyncratic than those of provisional intellectuals. In fact, don José is always leaning on local common sense, and his recitations are those of someone erudite in common knowledge. Most of the "capsules" that he recited began with either a folk saying, a famous biblical passage, or the words from an old song, and these cliches were then explained, exemplified, and applied to people's current problems. As opposed to Oralia Gutiérrez, then, don José is not an eccentric; he is unusual because of his extreme and specialized devotion to the central principles of organization of his society.

Indian Internal-Articulatory Intellectuals

I have already discussed some of the spaces for cultural coherence in several different intimate groups: Indian peasants from communities, mestizo peasants from pueblos, rancheros, and peones. I have also shown the incipient forces of the state and the kinds of provisional coherence created by its presence. This final section of the chapter is directed to the problem of coherence faced by Indian intellectuals who combine an internal with an articulatory need. I have already shown some of the main characteristics in the elaboration of Huastec Indian localist ideology, and have pointed out that syncretism between intimate culture and the interpretation of the culture of social relations is at the basis of this ideology. I have not had space, however, to deal with the culture of Indians who occupy an articulatory function in the *economy* of the community. In both of the communities best known to me there are a very few cases of Indians who take on the position of middlemen between the community and mestizo interests, and stand to gain personally from this position. In Tanchahuil there is a man who acts as coyote between a ranchero and community laborers; he contracts crews of men to go work on this man's ranch. This Indian is, however, looked down upon locally because he is taking on an exploitative position. However, in both Tanchahuil and Tenexo there are less extreme cases of Indian middlemen who are not so disliked internally. These are the small shop owners who also take on the job of buying local piloncillo during the week and saving it for the coyote's weekly rounds. These people can serve an articulatory function in the regional economy; however, they do not occupy the position of articulating the community's culture or needs to a wider audience, nor are they necessarily the internal representatives of localist ideological constructions.

The existence of an internal-articulatory Indian intelligentsia is questionable, because this kind of sustained position has perhaps existed only in the cases of Indian rebellion, as in the well-known rebellion of Juan Santiago in the 1880s. One kind of internal-articulatory function is carried out by the civil-religious authorities, particularly the juez. However, the juez is not an articulatory intellectual because he is not devoted to producing an image of Indian culture for the outside. One must bear in mind that jueces—like most other Indian local authorities—change every year; their transitory nature guarantees that they be true representatives of the Indian community vis-à-vis the outside, and they can also convey the desires of mestizo authorities to the members of the community. However, jueces do not create ideologies of articulation (the same can usually be said for communal agrarian authorities, when they exist[9]).

The only true case of internal-articulatory intellectuals is that of some of the bilingual schoolteachers who have been created by the national state. In most cases these bilingual teachers are "provisional" intellectuals who respond primarily to the state's need for Indian cultural synthesizers. To a certain degree the precarious position of the bilingual teacher is guaranteed by state policy itself, for it usually insists that a bilingual teacher work in a community different from his or her own. Thus the teachers are very often not members of the community, hold no communal land, and therefore do not participate in the activities that are most central to the community qua community; in addition, this distance between teacher and community allows the bilingual teacher to feel superior to the locals because teachers are "cultured" and receive a steady salary, meager though it is.

There are a few cases, however, in which the teachers attempt to take on both an internal and an articulatory function, and these cases are illustrative of what happens when the logic of Indian localist ideology (syncretism between intimate culture and the culture of social relations) breaks down.

My introduction to Eustaquio was in a restaurant/bar in the market town of Tancanhuitz. It was the day of Saint Michael, the patron saint, and Eustaquio was drinking with a friend. I was sitting at the table next to him, getting something to eat with my wife and son.

Because Eustaquio was not sober, he began conversing with us, and asked if we came on behalf of the Instituto Nacional Indigenista to see the fiesta, or whether we were anthropologists or indigenistas. It was obvious to him that we valued Indian culture and that we came here because of that.

Eustaquio told us that he was the principal of the grade school in a nearby Huastecan village and invited us to go visit him during the week. I later did this, of course, and it turned out that Tanchahuil—the village where he worked—suited my regional-cultural purposes quite well, so that in fact I did some ethnographic work there. Eustaquio identified himself as an Indian, a Huastecan Indian, and told us that he had studied at the Indian boarding school at Matlapa, perhaps the only still-functioning Indian boarding school from the times of Lázaro Cárdenas. He claims that he is proud of being Indian, and is happy that there is some recognition of Indian culture on the part of non-Indians like ourselves.

When Eustaquio mentioned that he had studied in Huejutla, I asked him if he knew Joaquín Tlaxcalli (the other internal-articulatory case that I am discussing here). The fact that I knew Joaquín brightened him up considerably. He said Joaquín had been his teacher at Huejutla and that he was a very talented painter whose work had even been shown in Bellas Artes in Mexico; he also had a job at the INI and, although he is important, still acknowledged his Indianness. Although he dressed like a white man, and may have had the luxuries of a white man, he did not deny his race. He proudly carried Indian blood.

Eustaquio then spoke a little about how mestizos in the region referred to Huastecan as a "dialect" when the ethnolinguists have proved that it is a language. Eustaquio asked us if we had not yet seen the dances, and he told us that although the main dances had been the night before, there were still some dances at the INI. He also told us that we had missed the selection of an "Indian Queen," a contest of beautiful young Indian women who (in the way that the ranchers select queens at their fairs) had been paraded all around the center of the village.

In Eustaquio's discourse one can perceive the kind of political and cultural dilemmas faced by an Indian when (s)he severs his or her links with the community in the name of a broader identification as an Indian. In opposition to localist ideologies as we saw them in Juan Santos, where the mestizo order was incorporated into the general religious world view, Eustaquio frames the relationship between Indian and national culture as an opposition between two equally valid cultures, which is to say that he frames Indian culture in Western terms, and looks to find in it a set of one to one equivalences with national culture. The effect of breaking down the syncretistic function in Indian localist ideology is that of inevitably distancing Eustaquio from "his" Indian culture, for if that culture cannot succeed in ideologically encompassing dominant society, then what remains will be strictly a subordinate, discriminated race. Put in rather abstract terms, what I am trying to say is that Indian cultural reproduction depends on a localist ideology *of caste,* where dominant national and mestizo societies are incorporated within a world view of order, hierarchy, and interdependence. National culture, and dominant regional ranchero culture as well, function on a liberal ideology that can cast Indian society only in one of two positions: as an independent culture, with its own values, language, and customs (which is the point of view of the indigenistas and of Eustaquio), or as a subordinate race that is stripped of cultural value and can be redeemed only through education, if it can be redeemed at all (this is the ranchero mode of racism). Because Eustaquio sees the logic of the state and of the dominant system as being separate from that of Indian internal culture, he is irredeemably split in his allegiances. His conception of Indian customs as a coherent totality must break down—because among these values and customs there are customs of subordination to national and regional society—and instead be substituted by a piecemeal revalorization of specific habits that he finds useful, superior, or congenial with those of the hegemonic culture of social relations.

Joaquín Tlaxcalli is a similar, though much more elaborate and successful, case. Joaquín had a post in the INI at Huejutla (Hidalgo) when I met him. He is a kind of obligatory acquaintance for anthropologists and historians working in the region. Joaquín is a well-educated Nahua Indian who has been to Europe and has a fair amount of local and regional success as a painter of murals with Indian themes. Unlike Eustaquio, Joaquín is eloquent in Spanish and shows an astute ability to classify outsiders. In what follows I will put forth fragments of an interview I held with him in his offices at INI late one night. The fragments are selected merely to illustrate the problems one must face in an attempt to become an internal-articulatory Indian intellectual.[10]

Says Joaquín:

And now you want to hear many stories, eh? Many stories that we have in Nahuatl or Spanish. If you want to know them, I will tell them to you in the end [he is, after all, a government bureaucrat as much as we were at the time], but what do you want them for, what purpose will they serve? . . . Look, believe me, I am already old in these things and some-times I get to thinking: there is an army of schoolteachers that wants to know everything about Indian traditions. But what will those teachers do? They come hear, they listen, they take notes, and one day, when they are having coffee with some statuesque secretary, they remember these inter-esting things [as a conversation topic]. Then this teacher becomes a univer-sity professor, but what does he care about the Huasteca? He will never set foot in a hut, of that I am sure!

The other day I got into a fight with some teachers from the Normal Superior, and I told them what they were.

"Oh, we have come to work. . . ."

"Don't make me laugh, you won't do a thing. The only thing you will do is come to snoop on how Indians live."

We began to fight, but I spent about five hours giving them a conference to shake them up a bit. In the end I said, "All right, come if you want to, but come and help us. Just don't help us get organized, because we are already organized—every community has its organization. Don't come as snoopers to organize because the Indians are more organized than every-one else." We decided that they would come and help with the ecological education of Indian children. "But don't do to them what you did to us when we were kids. You hit us so that we would learn Spanish. Instead, help the children feel less oppressed and less shameful about the fact that they live in such and such a place, and that will be of aid in getting them to know and to deal with the Indian world."

Also I explained to them that they should give information to the Indi-ans when they ask for it, because I have yet to see them give us authoriza-tion to study the people that live along, for example, the streets of Aris-totle or Edgar Allan Poe in Polanco [a rich Mexico City neighborhood], or one of those houses that are in San Angel or El Pedregal. I would like them to let me study how they earn those millions of pesos, and where they get those fancy cars. I am interested in all of that. Sincerely that was my proposal, and that still is my proposal, and whenever I go give a talk I say, all right, I will tell my stories, but tell me, how do you do it to have money in the banks of Switzerland? How do you multiply your money? How do you buy your cars? How is it that you have children here and there? Because you create contraceptive pills for us Indians, but you do not take them yourselves. I want to know all of these things. The people from the Normal Superior left in a huff, they said they had never met such a uncouth and conceited person.

In this part of his diatribe, Joaquín was taking on an internal-articulatory function because he was defending Indian communities from the unrestricted power of observation of the dominant classes. However, in this same discourse, the strength of his position as an internal intellectual is called into question. Thus, when he refers to the Indians, he slips continually between speaking about "us" and about "the Indians." The fragility of his identification as an internal intellectual is more apparent in what follows:

[In Xonteletl] I solicited the presence of the local authorities, and there were sixty of them. We started talking and I asked them, "What do you think about the Moon?"

Do you know what they answered? "We are stupid, we don't know anything."

I withstood that answer for a whole day. I would invite them to eat a little soup; I would bring some beers and aguardiente, and when we were all together I would ask again, "What do you think of the Moon?" or "What do you think of the stars?" I wanted to see whether I could complete my book of stories that I now have. But most of them would stop and tell me, "Listen, señor, if you want we can invite you to eat, but the truth is that in this village we are stupid, we don't know anything, we don't speak Spanish, we never went to school, we know absolutely nothing."

But then there came a storm and I was stranded in this village for the night. And I was sitting there listening to the radio when I asked the person who was with me, "And how about the rabbit, huh? That rabbit that was with the Moon" [the basis of a Nahua tale about the moon]. And then one of them began telling me, for over an hour, the whole story that I wanted to hear. He told it all. And afterwards he passed on to other stories, the one about the bulls, and the other on nixtamal. I came home mesmerized because I was able to prove everything that I had been compiling for years!

This part of Joaquín's discourse is more akin to tips on fieldwork for a fellow anthropologist than to a warning or defense of the interests of any particular Indian community. It shows the practical difficulties that an outstanding individual has in attempting a position of an internal-articulatory Indian intellectual. For Joaquín discovered the value of 'his culture' in Europe, and is now not ashamed to be Indian. However, he cannot solve the contradiction that exists between Indian intimate culture and the hegemonic culture of social relations, because he recognizes the difference between the two. Like Eustaquio (only with greater competence), Joaquín is drawn towards the aspects of Indian culture that prove the value and nature of Indian culture *in opposition to* Western culture. Like Eustaquio, too, he is forced to seek cultural coherence in especially "pure" realms of Indian culture when in fact what is essential to Indian culture (from the point of view of communities) is that its "purity" be articulated to the wider society in which it exists.

So, for example, Joaquín has spent years showing that every piece of Nahua embroidery—every design, every color—has a specific meaning.[11] Joaquín believes that Nahua painting is iconic and can be read exactly like a book. So he claims that the rays that Juan Diego painted around the Virgin of Guadalupe are an encoded message.[12] This obsession with hidden meaning most certainly has a basis in Indian culture, for it is in fact true that these groups have sophisticated mythologies that are rarely opened to outsiders. It is also in the nature of this kind of knowledge that an outsider never knows whether or not (s)he is getting the full, complete story, so the search for secret and hidden meanings is endless and, indeed, fascinating. However, there is also the temptation of believing that only this secret knowledge is the real truth, especially when, as in Joaquín's case, one is trying to find in Indian culture a parallel alternate to Mexican national culture. This kind of sophisticated secret knowledge is what Joaquín considers the "true" Indian culture. He does not consider, for example, that the answer "we do not know, we are stupid" is a part of the culture of the community. This search for a complex, hidden culture among the Indians is itself a symptom of the real distance between Joaquín and Nahua communities, for with them this complex knowledge is not valuable because it parallels European knowledge, it is valuable because it helps integrate a single world, in which they lead a subordinate existence to Westerners.

In the cases of Eustaquio and Joaquín we have seen that there is a social need on behalf of the state and—to a lesser extent—the communities for constitution of an internal-articulatory Indian intelligentsia. Nevertheless, the production of such an intelligentsia is extremely difficult because the moment an Indian takes on an articulatory function, a function of "explaining" Indian culture to outsiders, that person must accept the terms of the culture of social relations and tends either to downgrade Indian culture or to present it as an alternative to that culture of social relations (which it isn't). The syncretistic function that is basic to Indian localist ideology—the function whereby the explanation of the earth, the community, and social world is linked to the requirements of the culture of social relations—is broken, and the intellectual can never adequately represent his community again.

The alternate kind of internal-articulatory intellectual, the best example of which is Juan Santiago, the Indian rebel of the 1880s, is one in which an internal intellectual seeks to place conditions on hegemonic classes and learns to converse with them only for that purpose. Here he does not have to explain Indian culture, only Indian political demands, and therefore does not become unidentified with his community. The price for this kind of success has been, until now, the life of its bearer.

14

Epilogue

Power makes for a regional structure of places. This "structure of places" is made up of a set of loci for cultural interaction, and a set of ideologies about relative positions. "Places" are therefore both objective and subjective situations. Places are like games that engage you in the moment that you enter them. That is why they have a dialectic of their own. Because of this, there is room for distance between people's notions of themselves and the roles that people occupy in different places; migration, or the breakdown or construction of cultural coherence may create that sort of distance between culture and the self. Thus "culture" can be felt with conviction, or it can be played from an emotional distance.

The spatial structures of cultural production that we have explored so far show a kind of system to these processes of disaffection and conviction. People whose values have been molded in one intimate culture then live to see that culture undermined by changes in the organization of class; or else they move from one place to another and must go through the conscious experience of learning the new cultural "games" that are associated with a new place. The distance created in these processes can only be turned into new transformed versions of one's culture and one's self after many lived experiences; and these newly gained convictions can only be transmitted to one's children after inventing new rituals and myths.

Movement between places is like changing masks. In the theater, actors who use masks are supposed to let those masks transform their personae: the mask is not something that conceals actors; it is something that possesses them. In this sense, Octavio Paz did not take his interest in Mexican masks far enough, for Paz saw "masks" as reflections of solitude—as reflections of a personal and collective concealment because of their insecurity vis-à-vis others. In his view, Mexicans lamely resolved this insecurity with the mask: the mask of the humble Indian, the mask of the abnegated mother, the mask of the virile cacique. But, in fact, these masks are not really products of an identity crisis; they are a product of the vast differences between places in the Mexican cultural landscape: the wooden, formulaic behavior that Paz was so sensitive to, and that he saw as a fetter to true human communication, is a reflection of the importance of place in Mexico.

Those of us who have contemplated and thought about Mexican culture have traveled through this system of places. We are argonauts of national culture. We have been confronted with these masks, these trite and mythified roles that appear to hide the true person; but looking at these postures and gestures as concealment is only to reveal one's own position as traveler, for these masks do not only conceal, they also *possess,* and their triteness is comparable in function to the grotesque ritual masks of the Ndembu that Victor Turner once analyzed: it emphasizes a distinctive feature and proposes it as a key metaphor for everyone that is present. The freedom to take off one's mask may only arrive when people feel that their place is not so important; but this feeling rarely emerges, for the power relations that created those places is also "in place."

On the other hand, perhaps Paz was right about the transition that Mexican culture was going through when he wrote *The Labyrinth of Solitude.* The highly dramatized representation of one's place that he described could have been, in some cases, a reflection of social-spatial change. People were beginning to look at their own place with a little bit of distance. They had the inkling that their position, or the meaning of their position, would change. This distance—which was a product of changes in the regional political economy of culture—was met either with irony or with the conviction of the mask.

Paz claimed that Mexican history was the history of a man looking for his filiation. I would say that the malaise that produces meditations like that of Paz and, perhaps, also of my own, is a search for conviction. The geography of Mexican intimate cultures and of processes of mestizaje is a fundamental reference point for an anthropology of this nostalgia for conviction, of this "search for identity." Nostalgia for cultural coherence, nostalgia for the culture of one's community and home, nostalgia for forms of cultural hegemony that are today residual or gone. The ironic distance that has begun to separate person and place in some Mexican intimate cultures produces a will for a new coherence. When that will surges, national and regional spaces begin to get reimagined and reshaped.

Part Two

National Culture

15

Theory and Politics

In the mid-1980s, around the time I finished the dissertation which was the first version of this book, several books on national culture were published in Mexico. Three salient ones were Guillermo Bonfil's *México profundo,* Enrique Alduncin Abitia's *Los valores de los mexicanos,* and Roger Bartra's *La jaula de la melancolía.* In fact, the past few years have seen the biggest upsurge of production on the theme of Mexican national culture since the "golden age" of Mexican national culture studies, which was inaugurated by Samuel Ramos in the 1930s and which reached its climax in the late fifties. The three books are different, and yet they revive familiar contradictions.

Bonfil's book—as his title suggests—promotes the idea that there is a "deep" Mexico, a common Mexican culture, which is grounded in Indian culture:

> I have tried to show that the deep Mexico, which is the bearer of a civilization that has been negated, incarnates the developed product of an uninterrupted process: the Mesoamerican civilizatory process. During the past five centuries (which are but a moment in this long trajectory) the Mesoamerican peoples have been subjected to a system of brutal oppression that affects all of their lives and of their cultures. The resources of colonial domination have been many, and they have varied through time, but the stigma, the violence, and the denial have been constant. Despite this, however, Mesoamerican civilization is still present and alive, not only in the peoples who maintain their own identity and assert their difference [i.e., the Indians], but also in wide sectors of the population that do not identify themselves as Indians, although they organize their collective life

according to a Mesoamerican cultural matrix. All of them form the deep Mexico, which is systematically ignored by the imaginary Mexico that wields the power and that presumes itself to be the bearer of the only valid national project. (Bonfil 1987:244, my trans.)

Bonfil is outraged by the fact that the dominant national projects have imposed a false ("imaginary") vision of the country, and in so doing they have belittled, marginalized and discriminated the culture of the national majority. Instead of facing "outward," to Europe and the United States, Mexico must face "inward" to its civilizational roots and reconstruct a nationality from that vantage point.

However, although one may sympathize with Bonfil's ideals (I personally feel that he is right in denouncing the shallow and mechanical importation of development projects and in crying out against the belittlement of native Mexican culture), Bonfil's dichotomy of the subordinated "deep" or "real" Mexico and the dominant "imaginary" or "fictitious" Mexico is as old and as bankrupt as the ideology of the "imaginary" Mexico he so justly criticizes. It is a strain of the indigenismo which has existed since independence, and its main problem is that it fails to recognize that Mexico, like all the nation-states of the world, is a creature of modernity, and its roots cannot be traced further back than the colonial period. In this sense, the "imaginary Mexico" is still the only Mexico that has ever existed as a nation-state.

This does not mean that Bonfil is wrong when he points out that Mexico's indigenous culture and race are discriminated against. He is right about that. It does, however, call into question the ontological status of his "deep" and "imaginary" Mexicos, for on the one hand both ideologies are linked to sets of real practices and, on the other, both ideologies are products of the collective imagination. In other words, they are both "deep," and they are both "imaginary." In attributing "reality" to one and "illusion" to another, Bonfil is merely returning to the nationalist drawing board of the Mexican Revolution without having fully confronted the reasons why the "imaginary" Mexico has become so very real.

Bonfil's attempt to uncover a living commonality among Mexicans is undoubtedly related to a mood of nostalgia that permeated the life and works of Mexican intellectuals in the eighties. In Mexican political life, this nostalgia was crystalized around that "deepest" of Mexicans, Cuauhtémoc Cárdenas. Thus, Bonfil portrays a "deep Mexico" which seems to have come to life in Cárdenas's 1988 presidential campaign. It is humble, it has Indian roots, and it is community-oriented. Upon this true or real Mexico, capitalism has built a superstructure of supermarkets, malls, cars, and technocrats; but, although this asphalt superstructure does threaten to pave over everything, the deep Mexico survives.

> I have tried to uncover the fact that today's crisis is not the crisis of Mexico, it is only just the exhaustion of a model of development that ignored the deep Mexico. We have enough natural resources—although they are not unlimited—and we have a great variety of cultural systems through which those resources can be transformed into elements that can make for a more wholesome human existence, according to the aspirations that are implicit in the culture. I also tried to show how sticking to a single developmental model has led to an underutilization of what we do have and it provokes a kind of schizophrenia in which reality marches its way while the national project follows its imaginary route. (1987:245, my trans.)

Bonfil's book thus attempts to grapple with the old and difficult problem of national culture without the aid of a new theoretical perspective. He simplifies the relationship between national ideology and "the aspirations that are implicit in the culture" because he sees the state as ideally corresponding to "a nation" which has "a culture," whereas in fact any successful national project will articulate diverse local and regional cultures under the hegemony of a dominant class or of the state bureaucracy. By producing a new study of Mexican national culture that offers no new ideas as to *how* this study avoids any of the pitfalls of its predecessors (which, indeed, it does not), Bonfil has succumbed to the excitement of politics while forfeiting his critical capacity. Preoccupied—as many of us are—by the turn that life in Mexico has taken in the last few years (the frightening ecological problem, the decline of the peasantry, the dehumanization of cities, the intrusion of imported goods, fashions, and ideas), Bonfil nostalgically reconstructs the deep Mexico, which is a kind of transcendental Indian character that survives, practically unblemished, beneath the asphalt. And, despite the debility of this thesis as an intellectual construct, Bonfil finds that he is not alone in reaffirming the deep Mexico. A huge political movement has rallied around some of the same memories.

Another study of national culture is by Enrique Alduncin. This study is also reminiscent of the past. It is an attempt to bring the lights of science to national culture. Alduncin's position differs from Bonfil's in that it does not seek to find the underlying structure of Mexico's culture. It substitutes this desire with an earnest determination to portray what Mexicans are today. It is a kind of "lo mexicano" update, based on a broad use of questionnaires. Where Bonfil's motives are those of a kind of political millennarianism, Alduncin's are those of the technician.[1] He wants to know where Mexicans are at right now, who they are, what they think. While Bonfil plays with the fire of myth, Alduncin is looking for firewood. Alduncin provides bric-a-brac, Bonfil does bricolage.

Bonfil tries to show that, deep down, there is still a dominant (though negated) Indian culture that can still serve to forge a new nationality, whereas Alduncin is only convinced of the need to know the attitudes of Mexicans (i.e., that things are no longer known, that we need to redis-cover who or what we are). In other words, for Alduncin, using old views of Mexican culture that focus on community to confront today's atom-ized diversity is, to paraphrase Salvador Novo, like "diluting my grain of salt in the well of your indifference." And this conviction of Alduncin's resonates with the views of both the Mexican state and the private corpo-rations. The Mexican government has abandoned the view of Mexico that was created in the aftermath of the Revolution. It no longer has convictions about the nature of Mexican popular culture. And yet, the technocrats can hear the rumor of their unpopularity, of their detach-ment from that popular culture which Bonfil explores (whatever it is). So, some of the technocrats have put their ear to the ground; the situa-tion calls for a questionnaire! This may be the reason Alduncin no longer seeks the holistic approach of anthropology or psychoanalysis—no longer the structural visions of Marxism—but mere facts. All wood, no fire.

And yet Bonfil's approach is so traditional that it speaks only to our nostalgia. Although he tries to develop ideas on national culture, he is simply following an all too well-worn path in a new social context. And since, to twist a famous phrase, "the less it changes, the less it remains the same," Bonfil's study is not as interesting as the ones carried out in the "golden age" of national culture. Despite its eloquence and despite its timely intentions, it is intellectually derivative and stale; in its politi-cal implications it is mediocre, for it does not really explore the reason why Indian communalism has not been a successful national ideology.

The third national culture book of the eighties, *La jaula de la melancolía,* is by far the most interesting. Bartra comes out of a dialogue with contemporary European philosophy and social sciences, and ad-dresses the lo mexicano literature in a work that has two parallel texts. One of the texts is a critique of the lo mexicano literature, in which Bartra discusses the images which have been composed in that litera-ture. He concludes that the whole project of Mexican national-culture studies has its motivational roots in the romantic melancholia caused by the impact of modernization. It is a reaffirmation of a lyrically recon-structed peasant culture amid a process of accelerated proletarianiza-tion. On the other hand, the melancholia that spurred the intellectuals' projects became a cage, in that it has been used to construct an image of nationality in which the values of modernity are never fully attainable to Mexicans. Through the mythical Mexican, the Mexican intellectuals and politicians reproduce the source of their melancholia, which is really just a half-lived modernity. So, Mexican nationalism (as created through the imagery of the peasant and of the debased peasant, the lumpenproletarian) is an ideological tool that guards the state and the bourgeoisie from the full claims of modernity, such as democracy or socialism.

Parallel to this discussion, Bartra develops an allegory about Mexican nationality that humorously replicates most of the images in the lo mexicano literature. This is Bartra's "myth of the axolote." The axolote is, biologically, a very peculiar kind of salamander that has been thought of as a "Mexican" animal (it, like Alfonso Reyes's Mexicans, also bears the "x" on its forehead) and, like Mexicans, it fully reproduces and yet never completes its full evolutionary destiny, which is to become a true salamander. Like Paz's solitary Mexicans, axolotes never get past adolescence.

In other words, Bartra implicitly accuses the lo mexicano literature of a sort of complicity with the state's mythified Mexico. The state has no desire to represent the real Mexico. It prefers to invent that which it represents out of bits and pieces of images that are well known to all of us. This act of power stands in the way of the benefits of modernity (democracy) while it leaves the people vulnerable to its economic implications.[2]

Bartra's position is clearly opposed to Bonfil's. He believes that the full political consequences of modernity and postmodernity have yet to be felt, and that appeals to the premodern culture as a source of a national image tend to strengthen the Mexican authoritarian state. Evidently, Bartra's position is also distinct from Alduncin's, for although Bartra and Alduncin might agree on the idea that there is no prototypical "Mexican," in Alduncin this conclusion leads to the fabrication of a questionnaire that leaves the nature and contours of Mexican national ideology untouched, whereas Bartra's axolote myth is a caricature of the lo mexicano mythology. It is a myth proposed in irony; its political purpose is to struggle against some myths while still allowing people to create their own.

Bartra makes quite a strong case for the connection between modernization and the construction of images of Mexicanness. However, as we have seen in the discourses of local intellectuals, localist mythologies reveal about as much as they conceal. They express as much as they suppress. If modernity is suppressed by Mexican nationalism, it stands to reason that this nationalism is also expressing something about culture in the national space, perhaps something (outside the myth) that is standing in the way of democracy. Therefore, the fact, acknowledged playfully by Bartra, that the national myth reproduces itself is sociologically crucial and cannot be eschewed by a simple act of will. There is a real sociology of national culture that is protruding into the thought of intellectuals, and that is making them re-create these myths. This is why the works of Bonfil and Alduncin were written.

In sum, the works of Bartra, Bonfil, and Alduncin index, in very different ways, the politics of national culture studies. Bonfil proclaims the existence of a deep Indian Mexico that survives *malgré tout.* Politically, this position is (today) part of the cultural aura of Cardenismo. The book is more a symptom of a perceived political alternative than an analysis of national culture or of its true import. It is, in this sense, anthropology abdicating from its role as critical theory, in exchange for the popular appeal of myth.

Alduncin's book substitutes a study of national culture for a study of attitudes. It is the social scientist as pollster. It recognizes the staleness of our ideas about Mexicanness, and makes an effort to reach out and discover "what Mexicans believe." No need to theorize on ideology and what it is, no need to think about the nation-state and what it is.

Finally, Bartra's book clearly focuses on some aspects of national mythmaking, but it does not attempt to develop a sociology of national culture. This is reflected in the political implications of his work. Bartra's book is a call for democracy. Mexicans have borne the combined burdens of a capitalist economic system and a "traditional" political system for too long. Democracy is the only way out of this "cage of melancholy." Unfortunately, each and every one of the national alternatives in Mexico's current democratic contest are completely imbued in the national mythology. Mexican party politics are also built on this nostalgia for the Mexico that could have been. This is the never-ending story of Mexican national culture.

It is in this conjuncture that reanalyzing some of the past political uses of national-culture studies is most useful, because the politics of the national-culture literature of the eighties and nineties is not the same as that of the golden-agers. So, for example, in *The Labyrinth of Solitude,* Paz called for a *renaming* of Mexican culture:

> Our recent history offers numerous examples of this juxtaposition and coexistence of diverse historical levels: Porfirian neo-feudalism (I use this term in the hopes that a historian will someday classify our historical states in their true originality) utilized positivism—a bourgeois philosophy—to justify itself; Caso and Vasconcelos, the intellectual initiators of the Revolution, used Boutroux and Bergson's ideas against Porfirian positivism; there are revolutionary frescos on government buildings. . . . All of these apparent contradictions demand a new look at our history and our culture, which is a confluence of many currents and epochs. (1981a:11, my trans.).

This view of the uses of national-culture studies is still important. It is saying that we do not have adequate *terms* to describe our own reality, that there is a fissure between culture and ideology in Mexico. The lack of fit between "words and things" produces, within Mexico, a sense of powerlessness ("inferiority," Ramos said) in that many actions are defined negatively. Peasant knowledge is defined as ignorance (as Bonfil shows). The Mexican political system is simply "undemocratic." The Mexican economy is "backward." How can we get out from under these problems when they are defined in such a way that they lump together things we value with things that we abhor? "Corruption" is almost universally disliked in Mexico, but it is a practice that at times involves maintaining highly valued relationships such as friendship, family solidarity, and trust. For corruption to be strongly resisted in Mexico, it must be redefined in such a way as to be a more unambiguously negative experience for more Mexicans. The fissure between culture and social explanation is politically important, in that it implies that we are continuously involved in political projects that are not adequately conceptualized.

This cannot be resolved—as Bonfil attempts—by positing a simple opposition between colonizer and colonized and then calling for a return to the indigenous cultural matrix. Mexican culture is a mixture of European and indigenous elements, and the Mexican national state is a particular variation of (Western) modernism. Paz wants studies of Mexican culture history because he recognizes the analytical inadequacies that derive from the fact that European ideologies are applied in contexts that are qualitatively different from those in which they originated. In this sense, his work is a call for Mexicans to begin to think through and name the processes in which they are involved. This call is fundamental if Mexicans want to be social agents and not just victims.

Jorge Portilla also provides a few examples of the importance of a sociology of the culture in the national space:

> The result [of the weaknesses of communities in Mexico] is a weak political life, with all of the consequences that we have today. The thorny ambiguity of events in this political life; the hollow and demagogical tone of political speeches, proclamations, state addresses, etc.; a generalized insecurity regarding which principles apply where [*un general no saber a qué atenerse*]; a game of riddles which is the criterion for deciding probabilities; waves of rumors, etc. (1984:126, my trans.)

Portilla tried to propose a phenomenology of Mexican culture because that culture produces certain forms of power, such as the one quoted above, which he rejects. Although Portilla did not develop a sociology of his phenomenology (he only *names* a few Mexican cultural elements in their own terms), his cultural description is most certainly geared to changing specific aspects of Mexican culture. In this sense, Portilla's and Paz's works sound a cautionary note to Bartra's often perceptive reading of the lo mexicano literature. Like Bartra, Portilla seems to be writing because of his *frustration* with an incomplete modernization, and not out of nostalgia for the premodern. This frustration stems from the fact that he could already observe (in 1966) that "modernization" was just another one of those imported names that do not fully apply in Mexico.

In other words, the melancholic effect is perhaps stronger in Bonfil than it was even in Paz (to say nothing of Portilla). Moreover, the phenomenological bent of some of the earlier writers on Mexican culture was a useful beginning for a sociology of national culture, even though this sociology was never developed. But the Mexican national-culture literature of the eighties does show (1) that images of national culture often emerge out of a sense of nostalgia for that which modernization destroys; (2) that these nostalgic images can serve to justify a holistic, antidemocratic ideology that has been embodied in the post-revolutionary Mexican state; (3) that "naming" Mexican culture is not enough, we must try to contextualize and explain it as well.

The idea for this book originated while I was a graduate student at Stanford University in 1980. At that time I was reading for my doctoral exams and was struck by the interesting kinds of cultural descriptions that were developed in the Iberoamerican national-culture literature. I was especially inspired by the theoretical problem of how those descriptions could be cast in social-scientific terms. Thus, my first interest was theoretical. How can we embark on cultural descriptions of complex heterogeneous spaces like that of the nation-state?

Alongside this theoretical question, which has remained a constant throughout my work, were a set of political considerations which were not so clear to me then, and which have only found their place after many years. When I first became interested again in the lo mexicano literature, I had been asking myself: If I had to recommend a couple of books to a Californian who wanted to travel to Mexico, which would I choose? I thought that I would probably choose the *Labyrinth of Solitude* before choosing *Life in a Mexican Village,* or *Pedro Páramo* before *Tzintzuntzan.* At the time, however, I saw only the theoretical import of this question (i.e., how can an anthropologist reframe in sound methodological and theoretical terms whatever there is that is good in *The Labyrinth of Solitude?*), I did not see the political implications of the question.

Obviously I was interested in the issue of cultural translation (what book to give a foreign reader, for example), but, much more important, I was also interested in holistic description. *Life in a Mexican Village* is empirically richer, more detailed, and more precise than *The Labyrinth of Solitude,* but it is a case study in a sea of case studies and does not attempt to offer an interpretation of Mexican society. In this sense, the case-study tradition in Mexico was making anthropologists into technicians and leaving the view of the "whole" to others.

On the other hand, spatially insensitive forms of ethnography can, in some contexts, lead to misrepresentations of "national culture." In many anthropology courses in the United States, for example, studies of "other societies" serve students to think about their own culture. This is "anthropology as cultural critique." Nonetheless, the fragmentary descriptions provided by case studies are easily transformed into ideas about nationhood. Lewis called his study of Tepoztlán *Life in a Mexican Village;* many anthropological studies of Mexico suggest generalities about the country. On the other hand, the studies that actually confront Mexican national culture as such are, as we have seen, unacceptable to social science on theoretical and methodological grounds. Thus, our sciences have legitimized their own way of stereotyping national culture. Furthermore, stereotyping through case studies makes the subjects of stereotype appear as relatively powerless, for they are only small parts of an unfathomable system. The Mexican literature on national culture, like most "consciousness-raising" movements, was a way of discussing national culture that could—in some cases—lead to a feeling of empowerment. Arriving to national culture by implication (through case studies) leaves this possibility out.

When I began my studies in anthropology in Mexico (1974) there was an enormous sense of excitement and discovery surrounding the field. These sentiments grew out of a conviction that most interpretative work on Mexico had been invented from the vantage point of a library or a cafe, and was not based on a systematic investigation of the facts. We all looked upon the existing portraits of Mexican culture with anything ranging from distrust to disdain. Works like those of Samuel Ramos or Octavio Paz were compared to armchair anthropology which, at the time, was seen as the biggest of sins. If we were going to find out what Mexico was about, we had to go outside of ourselves to find it. There thus emerged a kind of Malinowskian fieldwork mystique, which very quickly got linked to a process of rediscovering the nation.

Fieldwork became the key to the anthropological endeavor and was formally taught in university training programs. At that time people kept saying that "anthropology is done with your feet" (by walking), and we were taught to distrust any secondhand written material on our field subject. We had to make fresh descriptions of all that we saw, from settlement patterns to agricultural systems, politics, and kinship. Everything needed to be understood firsthand, so much so that bureaucratically generated information was eschewed in favor of local information only available to someone "in the field." The anthropological texts of the period are littered with statements like "the population of Tepeji is 6,600 inhabitants, according to Don Silverio of the *barrio de arriba.*"

Because of all of this, "the field" was constructed as a kind of place of initiation, and fieldwork was like a baptism without which one could not confidently speak about Mexico. Anthropology became, then, a privileged producer of images of Mexico. As students, we were asked to enter the field ignorant of everything but a little anthropological theory and, after spending long months, or years, in a place—after many walks, and an infinite number of interviews and conversations—one would emerge with some true knowledge of Mexico. This process of immersion into reality captured the imagination of many, many people. Anthropology students introduced others to new idiomatic expressions. They legitimated a new interest in popular music. They helped popularize (or should I say gentrify?) peasant drinks and foods. Mexico was rediscovered and recreated in this anthropological dialectic. It was an exciting job.

True, there was a lot wrong with the views of Mexico that had been based on less firsthand experience in the field. The urban lumpenproletarian was usually not the familyless macho that Samuel Ramos thought. Peasant economy was not as idiosyncratic and inefficient as the members of the bourgeoisie and government thought. Capitalism and modernization affected even the most "pristine" Indian groups. Censuses *were* done carelessly. So the baptism of fieldwork and the rejection of prior texts did have some positive impact. On the other hand, the insistence on reconstructing Mexico from scratch produced a profound ingenuity in Mexican anthropology, while, at the same time, the populism created by the characteristics of fieldwork as a *rite de passage* provoked theoretical stagnation (the writer Jorge Ibarguengoitia told of an anthropologist girlfriend of his who spent two years in the Sierra de Puebla and finally wrote a report that he claimed he could have invented in two days).

It did not take too long for the misguided premises of Mexican anthropology's rediscovery of Mexico to catch up with it. The problems came on two sides. On the one hand, anthropologists began to pay a high price for ignoring all knowledge that had not been generated through anthropological fieldwork. Writers began discrediting the importance of fieldwork by charging that anthropologists were only rediscovering the obvious, while sociologists complained that anthropological information was not adequately linked to what was going on at "higher levels" of the system, and therefore was not "representative" of anything.

On the other hand, anthropological case studies began piling up, but no new theoretical understanding seemed to be emerging. Anthropology was providing plenty of food for thought, but anthropologists were not being trained to do the thinking. As consciousness of these problems spread, the promise of deriving important political conclusions from anthropology diminished, and the prestige of the discipline began to decline. Mexican anthropology's own (partly misplaced) claim to holism was corroded. Anthropology in Mexico is today unsure of its place and of the place of its analyses in national politics.

Many colleagues who were enthusiasts of anthropological analysis at the beginning of the eighties are today completely jaded and are looking to literature, to biology, to psychoanalysis—even to astrology—for truth. As anthropologists' misplaced pretensions of representing "the people" have declined, anthropologists have turned inwards. "How could we understand others when we did not understand ourselves?" But the result has not been "reflexivity" as much as a severe case of "literature-envy." So, one of my concerns in restoring national culture to anthropology in Mexico is to help revive the cultural critique to which anthropology aspired but which it never adequately reached.

My main aim in this work has been to develop a theory and methods that can help specify case studies and avoid their use in constructing an internally coherent and harmonious view of national culture. Being able to conceive of the state and of one's relation to it (something I have called "holism" in this chapter) is important for the construction of one's identity and, thence, for one's empowerment as a social actor. Nonetheless, this will to power cannot be a good thing if it is built on an entirely mythologized and fetishized view of the state.

In this sense, I believe that the thinking on national, regional and local culture in Mexico can be oriented to self-empowerment. The problem with most of the lo mexicano literature was that it was written in a period when the idea of modernization and development still seemed real to most Mexican intellectuals. They therefore tended to see Mexican culture as something to attack, as a kind of mask that hid a "real universal human." Today we (I at least) are less convinced about the attainability of some universal "modernity." We feel that to develop in desirable directions we need to nurture some things about Mexico that we like, but this is only possible if these elements are analytically named. A critique of the forms of consciousness in the Mexican national space is therefore fundamental.

The Pensadores' Descriptions as Questions

In this section I analyze a few key aspects of Mexican culture. The purpose of this limited inquiry is to take the mode of analysis that has been developed in part 1 and show how it can operate when we analyze "national characteristics." The stagnating pool of descriptions of national traits that were produced by the pensadores can be productively used to open up questions about culture in the national space.

What follows is only a limited list of (a) principles that are supposed to generate Mexican cultural practices, (b) paradigmatic cultural groups, and (c) cultural characteristics that have been proposed in some of the outstanding works on Mexican national culture:[3]

generative principles	groups	cultural characteristics
inferiority	Mexican men	machismo
solitude	Mexican women	defensiveness
relajo	Pachucos	closedness
	Pelados	formalism
	Indians	dissembling
	Intellectuals	relajo
	Politicians	attraction to death
		latent homosexuality
		extreme individualism
		passive stoicism

If we focus on these characteristics as propositions about a regional culture ("Mexican national culture") we notice that the most general problem is lack of clarity in the relations posited between groups, generative principles and cultural characteristics. The pensador tradition presents no satisfactory discussion of the organization of social groups in regional space. For example, the category of "Mexican women," present in Paz, contains no discussion of different sorts of women according to class, kind of locality, or kind of family organization. Mexican women in Paz's account are meant to represent (a) incommunicative, self-effaced, objects of lonely male veneration and (b) intrinsically "open"—and therefore intrinsically inferior—beings. It is clear that in this account women are not subjects of Mexican culture; they are only represented objects. Already here we can conclude that Paz is in fact detailing a particular male ideology and calling it "national culture,"[4] but let us go on to consider implications that are more fertile for regional research.

If we allow, without conceding, that women are best analyzed as representations and not agents of national culture (after all, Paz's description of Mexican national culture seems to refer mainly to the culture of the Mexicans who make up "public opinion"; in 1950 that may have meant that women only entered the picture as representations and not as actors), still we would have the problem of systematic regional differentiation in representations. Do landless day-laborers—whose ability to perpetuate family unity under patriarchal authority is undermined by lack of financial and cultural capital—value "closedness" (and thence virginity and the inherent inferiority of women) in the same way as peasants, whose base of patriarchal control is firmly established through property inheritance? Whatever the answer to this question is, it opens up a problem in the organization of national culture that is not present in the writings of any of the pensadores. The complexes (solitude, inferiority) that generate cultural practices are rooted in classes and groups that have particular histories and occupy specific places in the regional system. If the practices that are generated by these complexes extend themselves beyond their groups of origin, this extension implies other generative principles.

We could argue—with Octavio Paz—that the value or aesthetic of "closedness" is a kind of idiom of power wherein "penetration" stands for domination and "impenetrability" stands for power; but this realization still says relatively little about the areas of social activity where this aesthetic of "closedness" will apply. Perhaps the peasants characterized above bring this aesthetic to bear on a system of control over women's sexuality, while the day-laborers use it to build an image of the "macho" and the "weakling" that can be applied to men and women alike. The differences between the ways in which "closedness" relates to the cultural practices of our hypothetical peasants and day-laborers reflect the two groups' positions in society: each particular rendering of "closedness" is therefore tied to a specific set of "generative principles." These "other generative principles" are a major analytic problem. They are the mechanisms of ideological articulation of a regional culture. On the other hand, if there is in fact systematic variation in the meaning of women (for men) across different regional groups, can one point to common elements, or are these differences minimized by a dominant ideology of some sort?

Fruitful questions like these arise whenever we attempt to spatialize any one of the characteristics in the list above. For example, does "chaotic disorganization" (relajo) menace all purposeful collective action in Mexico or, alternatively, does it tend to appear only in particular frames of interaction in particular regional contexts? I have never seen the purposeful action of a peasant family seriously undermined by relajo, but I have seen this occur in student meetings, among employees and—especially—in bureaucratic offices. What is the spatial organization of relajo's subversions? What social relations and which collective actions does it most comically subvert?

The same kind of questions can be raised for Mexican etiquette, machismo, or "individualism" (*personalismo*). Is "machismo" the same for peasants as it is for peasant migrants in cities? Is "rudeness" (a breach of etiquette) defined the same way in a village as it is in Mexico City's middle classes? Where is "personalismo" tolerated (or encouraged) and where is it discouraged?

The ideas developed by the pensadores are internally incommensurable because they do not systematize the nature and relations between the cultural groups that compose Mexico, and because they do not investigate the ways in which different group ideologies are articulated. The result is that the characterizations of "Mexican national culture" which the pensadores have developed are connected only very loosely (or vaguely) to the social groups that occupy the national space. Because of this, each one of the pensadores' characterizations of "Mexican" culture can be constituted into a question or a problem for regional cultural explanation. The chapters of this section are an inquiry into a few of these national characteristics, specifically, caciquismo, caudillismo, presidencialismo, and race relations. The analysis of these features does not "solve" all of the enigmas of Mexican national culture. It does, however, clear the way for a more systematic resolution.

16

Racial Ideology and
Forms of Nationalism

So far I have presented various local and regional intellectuals vying to construct a place for themselves within a national whole. I have stressed the primary importance of the economic and political space in the construction of cultural differences and as a context for localist ideology. This perspective involves an exploration of the systematic intraregional and interregional cultural variations that allow for neither a homogeneous general description of "national culture" nor the vagueness of the notion of "popular culture." I have not, however, yet referred directly to the national ideology in which these localist ideologies are all operating; national ideology has only been described obliquely, through its empirical manifestations in what I called the regional "culture of social relations."

This second part is devoted to interpreting aspects of Mexican ideology and its relation to culture in the Mexican national space. This first chapter is an exploration of Mexican ideology, especially the relationship between racial ideology and the ideology of the national state. I use some of Louis Dumont's ideas on the relationship between hierarchy, individualism, and nationalism in Western Europe to explore the historical relationships among caste, color, class, and the characteristics of Mexican nationalisms.[1] The questions that I will concentrate on are: (1) How can we characterize the hierarchical ideology of the colonial period? (2) How were racial ideologies affected by the emergence of liberalism and Revolutionary nationalism? (3) What is the relationship between changes in racial ideologies and Mexican nationalism? In this chapter I leave aside the regional perspective and its implications for the dynamics of these ideologies. Some of these implications will be explored in the last chapter, which is a spatial analysis of Mexican political forms.

The Dynamics of Race and Caste in Colonial Ideology

The salience of nationalism in postrevolutionary Mexico has been universally noted. This nationalism has a protagonist, the Mexican; and that protagonist has a particular, historically forged cultural identity which has been inextricably linked to a racial category, the mestizo. I shall explore how and why this ideology emerged. Some readers may be disturbed by the fact that I begin with a discussion of race and caste in the colonial (prenational) period. I do this for two reasons: because Mexican national communities were first conceived in the frame of the Spanish empire, and because there are certain problems in our current understanding of colonial ideology that need to be resolved in order to analyze the dialectics of modern Mexican nationalism. This chapter is, then, an essay in historical interpretation. I will begin by painting a picture of the evolution of hierarchy and individualism. The problem that interests me is modernization, in particular, the implantation of modern individualism in Mexico.

A historiographical current, which includes José Antonio Maraval and Richard Morse, has stressed the importance of hierarchy and caste in the Spanish ideological system. Following Morse (1982), one might synthesize some of the general elements of ideology in Iberoamerica as follows: the Spanish state consolidated around a legal system premised on Aquinas's philosophy. The Spanish state encompassed a series of culturally diverse peoples who were interlinked in a chain of subordination and complementarity. This chain had the king and the pope at its apex.

The relationship between the king and the pope, between the terrestrial and the celestial powers, was also complementary and hierarchical. So, for example, the discovery and conquest of Mexico was represented as a chapter in the spiritual contest between God and Satan. Cortés and his men were seen as being subordinate to a spiritual force. Thus the sixteenth-century Franciscan Gerónimo de Mendieta argued that

> It ought to be well pondered how, without any doubt God chose the valiant Cortés as his instrument for opening the door and preparing the way for the preachers of the gospel in the New World, where the Catholic church might be restored and recompensed by the conversions of many souls for the great loss and damages which the accursed Luther was to cause at the same time within established Christianity. . . . Thus it is not without mystery that in the same year in which Luther was born in

Eisleben, in Saxony, Hernando Cortés saw the light in Medellín, a village in Spain; the former to upset the world and bring beneath the banner of Satan many of the faithful who had been for generations Catholics; the latter to bring into the fold of the Church an infinite number of people who had for ages been under the dominion of Satan in idolatry, vice and sin. (1876, III:174–175)

The subordination of the political order to religion was dramatized before the Indians by Cortés himself in his famous reception of the twelve apostle-missionaries who were sent to evangelize the Indians after conquest:

Kneeling on the ground in front of one after another, [Cortés] kissed their hands, followed by the other captains and knights. This act has been the subject of many paintings in New Spain, and has been told to the eternal memory of so great an act, the greatest which Cortés performed, not only as a human man, but as an angel from heaven by whose means the Holy Spirit operated in laying a firm foundation for his Holy Word. . . . It was Cortés's greatest act, for in it he overcame not others but himself. (Ibid., 211–212)

Cortés also provides us with a more reasoned, less ritualized, formulation of the nature of this hierarchical relationship in one of his early letters to the emperor Charles V:

[I]t is not without cause that God, our Lord, has permitted that these parts should be discovered in the name of your Royal Highness, so that this fruit and merit before God should be enjoyed by your majesties, of having instructed these barbarian people, and brought them through your commands to the true Faith. (letter of July 10, 1519, cited in Braden 1930:125)

And once Cortés had submitted the Indians, he urged them to "recognize the church as superior in the world and the pope as superior in matters spiritual and the king and queen as lords and sovereigns of this land" (letter cited in González Dávila 1649 I:3–5). In sum, the hierarchical relationship between Church and State was recognized even at the highest level of Spanish political ideology, and although this hierarchical relationship was not without some areas of tension, the ideology was in place throughout the colonial period and well into the nineteenth century.[2] The placement of the faith at the apex of the Spanish hierarchical order was also used to create a caste society based on the notion of purity of blood (*limpieza de sangre*). This process began during and immediately following the Spanish *Reconquista*. Thus, in the late fifteenth century "certificates of this [limpieza de sangre], that is, sworn

statements that the bearer had no Jewish, Moslem, or heretical antecedents, began to be required for holding the various church offices, or for
entry into religious orders, and often also for admission into the guilds"
(Braden 1930:15).

This notion of purity of blood is interesting, since it tied familial
honor to a kind of Spanish Old-Christian nationalism that was ultimately
used to create a caste society. Purity of blood was tied to honor in two
ways. First, it reflected the depth of a lineage's loyalty to Christianity
(and, thence, generally to an individual's trustworthiness); second, it
reflected the capacity of the men of "clean blood" to control their
women. Thus the Mediterranean ideology of honor, which is tied to the
virginity, chastity, and loyalty of the women, was reinforced when
limpieza de sangre was used as a way of gaining economic and political
advantages. Purity of blood was used in the realm of real earthly power,
and was not merely an index of moral superiority.

As in the case of the Spanish Inquisition, the notion of purity of blood
also led to a kind of nationalization of the Church and of the faith, in so
far as the "Old Christians" were the Spaniards, and the converted Indians, Jews, Moslems, and Africans were supposed to be spiritually unreliable and were therefore legitimately subordinated to the Spaniards.
Thus the Hispanicization of the Church through an ideology of racial
purity was a key antecedent to the construction of the racial hierarchy in
Mexico.

The political conquest of Mexico was seen as the temporal result of
the expansion of the faith. Because converted Indians were New Christians, they had to be watched by the Spaniards, and they could legitimately be made to pay for their spiritual debt through tribute and corvée
labor.[3] Thus, the Spanish concept of *nación* (nation) referred to a community of blood and it was distinct from the notion of *patria* (fatherland), which was merely the place where a person was born (see
Minguet 1979). The member of the newly christianized *naciones* were
subordinated to the Spanish nación.

There were, of course, some significant tensions in making evangelization into an ideology that legitimated political and economic subordination of Indians. These contradictions emerged especially in the early
period, and were later revived in the ideological battles that surrounded
the independence movement. The most famous critic of the use of evangelization as an excuse for economic and political subordination was
Fray Bartolomé de las Casas. It is worth reproducing parts of his arguments here, because Las Casas's ideology respected the hierarchical
relationship between church and state, but did not support the transformation of spiritual debts into perpetual serfdom:

Any incidental advantages which the princes may thus gain [through conquest of infidel territories] are allowable, but temporal ends should be wholly subordinate, the paramount objects being the extension of the church, the propagation of the Faith and the service of God. . . . Neither native rulers nor subjects should be deprived of their lands for idolatry nor any other sin. . . . Attempts [to evangelize] by force of arms are impious, like those of the Mahometans, Romans, Turks, and Moors; they are tyrannical and unworthy of Christians . . . and they have already made the Indians believe that our God is the most unmerciful and cruel of all gods. The Indians will naturally oppose the invasion of their country by a title of conquest and will resist the work of conversion. (Las Casas, cited in Braden 1930:181–183)

Las Casas's thesis clearly permits the imagining of a national independence in Mexico, and in fact the Mexican national community was imagined at least as early as 1550, when a Dominican priest was reported by a visitador as saying that "His Majesty has nothing here beyond what the pope has given him, and the pope could give land to no one save for the spiritual good of the Indians. The day when it [New Spain] has a government and it is instructed in the things of the faith, the king will be obliged to give the country over to the natives" (*Colección de documentos inéditos . . .* IV:370).

There was therefore a tension between institutionalizing the political and economic subordination of conquered people via the Hispanicization of the faith by means of the ideology of limpieza de sangre, and a view that tended to see the colonies as potential nations that were only subjected to the crown temporarily and that would be independent as soon as they had been evangelized. Evidently, the first ideology was dominant during the whole of the colonial period, although the second ideology was always present and eventually served to create the Mexican state.

Now that I have clarified the ideological basis of the Mexican caste system, we can turn to looking at its specific makeup. This subject is extremely important for understanding the logic of racial relations and its links to the construction of a Mexican national ideology. Moreover, it is a subject that has tended to be misunderstood because the liberal tradition that was implanted in Mexico in the nineteenth century clouds our understanding of the colonial system of values. This liberal view has tended to see relations of race in New Spain as a kind of color bar which tended to correspond in a direct way to economic class. So, for example, Palmer summarizes the dominant view of the colonial system as follows: "The Spaniards were ranked at the top, followed by the castas or racially mixed groups; then came the Indians, and finally the African slaves"

(1976:38). The image is thus one of simple stratification. However, this image is misleading from an ideological standpoint, since the way in which each of these groups was conceived varied. The colonial system of stratification was not a simple color bar.

The first important point in this regard is that Indians and Africans were incorporated in different ways to the Spanish political ideology. From very early on, the Indians were allowed to maintain a world of their own. As opposed to the African slaves, the Indians were recognized as having a right to a community and to a polity. The existence of value and of hierarchy *within* the Indian world was recognized and even reinforced since the conquest. In fact, Spaniards needed to rely on the Indian hierarchy in order to govern. Thus, for example, Cortés instructed one of his men in 1524, "Give each [Indian] chief to understand that he must enforce this order [from Cortés], and if evidence is found of its having been disobeyed, he shall suffer the penalty for permitting it to occur" (*Colección de documentos inéditos* . . . 26:151). In other words, Cortés promoted and relied upon a hierarchical relationship between Indian chiefs and Indian commoners. On the one hand, he recognized the chief's superiority to the commoner (nobility was acknowledged); the chief was seen as a representative who could stand in the place of the whole Indian community or polity.

The idea that the Indian communities had an internal hierarchy was still alive at the end of the colonial period, despite the impoverishment of the Indian nobility and the emergence of wage laborers. Witness, for example, the following document from the Indian town of Xocotitlán (1782):

> During the past thirteen years the macehuales [Indian commoners] have been occupying the government, against the dispositions of the Royal Laws and against the frequently renewed orders of His Majesty (may God keep him), where it is established that in the posts of governor and the other posts of the Indian Republics caciques [Indian nobles] should be preferred over plebeians, and if plebeians are elected to any of these posts, they must choose those with the best habits, who know to read and write, to speak Castilian and who can administer the royal tribute. The diametrical opposite of all of this is being practiced in the said village, because in the elections that they hold, they punctually elect the drunkards, the idiots, the people with the worst habits, none of whom know how to read nor write, much less to speak Castilian. And these people maliciously alternate in power without allowing the election of a cacique, despite the fact there there are some here who have even been governors. (cited in Chávez Orozco 1943:15, my trans.)

The acknowledgment of this hierarchical order was expressed in the notion of the Indian Republic. The fact that a certain wholeness was allowed to Indian society is part of what will explain, in later dates, the easy use of the Indian community—and especially of Indian nobility—in Mexican nationalism. The idea of the Indian Republic meant that the Spanish system recognized the existence of two nations with political representation within the Spanish state, the Spanish nation and the Indian nation, and the relationship between these two nations was meant to be paternalistic.

The difference between the Spanish/Indian and the Spanish/black relationship was that internal hierarchy was recognized for Indian society, whereas no internal hierarchy was ever allowed for slaves. In fact, although Africans too were thought of as a nación (a community of blood), the Spaniards tried to block the existence of a slave society.

The Spanish ideology of slavery was laid out in the *Siete Partidas,* a legal document which was forged in the thirteenth century. In this treatise slavery was seen as a condition that ran against natural law. In principle, slavery should be a transitory condition applied to individuals that belonged to nations that refused to allow evangelization. So, for example, the bills of sale that accompanied the purchase of African slaves in Mexico all contained the statement "captured in just war, subject to servitude, free from mortgage and other impediment" (cited in Palmer 1976:32).

The idea was, therefore, that slavery was a way of bringing individual infidels into a faith that their nations of origin rejected. Because of this, internal hierarchy was never allowed for the slave population.[4] Instead, the ideal was that, through intense surveillance by the Church and by their masters, *individual* slaves would earn their entrance to heaven and, in some circumstances, their or their children's manumission.

Palmer acknowledges that "the trend of active concern shown by the Church and the State for the Indian was never duplicated for the black slave. Under careful religious tutelage the slave would receive his paradise in heaven but not on earth" (1976:118). Yet, in a way, this statement is misleading; the Church showed no concern for Africans as a nation; their aim was to destroy these nations of infidels and to incorporate individual Africans into the faith via slavery. The Church's policy towards Indians was directed to the Indian nations, whereas their policy towards Africans was directed to the individual, for only individual Africans were redeemable.

The redemption of Africans could only happen as a result of their proven loyalty to the faith and to their masters. Thus, "a slave could . . . obtain his freedom by performing some meritorious deed, such as denouncing someone for treason, reporting the rape of a virgin, identifying counterfeiters or his master's murderer" (Palmer 1976:87). All of these "meritorious deeds" are proofs of loyalty to the new community, to the community of Christians. Moreover, the Inquisition was especially punctilious in punishing any sign of renunciation of the Christian faith. Blasphemy was a serious offense for slaves because the blasphemous slave was not deriving "the correct moral" from slavery. (Ideally, violence was being used to bring the slave into the fold of Christianity, not out of it.) Witness a typical Inquisition punishment for a blasphemous slave:

> We order that in the chapel of this Holy office he hears Mass, praying without a ribbon or a hat, with a wax candle in his hands and a rope tied to his neck and a gag in his mouth . . . that he be taken through the public streets of this city upon a beast of burden, naked to the waist, with the rope and the gag and with the voice of the crier making his offense known. (cited in Palmer 1976:149–150)

The public punishment of blasphemy stressed the relationship between infidelity to the Church and slavery: the slave was stripped almost naked, attached to a sign of submission (the rope), and gagged. The legitimacy of slavery was thus upheld at the same time that the blasphemer was punished. The public punishment of slave blasphemy can be understood as a mechanism that reinforced the idea that slaves were not yet fully convinced Christians and could easily renounce the faith. The public presentation of blaspheming slaves was a way of revitalizing the legitimation of black slavery; the slaves were New Christians that were still not eligible for unsurveilled freedom. These public events also reinforced the idea that blacks lacked honor and were untrustworthy.[5]

Thus, the humanity of the slaves as individuals was recognized by the Church and the State;[6] it was their existence as a viable community or nation that was consistently denied. This conclusion can be documented in the cases of slave rebellions. Palmer describes a 1608 coronation ceremony of a (rebellious) black king and queen, and the appointment of a whole noble stratum of dukes, counts, marquises, and princes (1976: 135–136). In the trials against the leaders of this conspiracy, one of the ringleaders is said to have claimed that "it was only a matter of time until the Spaniards and everyone else would become their [the blacks'] slaves" (137). Whether this was actually said by a slave or whether it was merely trumped up by the Spanish prosecution is questionable, but even in the latter case it is clear that the whole notion of black kings and a black kingdom was part of the phantasmagoria of Mexican society, where blacks were, on the one hand, treated as belonging to a discernible group while, on the other hand, the whole ideology of slavery was predicated on destroying those group identities and eventually absorbing the slave into the Christian world.[7]

Blacks were recognized as belonging to a group because of the political need to control slaves. Thus, since 1501 Ferdinand and Isabel denied "permission to come here [to Hispaniola] to Moors, nor Jews, nor heretics, nor reconcilables, nor persons converted to our faith, except if they are negro slaves or other slaves born in the power of Christians" (1976:7). This edict was renewed for the American mainland in 1543.

The whole issue can be clearly understood if we start with Las Casas's position regarding slavery in the New World. Las Casas argued that Indians not be subjected to slavery because they were allowing evangelization to proceed peacefully.[8] Accordingly, Indian slaves were not captives of a just war and they were thus illegitimately being deprived of their natural rights. Las Casas suggested that these illegitimate Indian slaves be substituted with *black or white* captives of just war (see Hanke 1959).

The Spanish Crown eventually supported Las Casas's argument against Indian slavery, except in the areas where Indians did not allow evangelization. However, as we have seen, the Crown also prohibited the importation of "white" slaves (Moors and Jews) because they were "considered to be intractable and rebellious" or "agents of Islam" (for a full discussion of the images of slaves, see Aguirre Beltrán 1972:155–175). African slaves were ideal in this respect precisely because they were easily distinguished from the Spaniards and thus would not confuse the Indian population.

In sum, Africans were recognized as a group for reasons of political control; however, they were not allowed to exist as a collectivity. Africans belonged to the Spanish Republic, while Indians had republics of their own. Indian society was superior to slave society at the ideological level, because Indians were allowed their own hierarchical organization, both within the family and in their republics. More precisely, Spanish ideology recognized an Indian society but denied a slave society. The relationship between the two cannot be ordered in a single model of stratification because the slaves were the bottom rung of the Spanish world, whereas the Indians were seen as having their own (subordinated) world.

An interesting and counterintuitive correlate of this is that, in certain respects, slaves were more valued as individuals than Indians. The life of a slave was worth more to a Spaniard than the life of an Indian, and their physical nature was more greatly admired. Although the spiritual nature of Indians was respected more than that of Africans by some,[9] they were seen as being physically inferior to them. For example, before the abolition of Indian slavery, black slaves sold for ten times the price of Indian slaves (Palmer 1976:35). Moreover, whites liked to make a show of their slaves in public places. The viceroy Martín Enriquez noted that "the Spaniards not only use them for labor and necessary tasks, but they honor themselves and have more pages and lackeys than there are ne-groes in Spain" (cited in Palmer 1976:43). African slaves were thus a part of the Spanish theatre of domination in the New World.[10]

The instability that characterized New Spain's organization of caste can be explained by these factors. Moreover, I shall argue that the specific dynamics of caste instability in New Spain explain much of the post-independence attitudes toward race and, as a result, they also help us understand the ways in which the national community was ideologically constituted.

Mexican slavery was unstable for several reasons.[11] First, according to Spanish law, bondage was inherited through the maternal side and slaves were allowed to marry non-slaves.[12] Second, two-thirds of the slaves imported to Mexico were men (Ibid.:11). Third, there were no slave breeders in Mexico (Ibid.:33). Fourth, the notion of limpieza de sangre is predicated on the importance of biological parenthood. Fifth, acculturation of Africans was considered to be both possible and important, and it was recognized as an asset for slaves.[13] Sixth, manumission was legal and was practiced.[14] African slaves were therefore logically (if not always actually) upwardly mobile. Moving "up" for them consisted in becoming free laborers within the Spanish world of cities, haciendas, ranches, mines, and obrajes.

The Indian sphere, in its turn, was unstable in a different way. Indian society continued to exist through the whole of the colonial period. However, Indian republics lost many individuals to the Spanish sphere through several mechanisms. First, many Indians emigrated out of their communities in order to avoid paying tribute and ended up working as wage laborers in Spanish mines, obrajes, or haciendas.[15] Second, some Indian communities lost their communal lands and individuals were forced to emigrate. Third, wealthy Indians could acquire privileges that were supposedly reserved for Spaniards and thereby fuse with certain sectors of Spanish and creole society.

From a class perspective the effects of the instability of slave and Indian castes seem simple and straightforward. The freeing of women and men through miscegenation, emigration, manumission, bribery, or acculturation created social classes of wage laborers, free artisans, and a preindustrial urban rabble of *léperos*.[16] From an ideological pespective, however, the effects of this process are much more complex, for they resulted in a whole culture of racial distinction.

Spaniards and descendants of Spaniards were recognized as being the elite, even if they were poor. Thus, Humboldt observed that "any white person, although he rides his horse barefoot, imagines himself to be of the nobility of the country" (cited in McAlister 1963:357). Despite the emergence of class, then, it is clear that many aspects of caste operated into the time of independence.

Beneath the Europeans were *las castas,* the free mixed-bloods who emerged out of slavery and out of the Indian republics. The castas were a product of the classificatory problems that emerged out of the ideology of blood purity and of the instability of the slave and Indian castes. The characteristics that were imputed to each of the castas were related to the dominant ideas regarding the nature of the Spanish, Indian, and African races, as well as to Spanish kinship and gender ideologies. On the other hand, the system of castas was also unstable, and transgenerational upward and downward mobility was possible. Thus, given the right resources and a few generations, one could come closer to the white, black, and Indian poles in a few generations through marriage strategies. Following is an example of an erudite classification of castas:[17]

1. Spanish and Indian: mestizo
2. Mestizo and Spanish: castizo
3. Castizo and Spanish: Spanish
4. Spanish and black: mulato
5. Spanish and mulato: morisco
6. Spanish and morisco: albino
7. Spanish and albino: torna atrás (turn back)
8. Turn back and Indian: lobo
9. Lobo and Indian: zambaigo
10. Zambaigo and Indian: cambujo
11. Cambujo and mulato: albarazado
12. Albarazado and mulata: barcina
13. Barcina and mulata: coyote
14. Coyote and Indian: chamiso
15. Chamiso and mestizo: coyote mestizo
16. Coyote mestizo and mulato: Ahí te estás (remain there)

Although this is not the place to decipher the meaning of las castas in detail, a few examples of the classificatory logic involved in their creation can clarify the nature of the system. It is particularly important to do so, because the system of classification of castas has all too often been treated as if it were unintelligible or as merely a curiosity of colonial racist thought. So, for example, in his excellent treatise on Mexican blacks, Aguirre Beltrán understands the logic of the *color* classifications that were used (for example, white mestizo, dark mestizo, black mestizo, black negro, and light negro), but he treats the elaborate classifications of *racial* combinations as follows:

> From simply reading the erudite classifications [of mixtures] above we see the tremendous confusion that their authors were in. The product of one same mixture is [sometimes] called by different names, and one same name [sometimes] serves to designate different mixes. Moreover, the classifications revived terms which had already been forgotten, such as *zambaigo* [the early term for the child of an Indian and an African], and other hateful names were invented, such as *albarazado, gíbaro, barcino, chamizo,* and *albino,* all of which are taken from the zoological vocabulary. We do not mention the etymologies of the categories *Ahí te estás* (remain there), *Salta Atrás* (jump back), *Torna Atrás* (turn back), *Tente en el aire* (stay suspended in the air), and *No te entiendo* (I don't understand you); they were not used in practice because they are positively unintelligible. Some of them, such as *Torna Atrás,* imply a regression to the black type in the products of a mixture. These regressions have been proven by modern research to be totally mythical. The erudite classifications had the defect of being unintelligible and impracticable, a logical product of an erudite mentality. (1972:177)

Let us look at the matter more closely. In principle, one could imagine a system with three poles (Spanish, Indian, and African) and a single racial category for all (free) mixed-bloods. This solution is close to what was adopted in Mexico after independence, when the ideology of race and caste was eliminated from the legal blueprint of the society. In the colonial period, there was a certain tendency for a system of this sort to operate in some rural areas, where people were either Spaniards, Indians, blacks, or mestizos. The urban areas, however, developed a much more fine-grained system of classification which can be understood by looking at the fundamental triangle of recognized races:

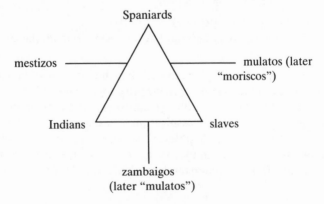

From this point secondary combinations could be made which tended to pull mulatos, mestizos, and zambaigos either closer to one of the pure poles or deeper into an ever-fouler mixture. For example, if a mestizo married a European, his or her progeny would be closer to the Spanish pole (a castizo), and if marriage with whites was repeated in the next generation, its offspring would be considered Spanish. Moreover, if one analyzes the erudite classifications which Aguirre discards one notes that they reveal interesting common principles: (1) By consistently marrying with Spaniards, the descendants of an Indian can formally be considered a full-fledged Spaniard in three generations. (2) The same cannot be said for blacks, who after four generations of marrying Spaniards get classified as *torna atrás* (turn back) and after five generations as *tente en el aire* (remain suspended in the air: a state from which they cannot advance); in other words, black blood can theoretically never be entirely fused into Spanish blood. (3) Persistent combinations of all three bloods create ever-viler products, which, after many generations, also have ending points beyond which it is no longer worth classifying (*ahí te estás* or *no te entiendo:* "there you shall remain" and "I don't understand you"). Thus the pure Indian and the pure black poles are also not technically generatable from mixtures. (4) In comparing different series of classifications one finds that when a same name refers to different kinds of mixtures, there is usually a reason. For example, *torna atrás* or *salta atrás* ("turn or jump back") can be either (a) a mixture of Spaniard and albina (turns back toward blackness), (b) a mixture of *chino* (an almost white black) with an Indian turns back toward the Indian pole, for the mixture of salta atrás and mulata is the same as the mixture between an Indian and an albina: a *lobo*; (c) a mixture of "no te entiendo" (which is a complex of nine generations of mixtures) with Indian (again it turns back towards Indian). In short, the category marks a return to a type of blood which dominates (either Indian or black) in situations beyond which the classificatory system is not willing to go. Another example is the term "lobo" (wolf), which is either (1) a mixture of Indian and torna atrás (in this case a whitened black), (2) a mixture of *chino cambujo* (a whitened black-Indian) and an Indian, or (3) a mixture of salta atrás (a whitened black-Indian) with mulato. In other words, the lobo is always a combination of the three bloods at a relatively early stage of mixture.

What does all of this mean? It means that Indian blood was entirely "redeemable," whereas African blood was not. It also means that once an Indian or an African began mixing they could never return to the pure pole, but they could go up or down the ladder of ascribed statuses. For example, a person of African descent could come so close to whiteness as to be placed in the limbo of tente en el aire, or she or he could descend as far down as the no te entiendo. Most of the animal names that Aguirre Beltrán discusses are low status, whereas there are high-status categories which are the product of simple combinations (between only two races): mestizo and *castizo* for people of Indian blood, and mulato (which derives from mule), morisco, albino, and tente en el aire for people with African blood.

The aspects of the colonial ideology of race which need to be emphasized are: (1) that the ascribed racial statuses were extremely important;[18] (2) that the black pole was easily incorporated into the proletarianized mass, whereas Indian communities were hierarchical societies in their own right; (3) that whiteness (or proximity to whiteness) could be achieved; (4) that the same principle which allowed for the construction of caste (limpieza de sangre) also provoked the extreme instability of caste; (5) that the peculiarity of the Spanish caste in this social system was that it was the only position in the society where prosperity and power were an ascribed status. "Whiteness" represented a kind of purity because it was the only position in which wealth, status and power could be in equilibrium.[19] In the turmoil of ethnic manipulation that characterized the Mexican eighteenth century, whiteness was the only position that people did not try to jockey out of.

How the Value of Whiteness Survived Under Liberalism

At independence the dynamics of race and class changed substantially. First, slavery was abolished. This meant that the whole of what used to be the castas plus the slaves were soon reclassified as "the masses." However, the Indian pole was not as easily abolished, and although public policy was bent on the destruction of the Indian community, this process was never successfully completed.

Thus, in 1821 the landlords of the Puebla region proclaimed that

> the greatest benefit that the government can give to agriculture is to consider and to remedy the disorder among the Indians, whose poverty has served as a pretext to protect them. This protection has worked against the Indians themselves, as well as against the agriculturalists [hacendados and ranchers] and agriculture. (cited in Chávez Orozco 1943:36, my trans.)

One of the main crusades of the liberals was that Indians had to cease being Indians and accede to the status of "citizens." The crux of the issue was summarized by José María Luis Mora's explanation of his discrepancies with congressman Rodríguez Puebla, who was an early indigenista:

The true cause of our opposition was related to public education, which conflicted openly with Mr. Rodríguez Puebla's desires regarding the future of what remains of the *Aztec race* that still exists in Mexico. This man, who claims to belong to that race, is one of the country's worthies because of his high moral and political qualities. His party is, in theory, that of *progress* . . . however . . . Mr. Rodríguez does not limit his sights to achieving liberty; instead he extends them to the exaltation of the Aztec race and consequently his prime objective is to maintain the existence of that race within society. In order to achieve this he has upheld the old [colonial] civil and religious privileges of the Indians, the *status quo* of their communal holdings, the houses of charity that were destined to help them, and the schools in which they exclusively received their education. In one word, although without explicitly confessing this, [Mr. Rodríguez's] principles and objectives tend visibly to establish a *purely Indian system.*

However, Farías's administration, like all of its predecessors, thought in a different way. Persuaded that the existence of different races in a single society was and would be a point of eternal discord, it not only denied the distinctions that were prescribed in the constitutional law of earlier years, but it also applied all of its efforts to speed the fusion of the Aztec race to the rest of the people [*la masa general*]. The Farías administration thus did not recognize the distinction between *Indians* and non-*Indians,* substituting it instead with that of *poor* and *rich,* and extending the benefits of society to all. (J.M.L. Mora, Obras Sueltas, vol. 1:262–263)

Mora thus recognized that the colonial constitution of Indian republics entailed acknowledging an Indian world, with its own internal hierarchy of values and its own political and social orientation. He and his fellow liberals believed that this situation could not be sustained in a modern nation-state because it meant having a nation within a nation. The Spanish system had encompassed many nations under the sovereignty of one king. The liberal state could not do so because the very idea of a democratic state supposes a single people who are all to be equal before the law; when sovereignty passes from the king to the people, the state has to coincide with a single nation.

Mora explicitly attempts to impose a class model over the old caste system. If the "members of the Aztec race" were to progress, they would have to be considered as (poor) citizens who could then aspire to climb the economic ladder through their work. The nineteenth century's political elites tried to abolish the Indian community by substituting communal property with private property, and by eliminating all laws which distinguished the Indian population from the rest (dress codes, tribute laws, residence laws, forms of surveillance through the Church).

On the other hand, despite the egalitarian rhetoric of liberalism, the ideal of whiteness did not disappear in nineteenth-century society. The dissolution of the castas into a "mestizo race" (referred to by Mora as *la masa general*) did not detract from the idea that whiteness was still the only position where wealth and high status were in homeostasis. This situation is made evident in the evolution of the category of "Indian" in the nineteenth century. With the dissolution of Indianness as a legal category that guaranteed a caste position, the use of the term "Indian" became synonymous with a combination of material poverty and cultural "backwardness." Class distinction was again framed in racial terms, so that poor mestizos—especially peasant mestizos—were called "Indians" by the upper classes (cf. Lomnitz-Adler 1979), while rich mestizos were "whitened" (cf. Knight 1990:73). Thus, the complex racial dynamics of the colonial period were simplified in the nineteenth century into a bipolar model (Indians/whites) with an intermediate class of "mestizos." This model, which was a direct result of liberal policies on the Mexican reality, later found some ideological support in Social Darwinism. For example, Justo Sierra explained that European migrants were needed "so as to obtain a cross with the indigenous race, for only European blood can keep the level of civilization . . . from sinking, which would mean regression, not evolution" (cited in Knight 1990:78).[20]

The passage from a caste to a class society therefore entailed a transformation—but not a complete elimination—of the old ethnic system. The nineteenth century kept the European and the Indian in opposite poles of an ideological system, and it also created (this was its novelty) an image of a dual society: one was a national society of citizens and social classes, the other was an Indian society of autarchic communities that, despite the national society's best efforts, survived. The dominant liberal ideology saw Indian society as standing on the margins of progress, on the margins of nationality and outside of history. For the Spanish colonists, Indian society was something to be overseen, for the liberals, it was something to be overcome. This fact combined with the class situation and provoked a positive valorization of whiteness in a complex that has come to be known as *malinchismo*.

In sum, the implantation of liberalism as the official ideology had the net effect of discarding certain aspects of the colonial racial ideology while it built on others. The pole of society that was identified as "the general mass" of citizens had "whites" at its apex, while the collectivities most recalcitrant to enter fully into a capitalist economy of wage labor, private property, and free enterprise were the Indians. Because of this, some of the colonial racial ideas were simply revamped, especially those that referred to the brutishness of Indians and, generally, to the inferiority of dark skin. Moreover, the nineteenth century also retained the colonial ideology of whiteness as an attainable status to which many people aspired. On the other hand, with the abolition of slavery and with the end of legal forms of racial discrimination, the castas blurred into a single mass which came to be known racially as "mestizos."

Thus, the results of liberal policy turned out different from what early proponents, such as Mora, imagined. Instead of achieving a nation of free and equal Mexicans, the country was almost entirely in the hands of a class of white hacendados and of national and foreign investors. "The Mexican citizenry" was a ragged mass of peons, peasants, and workers, many of whom were practically slaves. Democracy was never effectively implanted. The country belonged politically, economically, and culturally to the few.

The Mestizo and the Protectionist State

All of this led to the Mexican Revolution. On the racial front, the revolution provoked a reappraisal of the Indian and of the mestizo. The mestizo—not the creole—became the official protagonist of Mexican history, and Indian culture and the Indian past were revalorized in a movement which became known as *indigenismo*.

The phenomenon of indigenismo is interesting in several respects, for it served to reformulate the relationship between race and nation. Instead of seeing Indians as a nation encompassed by a Europe-oriented nation, indigenistas chose to see Mexico as the product of a clash between two independent and opposed nations, that of the Spaniards and that of the Indians. The new hero in the epic of Mexican nationality became the mestizo, who was physically both Indian and Spanish, and whose spiritual qualities avoided both the atavisms of Indian culture and the exploitative nature of the European.

An example of this is Manuel Gamio's racial interpretation of the Mexican revolution. "It is not the Indian who made the Revolution, nevertheless, its deepest roots grew and continue to grow in the Indian races" (cited in Knight 1990:77). The idea here is that the mestizo is the protagonist of Mexican history, but the mestizo's motivations are linked to his Indian side.

Molina Enriquez provides a particularly telling formulation of this ideology: "Over time, the anvil of Indian blood will always prevail over the hammer of Spanish blood" (cited in Knight 1990:85). Thus, Spanish:Indian::hammer:anvil::male:female. The roots and implications of this view are varied. On the one hand, it could be said that this position reflects a certain matrilineality, or at least matrifocality in the Mexican family system. This has been repeatedly argued in the lo mexicano literature's statements on Mexican national culture ("the Mexican's search for his father"), and especially in statements on Mexican machismo. It is difficult to tell whether the essays on this topic were mere reflections of the ideology of the revolution, or whether they were also describing an ethnographic reality. However, there is also a vein of matrilineality in colonial ideologies of race. So, for example, only the children of female slaves were born into slavery. The children who conquistadores had with Indian noble women made up the first generation of New Spain's Indian nobility. More generally, the Spanish notion of honor—whose links to the idea of limpieza de sangre I already explored—is predicated on male control over women's sexuality. Guarding a woman's virginity, having a say in her marriage decisions, and not being cuckolded by one's wife were a key part of one's honor, and all of this involves a hidden matrilineal principle since status is inherited through the purity or impurity of one's women.

In the case of indigenismo, this recourse to the matrilineal principle is laden with anti-imperialist implications. In emphasizing the mestizo's maternal side over his paternal side (the Indian side over the Spanish side), indigenistas claim the transcendence of a "Mexican soul" that is distinct from the "European" or "North American" soul. This is why indigenismo was so important in the justification of a protectionist state.

Indigenismo legitimated the active role of the Mexican state in subsuming the free market to the interests of the national community. It also allowed a reformulation of the hierarchical organization of that national community. This hierarchical organization has been constructed and institutionalized by the party of the revolution, today known as the PRI. Specifically, the official representation of the national community as a hierarchical order is evident in the sectorial organization of the party. The party's sectors have included a workers' sector, a peasant sector, a military sector (which disappeared in the 1940s), and a popular sector. The PRI's traditional hierarchical image was one in which nationalism and the protection of "the Mexican" were the sacred principle, and the national community was composed of a series of classes and occupational groups that were all complementary to one another. At the same time, the ultimate goal of progress for the whole community, the goal of reaching the level of development of the United States or of Europe was maintained.

This latter factor helps explain how the notion of "bettering one's race" (*mejorar la raza*) through "whitening oneself" (*blanquearse*) was retained in the postrevolutionary period. Dark Mexicans (mestizos) considered that obtaining and assimilating European culture and industry was both a right and a national goal. It is perhaps significant that male members of elite families often marry blond wives (cf. L. Lomnitz 1987). The slogan *gringos no, gringas sí,* and the high-status practice of marrying white women is not simply an act of "whitening," for whitening could just as easily involve mestizo women marrying white men; it can also be construed as an act of national appropriation of the dearest of European products.[21]

Thus, the choice of the mestizo as the new protagonist of nationality allowed both for the construction of a strong national state which buffered the influence of foreign power and for a retention of the Eurocentric goals of progress. Moreover, indigenistas used the image of the Indian community—which, as we have seen, retained its hierarchical organization in a way that mestizos never did—as a model of nationality. This was the purpose of Chávez Orozco's (1943) study of Indian "democratic institutions," it was behind Alfonso Caso's lists of "positive" and "negative" Indian traits, and, as we have seen, it is also Bonfil's (1987) strategy. In the recreation of a national community, the Indian comunidades served as a model of hierarchy, and thus as the antiliberal element that was necessary for the strong state and the "mixed economy" that were being proposed.[22]

The reappraisal of the mestizo, of the Indian and of the Spaniard created a formula that was anti-imperialist in the sense that the country's aperture to foreign interests was to be controlled by the national community. This national community was formally organized, and to a certain extent invented, in the official party's sectorial organization. On the other hand, indigenismo was not anti-imperialist in the sense that Mexico still aspired to modernization, the benefits of capitalist development, and access to European culture.

Revolutionary nationalism thus continued to value "whitening" for the community as a whole, but it was against merely turning the community over to the "whites." The development of this aspect of the revolutionary model is what Bonfil has identified as the development of an "imaginary Mexico" that negates the "deep Mexico" of Indian and Indian-influenced culture.

However, the model of upward mobility toward "whiteness" has had a "deeper" history and a wider social acceptance than Bonfil's notion of "imaginary Mexico" suggests. The ideology of castas allowed for this ideal of whitening, and it created a society where people manipulated their ethnic identity in order to scale the status hierarchy. Nineteenth-century racism provided a simpler mechanism for whitening—it was usually a matter of money. On the other hand, the main innovation of revolutionary indigenismo was to make "whitening" a process that was supposed to be in the control of the national state, and in the interest of the collectivity instead of merely in that of jockeying individuals.

Finally, the political developments of the 1980s and 1990s have led to yet another transformation of this ideological system. Mexico's economic aperture towards the United States is rapidly destroying the image of national community that the official party forged in earlier decades. The old sectors of the national community, the peasants, the unionized workers, the Indians, have been disappearing as politically represented collectivities. In a way, the civilization Bonfil feels is being denied is the postrevolutionary national community, that community which had an Indian soul, a mestizo body, and a civilized future.

It is being substituted by a Mexico that is still "imaginary" because its institutional makeup is still not clear, it is on the drawing board and in transition. That Mexico may be, as today's PRI seems to believe, the Mexico's long-awaited arrival to modernity, to democracy and to advanced capitalism. It may also be, as many others feel, the end of the Mexican national community and the transformation of the country into a mass of individuals whose best hope is to serve the economic interests of the United States.

The reason the nature of this transition is still unclear is that no new image of the national community has yet emerged, and the nature of the new political system is still unclear, for the current economic "modernization" would not have been possible without the powerful authoritarian state that grew out of the ideology of the Revolution. Are we to abandon the image of the national community only to retain the authoritarianism which that image fostered? Will democracy and racial equality finally arrive in the way José María Luis Mora had hoped? These are the current doubts. Their resolution will either involve rethinking the notion of the mestizo as the quintessential Mexican, or else it will preserve that notion and, with it, a hierarchical state.

Conclusions

Mexican ideologies of race have always seemed rather curious. On one side, Mexico is a society where Indian ancestry has been proudly acknowledged. On the other side, it is a society that clearly values whiteness as both a status symbol and as an aesthetic. Moreover, as opposed to racism in the United States, where blackness is marked (negatively) and whiteness claims the majority position, in Mexican racism it is whiteness that is marked (positively) and brownness claims the unmarked majority position.

Commentators on Mexican racial ideology have too often emphasized the continuity of racism from colonial times to the present. In their zeal against racism, they have ignored important aspects of the colonial caste ideology and they have minimized the nature of the changes in racial ideology in the post-Independence and post-Revolution periods. This mistake is easily made because in all three periods whites have been at the top of the economic and status ladder, and Indians, blacks, and mestizos have been undervalued and discriminated against.

In this chapter, however, I have shown that the changes in racial ideologies in these three periods were very important, and that these changes are related to the ways in which Mexican (and colonial) national ideologies have been shaped. The rise of liberalism in a society that had been built upon the Spanish hierarchical model gave rise to a particular form of discrimination against Indians and a particularly flagrant valorization of whiteness. The ideology of the Revolution, on the other hand, with its reappraisal of Indian cultures and its identification of "the Mexican" with "the mestizo" allowed for the reconstruction of a hierarchical ideology under the aegis of a protectionist state.

This argument also helps us understand why a lo mexicano literature emerged in the aftermath of the Revolution, and especially why the idea of a prototypical "Mexican" seemed acceptable to so many people then. The official (and also very popular) identification of the Mexican with the mestizo already meant that the lo mexicano literature was directed only to a certain field of persons: those who were fully part of the capitalist economy and of the political system and yet who were not foreign owners or identified fully with European stock. It is no wonder that Samuel Ramos believed that "the Mexican" had an inferiority complex: "the Mexican" (the mestizo) still had not risen to the apex of the society that was supposed, by revolutionary definition, to be his own.

The ideology of the Revolution had mestizo nationalism at its core. This ideology has supported the existence of a strong national state which systematically tries to encompass the social whole. This may be why the PRI has traditionally had no militants, and yet it has encompassed the majority of civil society. Until recently, the PRI stood for "the Mexican."

17

Regional Cultures and the Culture of the State

In the discussion of regional culture in Morelos and the Huasteca, I emphasized a dialectic between intimate cultures and used a core/periphery model to organize our understanding of this dialectic. The definition of "cultural centers" of regional culture was determined by the class relations which conformed these regions. I found cultural centers ("coherence") in the regional dominant classes and in the remote peripheries, and emergent forms of coherence in some of the more stabilized urban underclasses. These alternate loci of cultural coherence (alternate cultural centers) have important implications for the styles of political leadership and political discourse, and for alternate kinds of ideologies and policies.

Edward Shils (1975), Victor Turner (1967), and Clifford Geertz (1980 and 1983) have developed our understanding of the importance of centrality and marginality in symbolic systems such as politics and religion. The ritualization of centrality appears to be fundamental for renewing the charisma of political leaders, just as the play between marginality (or "liminality") and centrality is crucial for the dramatization of conflict and conflict resolution. However, these authors have tended to analyze the political culture of centers and margins without systematically exploring the polycentrism that always exists in complex regional political economies. The spatial perspective that I have developed on regional culture has, therefore, many implications for understanding alternate forms of legitimacy and leadership.

On the other hand, forms of political leadership and charisma have also been important in the literature on Mexican national culture. Special attention has been lavished on authoritarian political forms at local and national levels. In this chapter I shall suggest some of the implications of the regional cultural perspective for these issues. I shall focus especially on caudillos, caciques and postrevolutionary presidencialismo.

De la Peña (1986) recently summarized the main ideas regarding caudillos and caciques in Mexico. Caudillos were, everyone agrees, political phenomena of the nineteenth century. Their existence was related to the weakness of the newly created Iberoamerican states, and to the hacendados' economic incapacity to pull the countries together. Thus, caudillos were creole hacendados with a strong regional constituency, much power in the army, and aspirations to national power. Caciques, on the other hand, are regional and local leaders. They are usually mestizos or Indians. They are linked to the interests of both their local communities and the system of national power, and they command armed force which they can use either to suppress internal dissidence or to rebel against governments.[1] Whereas military caudillos were eventually substituted by the more institutionalized and more bureaucratized figure of "el señor Presidente," caciques continue to exist today in both rural and urban Mexico.

Despite the disappearance of the caudillo, many authors have stressed that the power of Mexican presidents is more than that of the mere administrator; so much so that the whole political system has been called a "presidentialist" regime. In *The Critique of the Pyramid,* Octavio Paz (1981*b*) called the postrevolutionary presidents *tlatoanis* (Aztec emperors). These presidents, Paz argued, are not like the individualistic—sometimes heroic, sometimes picaresque—figure of the caudillo; Mexican presidents have a kind of tellurian force. Their power is upheld by the vast pyramid of the state. The official party (PRI) has been in power for sixty years, and within each presidential cycle the president is an autocratic ruler. This combination between dictatorial power and cyclical change has given Mexican presidents an aura of deeply rooted power that is distinct from the personality cults of the caudillos.

The aim of this chapter is to demonstrate the implications of a spatial perspective for understanding the culture of the state, and to show how the state articulates cultural regions in Mexico. I shall begin by deconstructing the racial and class images that are present in the caudillo/cacique typology presented above. I mean to show that the dichotomy between "white" (creole) caudillos and "mestizo" or "Indian" caciques reflects a fundamental difference between the ideology of the state (which is an entirely fetishized entity, in that it is the level in which everyone's *place* is authenticated) and attitudes toward power at levels below that of "the nation." In this first part of the chapter, I shall argue that the historians who formalized the dichotomy between caudillos and caciques have simply adopted the dominant ideology about national power.

The second part of the chapter is an attempt to specify the kinds of mediating roles that "caciques" play in regional space. Whereas the alleged "whiteness" and the "wealth" of caudillos form an ideology that responds to the requirements of an exemplary center of national power, the kinds of cultural cores that are pertinent for the analysis of cacique power are more varied, and they frequently imply cleavages between regional cultural cores and regional cultural peripheries. The second part of the chapter illustrates the utility of a regional cultural perspective for understanding different kinds of "cacique" authority. The final section of the chapter discusses the routinization of both cacique and caudillo power by looking at the figure of the president of the republic and of powerful bureaucrats.

Caudillos and Caciques

The idea that caudillos were criollos and caciques are (and were) mestizos is very problematic. To begin with, the very division between criollo and mestizo is complex, for although criollos (Mexican-born Europeans) and mestizos were indeed legally distinguished in the colonial era (i.e., before caudillos), after independence the legal dichotomy between the two categories disappeared, leaving only racial discrimination to distinguish between them. Although, as we have seen, whiteness was, and still is, valued in Mexico, whites and non-whites have always intermarried. During the colonial era there was a tendency for women to marry (racially) "upward," insofar as many single Spanish men migrated to the colonies. After independence the legal barriers between races disappeared and social class became the most important form of distinction. However, race was retained as a marker of cultural distinction.[2]

Therefore, in the nineteenth century, using race to tell "criollos" apart from "mestizos" is quite difficult in any case. Moreover, if we actually look at both caciques and caudillos, there are several glaring exceptions to the racial and even to the class prototype. José María Morelos—the famous caudillo of independence—was a "mestizo," and so were Porfirio Díaz and Alvaro Obregón. On the other hand, there have also been some "white" caciques, such as Gonzalo Santos. In fact, many Huastecan caciques consider themselves to be white. Why, then, have some historians latched an ethnic or racial component onto their typologies of caciques and caudillos? In order to understand this issue, we must turn to the origins of Mexican nationalism and the ways in which national power was imagined. The construction of the idea of a Mexican nation was related to the exemplary centers of power that were built in the colonial period. In New Spain there was a spatially complex hierarchy of power centers, which culminated around the figure of the viceroy, who was the highest political authority. Gerhard (1972) provides a useful outline of the bureaucratic and ecclesiastical organization of New Spain. The viceroy was the supreme representative of all five branches of colonial government: *justicia, gobierno, militar, hacienda,* and *eclesiástico.* Because of this, the viceroy's court pooled outstanding members of all branches of government: the members of the *audiencia* in the juridical branch; the *alcaldes mayores* and *corregidores* in the government branch; the captain general, captains and lieutenants in the military branch; the royal officials (bookkeepers, accountants) in the hacienda branch; and the archbishop of Mexico and the representatives of the Inquisition and of the regular orders in the ecclesiastical branch. In addition to centralizing this particular mix of political and spiritual leaders, the court of New Spain also attracted the members of the economic elite, many of whom had influence in selecting officers to the posts of the five branches of government, or at least had constant dealings with members of one or more of these five branches of government.

Mexico City centralized all of the recognized branches of political, economic, and religious power in the social life of its elites, and in particular in the institution of the court. At the same time, one should note that there are two kinds of groups in this center of power. One is made up of native power personages who accede to the court through their independent wealth or through the favor of the viceroy or other officials; another's power is delegated from Spain: the viceroy, the members of the audiencia, the archbishop, and the Church hierarchy. The fact that the viceroy was at the pinnacle of power while he was, at the same time, a functionary that was named by the king, made for a political system that was oriented upwards and outwards.

Mexico was a society that had a court that was in every sense an exemplary center of power; it was the center of economic power, it was racially superior, it was the center of both administrative and military power, and it was the moral center of surveillance through both the justice of the Crown and the vigilance of the Church. As Lafaye (1977) has shown, all of this allowed for the creation of a national imagined community at least as early as 1600, if not earlier (see, for example, Liss 1975 and infra pt. 2, chap. 1). The fantasy of the national state was probably inspired by the fact that the pinnacle of local power was invested in the figure of the viceroy, who was not a ruler by divine right or by popular mandate, but a bureaucrat appointed by the king. This bureaucratic aspect of New Spain's political culture is perhaps what accounts for the lack of charisma of viceroys, whose power was as close to "rational bureaucratic" power as there has ever been in Mexico (cf. Rubio Mañé 1963).

The people of New Spain had experienced the centrality of power vividly. Economic, political, and religious power were combined in exemplary centers that culminated in Mexico City but had smaller centers that were hierarchically arranged in the regional system. All the local instances of power (the viceroy, the alcalde mayor, the priest, the bishop) were delegates, intermediaries, whose main characteristics were that they shared culture and ethnicity ("nationality") with the king and with the pope, but, in the end, were substitutes and were substitutable. True autonomous political power—"sovereignty"—was not to be found within the colony. Instead, there was a center with a self-effacing central figure, the viceroy.

Independence

It is well known that Independence was led by a combination of the lower clergy and low- and mid-level military officers ("creoles"), and that independence was premised on retaining the old idea of power centers, while acquiring a pinnacle ("sovereignty") within the administrative territory of Mexico. Several alternatives were engineered to create this new pinnacle. The first solution was culturally the simplest and most sound. Instead of a self-effacing center, Mexico would have its own charismatic center. Instead of having a viceroy, Mexico would have a king. This most obvious alternative was only tried out twice, once, very briefly, under Iturbide (1821), and once, in a more elaborate fashion, under Maximilian (1863–67). Both attempts failed. Iturbide's imperial aspirations lacked legitimacy. He was not Ferdinand VII (the deposed Spanish king who many leaders of independence wanted to instate as king of Mexico); he was just a leading creole military leader. By what privilege could he aspire to lead a ruling dynasty? Maximilian, on the other hand, attempted to create an empire too late. By the 1860s liberalism and nationalism had already taken root in Mexico, and so he appeared as both "unpopular" and "foreign" to too many people.

Instead of being ruled by a royal dynasty, Mexico adopted a republican system. But what exactly did that mean? Would presidents construct exemplary centers that paralleled those of the viceroy? If not, how would they differ? These questions, and the myriad political difficulties involved in reconstructing a national center of power, are the backdrop of caudillismo: military leaders attempting to control (and create) a national state.

It is extremely interesting to note, in this regard, that the emperor Maximilian spent an inordinate amount of energy creating a protocol for the Mexican empire, lavishing titles for a Mexican nobility that was Mexico-centered, establishing honorary titles on loyal subjects ("the order of Moctezuma," "the order of Guadalupe"), designing silverware and coats of arms, setting up imperial palaces, and centering the military around the figure of the emperor. Most historical treatments of Maximilian's empire present Maximilian's "inordinate" attention to the elaboration of a protocol as an example of how removed Maximilian was from the local social and political reality, and the picture that emerges from portraits of this imperial "adventure" are of a set of ideals fashioned in European courts encountering a social reality which was uninterested and untamable. Of course, this image is, in large part, true; but there is an aspect of it that is usually underplayed. Perhaps by the time Maximilian got to Mexico, the country had lived such intense political disquiet, such intense regional and ideological strife, that it was no longer possible to establish a hegemonic center unless it was to be under the liberal republican banner. But Maximilian was certainly right in understanding the crucial need to construct a center of power in Mexico if he was in fact to *reign*. The metaphors of the empire as an experience in which European civilization was swallowed by the Mexican jungle, in which "the Hapsburg was killed by the Indian" (Juárez), are in fact just one transformation of a phenomenon that plagued the whole post-Independence period: the center being undermined by the periphery.

Maximilian failed in establishing Mexico City as a real and as a symbolic center of national power, just as all Mexican leaders had failed since independence. The main difference was, of course, that Maximilian's failure also represented France's failure to impose this hegemonic order on Mexico, whereas the failures by Mexicans (Santa Anna, Bustamante, Nicolas Bravo, Guerrero, Iturbide, Commonfort, Juan Alvarez, Benito Juárez, Gomez Farías) represented the failure to construct hegemony from within. It was not until the triumph over the empire, or perhaps not until Porfirio Diaz came to power, that a national hegemonic system was more or less effectively established in Mexico. In this sense, Mexican political development went from bureaucratic forms of power in the colonial period, to charismatic forms in the early and mid-nineteenth century, to traditional forms in the Porfiriato.

Caudillismo and Caciquismo Reappraised: Regional Culture and the Culture of the State

The problem that political men faced in post-Independence Mexico was the (re)construction of a national center of power, of an investiture that could have compared with what the viceroy had had before independence. The administrative branches of the colonial government were severely impaired after independence. The political ties between the

State and the Church were uncertain. The Church itself was weakened both because of the loss of its Spanish ministers and because of the end of the Inquisition. The Wars of Independence left as a sequel several regional armies that were not incorporable into a professional army; and, finally, the Mexican hacendado class—although powerful enough in each of its regional domains—had difficulties in constituting itself as a national class. Creating a presidency with a "court" that could centralize and organize the nation's most powerful actors was an enormous problem. Given all of this, I can now return to the historians' typology of caciques and caudillos and ask the crucial question: why is it important that caudillos are "national" and caciques are "regional"?

It is obvious that not all caciques were missing ambitions of national power, just as not all leaders involved in national power were charismatic caudillos. The real issue that distinguishes different kinds of leaders has to do with reunifying the center, with recreating a center comparable to the one the viceroy had unified in his investiture. For example, Antonio López de Santa Anna—the prototypical nineteenth-century caudillo—had a lot of control over the professional army, as well as a strong regional base for maintaining his own independent force, while Gómez Farías, the liberal statesman, had support in certain parts of an emergent (liberal, federalist) "public opinion," but had no control over the army. Santa Anna thus proposed an alliance with Gómez Farías: "I will give you the esteem of the army, where I have many and very good friends, and you will give me the esteem of the masses, over which you have so much influence" (letter from Santa Anna to Gómez Farías, 1846; my trans.).[3]

This proposal betrays the importance of *personal* power (I have the army, you have the masses). However, Gómez Farías was not really the undisputed leader of "the masses," and politics in this period were not merely a question of "the people" versus "the army." Gómez Farías was a prominent leader of liberal public opinion; he could sway some of the elements of the state bureaucracy and perhaps some of the political groups that were linked to his Masonic lodge, but Santa Anna's alliance with Gómez Farías could in no way become routinized into a stable, institutionalized presidency. Gómez Farías's "masses" were really only a relatively small and localized set of people, and the Mexican state did not have the administrative capacity to expand its own institutional base. The most that such an alliance could achieve was to put Santa Anna (or Gómez Farías) into the presidency for a year or two. In fact, Santa Anna could—and did, on several occasions—ally himself just as easily with leaders of the conservative "masses." During the twenty-five years in which he was the most sought-after political figure in Mexico, Santa Anna's policies and alliances shifted from conservative to liberal, from federalist to centralist, from monarchist to republican, depending on whom he was coming in to "rescue" from a failure in national power. His only ideological "principle" was national sovereignty and independence. Everything else—the role of the Church, the independence of regions, democratic ideals—was negotiable.

The difficulty in constructing a center with a reliable democratic mandate from the people was bitterly noted by Agustín Iturbide after his abdication:

> Much is said of public opinion, and of the violence of its development. . . . Opinion has its crucible; its effects are not ephemeral, and this convinces me that we cannot yet ascertain what is the public opinion of the Mexicans, because either they have none, or have not yet manifested it. In the space of twelve years, one might count as many public opinions which were at least reputed to be such. (Iturbide 1823:152)

Thus one might say that there was no *national* hegemonic order during this period, which is why caudillos were so theatrically nationalistic. Nationalism was the only ideal that was abstract enough to permit coalitions with the diversity of groups that were necessary for state power. The struggle against the dismemberment of the country was important to most political groups in Mexico, and could be a banner that would weigh heavily in favor of anyone who could muster the military force to gain credibility.

Political speeches of the period claim that protecting the nation is a sacred duty, and there was no need to specify what "sacred" meant to each one of the actors in the national space. What was sacred to all was the will to thrive and reproduce. The defense of national sovereignty was thus compared to the defense of the community and of the family. In this sense, nationalism was a sacralized defense of intimate cultures. The maintenance and growth of local and regional power depend on the place of that locality or region within the national structure of power. Because of this, the symbols of state power (the president, the national capital, the national flag, the national anthem) also symbolized the possibility of sustaining growth and well-being in each and every place. The state was not seen as a *player* in the complex space of politics; rather, it was understood to be that space itself.

The connection between sovereignty and social reproduction is also reflected in the ideology wherein power wielded by Mexican nationalists was power wielded in good faith. When power was in the hands of a foreigner, there was bad faith in the sense that foreigners desired to prolong their control by keeping the people powerless, whereas fellow countrymen desire to prolong their control (vis-à-vis outside forces) by keeping the people strong. In this sense, many social injustices were blamed on the bad faith of the Spaniards (or, later, the Americans, British, and French), and popular classes were aroused with a call to justice wherein current injustice was blamed on bad faith, and not on the social and economic system. Nationalism was thus the only banner that could protect the existent power structures on the one hand, and move disaffected masses on the other. It was on the basis of these politics of "nationalism" and "good faith" that caudillos hoped to consolidate their personal power and eventually create an institutionalized center of national power. But, evidently, practically any leader who had a military following and some regional support could fashion his own nationalist banner and apply it for his own benefit.

It is in this context that the representation of caudillos as white creole aristocrats is significant. As we have already shown, caudillos were not consistently white; but they were consistently attempting to form an exemplary center of national power around themselves. These exemplary centers had to be built with two basic forces: military power, and the collective will that stemmed from being a "Good Mexican" (with capital letters). Military prowess was the subject of a lot of journalistic commentary, as well as of popular poetry and song. It was also the preferred form of visually representing caudillos (in military uniform, on horseback, in battle), but the "good faith" of the caudillos was just as crucial. Caudillos were routinely compared to Hercules, Mars, and Caesar, whereas the prowess of leaders who were perceived as being unnationalistic and self-serving was usually compared to that of Attila or of other "savages" (*salvages, selváticos, hotentotes*) or to bloodthirsty and ignoble animals (tigers, hyenas, vultures). On the other hand, the prowess of foreign military invaders was stained by their selfishness and greed. They were compared to the conquistadores—Hernán Cortés, Pedro de Alvarado, or Francisco Pizarro. They only sought to reinstate the "slavery" of colonialism.

One may ask, at this point, how it was that a caudillo came to be represented as a lion and not as a hyena, as a Hercules and not as an Attila, as a Cuauhtémoc and not as a Cortés. Evidently, during the first half of the nineteenth century national power was always so contested that there was no leader who did not get accused of being an Attila by one faction or another, and the title of "treasonous" was as important and as frequently utilized as that of "patriot." For this reason, caudillos worked hard on building their image of selfless patriotism.

The ways in which "good faith" was proven and represented invaded several cultural spheres, including all forms of self-sacrifice, because what caudillos needed to prove was that they stood for the general good, and not only for themselves. Their flaws were to be written off as "mistakes," not as bad will. After the battle with the French in which he lost a leg, Santa Anna, who thought he was at death's door, wrote a letter to the minister of war. It is said that this letter drew tears from the whole of congress, and it consolidated Santa Anna's reputation as a national hero:

> I also ask the government of my fatherland that my body be buried in these same swamps, so that my fellow men at arms know that this is the battle line that I mark for them: from now on let none of the unjust enemies of the Mexicans dare step on our soil with their filthy feet. . . . May all Mexicans, forgetting my political errors, at least grant me the only title that I hope to bestow on my children: that of being a *Good* Mexican. (1838; cited in Díaz y Díaz, 1972:145, my translation)

Caudillos, like Christ, were often portrayed as being "saviors" of the nation, and they insistently stressed their selflessness. They claimed to prefer the private life to public "service," and their leadership was based on their readiness for sacrifice. Once again, a precious example from Santa Anna:

> The good or bad name that I shall have in history has already been in-scribed in indelible letters that no one can erase, and they shall always read that, to my honor, I have made my career in the battlefield, defend-ing the rights of my country, and that the high position that I occupy in the army is not a prize that I have obtained in domestic conflicts: I have won it bodily defending national independence. And if anyone would dare to deny this, there is a mutilated member of my body [his leg] that can provide irrefutable testimony. (1843; cited in Díaz y Díaz, 1972:176; my trans.)

The basic importance of sacrifice (which helps explain the glorification of the army) is that it is the ultimate proof of selflessness. This selfless-ness, which was fundamental to establishing a caudillo's nationalism (his "good faith"), was also stressed by Santa Anna in his continuously re-hearsed gesture of "returning to his hacienda."[4] Whenever Santa Anna was elected president, he made sure that he was *called* into the presi-dency from his "civilian" life in his hacienda, Manga de Clavo. And often after he accepted the mandate of the presidency he would return there.

The theme of selflessness as the ultimate proof of nationalism and of one's credentials as a caudillo is continuously utilized to this day by politicians in Mexico (and elsewhere, I am sure), but it was of para-mount importance for the relatively uninstitutionalized power of ca-ciques and caudillos. The image reemerges with special potency during the Mexican revolution, as can be seen in the following stanza from a well-known revolutionary corrido:

> Fuí soldado de Francisco Villa
> de aquel hombre de fama inmortal
> que aunque anduvo sentado en la silla
> no envidiara la presidencial.
>
> [I was a soldier of Francisco Villa,
> that man of immortal fame
> who, despite having sat on the [presidential] chair
> never coveted the presidency.]

Given all of this, the fact that caudillos are represented as being white is important. The figures of the mestizo and the Indian were less convincing as representatives of selfless nationalism because they seemed more likely to look to political office as a way of bettering their social circumstances. Altruism seemed more plausible if it came from a white hacendado than if it came from a land-hungry mestizo. The image of "savior" could hardly be built out of a person who needed to be "redeemed." So the image of the creole hacendado served better than that of the uppity mestizo to represent the caudillo. On the other hand, "creoleness" was an image that could be manufactured. You could always buy an hacienda, wear a shiny uniform and marry a white woman. Porfirio Díaz is said to have whitened his face with powder. So, when it comes to caudillos, it is fair to say that some were born white, some achieved whiteness, and some had whiteness thrust upon them.

Even the figure of Benito Juárez, who recognized his Indian ascendance and was proud of it, reinforced aspects of this symbolic logic, for although Juárez was an Indian—more so than any other Mexican president before or since—he was an Indian who had overcome his Indianness (*se había superado*). Juárez was better educated than most statesmen of his time; in a context wherein whites were still known as *gente de razón* (reasoning people), Juárez had overcome the "ignorance" of his "race." He was, also, married to an elite creole woman. Particularly interesting is the fact that Juárez is always represented as a civilian; he was a statesman, not a caudillo. His abnegation of personal military power was symbolically related to his being a "civilized Indian." No lowly passions were allowed to him. Juárez is, thus, one of the very few Mexican politicians who have cultivated the image of the "family man."

This logic of caudillo charisma contrasts in interesting ways with the messianism of Indian political movements. Lafaye (1977) considers sixteenth-century Indian messianism, which involved appropriating the figures of Christ and king and making them Indian, as one of the antecedents to Mexican nationalism,[5] and indeed, both Indian messianism and caudillismo depended on the notion of sacrifice. But the Indians appropriated Christ (made him an Indian) in order to destroy the bonds of debt that tied them to the gente de razón. If Jesus was a European, and if he died for their sins, this legitimated Spanish tutelage and exploitation; an appropriation of Christ was fundamental for self-empowerment. Witness, for example, this prophecy from the Chilam Balam of Chumayel:

> This is the word of Our Father: the earth shall burn. There will be white circles in the sky on the day on which it shall arrive. It comes from God's mouth, it is not a lie. Ay! Heavy is the serfdom that comes with Christianity. It is coming! The words shall be slaves, enslaved shall be the trees, slaves the stones, slaves the men when it comes. It will come and you will see. (1952:158, my trans.)

Indian serfdom was legitimated through Christianity. Indian freedom and independence depended on an appropriation of Christ, for a return to the pre-Columbian religion was inconceivable:

> It is very important to come to understand that the stones that our fathers left here, the hard wood, the animals are what you have been worshipping. In the first periods here, among us, the men of majesty were worshipped like real gods. Those stones obstructed the coming of the true god our father, master of the sky and the land. Although they were ancient gods, perishable they were. The time for their adoration has ended. They were undone by the blessing of the lord of the sky when He finished redeeming the world, when the true God resuscitated, when He blessed the sky and the earth.
>
> Maya men, your gods have crumbled! Without hope you worshipped them. (Ibid., 61, my trans.)

The self-sacrifice of the caudillo is also, in some sense, an appropriation—a nationalization—of Christ. The patriot dies—or is willing to die—to preserve our families and our ways. And both Indian and caudillo leadership were founded on the idea that sharing nationality (Indian in one case, Mexican in the other) was the only possible basis for the "good faith" that was so badly needed. Moreover, Indian and caudillo messianisms shared difficulties in getting a hold of all the strings required to construct a polity. Both had difficulties in collecting revenues and administering a territory; both lacked sophisticated forms of controlling politically adverse cultural production.

The differences, of course, were that caudillos led an imagined (and half-built) state. This state image was constructed out of the colonial experience, and it inherited a functioning system of class relations. Because of this, many of the preexisting forms of power, such as the power of the Church and of the landowners, were compatible with the projects of caudillos, while they were incompatible with Indian "messianism." This fact is recognized in the terminology used for the Indian movements. They were referred to as "caste wars," not as regional independence movements. And this also helps explain why the messiahs of early nationality (caudillos) were represented as being white, whereas Indian movements were led by Indian Christs and kings. On the one hand, whiteness gave more credibility to a national messiah because whites (like Jesus) could be renouncers, whereas Indians were pariahs to begin with. On the other hand, a white sacrifice, a sacrifice from the *rich,* buttressed the solidarity between classes, which was indispensable for state formation. Indian messianism involved breaking faith with the gente de razón, and this was symbolized through the appropriation of Christ and king. This appropriation meant the end of the Indians' moral debt to the national society, and the creation of a new order.

Despite all of this, caudillos faced enormous difficulties in retaining their status of "saviors." Their power depended, in the last instance, on support from social sectors that expected privileges in return for their support. So, there were always several disenfranchised political groups that accused caudillos of being cowardly, unfaithful, self-interested and greedy; and the constant competition between the images of the hero and the villain produced an ever-louder skepticism around the messianic-cum-patriotic ideology of caudillismo. The theme of the political lie, of national politics as pantomime, and of the caudillo as buffoon became popular in the discourse of political commentators. The title of Francisco Bulnes's book, *The Great Lies of Our History,* is perhaps symptomatic of the ideological bankruptcy of caudillismo.

The notion of "the caudillos' lies" is in part a critique of the laxity of their philosophical principles (outside of nationalism). Readers will recall that the "good faith" of nationalism could be used to support or to challenge the status quo, and that caudillos depended on these ambiguities for their alliances. They were crucial to their capacity to sustain themselves in power for significant periods of time. The caudillos' shifting alliances were eventually understood to be proof of the self-interested opportunism of caudillos. Defending Mexico against outside forces was no longer enough; one needed principles in order to rule in good faith. In the Mexican nineteenth century there developed a critique of the politics that were built solely on a purposely ambiguous nationalism, and the consistent adherence to particular social programs became ideologically important for politicians around the middle of the century.

Another dimension of the development of a discourse on official lies has to do with print capitalism. Benedict Anderson (1983) has made much of the role of print capitalism in the emergence of nationalism in Spanish America and elsewhere. Although it is true that there was a vast expansion of printed materials in the region at the turn of the century, the relationship between this production and nationalism is quite complex. According to Anderson, the role of newspapers and novels was fundamental for constructing images of the national community, as well as for constructing a view of the world as a place that was made up of a set of national communities that were simultaneously developing through time.

The role of the press in the construction of the Mexican imagined community has not yet been explored by historians, and works of historians of Mexican nationalism such as Liss, Lafaye, and Brading seem to point to other—and earlier—sources for the construction of the Mexican imagined nationality. The dissemination of printed leaflets and books most certainly had an effect on the nature of the polity and of cultural regions in nineteenth-century Mexico. During the colonial period, the Crown and the Church controlled to a large extent the way the written word circulated. The Crown had a whole territorial organization of scribes who copied and circulated edicts and questionnaires. This system of scribes allowed for more or less effective administration of the territory. It kept the viceroyalty informed of the state of the different jurisdictions, and it kept the people informed of the changes in governmental policies.

In addition, the Crown and the Church both attempted to control what was printed in Mexico, as well as the flow of imported books. Through the Inquisition, the Church tried to uphold its prohibitions on reading materials. Crown and Church could collaborate in trying to keep the flow of reading materials under control. After independence this situation changed. Although the Church continued to offer a list of censored readings, it no longer had a judicial branch to uphold its prohibitions, and books that were censored were widely read by members of Masonic lodges, who included most of the active politicians in the country (see Guerra 1985). Independence seems to have had implications for the state's administrative capacity, and the state's systems of communications through scribes and justices decayed quite considerably.

Parallel to the decline of Church and state control over the circulation of written materials, the uncontrolled distribution of texts proliferated. Regional caciques and army coronels printed their own proclamations: the famous *pronunciamientos* of the period. There was not, at this time, a national "public opinion" in Mexico; as Knight (1986) has argued, that kind of opinion existed in Mexico City but spread very unevenly outside it. Urban public opinion was influenced by the regional powers that were specific to it. In this sense, print capitalism's uses in propagating an image of the shared national community (which, in any case, was formed thanks to both the viceregal "theater state" and the hierarchical ideology that legitimated the conquest in the first place) were somewhat offset by its antecedent role in the proliferation of dissent and in the creation of an ironic distance between caudillos and the readers of the caudillos' proclamations: this distance is reflected in the voices that accuse caudillos of being lying buffoons.

In conclusion, the typology that distinguishes between creole-hacendado-military-national "caudillos" and mestizo-regional "caciques" is merely an academic formalization of a dominant form of representing power in the Mexican national space. Moreover, the thinking involved in this typology does not address the key issue, which is why "national" charismatic leaders should be represented in a different way than "regional" charismatic leaders. In fact, what we have seen is that "caudillos" are key elements in the mythical construction of the state, whereas caciques (whom we will discuss in detail in a moment) are not. The relationship between caudillos and nation building is, in large part, what explains the caudillos' three characteristics: (a) caudillos are military leaders because only the military could aspire to control the countryside long enough to create a true political center, but they were also military leaders because of the key significance of self-sacrifice in the construction of national legitimacy; (b) caudillos were creoles more by popular representation than by fact; and (c) they were hacendados either because that is the way they achieved military power in the first place, or as a result of their military and political power. It was thus economically and symbolically important for caudillos to have *independent* wealth; their aristocratic image depended on their economic independence.

The distinction between caudillos and caciques turns out, then, to be fundamental only because the former are fetishes of nationality. In every other respect one could say that they are potentially interchangeable categories. The difference between them will always be in the nature of their "charisma": caciques have no possibility of extending their base of support outside their regions, while caudillos succeed in swaying outside groups through an appeal to national principles.

Caciques[6]

The phenomenon of "caciquismo" is so diverse—in terms of the kinds of power relations involved, in terms of the economic and ethnic characteristics of caciques, in terms of their position in society—that the utility of the term itself can be doubted. In Mexico, union bosses and agrarian leaders can be caciques, as can leaders of urban housing movements and wealthy rancheros. Evidently, the characteristics of different kinds of leadership implicit in caciquismo are equally diverse. Lázaro Cárdenas's image of benign patriarch of Michoacán, where the Indians called him "Tata Lázaro," contrasts with the arch-macho image of fear-inspiring caciques like Maximino Avila Camacho or Gonzalo Santos.

What is common to all caciques is that they mediate between the needs of the national state (or private corporations) and the actual on-the-ground situations of peasants and workers, that they derive power from this relation of mediation, and that this power takes on very complex cultural qualities because of the diverse natures of the caciques' mediating roles.

Because of this last consideration, de la Peña (1986) argues that caciques are not just "power brokers," they are also "cultural brokers." However, the nature of this "cultural brokerage" has not been systematically explored, both because of the great diversity in kinds of caciques and because analyses of caciquismo always stress only two levels of articulation; the state (or the corporation) and a particular constituency, whereas some caciques articulate more than one constituency.

In this section I will explore the relationship between caciques, regional culture and the state. I will focus especially on two issues: the effects that the cooptation of caciques has on the nature of the Mexican bureaucracy, and the relationship between the caciques' position in regional political economies and the caciques' ideological inclinations. As in the section on caudillismo, the exercise has the ultimate purpose of suggesting a relationship between the spatial organization of culture and different kinds of political leadership.

During the whole regnum of the Partido Revolucionario Institucional (1929 to date), there has been tremendous tension between rational-bureaucratic-democratic practices and practices that are founded on other kinds of principles, such as friendship, kinship, and personal loyalty. For example, in the PRI's 1988 presidential campaign there were a fair number of democratic rituals, and a lot of lip service was paid to democracy. The selection of the PRI's presidential candidate was publicly presented in a scenario of a democratic party primary, while, at the same time, the decision regarding the identity of the candidate was a top secret known only by the president (who made the final decision) and perhaps to a very few members of the cabinet.[7]

In most presidential successions even elections themselves were a formal ritual which merely served to authenticate decisions that were taken elsewhere. Analysts of the Mexican bureaucracy and of Mexican power elites (cf. Smith 1979, Camp 1980) stress that much of the internal organization of the bureaucracy is constructed on the basis of "informal ties" based on friendship, kinship, and the like, while the logic of political appointments is authenticated with a discourse of professionalism. In other words, even within the innards of the state we have a kind of "cultural brokerage" in operation. I shall resist the temptation of calling this kind of cultural brokerage "brocolage," although it does involve a creative, active cultural role which takes elements from different areas and works with them (bricolage). Within the bureaucracy, the bricolage works with elements of two discourses: that of the institutionalized, rationalized, democratic state, and that of friendship, enmity, and loyalty. These two kinds of ideologies and practices clash continuously in Mexico and, as François Xavier Guerra has demonstrated (1985), they have so clashed ever since independence.

What seems to distinguish caciques from most bureaucrats is that the cacique's power is greater than the power invested in whatever bureaucratic post they occupy, so much so that their power often predates or survives their dallying with public office. So, for example, the Caso family of Naranja used their bureaucratic positions as ejido or municipal authorities in ways that by far exceeded the formal attributes attached to those posts, and their power continued in periods in which they were ousted from one post or another (Friedrich 1986). When Gonzalo Santos was governor in San Luis he was practically an autocratic ruler of that state, and he succeeded in controlling the state for many years after his term had expired. Carlos Jonguitud Barrios, the cacique of the national schoolteachers union, carved himself a position parallel to the formal, "democratic" union structure, the "Vanguardias Revolucionarias." From that position he controlled the teachers' union, was once governor of San Luis Potosí, and is now a federal senator.

In other words, caciques play off a particular constituency (be it regional or professional) against the state, and vice versa. Because of this, they are often utilized in bureaucratic positions that relate to those constituencies. However, the contradiction between "rationalized and democratic" principles and the practices which are built on "relational" forms of sociability can also separate these leaders from their constituencies. Like the "good faith" of early nineteenth-century nationalism, the principles of bureaucratic rationality and democracy are necessary to construct cleavages that extend beyond the network of friends and followers of the president.

Governmental tactics to keep alliances with informal power leaders have usually involved using caciques as popular leaders in areas in which the government needs control, and offering posts outside a cacique's dominions when they seek to break up the cacique's informal power group. In both cases, the state presents the people with a bizarre combination of rational-democratic and personalistic politics. When caciques are chosen for bureaucratic positions within their constituencies, the selection is presented as a sign of democracy (insofar as the leader is identified with his constituency) while, at the same time, the leader's popularity is not based on a democratic vote, but on personal power within that constituency. On the other hand, if a cacique is offered a post outside his constituency, the choice is seen as being personalistic, because the cacique has no relationship to the people he will be working with and has been offered the position for reasons that are distinct from the cacique's professional abilities.

In other words, the utilization of caciques undermines a "rational-bureaucratic" ideology because it is a symptom of the real weakness of the administration; it depends on a local cacique because it lacks its own venues into that local constituency. The cooptation of caciques and their removal from their constituencies also violates the democratic-bureaucratic order, insofar as caciques must be offered posts for which they are neither professionally qualified nor elected to hold. Therefore, the relationship between the government and caciques tends to recreate the tension between a democratic-bureaucratic ideology and a relational ideology that values friendship, kinship, and loyalty.

Turning now to the position of caciques, one finds that they not only have to play in this dissected governmental cultural field in which rational democratic practices tensely coexist with the politics of social networks, but that they also have to construct complex cleavages among their followers, enemies, and potential followers. Gonzalo Santos presents an especially clear case with which to think these things through, because he operated as a cacique in many levels of the political system. By analyzing his case, I hope to suggest a way of thinking about the kinds of forms of leadership that caciques create.

The regional origins of Gonzalo Santos's cacicazgo are similar to all other Huastecan caciques of his generation. During that period, the Huasteca Potosina as a region was pulled together by the actions of the rancheros, who can be culturally distinguished from hacendados because they were not a class of absentee landlords. On the contrary, until the middle of this century, rancheros lived on their ranchos or in the towns closest to them, and they kept a personal command of the production that went on in them. At the same time, the ranchero class has always been in charge of keeping the classes of Indian laborers and peasants under control. This means that Huastecan rancheros tended to formulate a specific set of relationships of patronage with the cowboys on their ranches, and another kind of relationship with Indians from landed communities or those who were not involved in relations of production within the ranches.

This situation produced a complex cultural construction of ranchero power, for power over other mestizo cowboys was legitimated in terms of the superior individual qualities of the ranchero, while superiority over Indians was premised on the colonial organization of caste. The ideology of domination of rancheros over their mestizo cowboys was, therefore, easily wedded to nineteenth- and early twentieth-century liberalism, insofar as domination was based on the superiority of individuals competing on an equal basis, whereas the ideology of domination of rancheros over Indians was amenable to an aristocratic, conservative politico-cultural position.

To make things more complex, political relations between the ranchero class and the elites of the state capital (San Luis Potosí) and of Mexico City were equally difficult to reconcile with the ranchero liberal ideology of domination. We have already suggested that, at the national level, liberalism has never truly taken hold. Instead, the centers of bureaucratic power were weaned from their colonial existence by developing a contorted political discourse of ambiguity, in which lip service is paid to liberalism, but political practices are in fact predicated on a kind of personalism that ultimately reinforced a hierarchical and authoritarian political culture. Moreover, the adoption of indigenismo and of the mestizo as the national race meant that liberalism was subsumed into a protectionist regime that defined a national community made up of social sectors, and not merely of individual citizens.

In sum, ranchero caciques had to deal with three different kinds of power relations: relations of domination in their native relations of production (within ranches and in the towns built around ranch activities), relations of domination over Indians, and power relations with Highland Mexican political elites. In other words, the hegemonic core of the Huasteca had to develop power relations in that core and in the regional periphery, and it had to negotiate its position vis-à-vis national and state officials whose basis of power were markedly different from their own.

These regional cleavages are captured in the comments Gastón Santos made to me, and which were analyzed in another context in an earlier chapter:

> The Indians of the Huasteca [who, even today, are a majority of the population] are marginal economically, culturally and historically. Here, the Revolution (and all social movements) was carried out by the ranchero families. Why? Because they were richer, whiter, and more intelligent. And among the ranchero families of the Huasteca, we Santos were the richest and most intelligent.

This statement synthesizes the kind of cultural bricolage which the Santos family used to dominate regionally. The ideology of domination over mestizos (over other rancheros) is predicated on intellectual superiority and personal achievement (greater wealth), whereas the superiority over Indians is predicated on racial superiority. The ideology of domination over mestizos and other ranchers, therefore, had to be continuously proved, which explains why knowledge of ranch ways, and of the general characteristics and history of the region, is cultivated. This cultivation of the culture of the mestizo ranch workers by the regional elite has resulted in the ranchero manipulation of the cowboy point of view for their own political favor.

One of Gonzalo Santos's workers, a house painter, said that Don Gonzalo gave "La Tigresa," a famous Mexico City vedette, who was also the lover of a president, a statuette of the devil. He also recounted that he was commissioned to paint a slogan around the threshold of Gonzalo Santos's bedroom that read, "When God shuts the door, the devil opens a window for me" (*"cuando Dios me cierra la puerta, el diablo me abre una ventana"*). According to the painter, Gonzalo knew that he was going to hell upon his death.

Gonzalo Santos built his image as regional leader on motifs that are fully developed in the local rancher popular culture. In the egalitarian ideology of the ranch, rancheros like Santos explained their superiority over other cowboys in terms of greater intelligence and capabilities; but ranch peones explained the differences and the breach in *egalitarian* forms of reciprocity as a pact with the devil.[8] Gonzalo Santos made ample room for the reproduction of the peón explanation of domination in his own self-presentation, and so developed an image of an ultra-macho form of domination vis-à-vis local cowboys and peons.

This is already a long way from the image of the "traditional cacique," who bases his power on paternalistic patronage of peasants. This kind of caciquismo, which had a major exponent in San Luis in the figure of Saturnino Cedillo, and had comparable figures in Emiliano Zapata and Lázaro Cárdenas, is in fact just one way of articulating a cultural region. These "traditional" leaders, who were really no less traditional than Santos, were often conservative in the sense that they did not believe in the free hand of the market place and wished, instead, to guarantee a place for peasant communities within a national system; in this sense, they sought a social order which was legally more akin to that of the colonial period, except with the benefits of the "good faith" of nationalism (i.e., no deliberate exploitation of Mexicans).

What is interesting in Gonzalo Santos's case—and I suggest that this kind of articulation is common to practically all major caciques, be they "liberal" or "conservative"—is that his dominant source of power (the rancho and rancho culture) made him a liberal, but his power in the region was also predicated on paternalistic (conservative) relations towards Indians. So, for example, in his memoirs Gonzalo recounts how he had a large figure of Santiago made and delivered it personally, during the fiesta of the patron saint, to the Indians of Tampamolón:

> [I] knew the political significance that bringing their patron back had for me. I would explain to them that, although they saw Santiago burn [during the Revolution], he had not been burned because he is a saint, and that his ashes flew to the other side of the ocean [where Gonzalo hoped to have a replica made] where he was found, mounted on his horse again and angry at the Huertistas [the revolutionary faction that burnt the local church and who were mortal enemies of the Santos], and that he came back to lead the tribe again, and to give his full support to Gonzalo, in other words, to me. (1986:812)

Santos, like all other mestizo leaders of the region, supervised and reinforced Indian authorities, and made sure to develop a sense of personal loyalty with leaders of some communities by being personally responsible for the creation of a few ejidos. These ejidos were—as we have seen—created as a form of repayment for Indian support of Gonzalo's military campaign against the Cristeros in the states of Jalisco and Zacatecas.

In sum, Santos maintained a hierarchical, "traditional," form of behavior towards the Indians, while he constructed his main constituency on the basis of ranchero liberalism. This liberalism is the source of the discourse of "frankness" and "openness" which characterized Santos, and which he used consistently as a weapon vis-à-vis the elites of the highlands, in examples that I developed in part 1. Because Gonzalo's conception of domination was built on a model of individual assertiveness and dominance, he did not respect the courteous language of "normal" (national) political discourse, thereby confronting the political rhetoric of the bureaucratic classes with the sheer force of his machismo and his regional support. Thus, a crucial aspect of Santos's political use of Huastecan regional culture was his recourse (legitimated though liberal populism) to the "naked truth," with which he confronted the action of extraregional and national elites.

Gonzalo Santos's case suggests that to understand fully the nature of cacicazgos we need to look at more than just two levels (national and "regional"). In his case, he constructs his leadership with two different strategies in his regional core and periphery and then plays the complex result off against the culture of the urban middle classes and bureaucracies. Other cacicazgos also show this interesting kind of bricolage with different intimate cultures within a regional culture. So, for example, if we contrast the leadership of the different military and ideological leaders of Zapatismo we notice very distinct types of people with different kinds of relations to Morelos' intimate cultures. Zapata took on the imagery of the lowland "popular aristocrat" (the charro, the plateado) in his choice of clothing, in his well-groomed appearance, in his love of horses. Other leaders, like Otilio Montaño or Genovevo de la O, used the iconography of the Morelos peasant; while yet others (like the intellectuals of the movement) identified with the urban intellectual or proletarian classes. Each of these leaders, however, had certain ways of extending out locally beyond the kind of intimate culture which they themselves embodied; thus, despite his self-identification with the lowland mestizo, Zapata formalized cleavages with Indian communities by proclaiming some of his principles in Nahuatl and through extending his kinship networks. Zapata had godchildren, children and girlfriends in many different communities, thereby creating links across the Morelos regional system.

This very same kind of manipulative mix of intimate cultures for the construction of regional leadership can be found in the cases of other important agrarian leaders. In all cases, an analysis of their entourage is the key to the ways in which they combine in their own styles of leadership the different kinds of constituencies present in their regional cleavages. Several of the novels of the Revolution portray the tension between the leaders who actually construct these regional cleavages and their different military and civilian followings. The image that emerges is of regional leaders whose political vision is greater than that of the other competing leaders, but the competing leaders try to pry power away from them via a more direct and univocal (less mediated) appeal to only one constituency.[9]

These kinds of complex cultural cleavages can also be found in urban cacicazgos, but, of course, the nature of the cleavages are somewhat different. For example, the sorts of leadership provided by bosses of unions that are located in a single, stable, place (by the boss of, say, the textile mills of Atlixco or Orizaba) are different from the kinds of leadership that are necessary to control a national union. National bosses like La Quina (of the oil-workers union) and Jonguitud Barrios (of the schoolteachers union) had strong local constituencies in their local home unions. Apparently, both of these leaders built up impressive webs of patron-client ties in their local strongholds, where there were many people that were personally loyal to them. However, the process of extending union force outward implied creating cleavages with the government on the one hand, and with leaders of other localized unions on the other.[10]

The more successful these leaders were in their negotiations, the more resources they could funnel toward their faithful. In other words, personal bonds (built around kinship, friendship, compadrazgo, and on having a common place of origin—*paisanazgo*) could be expanded and strengthened thanks to the continual flows of resources, and so national leaders in fact construct two very different kinds of relations with their followers: one with very personal followers that are loyal to the leader and only to him, and another constituency that is relatively impersonal and that is renewed through negotiation, cooptation, or coercion.

Thus, for union leaders, the mixture between liberalism and other forms of political sociability contrast in interesting ways to those which we discussed for Gonzalo Santos or for Zapata. Paternalism is the main political form here. In this union context family is not only a metaphor for the social relations between unionized workers, it is also an important organizing principle behind unionism. One of the union leaders' main sources of power is the control they have over who is hired into unionized slots in the company. This control has usually been used in one of two ways: either leaders sell slots to the highest bidder (and thereby become a kind of labor aristocracy), or they give (or sell them cheaper) to members of their families or to members of families of other workers who exchange this favor for loyalty.

In this sense, one could say that family relations are the guiding relationship in the construction of a unionized labor force, and that these relations are only substituted in exchange for large sums of money. The money element enters this situation as a kind of degraded democratic element. People who are not friends or kinsmen can come in if they pay a ransom. People who do pay these high ransoms, especially in the well-paying governmental jobs at Pemex and the electric and telephone companies, are expected to keep a passive position vis-à-vis the union because, once they are in the system, they are beneficiaries of it, and they can expect to get their investment back either by working very little and collecting full pay, or by hiring a non-union person to carry out the work at a free-market (lower than minimum) wage.

Within the union, leaders try to have two kinds of constituents: clients (kinsmen and clients who owe their jobs or the jobs of their kinsmen to the leader) and tacit allies who enter the union through the "democracy" of the highest bidder. The kinds of political relations involved in the union leadership include (1) relations of negotiation with high governmental officials which have, as an outcome, the control of certain democratically elected governmental positions in the hands of the union, positions that allow the union leaders to adopt a "benign populist" kind of political rhetoric and practices in their local strongholds; (2) relations of mutual self-interest (disguised as democratic alliance) with the state and with union members who buy into the union; (3) relations of loyalty and patronage with allies and kinsmen; (4) relations of enemyhood to alternate leaders; (5) relations of alienation with large portions of the union's constituency. In sum, all of these "traditional" forms of leadership are "traditional" only insofar as they are constructed out of combinations of relationships which are not created or sanctioned by the law. What is more important, we can begin to distinguish between different forms of leadership by analyzing the relationship that the leadership has to its internally differentiated regional constituencies.

The different forms of cacique power and authority can be understood only in reference to the different poles of coherence in the regional core/periphery organization in which they operate. In this sense, the dichotomy between "modern" and "traditional" forms of leadership is terribly imprecise; different kinds of "traditional" power correspond to different intimate cultures, and cacicazgos always imply creating a space of power that spans and articulates several kinds of "traditional" and "modern" forms of leadership.

The spatial perspective that has been developed in this book allows us to specify the extremely diverse forms of leadership that have been created and classified as cacicazgos. One can do this by linking a cacique's power to the regional organization of cultural production. The "legitimacy" of caciques is a complex construct that depends on at least two, and frequently three poles of cultural coherence. Moreover, this perspective has facilitated understanding why the diverse forms of local and regional charisma[11] are distinct from the imagery of national leadership. The key situation of the national state in the construction of hegemony, in the construction of a sense of place, gives the national leadership a very particular kind of dynamics. It is interesting to note that historians and social scientists have assimilated the dominant ideology regarding national and regional power. By typing caudillos as creoles and caciques as mestizos, by typing bureaucrats "modern" and caciques "traditional," they have assimilated the fundamental postulates of Mexican nationalism.

Bureaucracy

In this final section, I shall sum up some of the implications of my spatial analyses of culture for the understanding of the third kind of political actor which I outlined in the earlier section: the bureaucracy. My analysis of the charisma of leaders allows me to begin to think about the relationship between the culture of the state and regional culture. A good starting point is a reconsideration of our notion of the "culture of social relations." This refers to idioms and frames of interaction between intimate cultures. The idioms are framed in contact events that are constricted and patterned by the logic of regional power. Frames include market places, loci of production, and political rituals. The actual idioms that are developed in the culture of social relations include articulatory symbols that connect different intimate cultures. Those articulatory symbols are constructed in two kinds of processes: mythification (the appropriation of a symbol by a dominant group and its resignification) and fetishism (the process of imputing autonomy and independent power to objects that are, in fact, dependent upon one's own work and actions).

The state is a major player in the construction of the culture of social relations. Because the state represents national society, it is continuously cutting across intimate cultures and constructing an image of itself as a transcendental whole that fully encompasses each one of the nation's intimate cultures. Yet the spatial diversification of cultural production is like a cultural frontier into which the state must expand if it is to create a hegemony. In other words, the state attempts to create interactional frames and articulatory symbols that are attuned to the spatial organization of cultural production.

One sees how each cacique actively molds the culture of social relations in order to construct his own appeal. The power of a cacique can be appraised in part by looking at the range and scope of the culture of social relations to which he is tapping in. At the same time, the rivalry between caciques for control of pieces of the state apparatus is part of the process of routinizing and bureaucratizing their power, and leaders who personally articulate a regional culture (via their power bases and via their construction of a political persona on the basis of the regional culture of social relations) tend to be substituted in their regional roles by others who have delegated powers from the top.

A very developed case of this kind of routinization of regional leadership is Morelos. The local Cuernavaca politicians have been reduced to a middle-level bureaucracy that is fundamental for state governors, but that has very little autonomous power in the state apparatus. Due to the relative efficacy of bureaucratic control in the region, the charisma of leaders who try to build political capital by mediating between different intimate cultures and the state is relatively limited, and the caciques who have emerged there tend to articulate one local group and not several with the state. In the wake of the cacique there emerges either an enormous indifference to the depersonalized state, or forms of fetishism wherein the state is cast as the active creator of social life.

Here are examples of these two processes. The production of indifference via the elimination of caciquismo can be seen in processes of transformation of *acarréo*. *Acarréo* is the popular word that refers to the custom of dragging people (typically peasants, workers, or bureaucrats) to political rallies. The capacity to mobilize actors has been fundamental for the power of the postrevolutionary Mexican regimes. (In this sense, the Leninist idea of the capitalist state as a demobilizer of popular classes is fundamentally incomplete in the case of Mexico.) When mobilization is carried out by a cacique, the acarreados can profess a kind of loyalty to the state through transitivity. Their support for the cacique strengthens the cacique's position vis-à-vis the state, and so it strengthens their own situation. Contrariwise, the acarreados who have been coerced by their caciques into attending will receive a lesson in the cacique's power by realizing the support he enjoys from the state.

When caciques are removed, access to state resources can be perceived to depend on principles other than those of personal loyalty. For example, they can be based on one's income. The moment the plutocratic principle overrides the personalistic one, the relationship to particular state institutions goes from relative commitment to relative indifference. Once the principle behind access to power is money, then any bureaucrat can be as good (or as bad) as another. There have been two main forms of access to political benefits in Mexico: one through personal ties, another through the "democracy" of money. This parallels DaMatta's conclusions regarding a "debased citizenry" in Brazil. A feeling of citizenship exists, but the principle of equality before the law is mediated by considerations either of money or of personal relations.

On a first level, then, bureaucratization simply means diminishing people's personal links to the state, and thence the growth in the plutocratic principle. The dialectic is not as simple as this, because with the decline of regional caciques, the importance of the national level increases, and the forms of fetishism observable in *caudillismo* grow and evolve with it. When relatively autonomous forms of local and regional power decline (they are far from disappearing, but merely spread to new niches), place in the nation becomes relatively more important.

Examples of the propagation of state fetishism include the nineteenth-century notion of *el supremo gobierno,* a phrase that peasants and others used to refer to the national government. Implicit in this notion was a sharp distinction between local and national authorities, especially the president of the republic. The ideology was that even though there could be injustices propagated by selfish politicians at all levels of the system, the president himself was innocent of these processes, and direct contact with the president would result in the impartment of justice. Contact with this fetishized president was ultimately the only way in which a group of people, or even an individual, could find or regain his legitimate *place* within the national whole.

Carmen Ramos has documented the correspondence between individuals and president Porfirio Diaz. This correspondence includes an enormous volume of letters asking don Porfirio to intercede in order to gain justice.[12] Here the president of the republic appears as the supreme arbiter and also as the holder of the ultimate power. I have already shown a political use of this ideology in the chapter on Morelos, where the governor, Lauro Ortega, institutionalized this aspect of the political culture as a way of galvanizing his appeal in a time of deep political and economic crisis. Once the power of the presidency became institutionalized, and an operating center of national power was reconstructed after the end of caudillos, the charisma of the president shifted from being linked to an ideology of selfless nationalism to a set of symbolic connections between the power of the president and the reproduction of the social whole. This power is a result of the persistent importance of personal relations in Mexican political power. Because people know that personal links are the prime form of access to political favor—and because this is especially so at the level of presidents, who, as in the case of caudillos, presumably do not need money, and therefore personal connections are more important for them than the plutocratic principle that guides ordinary bureaucrats—the president's personal relations become a kind of map of Mexican political society. His connections are the connections of the presidency. His story explains everyone's *place* during his regnum.

During presidential campaigns, the anecdotes and family history of the candidate are appropriated by "the nation" (i.e., by whoever is interested in negotiating a place in the next regime), and each one is amplified and extended in order to provide groups and sectors with a "personal" nexus to the candidate. The role of president fuses the life of one man with the shape of Mexican political society.[13] It is no wonder that in Mexico the president of the republic makes public appearances like a kind of deus ex machina who heals by mere contact. A person who makes contact with the president is renewing or reestablishing his place within the whole, his place in the nation and in the collectivity. The president alone has this magical position in which the private and the collective are entirely fused; and the process in which this fusion happens is, of course, the campaign tour, a pilgrimage in which a powerful bureaucrat becomes a collective representation of the polity.

The culture of the state grows and is transformed with institutionalization of the administration of socio-economic groups. At the same time, these processes of institutionalization have a different rhythm from the growth of different intimate cultures; the result is that there is always a complex politics around place in the state. There are many examples of this dynamic. The Mexican state has a complex institutional and discursive space for "the peasantry," yet many of the rural peoples who fit into this institutional category today are no longer peasants (as in the case of the peasantry within Cuernavaca, or the peasantry in Tepoztlán). The Indian communities, the official definitions of who are and are not Indians, do not coincide at all times with the processes of identity formation of the people that are being categorized, excluded or placed in these institutional frames. In part 1 we described the logic of regional cultural transformation (flows of mestizaje) in terms of residual, dominant, and emergent intimate cultures and localist ideologies. The state tends to construct its categories out of residual and dominant intimate cultures, and these categories with their institutional correspondents often outlive the cultures that they were created around. For example, the peasantry in Morelos is an important category in the discourse and institutional deployment of the government; this is because Morelos was Zapata's state, and it therefore has a privileged place in postrevolutionary nationalism. Nonetheless, the peasantry is no longer a majority in the state.

Understanding this process also helps us understand why caciquismo is not extinguished as a political phenomenon. Caciquismo flourishes where the state has not yet constructed a bureaucratized institutional structure to deal with an intimate culture. As the state expands into these areas, caciques are first incorporated into the state apparatus to fill the relevant bureaucratic slots. After the relationship with this intimate culture becomes somewhat routinized, caciques tend to be dislocated from their mediating roles (going either up, down, or out of the bureaucracy), and the relationship between the state and the intimate culture gets tainted by the combination of "indifference" and state-fetishism that I have described. As the coherence of the intimate culture begins to break down and new intimate cultures begin to emerge, the government's institutional and discursive apparatus becomes inadequate to deal directly with the new situations, and new leaders (caciques) emerge and are coopted into the system.[14]

Conclusion

Many analysts have pointed to the connections between nationalism and the sacred, and this connection certainly does exist. But the particular contents of these nationalist "religions" vary quite a lot, and they have different kinds of implications in different places within a nation-state.

In this chapter I have linked the nature and interconnections between intimate cultures with different kinds of political ideologies and with different sorts of charismatic leaders. Charisma is, here, the first symptom of the processes of mythmaking and fetishization that go into the state. Thus, I showed that the kinds of constituencies that caciques articulate explain the sorts of cultural bricolage that these leaders engage in. The "paternalism" of agrarian caciques like Saturnino Cedillo symbolizes the currency of reciprocal relations between him and "his" peasants (this is a crucial ideological need in his peasant groups of origin). The quick-witted aggressive machismo of Gonzalo Santos symbolized his personal superiority over other rancheros. Different kinds of intimate cultures (with their varying degrees of coherence) produce different materials for politicking. At the national level, the importance of the spatial perspective is that it allows an uncovering of the real differences between national and other kinds of local power. By contrasting caciques and caudillos, or presidents and bureaucrats, one understands much about the kinds of cultural articulations that operate within a nation-state. Since centrality and marginality are crucial in the construction of the sacred (including the sacred in politics), a regional-cultural perspective turns out to be indispensable for a systematic understanding of the forms that power takes within a system of hegemony.

On the other hand, I hope to have shown that the analysis of culture in the national space does indeed allow us to reframe some of the classical issues of the national-culture literature, such as the inferiority complex of "the Mexican," the fetishism of el señor presidente, personalismo as a political form, and the relationships among racial ideologies, nationalism, caudillismo, and caciquismo.

18

Spatial Analysis and National Culture

Most works on national culture attempt to single out a set of collective habits and traits, describe them, explain them, give them a genealogy, and then present them to the national audience with the hope that the portrait will make them reflect upon and then transcend the nation's cultural problems.

The works of the pensadores were just these kinds of *prises de conscience*. They were (mostly) produced during a time when Mexico's position in the world was being redefined, and there seemed to be hopes of achieving a kind of national autonomy and parity with other countries. With an effort, it seemed that Mexico could play a dignified role in the "concert of nations." Thus, most of the works on Mexican national culture emerged out of concern with the forms in which Mexico was or was not modernizing.

At the same time, however, the exercise of detailing national characteristics itself contributes to create an image of national culture. This is so not only because national-culture studies posit a common national culture; it is also that these critiques assume that there is a national public with a common goal (national welfare). These convictions regarding a common national welfare are, in the last analysis, what prompted people to find and analyze shared national characteristics.

The problem has been that this political impulse—which is, in many ways, quite good—has not been matched by the theoretical innovations that are needed to specify what a "shared" characteristic is. Someone might want to say that Mexican national culture is generally very *machista* (macho-oriented), but "machismo" does not mean the same thing for a man as it does for his wife. Although there may be some practices that are upheld between them (they are, therefore, "shared"), they are interpreted from distinct points of view. Routines that the husband interprets as assertions of his domination may be seen by the wife as part of a strategy for manipulating men ("men are like children!"). And when we consider culture in the national space, the problem of what "sharing" a cultural practice means is much more difficult to untangle, since it involves conceptualizing that national space.

This is the problem, for example, with Paz's otherwise brilliant analysis of etiquette and formality in Mexico. Paz provides us with an intricate description of the mechanisms of closure of "the Mexicans," one of which is *disimulo* (dissemblement): the Indian hides from others, he dissembles, and fuses into the landscape; Mexican women are silent and idol-like fetishes, they fuse into the night, the earth, the stone; the unimportant man is nullified (*ninguneado*) by others, and he disappears into the background. If one considers these examples further, however, one discovers that Paz's description is flawed on one point: the people whom he describes as hermetically sealed are only so vis-à-vis people of identity groups that are other than their own, and especially towards Paz's own class of well-established intellectual males. Indians fuse with the landscape only when they see a mestizo (whom they may suppose is a tax collector); they do not hide from one another. Mexican women may be silent idols for Mexican men, but amongst themselves they are known to be quite talkative. The man who was confused with the wall goes home and browbeats his children. In other words, what Paz saw as a culture of individual atomization through solitude, closure, and formality is in fact a hierarchical culture in which dominant classes and genders "mute" other classes and groups.

What is this hierarchical culture? How does Paz's insistence on formalism, rules of politeness, and violence fit into it?

The touchy defensiveness that Octavio Paz and Samuel Ramos identified, named, and criticized was the result of the distance and forms of interrelations between intimate cultures in Mexico. These distances are recognized by everyone in an idiom of respect, silence, ritual, and violence. People are conscious of the fact that "shared" experiences, including encounters between people, mean very different things for different participants: the Virgin of Guadalupe may be a national symbol that is shared by most Mexicans, but her precise significance is different for an atheistic politician than for a proclerical one, for an Indian than for a worker, for a shantytown dweller than for a university professor. People understand that they share frames and idioms of interaction ("a culture of social relations"), and, at the same time, they know that these sets of practices have different implications for the different actors.

Without a theoretical solution to this problem, works on national culture hinder as much as they help. By ignoring the ways in which a "shared" sign or a "shared" practice articulates very diverse kinds of experiences, these works falsify at the same time as they reveal. This is why they are *intriguing*. This is also why they have been put to so many different kinds of uses, both good and bad.

In this book I have tried to rescue the problem of national and regional culture from the residual position that it is currently in. The road that I chose in order to accomplish this was to rethink cultural production in internally differentiated regional and national spaces. This led me to a description of the culture of social classes in their localized settings, and to focus on the frames of interaction between them. I formalized a perspective that was designed for this task by discussing the relationships among what I have called "intimate culture," "the culture of social relations," "localist ideology," "mestizaje," and "coherence."

On some levels, these concepts have a lot in common with other formulations. For example, there are similarities between "intimate culture" and "mechanical solidarity"; "localist ideology" is similar to "ethnicity," "mestizaje" is similar to "deculturation," and "coherence" is a preexisting concept that is merely revamped for the analysis of intimate culture. The formulations that produced these other concepts (mechanical solidarity, ethnicity) were not developed for analyzing the spatial system of mediating structures that really makes up hegemony. I could not just expand, say, the notion of mechanical solidarity because it was designed to classify types of societies and forms of collective consciousness and representation. I preferred not to use acculturation, deculturation, and transculturation because these concepts were not tuned for the analysis of continuous regional dynamics.

By creating new concepts I have highlighted the conceptual problems involved in understanding regional culture. My ultimate purpose is not necessarily to promote a new vocabulary, although I have found this vocabulary quite useful; it is to instate the mode of analysis that I have proposed. This mode of analysis focuses on culture in space by juxtaposing several kinds of relations between cultural production and spatial systems and by analyzing the tensions and contradictions between these relations. One of these relations is the economy of sign transmission and distribution; another is the regional political economy of class; another is the spatial implications of dominant discourses. When we transpose all of this we finally begin to understand the places from which cultural understandings are produced. We also can begin to understand some of the systemic contradictions in different national hegemonic orders.

An analysis of the dialectic between these concepts led to an interpretation of culture in Morelos and the Huasteca, and of selected aspects of

Mexican national culture, especially certain forms of charisma and sociability. Throughout these analyses I emphasized that localist ideologies, including nationalism, cannot be analyzed without understanding their relationship to actual spaces of cultural production. These spaces help us pinpoint the elements of culture that ideologies pick up on, and they show the positions from which ideologies are created, and the kind of work that they are designed to do.

The analysis of regional and national culture also allowed me to point to some of the specificities of *national* culture versus culture at other complex spatial levels. Position in the nation-state is a fundamental aspect of all of the localist ideologies that were discussed in this book. This is because hegemony is established at the level of the state: "knowing one's place" is the fundamental requirement for sharing "a sense of reality" (i.e., for hegemony), and the state is the main available source of recognition of place. In addition, the importance of the state in the development of all localist ideologies makes it a particularly complex cultural phenomenon. The caudillo's mysterious whiteness is a product of this complexity; so is cultural salience of the Virgin of Guadalupe, and the tellurian power of el señor presidente. The contrast between the national space and other (lower-level) regional cultures also provides us with a cautionary lesson against jumping directly into the analysis of the national center. Nationalist ideology, national history, national leaders, all have to articulate these complex spaces in one way or another. This effort of articulation molds and transforms the characteristics of those histories, leaders, and ideologies. Nationalism cannot be understood without an analysis of culture in the national space.

Throughout this book I have also shown that the specific characteristics of national ideologies have important effects throughout the national space. The study of culture in the national space is therefore fundamental for the discussion of alternative forms of nationalism. I hope that the substantive and theoretical contributions of this book contribute to that discussion.

Notes

Introduction

1. "Each of us should look for America in his heart, instead of just lying in a delicious wait for the fruit to fall off the tree." In Reyes 1982:25.
2. Cited in Knight 1990:86.
3. Cited in Knight 1990:85.
4. The latent nationalism of Boasian relativism also found support in the culture and personality school. These anthropologists worked with the idea that different forms of social reproduction produced distinct dominant personality types, which in turn became projected onto culture in the form of "values." Cultures, said Ruth Benedict, "are individual psychology thrown large upon the screen, given gigantic proportions and a long time span" (1932:24). However, most anthropologists believed that this sort of "national" culture study was only feasible in small-scale societies that had relatively homogeneous populations and, after a demolishing critique from sociologists of complex societies (see Lindesmith and Strauss, 1950), anthropology shifted away from the study of national or protonational culture. Anthony Wallace (1961:2) aptly expresses this change: "[T]he problem for the theoretical anthropologist has shifted from the Linnean classification of cultures and their aspects on a temporal or geographic continuum to the discovery and analysis of the laws of cultural process."
5. My formulation of these problematics owes much to two important attempts to develop an anthropology of the nation-state: Julian Steward's (1956) *People of Puerto Rico,* and Roberto DaMatta's (1979) study of Brazilian national culture. These studies are fundamentally different. Steward's materialistic approach involved dissecting Puerto Rico spatially into a set of "subcultures" that corresponded to specific ecological niches. He made a substantial contribution to understanding the national space, but was not able to do an analysis of

national culture; he pointed to the subcultures, but never to the culture they were allegedly a part of. DaMatta's work, on the other hand, is an innovative examination of national culture through an analysis of ritual; he explores key aspects of Brazilian national culture without a full account of social differentiation in the national space. This book attempts to address the gap between Steward and DaMatta.

6. This also helps explain the enormous appeal of sociological topics to Latin American novelists and to their readers; only they have been able to describe in a wide-sweeping way the culture of cities and regions (as in Vargas Llosa's *Conversación en la catedral* or in Carlos Fuentes's *La región más transparente*), national political culture (as in Octavio Paz's *Sor Juana,* Carpentier's *El recurso del método* or García Márquez's *El General en su laberinto*) or even, more generally, the ways in which the diverse cultural understandings of Latin American classes and ethnic groups come together in single processes (as in Rosario Catellanos's *Oficio de tinieblas* or in Vargas Llosa's *Guerra del fín del mundo*). Liberated from the burden of having to produce a systematic body of data gathered through participant observation in each level of their complex descriptions, these writers have done research and fit pieces of materials into a whole vision of culture on a scale that has not been as fully developed in Latin American anthropology.

7. The ultimate proof of the utility of the popular-culture literature for Mexican nationalism has been the fact that the government has, since the 1970s, financed institutes that research and publicize Mexican popular culture. An undersecretariat of popular culture existed for quite a while, a Museum of Popular Cultures was created, and publications by the Ministry of Education on popular culture were heavily promoted. Moreover, some of the main political slogans of recent presidents promote this idea of cultural plurality; for example, José López Portillo's campaign slogan "La solución somos todos" ("we all are the solution") or Carlos Salinas de Gortari's "Que hable México" ("let Mexico speak") signal a shift towards a nationalism based on the recognition and approval of a certain state-guided diversity. This nationalism is better suited to a policy of free enterprise, to weaker state intervention, and to an open international market.

8. See, for example, the essays in Monsivais et al., *En torno a la cultura nacional* (1982).

9.

Mexicans	*United Statesians*
realists	utilitarians
macabre	hypocrites
pleasure in myths and legends	pleasure in fairy tales and detective books
they lie out of desperation or fantasy	they don't lie but eliminate portions of the truth
believers	gullible
get drunk to confess	get drunk to forget
nihilists	optimists

distrustful	open
sad and sarcastic	happy and humorous
desire to contemplate	desire to comprehend
relish their wounds	relish their interventions
health by contact	health by hygiene

1: Study of Regional Culture

1. By "regional analysis" I mean the school of spatial analysis that, in anthropology, has been championed by G. William Skinner (see, for example, 1964, 1977*a*, 1977*b*, 1985) and Carol Smith (1976, 1977, 1984). For a general introduction see Smith 1976.

2. Partial exceptions to this rule are Skinner (1977*b*) and Smith (1984); perhaps these examples demonstrate that many of the past excesses of regional analysis in cultural simplification are in fact superficial to the theory. Nonetheless, they are there.

3. Gregory (1985) has developed a critique of Hägerstrand's (1965) diffusion theory that often parallels my appraisal of regional analysis. Although regional analysis is much more attuned to sociological explanation and interpretation than Hägerstrand's theory, it is still the case that regional analysis concentrates most of its attention on observable human behavior and that its conceptualization of culture suffers from this methodological bias.

4. In fact, the exchange analogy is not even fully applicable to the case of information; so, for example, Hägerstrand's (1965) findings on innovation diffusion led him to distinguish between "public" and "private" information—"private" information affects innovation diffusion in a different way than "public" information does. Thus, even the supposed transparency of "information" is illusory: information, like all other forms of exchange, is built upon exchange relationships, which vary across cultures and contexts.

5. Skinner (1977*b*, 1985) has shown the importance of considering spatial systems for the study of selected aspects of culture, such as dialectical variation and ethnic relations.

6. An example of the ways in which a well-founded interest in images of regional culture can obfuscate the need for understanding the complexities of regional culture itself can be found in what is undoubtedly one of the most important books on nationalism: Benedict Anderson's *Imagined Communities* (1983). Anderson shows that "the nation" is an imagined community, by which he means not only that national feelings stem from the internalization of an *image* of community (that is, an image of interconnectedness, of sharing, of equal membership), but also that the nation is a false community. Because of this, Anderson does not really attempt to conceptualize the systemic processes of regional cultural differentiation and homogenization that are involved in "national culture," focusing instead on the analysis of a single state project: the mythologized imagined community that is designed to occupy the place that real (destroyed or fragmented) communities leave behind.

7. In his work on "the house" and "the street" as competing discourses in

Brazilian society, Roberto DaMatta (1985) shows that two fundamental ideological orientations, one holistic and hierarchical, with a fundamental imagery founded on family relationships, and one atomistic and competitive, with a discourse modeled on the life of the streets, compete at practically all levels of social life. Both of these ideologies have their relational and spatial correlates, which DaMatta ties to the formative impressions that the "house" and the "street" make on contemporary Brazilians.

8. In his analysis of "the dreaming," Myers (1986) shows how the practices of the Pintupi are ideologically rooted in interpersonal relationships that have a spatial expression. Places are charged with histories through which people conceive of their interrelations, and places therefore trigger sentiments about oneself and one's relationships; political conflict is conceived in terms of conflicts about place. See also Basso 1988.

9. See de Certeau 1984, for an enlightening and critical contrast between Foucault and Bourdieu.

10. I have also found important insights in the works of Marxist geographers such as Harvey (1985), Urry (1985), Gregory (1985), Gregory and Urry (1985), and Massey (1984). The works of these geographers are often epistemologically more compatible with cultural studies than regional analysis is. The perspective on social space which is being developed in this "radical geography" is in several ways a salutary synthesis of geography, Marxism, and theories of practice, and the findings, which have to do with the spatial logic of capitalism, are pregnant with implications for the study of culture. However, as in the case of Skinner and his school of regional analysis, these implications have not yet been elaborated theoretically.

11. In regional analysis, "region" and "regional" are analytic categories that refer to *any* nodally interconnected space within a spatial economic or political system. In other words, the term "region" can refer to large or small spaces of many different types. However, we can call a particular space a "region" only if that space is composed of different, internally homogeneous "zones." These zones are interconnected in terms of the logic with which one is regionalizing (for example, production, commerce, or political administration), and the system of interconnections (the "regional system") can be thought of as a hierarchy. I use these three criteria in the notion of "region" here. Although all of this spatial organization always involves geographic space in one way or another, it is important not to define the notion of region topographically, for the relationship between topography and region will depend entirely on the nature of the system of interaction that is being investigated. In agrarian economic regions, such as the ones that furnish many of the examples in this chapter, geography, orography, and land quality are fundamental for regional organization, but this should not lead us to reify these factors into the determining characteristics of regions in the abstract.

12. All Tepoztlán examples are taken from Lomnitz-Adler 1982 and in press.

13. The seats of Spanish power were located in the *cabeceras,* or political centers, of *Alcaldías Mayores* and *Corregimientos,* and the seats of Indian power were the *cabeceras* of Indian *jurisdicciones.* Haskett (1987) studied Indian government in the Alcaldía Mayor of Cuernavaca and showed that local Indian

government enjoyed a good deal of autonomy from the Spanish, so much so that there were many continuities between the colonial system of Indian authority and the pre-Columbian system. Lockhart, Berdan, and Anderson (1986) have edited and commented on the only local Indian town council (*cabildo*) records that are known to date.

14. In fact, in Morelos at least, the Crown had begun to push for the use of Indian wage labor in lieu of corvée labor since the early seventeenth century, and by the eighteenth century corvée labor through the *repartimiento* system was rare, except in the mines. However, the collection of tribute through the Indian communities and the Indians' access to communal lands maintained a spatially segregated ethnic system, despite the emergence of a multiethnic wage-earning class.

15. For cases of mestizos buying into barrio lands in Morelos, see de la Peña 1980; for a case of a Tepoztecan "Indian" governor who was later considered to be a Spaniard, see Archivo General de la Nación (AGN), Hospital de Jesús, vol. 309, exp. 5, f. 67v.; and for a case of a Spaniard who was occupying the office of Indian governor in Tepoztlán see AGN, Indios 7, 12v–13.

16. Although the documentation from Tepoztlán provides only a little information on the regional network of Spaniards (which most certainly existed); it is certain that Spaniards in Tepoztlán did have intense interactions with the local Tepoztecan elite. There are even some instances where Spaniards married into local Tepoztecan elite families (see, for example, in AGN, Hospital de Jesús, vol. 321, exp. 9, fs. 1–22). In the nineteenth century the old Spanish and Indian elite families fused into a single small-town group made up of a few last names: Ortega, Rojas, Zúñiga, Ortiz, Navarette, Lara, and one or two others.

17. Policies enforcing the ideological organization of space were continuously instated in places like Tepoztlán. Spaniards were discouraged from acquiring property there; mestizos and Spaniards were barred from holding offices in the Indian Republic; and Indians were punished for taking sacraments (especially baptism, marriage, and burial) out of the Church's hands and into their own.

18. It should be evident by now that I am attempting to dissect the notion of hegemony into components that occupy distinct aspects or contexts of social relations. In this sense I have misgivings about the benefits that can be derived from the holistic promise of the concept. So for example, Raymond Williams's definition of hegemony ("[I]t is, that is to say, in the strongest sense a 'culture', but a culture which has also to be seen as the lived dominance and subordination of particular classes" [1977:110]) is important because it stresses the power and domination that are present in culture, but it does not help us to understand the production of hegemony in space. Those studying hegemony have paid a good deal of attention to "lived dominance" and not enough to structures of mediation.

19. Some of these ideas have a history that can be traced as far as Greek notions of the "Wild Man," who lived outside of the polis and who lacked the ability to speak Greek (see Padgen 1982, ch. 1). Bartra (ms.) mentions that "Wild Men" had been a part of Spanish pageants in New Spain since at least the mid-sixteenth century.

20. In Marxist terms these two orientations could be described as money→ commodity→money + profit (M-C-M′) and commodity→money→commodity (C-M-C), respectively.

21. Therefore, the settlement is often an effective entry point for the study of regional culture. But, precisely because of this effectiveness, one must be wary of reducing a portrayal of regional culture to the description of settlement types. The settlement is one place of cultural interaction within a general hierarchical arrangement whose niches can include institutions such as households, neighborhoods, settlements, and formal organizations; however, settlements can easily be reified into the quintessential locus of cultural interaction. The settlement is useful as an entry point because of its organizational prominence in agrarian societies, where formal and informal ties revolve around the community, but the settlement must not be taken as the only—or even the best—place to begin the study of regional culture. The study of regional culture must privilege, first, the hierarchical organization of cultural interaction (communication). Once this has been considered, favorable criteria for regional typologies can be selected.

22. Readers may refer to Redfield 1930, ch. 6.

23. My use of the term "space" here is not the same as Taussig's (1987) in his notion of "space of death." In Taussig's usage, the space in which murder was executed was defined both by the concrete interactive contexts of colonialists and Indians and by the projected fantasies of the colonialists (alienation). My notion of the space of mestizaje refers only to frames of communication, to an interactional space, not an ideological one. I will not go into the subject of ideological spaces of mestizaje here, although the section on alienation in the construction of the culture of social relations suggests what an analysis of these spaces might look like.

24. Analyses of "subculture" like those of Stuart Hall (1976) or Dick Hebdige (1979) can be reinterpreted to some degree in this light: resistance from urban subcultures is often overcome via an expansion of the dominant order into ever-transforming "styles." Each time this happens, another generation of rebels seems to make its grudging peace with the dominant order; this phenomenon may help to explain the importance of generations in contemporary forms of resistance.

25. "By the mere fact that it is a *class* and no longer an *estate,* the bourgeoisie is forced to organize itself no longer locally, but nationally, and to give a general form to its mean average interest" (Marx 1988:80). Therefore, hegemony is achieved above all at the national level. It is a "mean average interest," which is why I have called it a relatively "diffuse" form of power, in comparison to the power needs of local dominant groups.

2: Morelos and the Huasteca

1. Ranchos existed during the nineteenth and earlier centuries, but were not the dominant form of production.

2. This version was published in the children's book *Así Cuentan en la Huasteca* (México: SEP, 1983) made with materials collected in the project

"Tradición oral y estructura social en la Huasteca" (SEP/CONAFE), which I directed; it was compiled by Lillian Scheffler.

3. And even to most Mexicanists. For example, Diehl (1981:506–507) claims that "[The Huasteca] is the least known region of Mesoamerica. . . The reason for this appears to be the Huasteca's marginality in the past. . . . [Its] inhabitants did not build many large ceremonial and urban centers." But precisely how many large urban centers do you need to become well known? The site known as Tantoc (or Tamtok), which has not been opened to the public or restored, occupies over a hundred hectares, has several major pyramids, a ball court, and countless mounds of lesser import. To a layman like me, the site looks to be about the size of any of Mexico's major pre-Columbian ruins.

4. Recent historiography recognizes the regional nature of the Revolution; however, the social bases of the movement in the Huasteca have not yet received full attention. Schryer (1980), Salamini (1978), and Márquez (1977) have made significant contributions in this direction, and Gonzalo Santos's memoirs (1986) are an invaluable source as well. But what seems to me to be most important in the present context is that, despite the multiregional nature of the Revolution, some of the movements have been officially recognized as more legitimate representatives than others.

5. Falcón (1984) mentions that Lárraga was supported by "his Indians" and states that the Indians that belonged to his ranch felt bonds of patronage that dragged them into the fray. This is possible, and certainly Falcón has found documents to support her case. However, in the two Indian communities where I and my students worked, both of which are very much in the zone of influence of the Lárragas and the Santos (municipios of San Antonio and Tampamolón) we found no memories of voluntary participation. On the contrary, people remember the capturing of members of the community—men and women—for their forced participation in the Revolution. My interviews with mestizo revolutionaries and relatives of revolutionaries all coincide on this point. They all claim that there were no Indian revolutionaries, although some were used as cannon fodder. They were, as Gastón Santos aptly put it, *voluntarios de a huevo* (forced volunteers). Stresser-Pean (personal communication, 1986) says that he met several Indian revolutionaries in his extensive travels in the region during 1938, especially around the area of Valles and Aquismón. Gonzalo Santos (1986) claims that Huastecan Indians were revolutionary and that Nahuas (of the region) were conservative. In any case, the situation is contradictory to the degree that it is still impossible to characterize Indian participation in the Revolution.

6. For colonial material on Central Mexican perceptions of the Huasteca see Vetancourt 1971 and Tapia Zenteno 1985. In the nineteenth century, the *modernista* poet Othón wrote about the Huasteca always in terms of its virginal exuberance, and this depiction of the region as wilderness has survived in today's journalism.

7. The Huasteca gets portrayed as having secret treasures even by John Huston, the American film director, in his realization of B. Traven's *Treasure of the Sierra Madre*. Here the gold-diggers (played by Humphrey Bogart, among others) recognize the secret wealth of the region and attempt to turn this recogni-

tion into their own personal prosperity. The region plays a trick on them, however, and resists their exploitation. Those who survive leave the Sierra Madre as poor as they arrived; the sand buries the gold that they dug up.

8. Most of my information on Axtla was collected by María del Carmen Hernández Beltrán. Practically all my information on Beto Ramón is from Hernández's work on medicine and curing in Axtla. The oral history I have from the village comes from Hernández Beltrán and Teresa Medina Mora, plus a few interviews of my own.

9. I have decided to use real names except in cases where I feel that the interviews would be harmful to an acquaintance's reputation.

10. Some of the remarkable genetic experiments conducted by Angel Castrillón and Manuel Berruecos (his highly specialized veterinarian partner) include the development of dwarf Brahman cows, and the development of sheep fit for the tropics.

11. Buñuel mentions in his autobiography that Sir Edward once offered him the services of an airplane to bomb Franco's Spain. He also sponsored Dalí when he was young, and owned an important collection of surrealist art. Edward James died in 1985.

3: Cultural Hegemony

1. In colonial times what is today the state of Morelos was subdivided into several Alcaldías Mayores. The most important was Cuernavaca, which was part of Cortés's grant as Marqués del Valle. Other Alcadías Mayores were Cuautla-Amilpas, Chalco, and Tetela del Volcán (Gerhard 1972). There were boundary disputes between these jurisdictions, especially between the Crown (Chalco) and the Marquis, so that their precise boundaries varied, especially during the sixteenth century. Each Alcaldía Mayor was composed of a set of *jurisdicciones* that had a seat of government (a *cabecera*); the main cabeceras were Cuernavaca (which has as its *sujetos* the whole of present-day western Morelos and was the seat of the Alcaldía Mayor), Yautepec (which had as sujetos the villages and towns of the modern municipios of Yautepec and Tlaltizapan), Tepoztlán (whose sujetos are today the villages of the municipio of Tepoztlán), Guastepec (Oaxtepec), whose sujetos were in dispute with the Cuautla jurisdiction, Yecapixtla, Cuautla (which was an Alcaldía Mayor), Huazulco, Ocuituco, Jumilpetepec, Totolapan, Tlayacapan, Atlatláhucan, and Tlalnepantla (Cuauhtenco).

2. At this time the state of Mexico shared the limits of the Archbishopric of Mexico, and was the largest, most important state in the union, covering the present-day states of Hidalgo, Mexico, Morelos, Guerrero, and the Federal District (see Macune 1970). The state of Mexico began to collapse from the moment Congress decided to extract Mexico City from it and transform the nation's capital into a Federal District. The state of Mexico had difficulties in locating its new capital, for each economic region within the state stood for its own interests. During a period of approximately thirty years, the state's capital moved among centers that were chosen because of their proximity to Mexico City (Texcoco and Tlalpan) and Toluca, the city with the most political weight in

the region. Finally, the capital stayed in Toluca, but several regions splintered from the state of Mexico and became states in their own right.

3. The state of Morelos was created after the refederalization of the country following the collapse of Maximilian's empire. There was at first some competition between Cuautla and Cuernavaca for the capital, but Cuernavaca was supported by the central government (see López González 1968; Diez 1930; Mazari 1968). The state of Morelos was subdivided into four districts: Cuernavaca, Cuautla (then known as "Morelos"), Tetecala, and Jojutla; twenty-eight municipios were created.

4. In 1970, Morelos had 36,726 hectares of irrigated land and 87,406 hectares of seasonal (Coordinación General, 1982c). It is interesting to note that very little has been invested in irrigation since the hacienda days in the Porfiriato, when there were 36,109 hectares of irrigated land in 1910 (González Herrera and Embriz Osorio 1984:290).

5. Morelos' economy was traditionally based on the commercial agriculture of its valleys. Today industry and the tertiary sector are more important than agriculture. In 1975 only 17.5 percent of the Gross Internal Product stemmed from agriculture, 31.1 percent came from industry, and 50.4 percent from the services. Although some of the industry is related to processing agricultural goods—sugar factories and rice mills—most of it is factories that have been "decentralized" from Mexico City.

6. The year-by-year agricultural statistics provided by the Dirección General de Estadísticas strike me as being unreliable for precise data on production, at least when compared to the municipios for which I and other anthropologists have data. Nonetheless, the importance of tomatoes and sorghum in peripheral municipios is registered.

7. Zacatepec has only become important since the construction of the Emiliano Zapata sugar mill in 1938. It was chosen for this site because of its central position with respect to cane production. I have not mentioned here towns whose importance is considerable but that have become practially industrial suburbs of Cuernavaca: Juitepec and Temixco.

8. There was interregional trade with the state of Mexico (trade was concentrated in Cuernavaca), with Guerrero (the main plazas were Jojutla, Cuautla, and Yautepec) and, to a lesser extent, with Puebla. This commerce worked with wholesale dealers that had *mesones,* or food warehouses, that were concentrated in the main settlements of the region. The 1900 census lists nine mesones in Cuernavaca, seven in Cuautla, four in Yautepec, four in Miacatlán, three in Xochitepec, three in Tepoztlán, three in Yecapixtla, and three in Jonacatepec.

The haciendas relieved some of their marketing needs on these towns; however, most of their trade was directly with Mexico City. All of the large haciendas had rail crossing their territory. I was fortunate to interview the late Alfonso Vélez Goribar, perhaps the last live hacendado of the region, before his death in 1985. Don Alfonso claimed that in the case of the haciendas of his family (Oacalco and Casasano) their main interactions with local merchants was in relation to money for paying labor. Rich locals supplied the haciendas with cash, and the hacendados paid them by check from Mexico City banks. The safety and peace in the countryside during this period was proverbial. The payer came and went on horseback from the towns to the haciendas with his satchels full of silver and was reportedly never held up.

According to Vélez Goribar, the hacendados also had dealings with the local pharmacists and to some degree with the general stores of the towns. There were also occasional get-togethers among hacendados and local dignitaries (the doctor, the pharmacist, the owner of the general store).

Sugar was always exported directly from the sugar factories to Mexico, never through local commercial networks; machinery and tools also came directly from Mexico. Although the dominant economy was the hacienda economy, it was not the main source of livelihood for the local and regional elites.

9. Until 1881 all transportation to and from Morelos was on horse, mule, or foot. There were two main roads from Mexico City, one to Cuernavaca crossing the Ajusco range at Tres Cumbres, and one to the Amilpas through Chalco, Nepantla, and Amecameca. According to travelers' accounts (cf. Prieto 1845) the road to Cuernavaca was in very poor condition; the voyage to Cuernavaca by carriage seems to have taken a full twenty-four hours—about the same as the journey on foot.

In 1881 the government built the first railroad to Morelos, the Ferrocarril Interoceánico. It went to the Amilpas, with stops at Cuautla, Yautepec, Jojutla, and Puente de Ixtla, and with connections to Puebla via Axochiapan. The prosperous haciendas of this region financed rails that connected the sugar factories with this line (cf. Diez 1930:38). The railroad allowed for relatively easy communication (given a seven- to ten-hour ride) between Mexico City and the Amilpas. The rail to Cuernavaca and down to Balsas was built in 1897. The construction of these rails shortly followed the pacification of the region (which was bandit-infested into the 1870s) as well as the modernization of the regional haciendas.

I do not know to what extent exchange between Morelos and the states of Mexico and Puebla was channelized through Mexico City because of the rail. Mule trains were used into the 1940s, especially to and from Guerrero, but also to Toluca and Puebla. It seems certain, in any case, that the rails did exacerbate the tendency for Mexico City to centralize all agricultural goods from the different ecological niches of the central valleys and for Morelos to acquire the cold-country goods through Mexico City.

During the Revolution the railroads were continuously assaulted by the Zapatistas, and rebuilt by government troops. Long-distance commerce was risky, and all sorts of pacts between merchants and different armed forces were necessary for the maintenance of commerce in the different zones (cf. López González 1980:245–247; other examples are available for Tlayacapan and Atlatláhucan).

10. Information on migratory labor to the United States is scanty. In the case of Tepoztlán this seems to have been an important alternate (or complementary) source of work in the 1950s (with the Bracero Program); this also seems to be the case in the southeastern villages in the district of Tetecala. It seems likely to me that the economic crisis of the 1980s may have induced a new wave of emigration

to the United States, but my field research in Morelos was done too early to observe this (1983–85).

11. In my work on Tepoztlán (1982) I distinguished four kinds of central places, which I called hamlets, pueblos ("villages"), central market towns, and regional cities. Of these, hamlets and pueblos exist in both the core and the periphery, whereas central market towns and regional cities exist only in the core. In the 1900 census the differences in the servicing capacity of the regional cities, the central market towns and the peripheral pueblos were not very important: Cuernavaca had 336 people working in commerce, compared to 109 in Yautepec, a central market town (32.4 percent of Cuernavaca), 47 in Tepoztlán, a larger peripheral pueblo (13.4 percent of Cuernavaca), and 20 in Tlalnepantla, a small peripheral pueblo (or 5.9 percent of the number of merchants in Cuernavaca). In 1976 Cuernavaca had 1,486 commercial establishments, Yautepec had 341 (only 22.9 percent of the number in Cuernavaca), Tepoztlán had 86 (5.8 percent), and Atlatláhucan had 33 (2.2 percent). In addition to the quantitative growth in the gap between levels of the central place hierarchy, we also have a greater qualitative difference in kinds of commerce, because certain products today are only available at the regional city level (for example, agricultural machinery) and others exist only at the central markets and regional cities (automobiles, shopping-center goods such as specific types of clothes, cloth, shoes, and the like).

12. The first road from Cuernavaca to Cuautla was begun shortly after the Revolution. In 1933 the first federal road from Mexico City to Cuernavaca was built. In 1936 Cuernavaca was connected to Tepoztlán. In 1965 the new highway between Mexico and Cuernavaca (with a branch to Tepoztlán, Yautepec, and Cuautla) was built. Cuernavaca is today scarcely an hour away from Mexico City; Cuautla is an hour and ten minutes away. There is probably no cabecera in Morelos farther than two and a half hours away from Mexico City, and Morelos' most distant villages (such as Hueyapan, Cuentepec, and Huautla) can be reached in five hours or less. Most villages today are connected to their cabeceras by passable roads, though many of them are dirt and gravel.

13. This initial period presents, in several aspects, continuities with the colonial organization of the region, which was temporarily thrown into chaos by the lawlessness that followed independence.

14. Travelers of the seventeenth century complained of the transportation problem between Acapulco and Mexico City (e.g., Gemeli Careri 1699), but even transportation between Cuernavaca and Mexico City seems to have been appalling (see Prieto 1845) until the construction of the Ferrocarril Central to Balsas in 1897.

15. The most contested governorships in Morelos history cannot said to have been contested by the regional elites. This is even the case of the movement against Escandón in 1909.

16. Since Zapatismo there have been a few rebellions in Morelos, most of them of a local nature. In the early 1940s the people in the eastern rim of the state rebelled against the draft for World War II; however, this movement was short-lived. The rebellion has been described by Ramírez (1974). I was fortunate

to interview Jesús Castillo López, who was the state governor at the time and who gave a substantially different version of events, including the key importance of the priest of Zacualpan in the movement and of how the rebellion was quelled via direct negotiation with the governor. For this purpose Castillo López made a tour of eastern Morelos on horseback, which took several months. Today the trip can be made by road in a day.

Other rebellions of minor import in the state have been the Cristero Revolt, which affected mostly the towns of Tepoztlán and Xochitepec, but also Cuernavaca to a lesser degree; and the Jaramillista movement, which ended in the assassination of Jaramillo and his family by government troops in 1962. Other recorded uprisings have all been local and usually related to land tenure and difficulties between peasants and government officials; this is the case of the assassination of eight members of the notorious Policía Judicial by peasants from Santa Catarina (Tepoztlán) in the 1950s and similar uprisings in other localities.

17. The size of the landholdings of local caciques has been discussed by Crespo and Frey 1982, and Crespo and Vega in press. Some information for specific villages is also available in Elizondo-Mayer 1984, Lewis 1951, and Lomnitz-Adler in press.

18. Although the history of this process is now difficult to retrieve, it would seem that these local caciques were more important in the regional peripheries than in the hacienda-dominated core. The Archivo General de la Nación abounds in information for the colonial period, but most of the nineteenth-century material, particularly after the separation of Morelos from the state of Mexico (1869), was burned during the Revolution. The existence of a local dominant class in almost all Morelos pueblos has been documented by Crespo and Vega (in press).

19. Crespo and Frey (1982) have argued that in most cases the amount of land that the pueblos lost to the haciendas as a result of the Juarez Reform has been grossly overstated. The possibility of compromise between haciendas and pueblos clearly existed in the first years of the Revolution, and it is quite possible that, had the hacendados rallied around more enlightened leaders, they would have been able to strike a bargain with the Zapatistas relatively cheaply. In my study of Tepoztlán (in press) I found that the haciendas appropriated communal lands shortly after independence.

20. For example, Augustín Güemes, one of Cuernavaca's oldest, most lucid, and most venerated schoolteachers told me that he was able to continue teaching in Cuernavaca through most of the Revolution. When Zapata occupied Cuernavaca, he paid the teachers to continue with their work. Activites fully stopped only during the siege of 1914 and in the final evacuation of the city in 1918.

21. There are only three or four "old" (i.e., elite) families in Cuernavaca today. None of them are very powerfully locally or regionally.

22. I have been told that machinery from the old Morelos mills has been seen in some of the Veracruz plants that were owned by Carrancista generals.

23. However, the politics of land reform in the region were complicated. There are testimonies from several villages to the effect that the first and best lands to be distributed went precisely to the wealthy families of the village (cf.

Elizondo-Mayer 1984), but this does not seem to have been the case everywhere. It is certain that many peasant families were frightened of asking for ejido grants at first, especially because the Church counseled against it. Nonetheless, it would be false to say that agrarian reform in Morelos uniformly concentrated wealth in the hands of the old caciques.

24. This is the case of Tepoztlán (Lomnitz-Adler 1982), but also of Tlayacapan (de la Peña 1980) and of eastern Morelos (Warman 1976). Perhaps the most important caudillo of the state in this period was Genovevo de la O, who kept strict control over his village of Santa María Ahuacatitlán, north of Cuernavaca.

It is interesting to note that there were no real regional caudillos in Morelos in this period. One must remember that Zapatismo was militarily defeated, and then politically reinstated in a position that was extremely dependent on support from the federal government.

25. Estrada Cajigal's birth place is a debated point. His supporters say he was born in Cuernavaca, while his adversaries claim he was from Michoacán. It is certain that Estrada had family ties in Michoacán, but his family remains grounded in Cuernavaca.

26. This is the period in which Malcolm Lowry wrote *Under the Volcano*. In it one catches a glimpse of the kinds of visitors that Cuernavaca received: wealthy and sophisticated Americans and Europeans who owned villas and stayed for extended periods of time. This was also the time, of course, when all of Mexico's top politicians had homes in Cuernavaca. It was the beginning of the creation of what a friend has called "the secret city" in Cuernavaca, the web of relations that exists among powerful members of society who have scarcely any contact with local Cuernavaca society.

27. The social history of the peasantification of the governorship in 1934–38 is yet to be written. Those who remember have many anecdotes of Bustamante's picturesque ways: kidnapping young girls from ranches to serve as concubines, peasantification of the governor's palace, and so forth.

28. Until the early 1950s there were still a few other privately owned mills that worked, the most important being Oacalco, Casasano, and Miacatlán. Oacalco and Casasano were originally owned by the Vélez Goribar family, but they sold Oacalco to Aarón Saenz, who was leader of the national sugar distributing syndicate. Saenz was a leading politician-capitalist of the period, a prominent Obregonista, owner of a mansion in Cuernavaca, and booster of local industry. Several of the more important businesses for the Cuernavaca elite of this period came precisely from partnerships with this combination of politician and impresario, a trademark of the Sonorense group. This is the case of the Salinas family of Cuernavaca, and also of Estrada Cajigal and his political associates.

29. In the postrevolutionary history of Morelos one might distinguish periods characterized by different kinds of governorships. The first is the 1920s, when governors were interim (usually military) rulers of the state whose main task was to maintain control over the region, to pacify whatever outbursts of violence there might still be, and to carry out agrarian reform.

The second period is perhaps the most difficult to define because it is not fully continuous, but might include the times when regional parties were active and governors were tied to their state (1930–46). The period might also be characterized by the severe financial difficulties of state government, in which case it would have to be extended until about 1954.

The period following (1955–75) has as its most outstanding characteristic the politics of urbanization of Morelos, and the participation of governors in the project to make Morelos the locus of industrial investment and of private investment in housing and recreation. In this period Morelos was radically changed; it shifted from being primarily agricultural to being an industrial and tertiary region. It is interesting to note that although industry and the services now dominate Morelos' economy, Morelos must still be represented by the peasant sector (CNC) in the Federal Congress. The seat of Zapatismo cannot easily accept its current suburban status.

The current period is one where the effects of an unplanned, predatory urban and industrial expansion have set in. Ecologically the state is in serious peril. A large proportion of the central valleys have become urban centers with great urban problems. Morelos has begun changing into an urban and semiurban periphery of Mexico City.

30. Until 1970 terms lasted only two years.

31. In Morelos there is only one cabecera, that of Tlalnepantla, that seems to fit this position, although Axochiapan may, arguably, fit this position.

32. Readers should bear in mind that the "ethnographic present" is 1983–86; this situation has probably changed to some degree in the aftermath of the 1988 presidential elections.

33. Again, "current" here means 1986.

4: The Cultural Region

1. Valentín López told me that in his period as municipal president of Cuernavaca large sums of money were expended for the creation of a plan of urban development, which has been buried since its creation. I would not be surprised if in fact the construction of this kind of master plan were a routine activity of governors and municipal presidents. All of these projects, however, die along with the power of their creators.

2. I shall provide a description of the basic elements of Morelos peasant culture in chapter 6; in this chapter I present only some of the formal aspects of culture in the context of the formation of what I am calling Cuernavacan baroque.

3. Until the 1950s, each of these villages was peopled by about four or five large patrilocal families. Intermarriage between the villages was common.

4. This debate can be documented through most of the numbers of the *Corréo del Sur* in 1961.

5. For example, this newspaper article on the annual fiesta at San Antón (1961): "We lament the loss of folkloric elements in the popular dances. The 'pantomime' that they organize is a long cry from the autochthonous dances (the way the men and women dress is repugnant), what they spend on the dance and on alcoholic beverages should be used on costumes and on the preparation of

some of the many types of Indian dances, for the good of this beloved corner of our fatherland and even for selfish reasons, such as the attraction of tourists" (*Corréo del Sur,* June 18, 1961).

6. In Mexico City associations of workers from different regions celebrate their local fiestas in the city, and such disparate niches as ice-cream vendors, juice makers, stonecutters, and many others are organized to a large degree around ties of trust built around village of origin.

7. In 1984 there were about 140 priests in Morelos; half were for liberation theology and half were against it.

8. Among useful literary sources there are Pablo Robles's *Los Plateados de Tierra Caliente* (1891) and Ignacio Altamirano's *El Zarco,* although these books are inspired on the Cuautla region of Morelos. Other well-known sources include Salinas 1924, Diez 1930, Mazari 1968, and many diverse titles that were reedited in past years by Valentín López González (Mayer 1843, Robelo 1894, Rivera Cambas 1883).

5: Central Places

1. These enclaves were the loci of agrarian problems since the early eighteenth century (cf. Hernández Orive 1973). The rich lands of the pueblos were the first to be invaded by haciendas from the sixteenth century onward. Pueblos that were in the core tended to lose all or almost all their lands, as was the case with Cuautla, Cuernavaca, Xochitepec, and others. Pueblos whose lands were predominantly marginal, such as Tepoztlán, Santa María or Tlalnepantla, lost much smaller portions of land.

2. I worked out this central place hierarchy in my book (1982) on Tepoztlán, however, in that piece I gave primary weight to marketing, and insufficient attention to position in the core/periphery organization. More important, I did not distinguish between two periods of spatio-economic organization, and gave primacy to the "old" core-periphery organization, probably because it is the only way to explain the *cultural* organization of regional space. I hope to make up for these shortcomings here.

The typology that I develop here comes out of an analysis of censuses and various government documents. It has also benefitted from the work of two geographers (Holt-Buttner 1962, Girault 1966). Mostly, however, the typology is a result of my own field research, interviews, and ethnohistorical research and of an analysis of works by other ethnographers. For ethnographies of hamlets, see Romanucci-Ross 1973, Fromm and Maccoby 1970, Varela 1984, Warman 1974, and Friedlander 1975; for villages, Redfield 1930, Lewis 1951, Warman 1974 and 1976; de la Peña 1980, Lomnitz-Adler 1982, Arias and Bazán 1979, Henschell and Pérez 1976, Varela 1984, and Ingham 1988; for market towns, Rounds 1977, Warman 1976, Varela 1984; for regional cities, Arias and Bazán 1977. The works by de la Peña and Warman are complex and rich accounts of parts of Morelos' regional organization, but neither pays sufficient attention to the problem of localities. For a review of the anthropology of Morelos, see Lomnitz-Adler 1984.

3. In the 1900 census, the smallest Morelos localities were of approximately seventy inhabitants, but these were invariably haciendas or train stations, most of which disappeared (as such) in the 1920s. Morelos' villages had a minimum of about two hundred inhabitants. It is possible that this has been the case since the Spanish policy of concentrating Indians into villages, that in Morelos was carried out in 1540, but mostly between 1601 and 1603 (Hernández Orive 1973). As we shall see, this kind of settlement pattern contrasts with that of the Huasteca, where ranchos of less than fifty inhabitants have always been quite common.

4. In the official nomenclature "hamlets" fall under the categories of *rancherías* and *congregaciones;* in colonial times these kinds of localities were known as *barrios, pueblitos, ranchos,* or *sujetos.* However, because there are ambiguities involved in all of these alternate terms, I use "hamlet."

5. In Rubén Jaramillo's autobiography (1967) we can appreciate that most southern hamlets in the 1940s had to be reached by foot or horse. Much of the northern periphery, however, got connected to highways in the forties and fifties.

6. This is variable, for many hamlets in Morelos have their own—sometimes colonial—churches, but rarely their own priest, so that mass may not be offered every Sunday, and certainly not every day.

7. When considering the characteristics of the "general stores" that are important in Mexican social history, one must take into account the fact that the owner was usually also a major local landowner and the town's source of credit. The specialization of stores goes hand in hand with changes in both land tenure and access to credit.

8. *Papelería* = school supplies; *ferretería* = hardware store; *mercería* = pins, needles, thread, yarn, cloth; *abarrotes* = packaged food, soft drinks, cigarettes, candles, and other sundries.

9. *Pulquerías* are not found in all Morelos pueblos, for pulque is a cold-country product and is especially popular with peasants (or workers from predominantly peasant backgrounds, typically construction workers).

10. Until about fifteen years ago, prostitution was legal and all brothels were supposed to be recorded in governmental records and monitored by health officials. In the past decade or so, prostitution has gone from the brothel to the streets because of anti-prostitution laws. The brothel was rare in villages, and was more a characteristic of the larger market towns, which have or have had "red zones" that are visited by people from the pueblos and hamlets. Pueblos have had a kind of traveling brothel at the major fiestas and ferias, where there are *carpas* (tents) with prostitutes.

11. The pharmacy is an institution that was important in the larger towns at least since the nineteenth century (cf. 1900 census, where pharmacists are listed for the major market towns). The pharmacist was a surrogate doctor even in Cuernavaca. Chemicals were prepared and mixed in the pharmacy. Today the pharmacist is a less prestigious and powerful character, although (s)he still plays a part in local curing. Also, pharmacies are much more spread out and can be found in almost any pueblo.

12. Not all pueblos have hotels, though usually they have rooms for rent.

The major centers of the Morelos hotel industry have to do with tourism, not with commerce.

13. Tourist-ridden pueblos and ranchos aside, the restaurant is an institution that is characteristic of the central market town and the roadside. Pueblos may or may not have *fondas* or a few eating stands.

14. There are some borderline cases, such as Puente de Ixtla and Tetecala. Their indeterminate situation is due to the respective rise and fall of these two places, making them difficult to situate squarely in the category of pueblo or central market town.

15. Merchants from these towns also travel out and sell goods that are not bought every day in hamlets and pueblos. Examples of this are regional newspapers, perfumes, jewelry, furniture, electrical appliances, and some kinds of clothing. These market town-based traveling salesmen were particularly important in the commercial hinterlands of Cuautla.

16. Until the 1960s hamlets very rarely had schools; pueblos typically had one or several grade schools, and market towns had junior high schools and technical training. Today most hamlets have grade schools, and junior high schools are common in pueblos.

17. Wholesaling seems relatively unimportant in Morelos' towns and cities because of the primacy of Mexico City. Wholesaling was important in the nineteenth century and a prerogative of the major market towns. Today only locally produced goods are subject to wholesaling, and there is not much money to be made from the warehouse.

18. Marginal agriculture was of three main kinds: plow culture of non-irrigated lands, slash-and-burn hill agriculture, and exploitation of grasses and forests.

19. At the same time, industrialization has changed some aspects of the old core/periphery logic. Peasant production around many of the towns diminished in the periods of industrialization (1965–75), when peasant family and land resources acquired another kind of value. Peasants in Morelos became less concerned with the productivity of their small plots and used them as a kind of insurance. Agricultural workers who were and are paid less than urban workers began coming from Guerrero and Oaxaca, even to work in the agricultural periphery.

20. For a detailed account of these cycles in eastern Morelos see Warman 1976.

21. In fact there are peasant cultures in all levels, including that of the regional city, in that the working classes of the cities are made up of peasant migrants.

22. Inhabitants of peripheral hamlets do have, of course, relationships with extralocal caciques; however, because they do not belong to the same local community, the ritual activities of this elite do not invade their communities. On the other hand, some hamlets in Morelos have their own caciques. These caciques are not merchants; rather, they usually base their power on political control over the *ejido* (for example, the family of Genovevo de la O, the Zapatista general, have had control over the ejido of Santa María Ahuacatitla for many decades).

23. So, for example, Francisco Gutiérrez Hormigo, who was the administrator of Morelos' largest hacienda—Tenango and Santa Clara—in the years immediately following the Revolution told me that, before allowing the government to decide who was to receive hacienda lands through agrarian reform, the García Pimentel family distributed much of the hacienda's lands to their *peones acasillados*. These peones, who lived in core hamlets, did not initially have the right to land because their settlements were not officially considered to be pueblos, but the hacendados preferred to give the land to these peones, who had had close ties with the administrators and hacendados, than to the inhabitants of villages. In her work on the hamlet of Chiconcuac, Romanucci-Ross notes that the inhabitants were so fearful of (perhaps also loyal to?) the hacendados that they did not ask for ejido lands, and most of the allotments in the hamlet went to migrants who came in especially from Guerrero.

24. Information on this class can be found in Womack 1969, Huerta 1984, Von Wobeser 1988, and Crespo and Vega (in press). My information on the social life of the hacienda is mainly based on interviews with the late Alfonso Vélez Goríbar, who still remembered these things.

25. Crespo and Vega (in press) point out that Morelos' irrigation projects were almost entirely undertaken by the hacendados during the Porfiriato; they were much more investment- and technology-oriented than the government or the peasants have been in this century.

6: Rural Cultures

1. Both Warman (1976) and de la Peña (1980) agree that the period between the Revolution and (vaguely) 1940 or 1950 is economically one of peasantification. De la Peña has also argued that the emigration of priests after the War of Independence produced an upsurge in popular Catholicism. However, the nuances and full implications of the peasant appropriation of the Church have not been spelled out. Because of this, the full impact of the appropriation and disqualification of local knowledge by Church and State since the 1950s has not been fully understood.

2. For a discussion of all this, see Lomnitz-Adler 1982 and Ingham 1970. Limón (1989) has recently taken up some of these same issues.

3. As was the case in Tepoztlán, where the peasants attempted to gain control over municipal politics, but ultimately failed (Lewis 1951, Lomnitz-Adler 1982). Evidence of this kind of political struggle in the early postrevolutionary period also exists for Atlatláhucan (see Elizondo-Mayer 1984) and Hueyapan (Friedlander 1975). I think that the phenomenon is widespread in Morelos' peripheral villages, but it has not yet been adequately documented.

4. Coherence is to do with how well elaborated and planned out are the stages in social reproduction. It is the extent to which culture is organized into a full complementary cycle of events and rituals, the extent to which different particular ideologies are synthesized into wider systems of belief. One of the by-products of the community study has been taking coherence as a given. Because

some degree of coherence exists in any class or community, it has always been found. However, the moment one focuses on *regional culture,* one is immediately struck by variations in the "force" of different local and class cultures.

Recent critics of the extremely coherent view of culture produced by anthropology, such as Taussig (1987), stress the basic incoherence, the basic uncertainty that actually operates in culture. Although this point is essential for all praxis theory, it unfortunately obscures the fact that there is more and less coherency in the culture of different classes, and communities. The problem with this debate is that it has given too much emphasis to coherence versus chaos as basic principles for culture, instead of focusing on the systematic differences in coherence within a hegemonic regional culture.

7: The Localist Ideology

1. This expression could also be interpreted to mean that every individual has his or her own patron, but usually it means that individuals work for their own cause.

2. For a related and similar situation see Elizondo-Mayer 1984.

3. So, for example, during my field research the director of the Dirección de Investigaciones Históricas (DIHAC) was the publisher of one of these newspapers.

4. It is interesting to note that several anthropologists have also justified their studies of Morelos in terms of its alleged representativeness of Mexico. So, for example, Lewis (1961) justifies studying Tepoztlán because it is a "typical" Mexican village, by which he means that it is very close to the national rural mean of wealth, population density and kind of predominant activity, thence the titles of his books and articles: *Life in a Mexican Village, Medicine in a Mexican Village,* and so on. Fromm and Maccoby (1970) also legitimate their work with the same pretense of representativeness ("Social Character in a Mexican Village"). In his study of local-level politics, Dávila (1976) gives "his" village the pseudonym of "Azteca," as does Lewis in *Pedro Martínez* and *Five Families.* In a more subtle way, the same is true for many studies carried out by Mexicans, where specific classes and social groups of Morelos become abstract classes, as, for example, in the subtitle of Warman's "We Come to Object: The Peasants and the National State."

5. There is an implicit thesis here—which is quite widespread—in the sense that "to walk is to know." Walking, sweating, doing physical labor, are constituted into a privileged form of knowledge for the intellectual classes. In my view this is due to an operation that is analogous to that described by Turner for Ndembu ritual: walking and sweating in the sun are, to intellectuals, like periods of liminality, where the transposition of one's person to a new context of supposed communion with peasant hardship allows an understanding of the peasants and lends authority to the intellectual's account, as if the sun felt the same for the peasant and the intellectual. Walking is to identify with the peasantry as charrería is to identify with the hacendados and rancheros.

8: Peasant Localism

1. On an economic and political plane, this is Crespo and Frey's (1982) and Crespo and Vega's (in press) main point. The traditional view of Zapatismo is that the expansion of hacienda holdings into pueblo lands produced the Revolution. Crespo and associates show that in fact hacienda expansion during the nineteenth century was minimal, and that the most important effect of the anticorporate Juarez reforms was social differentiation and concentration of land *within* the pueblos.

2. These include works by Robert Redfield, Oscar Lewis, Sotelo Inclán; the oral-history archive coordinated by Eugenia Meyer (now housed in the Instituto J. M. L. Mora); the interviews collected by Laura Espejel, Salvador Rueda, and others (based at the library of the National Anthropology Museum); and interviews carried out by many other anthropologists.

3. The romanticization is nowhere more apparent than in many intellectuals' conception of the relation between communities and Zapatista troops during the Revolution. Although it is certain that the unrevolutionary peasants (*los pacíficos*) preferred Zapatistas to Federales, I do not think that they conceived of themselves as an extension of the same social being. I have gathered several testimonies from pacificos to the effect that they hid from both Zapatistas and Federales. Elizondo (1984) reproduces the testimony of an old Atlatlahuqueño that recounts the way in which the pacificos set up two committees, one to receive Zapatistas and the other Federales.

4. So, for example, in a confrontation over acquisitions of communal land between the peasants of Tepoztlán and a (private) tourist development company, the peasants complained that "foreigners" were taking over lands that had been in the hands of (Tepoztecan) Mexicans for centuries. The press took up this part of their complaint quite loudly, and the owners of Montecastillo published letters (and sent copies to the government) explaining that they were a company owned by Mexican citizens who were interested only in the progress of the nation (see information in the Archivo de la Reforma Agraria's Tepoztlán files).

9: Huesteca as Hegemonic Region

1. Excellent discussions of Huastecan regional ecology can be found in Puig 1976 and in Alcorn 1984.

2. The commercial orientation towards the border began with the construction of the Panamerican Highway, which crosses the entire Huasteca Potosina on a north/south axis, and especially since the 1960s. Commercial relations with Mexico City have existed for many years, insofar as the cattle from the region were sold in Mexico City even during the nineteenth century; yet these are forms of specialized commerce, and trips to Mexico City for buying products are infrequent. Commerce with San Luis has intensified since the construction of the San Luis-Rio Verde-Valles-Tampico road in the 1960s.

3. In this study I have paid little attention to the municipio of Ebano. Ebano was originally a part of Tamuin, and was the seat of the petroleum industry in the

Huasteca. I did not include it in the study because it is economically oriented toward Tampico, and not to Ciudad Valles.

4. In 1970 the region had 456,991 head of cattle (Coordinación General . . . 1982*d:* 369), which means that they exported a minimum of 200,000 head a year. Knowledgeable local ranchers claim that they once exported as many as 300,000 cows for slaughter per year.

5. There are no recent official figures on livestock production in the region. Ranchero informants claim that the regional exportation of cattle is down to approximately 100,000 cows per year.

6. Between 1955 and 1970, the prices of piloncillo remained completely stagnant at 80 centavos to the kilogram (about 7 cents). Prices began to go up slowly after 1970; in 1980 the price of pilón was 4 pesos (about 17 cents; but no inflation in the U.S. dollar is calculated); in 1985 the price was 61 pesos (about 24 cents). However, these are the prices at which merchants sell the piloncillo to liquor factories, the merchants pay the Indians about 25 percent less. In the peasant economy of this region, a family cannot work more than about one hectare of cane for piloncillo per year; the ideal plot from the point of view of familial labor is one hectare of grown cane (which is cut slowly, between October and May), one hectare of newly planted cane (for next year's crop), and one hectare of maize that will be worked between May and October. The hectare of cane yields about U.S. $1,350 a year in 1985 prices (without counting any expenditures whatsoever).

Because of these extremely low prices, all of the attempts to industrialize the production of piloncillo in the region have failed. The largest attempt, by Javier Gallegos, a Ciudad Valles merchant and ranchero, was a factory that produced 5 tons of molasses per day; an Indian family mill will produce 50 kilos per day and will work about 150 days in the year.

7. According to my best-informed estimates (there are no reliable official figures for production and marketing of piloncillo), about 10 percent of the regional production is sold to regional aguardiente factories, over half goes to tequila factories in Jalisco, and the rest is distributed among medium and small rum and brandy factories.

8. It is interesting to note that during the Porfiriato and into the 1920s and 1930s parts of the Huasteca—especially the municipios of Tamuín, San Vicente, and Valles—exported maize. This is no longer the case.

9. Piloncillo is only worth making for peasants because it is a sure source of cash and allows extremely flexible allocations of work throughout the year, as well as the utilization of "unproductive" familial labor. All information presented here on piloncillo was compiled in interviews by my students and myself in 1985.

10. Population density in the Huasteca in 1970 was 35.3 inhabitants per square kilometer, whereas the corresponding figure for Morelos was 124.7.

11. The fullest treatment of the topic of Indian communities in the region is Stresser-Pean 1967; Alcorn (1984) has produced the most significant ethnography of Huastec Indian culture; Márquez (1977) provides land-tenure data for haciendas. The ecological transformation during this century, the clearing

and settlement of densely wooded jungles, is vividly noted in Santos's (1986) memoirs.

12. Márquez (1977) provides data to the effect that most of the region was subdivided into extremely large properties. If we turn to the censuses, we note that there are only 63,931 hectares of Indian communal lands (which presumably existed before the Revolution; otherwise they would be ejidos) in the whole of the Huasteca: less than 6 percent of all available land.

13. Gonzalo Santos is said to have maintained that the Huastecan rancheros went to the Revolution out of boredom: "We led a good life then, we had nothing to do but play conquian in the bars, plenty of food and lots of Indians to serve us. We went to the Revolution out of boredom." This personal account contrasts with the contents of his recently published (1986) memoirs, where Santos explains the intense factionalism that pervaded between his family and the Porfirio Diaz-supported Martell family, but it is in no way contradicted by it: there were intense struggles in the region among elite families, especially extraregional hacendados and local rancheros, but they were all equally well served by the Indian population.

14. For general accounts of this, see Santos 1986, Falcón 1984, and Ankerson 1984. Agrarian reform was used as bait for the recruitment of Indians to fight Cristeros in the Bajío (in the Huasteca this is especially the case in the municipios of Axtla, Tamazunchale, and Xilitla). In an interview with Gonzalo Santos's son, Gastón, I brought up the question of how Gonzalo helped recruit volunteers for the Cristiada. When I mentioned the word "volunteers," Gaston said: "*Bueno . . . voluntarios de a huevo, ¿no?*" (unvoluntary volunteers, stated in a more prosaic form).

15. Sharecropping is still used in some ranches, particularly those that are not well tended by their owners. Ranchers also make use of nonremunerated peasant labor for the clearing of forested or untended areas with a system wherein peasants are allowed to cultivate a forested area for free during one or two years. The payoff for the rancher is that the peasants clear the forest in order to plant. They are allowed the use of a plot for one or two years in exchange for clearing the fields.

16. Some of the ejidos attempt relatively capital-intensive export production. This is especially the case of the ejidos created under the auspices of the Pujal-Coy project, which have received a fair amount of credit and technical assistance. Other ejidos have access to credit facilities for commercial production through the state-financed agricultural banks; however, the situation for technified commercial ejido production is not always favorable due, in part, to the tendency for political factionalism to develop within ejidos and due also to the bureaucratized forms of operation of the credit-providing banks. Collective ejido projects for capitalized agricultural production have not been very successful in the region.

17. During my stay in the Huasteca, rural daily wages were less than a third of those paid in Mexico City.

18. The main historical studies of land tenure in the region are Márquez (1977 and 1982) and Stresser-Pean (1967). Márquez focuses mainly on the trans-

formations suffered by large landed property. He does not discuss the formation of Indian communities and suggests that all of them were created in the regime of the Republica de Indios. A full discussion of this is available in Stresser-Pean's article. In the case of the two Indian communities in which I and my students worked (Tanchahuil, municipio of San Antonio, and Tenexo, municipio of Tampamolon) there exists tne tradition that the origin of the communities was in a sale of land by a large rancho. These communities appear to have been purchased by a few families of Indians and all decisions regarding ownership of land within the community, as well as all work necessary for the community, are done communally.

19. In Tanchahuil and Tenexo, for example, there are many families that live closer to the stores or schools of the neighboring communities. Village exogamy is common—though virilocal residence upon marriage is the preferred rule—so that social and commercial relations between communities can be very intense.

20. In 1985 mestizo merchants bought piloncillo from Indians at 43 pesos per kilo and later sold to liquor companies at 65 pesos per kilo. Local comunidad Indian merchants bought piloncillo from other Indians at 42 pesos and sold to the mestizo *coyotes* at 43.

21. This is not quite the local terminology, since people in the region use the word *comunidad* exclusively for Indian communities.

22. Several teachers complain that parents from the community in which the school is based try to send their children to the boarding school in order that they might eat free meals. This is a sign of the poverty of most Indian families of the region. Children in the boarding schools have to work before and after school in school-owned plots.

23. Tamazunchale has at least two, Matlapa and Chapulhuacán; Valles has Rascón; Huehuetlán has Huichihuayán; Tamasopo has El Naranjo.

24. The exceptions to this generalization are the members of the emerging, but still relatively unimportant, working and professional classes, who are spatially concentrated in the towns with sugar mills or in Ciudad Valles.

25. At the fairs of Axtla, for example, a friend of my students lost 400,000 pesos in one weekend, which at that time was the equivalent of five months of my salary as a young professor at a Mexico City university. It was about twenty months of a peon's salary.

26. The regional power of rancheros was maintained even throughout the period when Saturnino Cedillo, an agrarista revolutionary peasant, controlled the state of San Luis (1926–39); Cedillo had a working relationship with Gonzalo Santos wherein Santos and the Huasteca supported Cedillo, and Cedillo respected—by and large—Santista power in the region.

10: Class Culture

1. Because of the prominence of interethnic relations in the Huasteca, I will use the term *mestizo* here in its ethnic connotation: Spanish-speaking non-white Mexicans. However, the terms *mestizaje* and *mesticized* will still be used in the same way they have been throughout the text.

2. It is quite interesting to note that this ideology is entirely different from that of the regions where the elites are truly urban, as in Morelos. In those cases, elites clearly distinguish themselves from the populace and base their hegemony on a lack of identification, on the possession of cultural and material goods that cannot be reached by the subordinate classes. In the case of the Huasteca, the ranchero class cultivates the tradition of being supreme experts on popular knowledge. Perhaps this is functionally related to their very real interest in, and hegemony over, the region. Examples of this are offered, again, by that supreme ranchero leader Gonzalo Santos. In his luncheons with the important Huasteca rancheros, he is known to have drilled them on such crucial questions as, "What is the name that we Huastecos give to this ant?" He was also famous for brandishing regional popular wisdom on his political opponents.

3. In the municipios where the contrary is the case, for example in Tancanhuitz, Aquismón, Xilitla, Tamazunchale, or the Huasteca Hidalguense, the rancheros very often spoke—and a few of them still do speak—Indian languages. This phenomenon has been aptly described by Stilles (1982), who claims that the mestizo elites of Hidalgo spoke only Nahuatl to the Indians in an attempt to keep them in an inferior position vis-à-vis regional and national elites. I believe that there was also a problem of the proportion of mestizos to Indians in these municipios. Until very recently (and this is still the case in some of the municipios of Hidalgo and Veracruz) the mestizo elites were truly a minuscule proportion of the population. Merchants had to learn Nahuatl or Huasteco to compete in trade with the Indians. I have even recorded the case of Italian merchants who reached the villages of Axtla and Xilitla in the beginning of the century and had to learn Nahuatl for their trade to prosper.

4. The narrator I heard was saying that Nahuas make much more reliable workers than Huastecos, because Huastecos practically have no houses. They lead a savage existence in the sierra, they have no culture. In pre-Columbian times, Aztec prejudice made Huastecos out as promiscuous drunkards. This reputation has survived to this date among some rancheros.

5. The extreme case of ranchero control over a village is that of Tamuín, Gonzalo Santos's village of adoption. Until very recently no federal police were allowed in Tamuín. Law and order was entirely in the hands of the municipal police, run by the gunmen of Gonzalo Santos.

6. This case is from M. Hernández Beltrán's diaries. The doctor established relations of reciprocity with other middle-class town mestizo; she often didn't charge for house calls and received many services in return. Political alliances were also ratified through her services.

7. This is one of the factors that make petitions for ejido land grants in one's ranch difficult, for one runs the immediate risk of being thrown out. In the case of Piedras Chinas, my ethnographic acquaintances were very active in demanding a land grant, but they made sure the petition was for land from a ranch whose owner was not to the liking of their patrons.

8. The descriptions here are constructed mostly out of my and my students' firsthand materials. The main published source on the Huastecs is Alcorn's (1984) superb ethnography. See also Stresser-Pean 1953 and 1967.

9. Gastón Santos recounts that his father would wake them up in the mornings, hollering, *"Ya tocaron la Diana; ya hay caldo en las fondas. A levantarse todos a darle gracias a Dios por haberlos hecho mexicanos sin merecerlo, pues si fueran suecos, hablarían ocho idiomas, serían ingeneros químicos y estarían de meseros en un café."* (Santos 1986:920) Roughly: "Everybody wake up and give thanks to God for making you Mexicans without deserving it, because if you were Swedish, you would all speak eight languages, be chemical engineers, and work as waiters in a restaurant."

A concept similar to *desmadre, relajo* was explored years ago by Portilla (1984), although for some reason his analysis has not been fully utilized or assimilated in Mexican cultural studies.

10. A touching and ethnographically rich rendering of this kind of situation can be found in the Peruvian antropologist-novelist José María Arguedas's *Los ríos profundos*.

11. I have described processes of this kind for communities of the state of Morelos (see Lomnitz-Adler 1979).

12. This, of course, has been discussed in urban anthropology at least since the studies of African urbanization, and in Mexico since L. Lomnitz's (1975) and Arizpe's (1978) studies of migration.

13. This process is a slow one that is especially deterred, among other things, because of the great availability of cheap labor in the ranches. Because of these conditions of uncertainty in rural work, the rancheros can still keep relations of loyalty and clientelism.

11: Ranchero Ideology

1. In particular, I stake out the major elements for a comparison between santismo and cedillismo, in order both to disentangle some notions about caciquismo and its relation to peasant culture, and to show some of the political and tactical alternatives in the use of local culture for politics.

2. Márquez has reconstructed the history of the Santos family during the Porfiriato and is currently working on a full-fledged history of the family since the eighteenth century. One of the fascinating elements of the work that is already available to the public is his discussion of the condueñazgo system of landholding: ranchos in the Huasteca were communally owned by families (or "clans," as Márquez puts it). The division of property and power within the family was informally decided through a set of conflicts whereby patriarchal leadership was established. Evidently, this system of competition between males of the ranchero families, and of intense solidarity within the condueñazgo families, does much to explain the development of ranchero culture.

3. Santos has provided us with a vivid account of the violent relations that existed between his family and the Diaz-backed Martells in Tampamolón.

4. When Gaston Santos explained the Revolution in terms of conflict between elites for who got the bigger slice of cake, Gaston's cousin—a nephew of don Gonzalo—interjected that there were also pure ideals in the Santos family;

for example, the case of Pedro Antonio, who was an idealist and a revolutionary, and who was the family's main revolutionary figure until his death. To this Gaston retorted that it was true that Pedro Antonio was an idealist, and that revolutions always begin thanks to the fiery idealism of a few, but that Pedro Antonio was certainly not the man to carry out the Revolution that he helped to create. He even declined the governorship of San Luis because he was not yet of legal age! When revolutions are afoot, and the task at hand is to govern a country or a region, Pedro Antonio was worried about legal age! But then, that was typical of the idealists who started revolutions. "Just look at Francisco Madero! [Madero was the initiator of the Mexican Revolution.] Madero was crazy. He believed in spirits and had seances, he never slept with a woman before he got married, and after he got married he slept only with his wife! He was crazy. Men like him, or like Pedro Antonio, begin revolutions and set down some ideals, but the men who actually carry them out are always careful and ruthless, like Carranza, who waited in El Paso for Maderismo to really take hold before coming into the country, like Obregón, or like my father."

5. Falcón (1984) provides an excellent description of the Revolution in the state of San Luis. Lárraga is described in my interview with Gastón in the following terms: "Lárraga had no importance whatsoever; people have flaunted Lárraga in my father's face quite often, but the truth is that the only reason why Lárraga became important is because my father never bothered to kill him. He was only a thief, a pillager. He never carried more than about twenty armed men and all they did was go around in the countryside stealing chickens. The only important revolutionary family in the Huasteca was mine." Gonzalo himself minimizes Lárraga's importance in the Huasteca.

6. This pun doesn't work in English. In Spanish, *mora* is blackberry and *la moral* is morality, but it could be twisted into meaning a blackberry bush; so Santos says that the only "morality" he knows is the one that produces blackberries.

7. I have heard three versions on the reasons for this feud. The first is that Lárraga's men killed a close cousin of the Santos brothers, the second that Lárraga's men helped capture Pedro Antonio Santos, and the third is that the Santos had Leopoldo Lárraga (Manuel's brother, also a revolutionary of the "idealist" genre that was crudely depicted by Gaston above) killed. Of these three versions I think that the one about Pedro Antonio has no substance, while the other two versions may both be true.

8. Although the differences between the ideology of Cedillo and Santos are evident, there was a need for an alliance between these two interest groups. Cedillo's leadership in the Huasteca was never direct; it depended on support that he might achieve from regional caudillos. He and Gonzalo struck a—sometimes rather tense—bargain.

9. In my first conversation in Valles I was introduced to this history. I was talking to someone about renting a house for my family and myself and explaining that I was an anthropologist. So this person told me a story about an anthropologist, later repeated to me several times.

This took place at the time when Mano Negra, Gonzalo's main hit man, was chief of police at Tamuín.

Scene 1. In the police station. Mano Negra is sitting around. Enter a police officer.

Officer: "Con la novedad mi capitán de que hay un arqueólogo rascando ahí por La Concepción." ("There is an archeologist scratching [he meant digging] at La Concepción.")

Mano Negra: "¿Un qué?" (A what?)

Officer: "Un arqueólogo." (An archeologist.)

Mano Negra: "Mátalo y tráemelo." (Kill [him or it] and bring [him or it] in.)

Scene 2. Hours later, at the police station. Enter Mano Negra. In the room is the officer with the corpse of a redhead.

Mano Negra: "¿Qué es esto? (What's this???)

Officer: El arqueólogo, mi capitán. (It's the archeologist, captain.)

Mano Negra: "¡Ah chingaos! ¡Yo creí que era un animal de uña que estaba rascando por ahí!" (Fuck! I thought you meant that there was a clawed animal that was scratching [digging] out there!)

The moral of this story was that I should introduce myself to municipal authorities before beginning my work lest I be mistaken for a ferocious animal and shot.

10. Gonzalo is said to have divorced this wife on account of her affair with Capdevielle. Gonzalo had a son by this first marriage, also called Gonzalo, who has not been associated with the family ranches or business.

11. A good documentary example of middle-class resentment of santismo is Estrada (1963).

12. When time came for the selection of municipal authorities in the Huasteca, people from the different municipios would travel to Tamuín to speak with don Gonzalo about their candidates. However, in many cases Gonzalo had a lesser cacique in each municipio that would suggest an adequate candidate. So, for example, the Terrazas family in Axtla, Chimino Zúñiga in Tanquián, Braulio Romero and Quirino Balderas in Tamuín, the Contreras family in Tancanhuitz, and the Ortas in San Antonio were the power behind the throne in their municipios.

13. This anecdote was transcribed by Guillermo Antunes as it was told to him by Oliva. Mr. Antunes has been preparing a book of Gonzalo Santos anecdotes. My translation of the text is rough (Santos's language is very colloquial).

14. My first ranchero friend in Tamuín is a man who has lived and studied in Mexico City and Canada, but is from a Spanish-origin Tamuín family of rancheros. On our first account I was a little taken aback by his fast-flowing, aggressive, smutty language. Angel noticed this and said: "Please excuse my lexicon. You see, if you say *"por favor páseme esa pala"* here (please give me the shovel), no one will listen. One must say *"oye, dame esa chingadera."* (Hey, gimme that [fucking] thing!) I soon began using similar language.

15. Gonzalo Santos added the "N." to his name in order to avoid its having thirteen letters. It is not the initial of a name.

12: Indian Localism

1. I was so intrigued by the results of my interview with Juan that I solicited, and received, a grant from the Instituto Mexicano de Psiquiatría for a study on the culture of alcohol consumption in two Indian communities, Tanchahuil (municipio of San Antonio) and Tenexo (Tampamolón). Thanks to this opportunity I was able to pursue research in Tanchahuil.

2. Evidently, this defense mechanism can just as well work the other way around; people from outside the community cannot easily find a person by knowing their "real name"; it is interesting, however, that Juan emphasized defense against people from within. Another extremely important point for anthropologists and historians is that it is tricky to use birth records for any kind of extended family histories in Indian communities in the region (we found the same problem with names in Tenexo, a nearby Nahuatl community) because the last names used in the Civil Registry often change in every generation. Patrilineally related kin are best located in terms of a physical spot (for example, Mushi'), that is, the place where they have their land and build their houses.

3. When I recorded this Huastec cosmogony, it was the first I had ever heard of these views. Later Alcorn's (1984) ethnography appeared with a discussion of Huastec cosmology. Alcorn's book is the first full-fledge ethnography of the Huastecs. Nevertheless, it is worth presenting my materials here (despite some repetition with Alcorn) because the order and way in which these stories were told are important to the ideological analyses that were not a part of Alcorn's preoccupation.

4. The arch is a necessary element in all Huastecan respetaciones, and all households have an arch for small domestic ceremonies. Larger arches are built and adorned for the major repetaciones, such as this. Flowers are also indispensable and are planted near all houses for these purposes; bolimes, aguardiente, and copal are all, as we shall presently see, indispensable for these rituals.

5. An interesting point in regard to this striking view is that most respetaciones involve offerings to the posts (*horcones*) that sustain Huastecan houses, for example at New Year's, and also during several kinds of curing ceremonies. Also many respetaciones involve pouring wine (aguardiente) at the four legs of the table upon which the shrine is placed.

6. Miguel Angel Riva Palacio, field notes 1985.

7. There is also the notion in the community that Tz'ahuil is a bird that used to exist in these parts.

8. Tancanhuitz de Santos is the most important nearby cabecera. San Antonio, the cabecera to which Tanchahuil belongs, is very small—today, it has fewer inhabitants than Tanchahuil, although among them are the only mestizo ranchers of the municipio. The El Jolol-Santos-Tampamolón-Tanquian road was built in the 1940s, and the offshoot to San Antonio in the 1970s. Tanchahuil is located along a dirt track that terminates on the San Antonio road.

9. The concept *cerro* (hill or mountain) is not unlike *monte*. It implies *forested* terrain.

10. The image of the government as pacifier and protector of the Indians was

reinforced in my mind by the poster of López Portillo, Mexico's past president, that was pinned on the door. Juan had gone along with the dancers from Tanchahuil to greet López Portillo and later Miguel de la Madrid when they were on their presidential campaign tours. Many Indian houses have posters of the president or of some official government campaigns, such as drives against malaria. I attribute this in part to the fact that people like to have something modern and industrial hanging on their wall; but also there is a certain veneration towards the figure of the president. The colors of the PRI and the flag are associated with the Virgin of Guadalupe and with Miguel Hidalgo, to whom, as we saw, Juan gives the status of patron saint. Political leaders are honored with festivities that are in many senses comparable to those rendered to the patron saints; and religious festivities are sometimes interfered with by political institutions, such as the Instituto Nacional Indigenista (INI), with no Indian resistance whatsoever. Such is the case, for example, of the Huastecan dances in the fiesta of San Miguel in Tancanhuitz. The INI has relocated the dances in its patio, and has instated a dance contest. When I attended this contest—which includes the selection of an Indian beauty queen—I found that the five judges were all INI anthropologist/bureaucrats. This fact did not seem to perturb the participants. There must have been some four hundred Huastecans in native dress there. My wife, my child, and I were, in addition to the judges, the only non-Indians present. Upon our arrival a very drunk Indian dancer came up to me speaking in Huastecan and kissed my hand, possibly imagining me to be a priest.

11. This is in fact true. There were remarkably few priests in the Huasteca after the Revolution. I was fortunate to interview the locally famous Padre Javier of Valles shortly before his death. This man was for a time the only priest in the entire Huasteca Potosina.

12. At this point in the interview we discussed whether someone that was Huasteco could become mestizo. Both Juan and Cayetano considered that they could not, even if they learned Spanish, forget Huasteco and leave the community. They remained Huastecos because their parents were Huasteco, because they had Huasteco blood. They gave some examples of this. I then asked them what I was. I am Laab (*español*) which is not the same as mestizo. Mestizos and Laabs both speak Spanish, but we speak it differently.

13. I asked Juan whether those women did any agricultural work and he answered that they did not because they married the men who made the milpas while they made tortillas. Juan prefers women in the traditional attire, while Cayetano prefers modern dress. Juan's wife (he is a widower) wore the petope when they married, but later changed to dresses for economic reasons. Let it be said in passing that the "modern" dresses still allow observers to distinguish an Indian from a mestizo woman.

14. I have already analyzed in full a parallel ideology in Tepoztlán (1982). In this case the animal names of the people of the barrios are, as Redfield noted, associated with different characteristics that are attributed to the members of the different barrios, which were made up of one or several interrelated groups of patrilineal kin. I have shown that this ideology of differentiation between barrios had its origins and material base in the barrio-owned communal lands and the

barrio-organized communal labor for tribute and internal betterment. Evidently this situation is more vivid in the case of Indian communities in the Huasteca, where communal land and communal labor is still extremely important, where communities are made up of a small number of patrilineally related grand families, and where neighboring communities are interrelated through marriage.

15. "Pedro Antonio Santos" replaced "Tancanhuitz" and "Alfredo M. Terrazas" replaced "Axtla"; during Cedillo's regnum "Ciudad del Maíz" was transformed into "Magdaleno Cedillo."

13: Local Intelligentsia

1. If we add the orientation (internal, articulatory, or internal-articulatory) of the intellectual to the problem of whether the culture that (s)he synthesizes is residual, emergent, or dominant (see R. Williams 1977) we come up with a more complex typology of intellectuals in regional culture. Theoretically we would have nine different types: internal, articulatory and internal-articulatory residual intellectuals; internal, articulatory, and internal-articulatory dominant intellectuals; and internal, articulatory, and internal-articulatory emergent intellectuals.

2. These people will not be extensively treated here because their ideologies generally are blended into the ranchero-class ideology that has already been discussed.

3. A handful of people have been charged with this function in the region. The most important of these live in the major towns (Valles and Tamazunchale). There are exceptional cases in some of the other pueblos and cabeceras, but these intellectuals rarely claim to represent the culture of the *region*.

4. One day her Indian friends asked her to come with them to Popol. "What is Popol?" asked Oralia. "Popol is the place where corn was created." So they walked until they reached a valley that only had access on foot, and there was a mountain called Popol. "In other words, the Popol Vuh is of Huastecan origin."

5. Oralia does not distinguish between her interest in archaeology and her interest in the geography and ecology of the Huasteca. To her these categories all fall under her more general purpose, which has been "the quest for beautiful things" (*cosas bellas*). So, Oralia claims to have "discovered" the El Tamul falls forty years ago. In what is yet another version of the hidden treasure theme, she also found a mine of precious green stones that the Indians had worked; in that mine one can still hear the sound of the picks that the Indians used for centuries. She has not given the location of this site away; it is not exploitable by anyone with greed in his heart.

6. In this aspect it is perhaps important that Oralia is not wealthy. If she were so, she might choose to give "centrality" to her life by moving out of the region.

7. If this were not the general principle governing Oralia's intellectual drive we would not be able to explain her interest in the international diffusion of her findings. She is always very interested in speaking to foreigners and seeks to publish her results in journals with international readerships, especially that of

the Sociedad de Historia de San Luis and de Tamaulipas, which supposedly publishes in thirty-five languages.

8. This fact does not mean that there is perfect confluence in interests between this kind of "provisional" intellectual and the state. On the contrary, we have seen in Oralia's case how she disapproves of the selfish motivations of politicans. But that has never stopped her from seeking their support and recognition, and when she does achieve this kind of recognition she considers it a triumph that is not merely personal but general to her cause.

9. Except that, in my experience at least, agrarian authorities usually have to be better acquainted with mestizo ways than the juez, in that they have to deal more actively with Spanish-speaking bureaucrats.

10. This interview, like the one with Don José, was held on my first visit to the Huasteca in 1982. I was accompanied by my three assistants from the aforementioned project of folklore collection through the Ministry of Education.

11. Joaquín showed us that the blouses of the women have different kinds of designs for different social categories: girls, unmarried women, prostitutes, married women, old women. He didn't say whether this is the case in all communities, but Stilles (1982) attributes this only to the Hidalgo community of Chililico. Joaquín also says that the colors mean different things, and that each motif is an allusion to an aspect of Nahua cosmogony.

12. Juan Diego was the Indian to whom the Virgin Mary appeared on the hill of Tepeyac in 1531. The story says that the bishop asked him for proof of the apparition, so Juan Diego returned to the hill and the Virgin instructed him to wrap a bouquet of flowers in his cape and take it to the bishop. When Juan Diego opened the cape in front of the bishop, the flowers had disappeared and a painting of the virgin appeared. This is the revered image of the Virgin of Guadalupe. Joaquín's interpretation is that Juan Diego painted the image and, because he was a Nahua Indian, encoded a message in the rays that surround the image.

15: Theory and Politics

1. "We tried to confirm [Samuel Ramos's] hypothesis that all Mexicans, regardless of our condition or circumstance, suffer from an inferiority complex which provokes a feeling of being personally unworthy. It is invalid in practice. Nevertheless, over the years it has contributed, along with other sayings and generalizations, to create a distorted and false image of Mexico and of its citizens. In this study we conclude that it is possible to outline the profile of men and women, but that the reality of what we are as Mexicans is ungraspable" (Alduncin 1989:13, my trans.). This quote also shows that even Samuel Ramos can be trivialized by number-crunching technocrats.

2. Bartra's argument here has some continuities with his view of caciquismo. Bartra views caciquismo as a form of mediation utilized by the state to diminish class struggle. In his view, the cultural creation of the semi-popular, semi-autocratic leader is really designed to avoid the creation of (class-based) forms of local and regional power that contest the state. So, like caciquismo, the

national mythology about the Mexican is a device that mutes people's real political positions.

3. The main works I use here are Ramos 1934, Paz 1950, and Portilla 1984, but many of these same characteristics have been developed by other authors as well. For reviews of the literature, see Schmidt 1978 and Bartra 1987.

4. Paz is keenly aware of the fact that sexual relations are a metaphor for exploitation and domination in Mexico; in my study of Tepoztlán (1982:209–308) I discuss how metaphors of gender and sexual intercourse are used to conceive of the political domain. A similar point has been made by Limón (1989).

16: Racial Ideology

1. Louis Dumont (1986) has developed one of the most fertile perspectives for the study of national ideology. He works from a contrast between hierarchical (or holistic) ideologies, which see society as being composed of a set of distinct groups whose interrelations are simultaneously of opposition, of complementarity and of subordination/domination (society as *universitas*), and individualistic ideologies, which understand society to be the result of a pact or contract between free individuals (society as compact or *societas*). A hierarchical relationship is defined as a relationship of opposition, complementarity, and subordination. Dumont offers the example of Adam and Eve. On one level, Eve is opposed to Adam and complementary to him. On another, she is subordinated to and encompassed by him. In hierarchical relationships the dominant part encompasses the subordinate part and it can represent the whole; thus the term "man" was used to represent both men and women.

The reason why this very general distinction has bearing on the analysis of nationalism is that the nation-state is supposed to embody the social whole. Therefore the specific hierarchical ideologies that operate in a society, and their relationship to individualistic ideologies, such as liberalism, will be forces that help shape the particular forms which nationalism adopts.

Dumont's theory is also important because, although individualism has become common sense in most Western societies, there are always social sectors who yearn for hierarchy: hierarchy between the sexes, hierarchy between social classes, or hierarchy between technological innovation and communal needs. Thus, although individualism denies hierarchy, it still operates in relation to it. Its tendency, at least in some societies, is to transgress more and more hierarchical values in a crusade for legal individual equality and freedom, but these transgressions also produce reactions that find expression in national ideologies.

2. There was, to a certain extent, a tendency for the Spanish state to run the Church as a national institution that was subordinated to the Crown. Thus, in 1478 the pope authorized Ferdinand and Isabella to appoint and remove inquisitors, thereby making the Inquisition a branch of the state. The viceroy in New Spain also had the right to appoint priests and compose ecclesiastical courts. Moreover, in 1501 the pope conceded the tithes of the Indies to the king: "The king conceded to the church almost the whole of the tithes. The pinch came

principally, however, in the fact that the control of these funds gave the king a very direct control of the church and clergy" (Braden 1930:198). An example of this tendency for the church to be subordinated to Spanish national interests is that, during the Wars of Independence, Hidalgo and Morelos, the rebellious creole priests, were excommunicated.

3. Witness, for example, the following document from the early Franciscans: "At daybreak the Indians are gathered into the patio of the church. . . . Those who are recalcitrant about coming when they are obliged to are given half a dozen lashes. . . . This is the punishment they have always known, even for very light offenses. To take this away, in the temporal as well as in the spiritual government, would be to take away the only way of controlling them, for they are like children and to control them properly it is necessary to do just what the schoolmasters do when children fail to get their lessons or get into mischief— give them half a dozen lashes" (*Códice Franciscano,* cited in Braden 1930: 169).

4. Practically all forms of association among slaves were prohibited. An exception to this rule was the formation of black religious *cofradías,* but these too were considered politically dangerous and were sometimes outlawed (Palmer 1976:54). Slave women were not allowed to wear gold, silk, or jewels, or to take on the dress of Indian women (signs of internal hierarchy were thereby discouraged). Palmer also notes that "the social divisions among the slaves were not as clearly marked as those existing within the other two groups [Spaniards and Indians]" (37). The main distinction, which I shall discuss below, was between hispanicized Africans (*criollos*) and non-hispanicized Africans (*bozales*).

5. "The African was considered 'naturally evil,' of 'bad race,' and 'bad caste.'. . . [They were] 'people of little shame and trust' " (Palmer 1976:42). Again, "blood" or "race" is tied to the notion of loyalty and honor.

6. This definition of the slave as a moral person, worthy of being christianized and capable of being free, was contradicted to a certain extent by the economics of slavery. Thus, slaves were referred to commercially as *piezas de esclavo:* "A pieza de esclavo was the proverbial ideal or standard slave, generally a young man in good physical condition" (Palmer 1976:14). This meant that, economically, the human wholeness of each individual slave was not recognized, and some slaves counted as less than one pieza de esclavo.

7. Palmer also cites elections of black kings in several other seventeenth-century rebellions. In a 1611 rebellion a priest, Fray Juan de Tobar, apparently betrayed the secrets of the confessional and sounded the alarm (1976:139), thus showing, once again, the complicity between the Church and the Spanish state. Maroon societies in Mexico were also known to elect kings (52–53).

8. This argument was also made by Indian writers of the late sixteenth and seventeenth century. Thus Fernando de Alva Ixtlilxochitl claimed that his grandfather, the king of Texcoco, was born on the same day as Hernán Cortés, and that their destinies were linked by the fact that both were instrumental to spreading the Christian faith in the Americas (see 1891 I:360–363). The Peruvian writer Felipe Guamán Poma de Ayala makes the even more radical claim that the Peruvians willfully surrendered to the Spaniards in order to accept Christianity (for a discussion of this see Adorno 1986).

9. Palmer (1976:91) notes that treatises praising black character are absent from the Mexican colonial literature. Works that praise Indian character abound. (However, so do works that criticize Indian character.) The works that praise Indian character see Indians as being childlike and pure, whereas blacks are almost always described as being untrustworthy and vile. This difference relates to the difference in the status of African and Indian peoples vis-à-vis the faith.

10. Throughout the sixteenth and seventeenth centuries authorities tried to keep blacks out of Indian villages, and there were many examples of Indians being mistreated by slaves (Palmer 1976:60). I believe that this was because slaves were protected by Spaniards because they were their property. However, it also reflects the fact that blacks were part of the repertoire of signs of Spanish power, whereas Indians were the subjects that needed continual intimidation. In the words of Ixtlilxochitl, the Spaniards "belittle [apocan] the natives so much that it is shameful, and lacking in all truth and reason" (Alva Ixtlilxóchitl I:420).

11. A study of marriage among African-Mexicans shows that between 1646 and 1746 fully 74 percent of Mexico City's population of African descent was free, while only 21 percent were slaves (Love 1971). Naveda Chávez-Hita (1987: 62–65) shows that in the district of Córdoba, Veracruz, in the period between 1746 and 1788 the percentage of slaves fell from 79 percent to 16 percent of the population, whereas the proportion of free mixed bloods of (partial) African descent went from 21 percent to 84 percent.

12. In 1574 the viceroy Martín Enriquez tried to create a stable caste of slaves by proposing that the children of male slaves also be slaves (see ibid.: 63). However, his petition was not accepted by the king, and the racial instability that worried Enriquez continued to develop and intensify throughout the colonial period.

13. "Criollo" slaves were worth more than "bozales" (unacculturated Africans), and they occupied the more prestigious position of houseservants, whereas bozales were used on plantations, mines, and obrajes. Being a criollo slave was probably a sine qua non for manumission.

14. Palmer notes in most cases slaves were either manumitted at birth or on the deathbed of their masters. This is consonant with the basic premises of the Spanish ideology of slavery; to free a slave at your deathbed is to recognize that the individual has already learned and paid for past vices through bondage and that it is now fair to set the person free. To free a slave at birth is to recognize that their parents are already Christians and that the newly born infant need not inherit the whole stain of infidelity.

15. In 1597 the main mines of the Morelos region (Guautla and Taxco) occupied more free Indian labor than corvée (repartimiento) Indian labor (Palmer 1976:83).

16. Israel 1975, Chance 1978, W. Taylor 1972, Van Young 1981, and Brading 1971 have explored some aspects of the transition from caste to class in New Spain. Viqueira 1987 studied this transition from the perspective of urban popular culture.

17. From the Riva Palacio collection, cited in Aguirre Beltrán 1972:175–177. Aguirre reproduces another two series, and many others exist. A full analysis of the issue would require analyzing all of them. Here I make reference to the other two series provided by Aguirre, but I only reproduce this one for the readers to have an idea of the nature of these lists. Lists differ somewhat in their content, especially regarding some of the combinations that they choose to name and also in some of the names used for the combinations.

18. Aguirre Beltrán (1972:154) points out that "passing" upwards was not easy, because there was a lot of social surveillance around this issue; however, it seems to have been quite common regardless. Aguirre claims that the most common type of passing was from mestizo to criollo.

19. In fact the Spaniards thought of their color as being red (bermejo) and not white (Aguirre Beltrán 1972:166). I use the term "white" for easier communication with my readers.

20. Chávez Orozco notes that "as the nineteenth century progressed, the complex of ideas regarding the total incapacity of Indians matured and, what is worse, a prejudice was created wherein Mexico's backwardness and its difficulties in becoming democratic were attributed to the fact that Mexican nationality had to bear the enormous weight of the retrograde Indian conglomerate" (1943:47, my trans.).

21. Knight (1990:97) claims that no Mexican president has ever married a woman who was darker than himself.

22. There are some interesting parallels between indigenismo and other forms of Latin American nationalism of the turn of the century. For example, Martí and Rodó, who came from countries that had no Indians, both emphasize a Latin American soul that contrasts with the "greed" that reigned in the United States. Latin America thus became an alternative civilization, instead of a cultural backwater. Like the indigenistas, some of the successors of this line of argument (cf. Fernández Retamar 1971) have argued for the necessity of strong states in order to protect our countries against U.S. influence.

17: Regional Cultures

1. These characteristics were taken from Chevalier 1962, González Navarro 1968, and de la Peña's (1986) excellent discussion.

2. In Tepoztlán the local Spanish elites intermarried with some of the wealthy Indian families in the eighteenth century. However, "Spaniards" and "naturales" (Indians) were legally separated. After independence, the two elites fused into a single group that referred to itself as "los notables." In nineteenth-century Morelos, as in most of Mexico, the term "indio" was transformed to mean poor peasant, and the category of "mestizo" and "criollo" both were lumped together in either a class of wealthy and distinguished people (*los notables*) or a class of poor popular classes (*el pueblo*).

3. Cited in Díaz y Díaz 1972:192.

4. The same theme is insistently developed in Iturbide's memoirs (1823).

5. For a discussion of the history and characteristic of this kind of political

movement, see Bricker 1985, Gruzinski 1988, and Reed 1964. See also Castellanos 1962.

6. The literature on caciques is vast. I shall not swell this text with references, for it has no pretense to novelty from the point of view of data. Instead I wish to clarify the implications of the regional cultural perspective for understanding a phenomenon that has not been adequately understood precisely because of its complex position in the Mexican national space. De la Peña (1986) offers a superb overview of the literature on caciquismo. Some of the valuable works on the subject include Friedrich 1970 and 1986, Cornelius 1975, Falcón 1984, Brading 1980, Bartra 1975, Knight 1986, and Guerra 1985. But this is a very long way from being a comprehensive list.

7. For an ethnographic account and cultural analysis of the public rituals of the PRI's presidential campaign see Lomnitz, Lomnitz A., and Adler 1990. For parallel discussions on the competition between "democratic" and "relational" discourses in Brazil, see DaMatta 1979 and 1985.

8. This has many similarities with what Taussig (1980) observed in Colombia, except that in that case, the belief in the pact with the devil led to resistance towards a capitalist work ethic, whereas in this case, the idea is utilized to explain (and so to tolerate) a form of political power.

9. For example, see Mariano Azuela's *Los de abajo* and Martín Luis Guzmán's *La sombra del caudillo*.

10. For an overview of these issues see Bizberg 1990. For other descriptive material see Novelo 1987.

11. De la Peña (1986) and Friedrich (1986) have both argued that the notion of "charisma" is not applicable to caciques, for their mediating roles make their forms of leadership almost transparently pragmatic to their "constituencies," and their use of coercive force gives compliance an undertone of fear and not of commitment.

However, Friedrich does suggest that caciques (in Naranja) gained legitimacy from the fact that people in the village recognized a need and a place for a mediating position. This suggests that although in Friedrich's experience the attitudes of the cacique's "constituency" went from indifference to alienation, they might have shifted towards the commitment that charisma produces, had the mediating role of the cacique coincided in a different way with their moral and political longings. In other words, the issue of charisma is very much germane to the question of caciquismo, and it can help us understand the phenomenon in its historical and spatial complexity.

12. Personal communication.

13. For a cultural study of a presidential campaign, see Lomnitz, Lomnitz-Adler, and Adler 1990.

14. Occasionally, caciques can successfully retain their key bureaucratic positions for very long periods of time. In my view, when this happens it is an index of a somewhat different problem than what I have been focusing on: the fact that the logic of bureaucratic power is inadequate to the task of long-term control. For example, long cacicazgos are characteristic in sectors of society that need to be controlled (mobilized or demobilized) by the government and yet are not part

of the government, for example, trade unions and occupational organizations. These cacicazgos are based on the state's need for continuity in its dealings with particular groups of people. This need for continuity is either a need for guaranteed continued social control, or it reflects the state's need to have a real-live counterpart to its institutional and discursive arrangement of the national order. So, for instance, the state has its officially recognized Indians, its workers, its intellectuals, its peasants; the caciques of these groups have longevity because they have relatively little independent power. They are, really and truly, brokers. They have not built a power base in which personal loyalties at the bottom are strong; their main source of credibility stems from the government.

References

Adorno, Rolena
1986   *Guaman Poma: Writing and Resistance in Colonial Peru.* Austin: University of Texas Press.
Aguilar Mora, Jorge
1978   *La divina pareja, historia y mito: Valoración e interpretación de la obra ensayística de Octavio Paz.* México: ERA.
Aguirre Beltrán, Gonzalo
1972   *La población negra de México, 1519–1810.* México: Fondo de Cultura Económica.
Alcorn, Janis
1984   *Mayan Huastec Ethnobotany.* Austin: University of Texas Press.
Alduncin Abitia, Enrique
1989   *Los valores de los mexicanos.* Mexico: Fomento Cultural Banamex.
Altamirano, Ignacio Manuel
1986   *El Zarco.* Chilpancingo: Universidad Autónoma de Guerrero.
Althusser, Louis
1971   *Lenin and Philosophy.* London: New Left Books.
Alva Ixtlilxóchitl, Fernando de
1891–92   *Obras históricas.* Edited by Alfredo Chavero. 2 vols. México: Oficinas Tipográficas de la Secretaría de Fomento.
Anderson, Benedict
1983   *Imagined Communities: Reflections on the Origin and Spread of Nationalism.* London: Verso.
Ankerson, Dudley
1984   *Agrarian Warlord: Saturnino Cedillo and the Mexican Revolution in San Luis Potosí.* DeKalb: Northern Illinois University Press.

Araoz, Luis
1984   El sector agropecuario de Morelos, 1960–1980. In *Morelos: Cinco Siglos de Historia Regional.* Edited by Horacio Crespo and Brígida Von Mentz. Mexico: CEHAM.

Arguedas, José María
1967   *Los ríos profundos.* Santiago: Universitaria.

Arias, Patricia, and Lucía Bazán
1977   *CIVAC, Un proceso de industrialización en una zona campesina.* México: Cuadernos de la Casa Chata, Num. 1.
1979   *Demandas y conflictos: El poder político en un pueblo de Morelos.* México: Nueva Imagen.

Arizpe, Lourdes
1978   *Migración, etnicismo y cambio económico: Un estudio sobre migrantes campesinos a la Ciudad de México.* México: El Colegio de México.

Azuela, Mariano
1930   *Los de abajo.* Madrid: Espasa Calpe.

Barth, Fredrik
1969   *Ethnic Groups and Boundaries.* Boston: Little, Brown.

Barthes, Roland
1957   *Mythologies.* Paris: Editions Seuil.

Bartra, Roger
1975   Campesinado y poder político en México. In *Caciquismo y poder político en México.* Edited by Roger Bartra. México: Siglo XXI.
1987   *La jaula de la melancolía.* México: Grijalbo.
n.d.   Los orígenes del "Hombre Salvage." Paper presented at the Center for Historical Analysis, Rutgers University.

Basso, Keith
1988   "Speaking with Names": Language and Landscape among the Western Apache. *Cultural Anthropology* 3(2):99–130.

Benedict, Ruth
1932   Configurations of Culture in North America. *American Anthropologist* 34:1–27.
1934   *Patterns of Culture.* New York: Houghton Mifflin.
1946   *The Chrysanthemum and the Sword.* Cambridge: Riverside Press.

Bernardez, Enrique
1982   *Introducción a la lingüística del texto.* Madrid: Esparsa Calpe.

Bizberg, Ilán
1990   *Estado y sindicalismo en México.* México: El Colegio de México.

Blasio, Jose Luis
1966   *Maximiliano íntimo.* México: Editora Nacional.

Bock, Philip K.
1980   Tepoztlan Reconsidered. *Journal of Latin American Lore* 6(1):129–150.

Bonfil Batalla, Guillermo
1971   Introducción al ciclo de ferias de cuaresma en la región de Cuautla, Morelos. *Anales de Antropología* 8:167–200.

1987   *México profundo*. México: SEP.
Bourdieu, Pierre
1971   (1973) The Berber House. In *Rules and Meanings*. Edited by Mary
        Douglas. Harmondsworth: Penguin Books.
1979   (1972) *Outline of a Theory of Practice*. Cambridge: Cambridge University Press.
Braden, Charles
1930   *Religious Aspects of the Conquest of Mexico*. Durham: Duke University Press.
Brading, David A.
1971   *Miners and Merchants in Bourbon Mexico, 1763–1810*. Cambridge:
        Cambridge University Press.
1972   *Los orígenes del nacionalismo mexicano*. México: ERA.
1980   *Caudillo and Peasant in the Mexican Revolution*. New York: Cambridge University Press.
Bricker, Victoria
1985   *The Indian Christ, the Indian King*. Austin: University of Texas Press.
Bulnes, Francisco
1960   (1904) *Las grandes mentiras de nuestra historia*. México: Editorial
        Nacional.
Camp, Roderic
1980   *Mexico's Leaders, Their Education and Recruitment*. Tucson: University of Arizona Press.
Casas, Bartolomé de las
1951   *Historia de las Indias*. México: Fondo de Cultura Económica.
Castellanos, Rosario
1962   *Oficio de tinieblas*. México: Joaquín Mortiz.
Certeau, Michel de
1984   On the Oppositional Practices of Everyday Life. *Social Text* 1(3):3–
        43.
Chance, John
1978   *Race and Class in Colonial Oaxaca*. Stanford: Stanford University
        Press.
Chávez Orozco, Luis
1943   *Las instituciones democráticas de los indígenas mexicanos en la
        época colonial*. México: Instituto Indigenista Interamericano.
Chevalier, François
1962   "Caudillos" et "caciques" en Amérique: Contribution a l'étude des
        liens personnels. *Mélanges offerts a Marcel Bataillon par les Hispanistes Françaises, Bulletin Hispanique*, vol. 61 bis.
*Colección de documentos inéditos relativos al descrubrimiento, conquista y colonización de las posesiones españolas . . . sacadas en su mayor parte del Real
Archivo de Indias*
1864–84 42 vols. Madrid: n.p.
Coordinación General de los Servicios Nacionales de Estadística, Geografía e
Informática
1982a   *X Censo General de Población y Vivienda, 1980*. Cartografía Geo-

estadística del Estado de Morelos. 2 vols. México: Secretaría de Programación y Presupuesto.

1982*b*   *X Censo General de Población y Vivienda, 1980.* Cartografía Geoestadística del Estado de San Luis Potosí. 2 vols. México: Secretaría de Programación y Presupuesto.

1982*c*   *Manual de Estadísticas Básicas del Estado de Morelos.* 2 vols. México: Secretaría de Programación y Presupuesto.

1982*d*   *Manual de Estadísticas Básicas del Estado de San Luis Potosí.* 2 vols. México: Secretaría de Programación y Presupuesto.

1985*a*   *Síntesis Geográfica del Estado de Morelos con Anexo Cartográfico.* México: Secretaría de Programación y Presupuesto.

1985*b*   *Síntesis Geográfica del Estado de San Luis Potosí con Anexo Cartográfico.* México: Secretaría de Programación y Presupuesto.

Cornelius, Wayne
1975   *Politics and the Migrant Poor in Mexico City.* Stanford: Stanford University Press.

Crespo, Horacio, and Herbert Frey
1982   La diferenciación social del campesinado como problema de la teoría de la historia, hipótesis generales para el caso de Morelos, Mexico. *Revista Mexicana de Sociología* 1982/1:285–313.

Crespo, Horacio, and Enrique Vega V.
In Press   *Tierra y propiedad en el fin del porfiriato, Tomo I, En los orígenes del zapatismo: Crecimiento económico y diferenciación social campesina.* Cuernavaca: CEHAM-UAEM.

Crepo, Horacio, and Brigida von Mentz (editors)
1984   *Morelos: Cinco Siglos de Historia Regional.* México: CEHAM.

Dakin, Karen, and Diana Riesky
1975   Morelos Nahuatl: An Ethnolinguistic Survey. Mimeographed.

Dávila, Mario
1976   Patronage and Political Process in a Mexican Village. Ph.D. diss. Department of Anthropology, University of California, Berkeley.

Díaz Cruz, Rodrigo
1984   El rumor de Tetelcingo. Licenciatura thesis, Department of Anthropology, Universidad Autónoma Metropolitana (Mexico).

Díaz y Díaz, Fernando
1972   *Caudillos y caciques.* México: El Colegio de México.

Diehl, Richard A.
1981   Review of Lorenzo Ochoa's *Historia Prehispánica de la Huasteca.* *Hispanic American Historical Review* 61(3):506–507.

Diez, Domingo
1967   (1930) *Bosquejo histórico-geográfico de Morelos.* Cuernavaca: Editorial Tlahuica.

Dirección General de Estadística
1918–20   *Tercer Censo General de Población, 1910.* México: Oficina Impresora de la Secretaría de Hacienda.

1925–28   *Cuarto Censo General de Habitantes, 1921.* México: Talleres Gráficos de la Nación.

1933   *Quinto Censo General de Población, 1930*. México: Secretaría de la Economía Nacional.

1943   *Segundo Censo Agrícola, Ganadero y Ejidal, 1940*. México: Secretaría de Economía.

1943   *Sexto Censo General de Población, 1940*. México: Secretaría de la Economía Nacional.

1973   *Noveno Censo General de Población, 1970*. México: Secretaría de Industria y Comercio.

1975   *Sexto Censo Comercial, 1971*. México: Secretaría de Industria y Comercio.

Dumont, Louis
1970   *Homo Hierarchicus: The Caste System and Its Implications*. London: Weidenfeld and Nicolson.

1986   *Essays on Individualism*. Chicago: University of Chicago Press.

Durkheim, Emile
1960   *The Division of Labor in Society*. Glencoe: The Free Press.

1965   *The Elementary Forms of Religious Life*. New York: The Free Press.

Elizondo Mayer, Norma
1984   Las relaciones de poder en Atlatláhucan, Morelos. Licenciatura thesis, Department of Anthropology, Universidad Autónoma Metropolitana (México).

Espejel, Laura
1984   El Cuartel General: Órgano rector de la revolución zapatista, 1914 y 1915. In Crespo 1984.

Estrada, Antonia
1963   *La Grieta en el Yugo*. México: Jus.

Falcón, Romana
1984   *Política y caciquismo en San Luis Potosí, 1918–1939*. México: El Colegio de México.

Fernández Retamar, Roberto
1971   *Calibán, apuntes sobre la cultura en nuestra América*. México: Diógenes.

Florescano, Enrique
1980   *El poder y la lucha por el poder en la historiografía mexicana*. (Cuadernos de Trabajo 33). Mexico: INAH.

1987   *Memoria mexicana*. México: SEP.

Foster, George
1973   (1948) *Empire's Children: The People of Tzintzuntzan*. Westport: Greenwood Press.

Foucault, Michel
1988   (1966) *Madness and Civilization*. New York: Vintage Books.

Friedlander, Judith
1975   *Being Indian in Hueyapan: A Study in Forced Identity*. New York: St. Martin's.

Friedrich, Paul
1970   *Agrarian Revolt in a Mexican Village*. Englewood: Prentice Hall.

1986   *The Princes of Naranja*. Austin: University of Texas Press.

1989   Language, Ideology and Political Economy. *American Anthropologist* 91(2):295–313.

Fromm, Erich and Michael Maccoby
1970   *Social Character in a Mexican Village.* Englewood Cliffs: Prentice Hall.

Gamio, Manuel
1916   *Forjando Patria: Pro nacionalismo.* México: Porrúa.
1979   (1925) *La Población del Valle de Teotihuacan.* México: Instituto Nacional Indigenista.

García Mora, Carlos (editor)
1988   *La antropología en México: Panorama histórico.* México: INAH.

Geertz, Clifford
1980   *Negara: The Theater State in Nineteenth-Century Bali.* Princeton: Princeton University Press.
1983   Centers, Kings and Charisma: Reflections on the Symbolics of Power. In *Local Knowledge,* 121–147. New York: Basic Books.

Gemelli Carreri, Giovanni
1976   (1699) *Viaje a la Nueva España.* México: Universidad Nacional Autonoma de Mexico.

Gerhard, Peter
1970   A Method for Reconstructing Precolumbian Political Boundaries in Central Mexico. *Journal de la Société des Américanistes* 59:27–41.
1972   *A Guide to the Historical Geography of New Spain.* Cambridge: Cambridge University Press.

Gibson, Charles
1964   *The Aztecs under Spanish Rule.* Stanford: Stanford University Press.

Girault, Christian
1966   La Vie Urbaine dans l'Etat de Morelos (Méxique). Ph.D. diss., Department of Geography, University of Paris (Sorbonne).

Goffman, Erving
1975   *Frames.* New York: Basic Books.

González Dávila, Gil
1649   *Teatro eclesiástico de la primitiva iglesia de Las Indias.* 2 vols. Madrid, n.p.

González Herrera, Carlos, and Arnulfo Embriz Osorio
1984   La reforma agraria y la desaparación del latifundio en el Estado de Morelos, 1916–1927. In Crespo and von Mentz 1984.

González Navarro
1968   *La Confederación Nacional Campesina (un grupo de presión en la reforma agraria mexicana).* México: Costa Amic.

Gramsci, Antonio
1971   *Selections from the Prison Notebooks.* New York: International Publishers.

Gregory, Derek
1985   Suspended Animation: The Stasis of Diffusion Theory. In Gregory and Urry 1985.

Gregory, Derek, and John Urry (editors)
1985   *Social Relations and Spatial Structures*. New York: St. Martin's Press.
Gruzinski, Serge
1988   *La colonization de l'imaginaire: Sociétés indigènes et occidentaliza-tion dans le Mexique Espagnol, XVI–XVIII siècle*. Paris: Gallimard.
Guerra, François Xavier
1985   *Le Mexique dans l'Ancien Régime*. 2 vols. Paris: Harmattan.
Guzmán, Martín Luis
1989   *La sombra del caudillo*. Mexico: Porrúa.
Hägerstrand, Torsten
1965   *Innovation-Diffusion as a Spatial Process*. Chicago: University of Chicago Press.
Hall, Stuart (editor)
1976   *Resistance Through Rituals: Youth Subcultures in Post-War Britain*. London: Hutchinson.
Handler, Richard
1988   *Nationalism and the Politics of Culture in Quebec*. Madison: University of Wisconsin Press.
Hanke, Lewis
1959   *Aristotle and the American Indian*. London: Hollis and Carter.
Harvey, David
1985   The Geopolitics of Capitalism. In Gregory and Urry 1985.
Haskett, Robert
1987   Indian Town Government in Colonial Cuernavaca: Persistence, Adaptation, and Change. *Hispanic American Historical Review* 67(2):203–231.
Heau, Catherine
1984   Trova popular e identidad cultural en Morelos. In Crespo and von Mentz 1984.
Hebdige, Dick
1979   *Subculture: The Meaning of Style*. London: Methuen.
Henschel Ariza, Elizabeth, and Juan Pérez Quijada
1976   Estructura en el Cambio. Licenciatura thesis, Department of Anthropology, Universidad Iberoamericana (Mexico).
Hernández Orive, Alicia
1973   Haciendas y pueblos en el estado de Morelos, 1535–1810. Master's thesis, Centro de Estudios Históricos, El Colegio de México (Mexico).
Herzfeld, Michael
1982   *Ours Once More: Folklore, Ideology, and the Making of Modern Greece*. Austin: University of Texas Press.
1990   *The Social Production of Indifference*. Unpublished manuscript.
Hobsbawm, Eric, and Terence Ranger (editors)
1983   *The Invention of Tradition*. New York: Cambridge University Press.
Holt-Buttner, Elizabeth
1962   Evolución de las localidades en el estado de Morelos según los

censos de población (1900–1950). *Anuario de geografía*. México: UNAM.

Huerta, María Teresa
1984   Formación del grupo de hacendados azucareros morelenses. 1780–1840. In Crespo and von Mentz 1984.

Ingham, John
1970   On Mexican Folk Medicine. *American Anthropologist* 72: 76–87.
1986   *Mary, Michael, and Lucifer: Folk Catholicism in Central Mexico*. Austin: Texas University Press.

Israel, Jonathan
1975   *Race, Class and Politics in Colonial Mexico*. Oxford: Oxford University Press.

Iturbide, Agustín
1971   (1823) *A Statement of some of the Principal Events in the Life of Agustín Iturbide, Written by Himself.* Washington: Documentary.

Jaramillo, Rubén
1967   *Autobiografía*. México: Nuestro Tiempo.

Kapferer, Bruce
1988   *Legends of People, Myths of State*. Washington: Smithsonian Institution Press.

Keen, Benjamin
1971   *The Aztec Image in Western Thought*. New Brunswick: Rutgers University Press.

Knight, Alan
1986   *The Mexican Revolution*. Cambridge: Cambridge University Press.
1990   Racism, Revolution and Indigenismo: Mexico, 1910–1940. In *The Idea of Race in Latin America, 1870–1940*. Edited by Richard Graham. Austin: University of Texas Press.

Kroeber, A. L.
1944   *Configurations of Culture Growth*. Berkeley: University of California Press.

Krotz, Stefan
1974   El poder político en un pueblo de Morelos. In *Los campesinos de la Tierra de Zapata, III, Política y conflicto*. México: SEP/INAH.

Lafaye, Jacques
1977   *Quetzalcoatl y Guadalupe: La formación de la conciencia nacional en México*. México: Fondo de Cultura Económica.

Leach, Edmund R.
1956   *Political Systems of Highland Burma*. London: ASA Monographs.

Leonard, Irving
1959   *Baroque Times in Old Mexico*. Ann Arbor: University of Michigan Press.

Lévi-Strauss, Claude
1962   *Le totémisme aujourd'hui*. Paris: Presses Universitaires de France.
1974   *Anthropologie structurale*. Paris: Librairie Plon.

Lewis, Oscar
1951   *Life in a Mexican Village: Tepoztlán Restudied.* Urbana: University of Illinois Press.
1961   *Tepoztlán, A Village in Mexico.* New York: Holt, Rinehart and Winston.
1966   (1964) *Pedro Martínez.* Mexico: Joaquín Mortiz.
1969   *Five Families.* New York: Random House.
1970   *Anthropological Essays.* New York: Random House.
Limón, José
1989   Carne, Carnales and the Carnivalesque. *American Ethnologist* 16(3): 471–486.
Lindesmith, Alfred R., and Anselm L. Strauss
1950   A Critique of Culture-Personality Writings. *American Sociological Review* 15:587–600.
Liss, Peggy K.
1975   *Mexico Under Spain 1521–1556: Society and the Origins of Nationality.* Chicago: University of Chicago Press.
Lockhart, James, Frances Berdan, and Arthur J. O. Anderson
1986   *The Tlaxcallan Actas.* Salt Lake City: University of Utah Press.
Lomnitz, Larissa
1975   *Cómo Sobreviven los marginados.* México: Siglo XXI.
1979   Anthropology and Development in Latin America. *Human Organization* 38(3):313–317.
1987   *A Mexican Elite Family.* Princeton: Princeton University Press.
Lomnitz, Larissa, C. Lomnitz-Adler, and Ilya Adler
1990   El fondo de la forma: Actos Públicos de la Campaña Presidencial del PRI, 1988. *Nueva Antropología* 38:45–82. English translation in *Politics and Culture in Latin America.* Edited by Daniel Levine. Ann Arbor: University of Michigan Press (in press).
Lomnitz-Adler, Claudio
1979   Clase y etnicidad en Morelos: Una nueva interpretación. *América Indígena* 39(3):439–475.
1982   *Evolución de una sociedad rural.* (Sepochentas Num. 27.) Mexico: SEP/Fondo de Cultura Económica.
1984   Los estudios de campo en Morelos, 1930–1983. In Crespo and von Mentz 1984.
(forthcoming) *Tepoztlán.* Norman: Oklahoma University Press.
López González, Valentín
1968   *Como Nació el Estado de Morelos a la Vida Institucional, 1869.* Cuernavaca: Editorial Tlahuica.
1980   *Los Compañeros de Zapata.* Cuernavaca: Gobierno del Estado Libre y Soberano de Morelos.
Love, Edgar
1971   Marriage Patterns of Persons of African Descent in a Colonial Mexico City Parish. *Hispanic American Historical Review* 51:79–91.

Lowry, Malcolm
1965   *Under the Volcano.* Philadelphia: J. B. Lippincott.
McAlister, L. N.
1963   Social Structure and Social Change in New Spain. *Hispanic American Historical Review* 43:349–370.
Machlachlan, Colin M., and Jaime E. Rodríguez O.
1980   *The Forging of the Cosmic Race: A Reinterpretation of Colonial Mexico.* Berkeley: University of California Press.
Macune, Charles William
1970   *A Test of Federalism: Political, Economic and Ecclesiastical Relations Between the State of Mexico and the Mexican Nation, 1823–1835.* Austin, Texas: Graduate School of the University of Texas at Austin.
Maraval, José Antonio
1944   *La teoría española del Estado en el siglo XVII.* Madrid: Instituto de Estudios Políticos.
Marcus, George, and Michael Fischer
1986   *Anthropology as Cultural Critique.* Chicago: University of Chicago Press.
Mariátegui, José Carlos
1979   *Siete ensayos de interpretación de la realidad peruana.* México: ERA.
Márquez, Enrique
1977   *La Casa de los Señores Santos.* Master's thesis, Centro de Relaciones Internacionales. El Colegio de México (Mexico).
1982   Las Tierras de Felipe Barragán. In *Después de los latifundios: La desintegración de la gran propiedad agraria en México.* Edited by Heriberto Moreno García. México: El Colegio de Michoacán.
Martí, José
1977   *Política de nuestra América.* México: Siglo XXI.
Martin, Cheryl English
1982   Haciendas and Villages in Late Colonial Morelos. *Hispanic American Historical Review* 62(3):407–428.
Marx, Karl
1988   (1846) *The German Ideology.* New York: International Publishers.
Massey, Doreen
1984   *Spatial Divisions of Labor: Social Structures and the Geography of Production.* New York: Methuen.
Matta, Roberto da
1979   *Carnavais, Malandros e Herois: Para uma Sociologia do Dilema Brasileiro.* Rio de Janeiro: Zahar Editores.
1985   *A casa e a rua: Espaço, cidadania, mulher e morte no Brasil.* São Paulo: Brasiliense.
Mayer, Brantz
1982   (1843) Un viaje a la tierra caliente [Published extract from *México, lo que fue y lo que es*]. Cuernavaca: Summa Morelense.

Mazari, Manuel
1968   *Bosquejo Histórico del Estado de Morelos*. Mexico: Private Edition.
Meade, Joaquín
1970   *Historia de Valles*. San Luis Potosí: Sociedad Histórica Potosina.
Melville, Roberto
1979   *Crecimiento y rebelión: El desarrollo económico de las Haciendas azucareras en Morelos, 1880–1910*. México: Nueva Imágen.
Mendieta, Gerónimo de
1876   *Historia eclesiástica indiana*. 3 vols. México: Edición Joaquín García Icazbalceta.
Minguet, Charles
1979   El concepto de nación, pueblo, estado y patria en las generaciones de la Independencia. In *Récherches sur le monde hispanique au dix-neuvième siècle*. Lille: Editions Universitaires.
Monsivais, Carlos
1982   La Nación de unos cuantos y las esperanzas románticas: Notas sobre la Historia del término "cultura nacional" en México. In *En torno a la cultura nacional*. Mexico: SEP/Fondo de Cultura Economica.
Mora, José María Luis
1963   *Obras sueltas*. México: Porrúa.
Morse, Richard M.
1982   *El espejo de Próspero: Dialéctica del Nuevo Mundo*. México: Siglo XXI.
Myers, Fred
1986   *Pintupi Country, Pintupi Self: Sentiment, Place, and Politics among Western Desert Aborigines*. Washington: Smithsonian Institution Press.
Naveda Chávez-Hita, Adriana
1987   *Esclavos negros en las haciendas azucareras de Córdoba, Veracruz, 1690–1830*. Jalapa: Universidad Veracruzana.
Novelo, Victoria (editor)
1987   *Coloquio sobre cultura obrera*. Mexico: CIESAS.
O'Gorman, Edmundo
1977   *México, el trauma de su historia*. México: Universidad Nacional Autónoma de México.
Olsen, Stephen M.
1976   Regional Social Systems: Linking Quantitative Analysis and Field Work. In Smith 1976, vol. 2:21–55.
Padgen, Anthony
1982   *The Fall of Natural Man*. New York: Cambridge University Press.
Palmer, Colin
1976   *Slaves of the White God: Blacks in Mexico, 1570–1650*. Cambridge: Harvard University Press.
Paz, Octavio
1981a   (1950) *El laberinto de la soledad*. México: Fondo de Cultura Económica.

1981*b*   *(1970). Postdata.* México: Fondo de Cultura Económica.

1982   *Sor Juana Inés de la Cruz o las trampas de la fé.* México: Fondo de Cultura Económica.

Peña, Guillermo de la

1980   *Herederos de promesas: Agricultura, ritual y política en los Altos de Morelos.* México: Casa Chata.

1986   Poder local, poder regional: Perspectives socioantropológicas. In *Poder local, poder regional.* Edited by Jorge Padua and Alain Vanneph. México: El Colegio de México.

Pétonnet, Colette

1982   *Espaces habités: Ethnologie des Banlieues.* Paris: Editions Galilee.

Plancarte y Navarrete, Francisco

1982   (1911) *Tamoanchan: El estado de Morelos y el principio de la civilización en México.* Cuernavaca: Summa Morelense.

Portilla, Jorge

1984   *Fenomenología del relajo.* México: CREA/Fondo de Cultura Económica.

Prieto, Guillermo

1982   (1845) *Un paseo a Cuernavaca.* Cuernavaca: Suma Morelense.

Puig, Henri

1976   *Végetation de la Huasteca, Méxique.* México: Mission Archeologique et Ethnologique Française au Méxique.

Rama, Angel

1982   *Transculturación narrativa en América Latina.* Mexico: Siglo XXI.

Ramírez Melgarejo, Ramón

1974   La bola chiquita, un movimiento campesino. In *Los campesinos de la tierra de Zapata,* vol. 1. Mexico: SEP/INAH.

Ramos, Samuel

1934   *El Perfil del hombre y la cultura en Mexico.* México: Imprenta Mundial.

Redfield, Robert

1930   *Tepoztlán: A Mexican Village.* Chicago: University of Chicago Press.

1941   *The Folk Culture of Yucatan.* Chicago: University of Chicago Press.

Reed, John

1964   *The Caste War of Yucatán.* Stanford: Stanford University Press.

Reina, Leticia

1980   *Las Rebeliones Campesinas en México 1819–1906.* México: Siglo XXI.

Reyes, Alfonso

1982   *Posición de América.* México: Nueva Imágen.

Riding, Alan

1985   *Vecinos distantes.* México: Planeta.

Rivera Cambas, Manuel

1981   (1883) *México pintoresco, artístico y monumental (estado de Morelos).* Cuernavaca: Summa Morelense.

Robelo, Cecilio
1982   (1894) *Cuernavaca*. Cuernavaca: Summa Morelense.
Robles, Pablo
1982   (1891) *Los Plateados de tierra caliente*. México: La Matraca.
Rodó, José Enrique
1962   *Ariel*. Buenos Aires: Kapelusz.
Roheim, Geza
1950   *Psychoanalysis and Anthropology*. New York: International University Press.
Romanucci-Ross, Lola
1973   *Conflict, Violence, and Morality in a Mexican Village*. Palo Alto: National Press.
Rounds, Christopher Robert
1977   From Hacienda to Ejido: Land Reform and Economic Development in Yautepec, Morelos, 1920–1970. Ph.D. diss., Department of History, State University of New York, Stony Brook.
Rubio Mañé, Jorge Ignacio
1963   *Introducción al estudio de los virreyes de la Nueva España, 1535–1746*. Mexico: UNAM.
Rueda Smithers, Salvador
1984   La dinámica interna del zapatismo: Consideración para el estudio de la cotidianeidad campesina en el área zapatista. In Crespo and Von Mentz 1984.
Ruiz de Alarcón, Hernando
1984   *Treatise on the Heathen Superstitions That Today Live Among the Indians Native to This New Spain, 1629*. Edited by J. Richard Andrews and Ross Hassig. Norman: University of Oklahoma Press.
Sahlins, Marshall
1976   *Culture and Practical Reason*. Chicago: University of Chicago Press.
1985   *Islands of History*. Chicago: University of Chicago Press.
Said, Edward
1979   *Orientalism*. New York: Vintage Press.
Salamini, Heather Fowler
1978   *Agrarian Radicalism in Veracruz, 1920–1938*. Lincoln: University of Nebraska Press.
Salinas, Miguel
1981   (1924) *Historias y paisajes morelenses*. México: Imprenta Aldina, Rossel y Sordo.
Sangren, Steven
1984   Great Tradition and Little Tradition Reconsidered: The Question of Cultural Integration in China. *Journal of Chinese Studies* 1(1):1–24.
1988   Rhetoric and Authority in Ethnography: "Postmodernism" and the Social Reproduction of Texts. *Current Anthropology* 29(3):405–436.
Santos, Gonzalo N.
1986   *Memorias*. México: Grijalbo.

Secretaría de Fomento, Colonia e Industria
1903   *Censo General de la República Mexicana 1900.* México: Oficina Tipográfica de la Secretaría de Fomento.
Schmidt, Henry C.
1978   *The Roots of Lo Mexicano: Self and Society in Mexican Thought, 1900–1934.* College Station: Texas A & M University Press.
Schryer, Franz
n.d.   Stories of Hidden Treasure and the Idea of Limited Good. Unpublished manuscript.
1980   *The Rancheros of Pisaflores.* Toronto: University of Toronto Press.
1990   *Ethnicity and Class Conflict in Rural Mexico.* Princeton: Princeton University Press.
Shils, Edward
1975   *Center and Periphery: Essays in Macrosociology.* Chicago: University of Chicago Press.
Las Siete Partidas del rey Alfonso el sabio.
1807   3 vols. Madrid: La Imprenta Real.
Singelman, Peter, Jesús Tapia, and Sergio Quesada
1979   El desarrollo capitalista periférico y la transformación de las relaciones de clase en el campo: El papel de los campesinos cañeros en la industria azucarera de México. *Revista Mexicana de Sociología* 4:1167–1181.
Skinner, G. William
1964   Marketing and Social Structure in Rural China. *The Journal of Asian Studies* 24(1–3).
1977a   Cities and the Hierarchy of Local Systems. In *The City in Late Imperial China.* Edited by G. William Skinner. Stanford: Stanford University Press.
1977b   Regional Systems in Late Imperial China. Second Annual Meeting of the Social Science History Association, Ann Arbor, Michigan.
1985   The Structure of Chinese History. *Journal of Asian Studies* 44(2):271–292.
Smith, Carol A.
1976   *Regional Analysis.* 2 vols. New York: Academic Press.
1977   How Marketing Systems Affect Economic Opportunity in Agrarian Societies. In *Peasant Livelihood: Studies in Economic Anthropology and Cultural Ecology.* Edited by Rhoda Halperin and James Row. New York: St. Martin's Press.
1984   Local History in Global Context: Social and Economic Transitions in Western Guatemala. *Comparative Studies in Society and History* 26(2):193–228.
Smith, Peter
1979   *Labyrinths of Power: Political Recruitment in Twentieth-Century Mexico.* Princeton: Princeton University Press.
Sotelo Inclán, Jesús
1979   *Raíz y razón de Zapata.* México: Secretaría de Educación Pública.

Steward, Julian H.
1956   *The People of Puerto Rico*. Urbana: University of Illinois Press.
Stilles, Neville
1982   Nahuatl in the Huasteca Hidalguense: A Case Study in the Sociology of Language. Ph.D. diss., Centre for Latin American Linguistic Studies, University of Saint Andrews, Scotland.
Stresser-Pean, Jean G.
1952–53 Les Nahuas du sud de la Huasteca et le l'ancienne extension meridionale des Huastetèques. *Revista Mexicana de Estudios Antropológicos* 13:287–290.
1953   Les Indiens Huasteques. *Revista Mexicana de Estudios Antropológicos* 13:213–235.
1967   *Problèmes agraires de la Huasteca ou region de Tampico*. Paris: Centre National de la Récherche Scientifique.
Tapia Zenteno, Carlos de
1985   (1767) *Paradigma apologético y noticia de la lengua huasteca*. Mexico: UNAM.
Taussig, Michael
1980   *The Devil and Commodity Fetishism in South America*. Chapel Hill: University of North Carolina Press.
1987   *Shamanism, Colonialism, and the Wild Man*. Chicago: University of Chicago Press.
Taylor, Peter
1987   The Paradox of Geographical Scale in Marx's Politics. *Antipode* 19(3):287–306.
Taylor, William
1972   *Landlord and Peasant in Colonial Oaxaca*. Stanford: Stanford University Press.
Todorov, Tzvetan
1984   (1982) *The Conquest of America: The Question of the Other*. New York: Harper and Row.
Turner, Victor
1967   *The Forest of Symbols: Aspects of Ndembu Ritual*. Ithaca: Cornell University Press.
Uranga, Emilio
1952   *Análisis del ser mexicano*. México: Porrúa y Obregón.
Urry, John
1985   Social Relations, Space and Time. In Gregory and Urry 1985.
Valverde, Sergio
1933   *Zapatismo: Apuntes para la historia de la revolución y de la política en el estado de Morelos desde la muerte del gobernador Alarcon, pronunciamiento de los grales: Pablo Torres Burgos y Emiliano Zapata Mártires, hasta la restauración de la reacción por Vicente Estrada Cajigal Impostor*. México.
Van Dijk, Teun
1978   *La ciencia del texto*. Buenos Aires: Paidos.

Van Young, Eric
1981   *Hacienda and Market in Eighteenth-Century Mexico.* Berkeley: University of California Press.
Varela, Roberto
1984   *Expansión de sistemas y relaciones de poder: Antropología política del estado de Morelos.* México: Universidad Autónoma Metropolitana.
Vasconcelos, José
1983   *La raza cósmica.* México: Asociación Nacional de Libreros.
Vetancourt, Agustín de
1971   *Teatro mexicano.* México: Porrúa.
Viqueira, Juan Pedro
1987   *¿Relajados ó reprimidos? Diversiones públicas y vida social en la Ciudad de México durante el siglo de las luces.* México: Fondo de Cultura Económica.
Von Mentz, Brígida
1984   La región Morelense en la primera mitad del siglo XIX: Fuentes e hipótesis de trabajo. In Crespo and Von Mentz 1984.
Von Wobeser, Gisela
1988   *La hacienda azucarera en la época colonial.* México: SEP/UNAM.
Wallace, Anthony
1966   (1961) *Culture and Personality.* New York: Random House.
Warman, Arturo (editor)
1974   *Los campesinos en la tierra de Zapata.* 3 vols. Mexico: SEP-INAH.
1976   *. . . Y venimos a contradecir.* México: Casa Chata.
White, Hayden
1973   *Metahistory: The Historical Imagination in Nineteenth-Century Europe.* Baltimore: Johns Hopkins University Press.
Williams, Gwynn
1961   The Concept of "Egemonia" in the Thought of Antonio Gramsci: Some Notes of Interpretation. *Journal of the History of Ideas* 1:586–599.
Williams, Raymond
1977   *Marxism and Literature.* Oxford: Oxford University Press.
Wolf, Eric
1957   Closed Corporate Communities in Mesoamerica and Java. *Southwestern Journal of Anthropology* 13:1–18.
1959   *Sons of the Shaking Earth.* Chicago: University of Chicago Press.
1984   *Europe and the People Without History.* Berkeley: University of California Press.
Womack, John
1969   *Zapata and the Mexican Revolution.* New York: Alfred A. Knopf.

Index

Designer: U. C. Press Staff
Compositor: Huron Valley Graphics
Text: 10/12 Times Roman
Display: Helvetica
Printer: Braun-Brumfield, Inc.
Binder: Braun-Brumfield, Inc.